UNSUNG HEROES

Unsung Heroes

The Twentieth Century's Forgotten History-Makers

Erik Durschmied

CORONET BOOKS

Hodder & Stoughton

A CIP catalogue record for this title is
available from the British Library

ISBN 0 340 82520 0

Typeset in Sabon by Palimpsest Book Production Limited,
Polmont, Stirlingshire
Printed and bound in Great Britain by
Clays Ltd, St Ives plc

Hodder and Stoughton
A division of Hodder Headline
338 Euston Road
London NW1 3BH

For those that history has forgotten

For you I faced hell-fury and despair;
The reeking horror of it all I knew.
I flung myself into the furnace there;
I faced the flame that scorched me with its glare;
I drank unto the dregs the devil's brew.
Look at me now – for you and you and you . . .

Robert Service, *The Faceless Man*

Contents

Acknowledgements

Any work that attempts to recreate a moment in history owes all to records and personal recollections, without which the rest is nothing. I hope that those who offered their time to share with me their version of events, will forgive me for reviving some painful memories.

I would like to thank in particular those whose recollections have been indispensable; I appreciate the unique advantage, and the obligation to be cautious in mentioning names, having been allowed access to some closed records: Geneviève de Galard, the 'Angel of Dien Bien Phu'; Judith Maleter, widow of Hungarian General Pal Maleter; Israel Ludwig and Beth Slotin Shore, relatives of Canadian nuclear physicist Dr Slotin; the Danish fishermen Gunner Sylow and others for their wartime accounts of 'the dangerous crossing'; the Canadian journalist Martin Zeilig, Gen. Ahnfeld-Møllerup and Sven Dabelsteen (Denmark), Ailie Collins (France), Katalina Venczel (Hungary), Col. Ken Hamburger and Danny Crawford (USA), Wolfgang Käberich (Germany), Michael Paterson, Craig Cabell and Major Rebbeck (United Kingdom). Thanks also to those who have given me leads on sources and provided inspiring conversation on the persons dealt with. I wish to thank Rupert Lancaster, Kerry Hood and Luigi Bonomi for their editorial counsel and support. To all, my sincere gratitude.

E.D.
Valensole, France, Autumn 2002

Prologue

'*Reprendre courage est le courage de l'improviste* . . . to take heart is the unexpected courage. Moral consideration accounts for three-quarters, the balance of actual forces only for the other quarter.'

Napoleon, on the eve of the Battle of Austerlitz, 2 December 1805

No man is born a hero.

To believe such would be pretentious conceit; nor is heroism shallow vanity or self-glorification. In each man lies the root of an absolute certainty of his own merit, that, being endowed with greater wisdom or courage than others, he owes it to his own mankind to be free to do what he thinks best on behalf of others. What then is his motivation? Inspiration, incentive or impetus varies: it can be man's prime instinct for survival, or the quiet, self-effacing heroism, the I'm-better-than-thou challenge, a profound sense of duty, a sacrifice in the defence of the motherland, or taking a moral stand against inhuman acts. Courage and bravery – physical or moral – is normally seen as an absolute quality: you have it or you don't. There are some born into a cult of spiritual courage and physical endurance. First and foremost among them is the select group of brave men, inspired by a nationalistic fervour, to defend the motherland against all evil. They feel it honourable to lay down their lives for their king, or struggle on in a quest for their people's liberty. Tales of such heroic exploits form an integral part of a nation's history.

This is all about some men and women who took risks, about courage meeting up with incredible odds, and about the nature of chance; about the oppressive weight of official secrecy; about tragic events, and the many versions of the truth.

Frequently, heroism stems from action performed instinctively in the heat of the moment, brought on by circumstances beyond control. There is the notion of 'they fought to the last men and the last round', selling their lives as dearly as possible in the hope of relief, when extermination seems inevitable and only the ultimate sacrifice can give them the slightest chance of prolonging their lives. Many were those who refused to surrender; in the Second World War the Japanese did so due to a religious conviction that their lives already belonged to their Emperor. There is the 'laudable conduct in battle', an *esprit de corps* used as fierce motivation; with it, a soldier accepts the demands of duty, discipline and tradition and prepares for death. His great fear is to be shamed in front of his comrades. This can be driven to the point of absurdity when a commander demands of his unit to behave courageously and 'to hell with it'. One of the most bizarre incidents took place during the Battle of the Somme in 1916. When the battalion commander's whistle blew for the men of the 8th East Surreys to go over the top, a Captain Neville came up with the barmy idea of having his company kick a football across no-man's-land and chase it all the way to the German lines. The battalion was cut down, including their whistle-blowing captain.

Stupidity mustn't be confounded with simplicity. Some incredible feats were born from simplicity (only the envious call it stupidity) – that simple courage, not yet eaten away by over-intelligence. In difficult times simplicity can be a most priceless gift, a magic cloak that conceals the danger into which no super-bright will venture. Recently, a new kind of insane valour has emerged: a heroism confused with self-sacrifice. To fall on to an enemy's grenade that has rolled into a dugout, thereby saving the lives of many, can be truly called brave. To immolate oneself with a belt of dynamite sticks lashed around the belly is madness – even in the fulfilment of some sacred cause. The spiritual soul masters who instil in their youngsters a desire to become 'the salt of the earth, the engines of history, the most honourable amongst us', are reckless criminals; suicidal acts by their fanatical disciples can never be called heroic. Their only inspiration is self-destruction, while causing the deaths of many by using passenger planes as their flaming swords.

Taken from a great multitude, the characters here are possessed with one of the many elements that make a hero: basic instinct for survival, physical courage in action, resolution and determination, moral fortitude and moral courage, personal reliability, tenacity, quiet resolution and calm determination and boldness.

Time and again, heroes are like Shakespearean characters; they rise swiftly, are betrayed by their peers and stabbed in the back by their admirers; eviscerated by changing priorities, they lose everything and, finally, are misunderstood by all. Often, a brave man has to live by his wits rather than his weapon; he knows the risk involved and shows a willingness to bear it. Self-preservation is not his overriding motive; he pits good against evil, and by his individual act tries to rectify an injustice to help others without asking for recognition or reward. He is one who represents the very embodiment of the pure spirit of courage and dedication. We seldom hear of him: a faceless hero.

Feldwebel Kunze, A hero in spite of himself

'*Dieser Tag ist ein neues unwiderlegliches Zeugnis für das historische Gesetz, dass Männer Geschichte machen* – This day provides unquestionable proof to the historic law that it is men who make history.'

German *Reichs Archive*, 25 February 1916

His name was Kunze. Not Otto, not Wilhelm. Just Kunze. The friends, of whom there were just three left since they had set off into the slaughter in August 1914, called him 'Kunze'. The fresh replacement addressed him as 'Herr Feldwebel'. For the officers he was simply 'F'webl Kunze'.

Now, this Kunze was lying face down down in the muck with his finger anchored in dirt. He clenched his teeth, trying to forget the aftermath of yesterday's attack, when the dawn had revealed the corpses of the infantry bobbing in water-filled shell craters. Some of those bobbing bodies had been his men; they had drowned in two feet of water, struck down by bullets from French *mitraillettes*. He was on the bottom of such a shell crater, knee-deep in mud; all he could see in the pale winter's light was the dubious comfort of a steep earthen wall all around him, clumps of earth that an explosion had heaped up, humpy and uneven. Must've come from one of the big calibre *Krupps* to punch a hole like this. It was freezing cold and yet he could feel the sweat running down his chest. '*Scheisse, dieser Krieg, oh Junge* – Oh Boy, I hope you know what you're doing . . . it's all so bloody stupid, if you ask me . . .' he mumbled to no one, since he was all alone. Up to his neck in shit and not about to get out of it. That war wasn't going anywhere and neither was he. He heard the soft whistle of a shell slicing through the air, racing towards him . . . an ear-splitting explosion . . . all hung in suspension while he lay there shaking, with a ringing in his ears. In that elongated aftermath beyond rational thought, he knew instinctively that he had to get the hell out of that hole – *ahead*, because shells were beginning to explode *behind* him. He could tell by the noise, because he had become an expert; the first was a puny 7kg shell, the second was spit out by a 150mm and weighed a lot more. The third came from a 420mm and weighed a bloody ton. The man in his muddied field grey, with water rushing from his boots, scrambled up the crater wall and raced on through smoke. Straight forward.

Feldwebel Kunze was no charmer. Even his best friends would agree on that. Of friends he had only two left: Karl Stallwart and Heinrich Stieglitz. All the others were lying in some foreign field, with their steel helmets planted on a stick in the ground. Kunze was stocky, with a jaw like a wedge sticking out from a bullet-shaped head. His blond hair was cut down to stubble, not because of some stupid army regulation, but to avoid giving lice a chance. He was steady, strong and not greatly educated, but possessed with this a certain country smartness which, combined with toughness, comes from working the fields. When the Junker back home said: 'The field of barley beyond the lake looks ready . . .' the overseer would call Kunze and tell him to mow it. They had none of that modern farm machinery; everything had to be done by hand and, come evening, stroppy young Kunze would barely have the strength to take off his clothes and fall into bed, knowing that his next day began at three. Only Sunday was a holiday, when he went to church. The pastor had preached kindness, goodness and peace among all men, and sermoned them about unquestionable fidelity to the Kaiser and the Junker. The meal afterwards at the estate was the main event of the week: a thick bean stew with a slice of *Speck* (bacon) and potatoes with onions – that is, if that year the blight had not struck.

When winter storms whipped across the country, it was time to convert the hogs into *Speck* (for the farm hands) and ham (for the Junker's family). Kunze had taught himself the trade of slaughtering the pig, and he was proud of his skill. He would lead the hog out of the stall, tie a rope around its feet, knock it down and stick it in the neck. He had never received more than the basic schooling prescribed by law; he was instead a strong young man who took all his orders from the overseer and executed them without question. That avoided thinking. When war came, Kunze was the ideal mechanical robot to advance unquestionably into the death-spraying French *mitraillettes* (machine guns). He never volunteered for an attack; however, when he received the order to advance, he would look without expression at his officer, plant the bayonet on his rifle and, with a '*Jawohl, Herr Leutnant!*', march out into no-man's-land. For this, and also because he was one of the few survivors from the original bunch that had gone forth in 1914, he was promoted in the field to Vice-Feldwebel (1st sergeant). Kunze was no different from other soldiers. Every soldier grumbles, and then goes forth and does his duty. It was no different in 1914, 1915 or 1916. The front in France was hell. They were either shelled or bayoneted, or drowned in mud in their trenches during the rainy season. Grumbling was good for the soul, grumbling cleared the air, grumbling about the '*Frass*' (food) they called '*Stacheldraht*' (barbed wire), their meagre '*Schmalzportionen*' (fat portions), and their dissatisfaction with the fact that only officers were decorated with the '*Blaue Heinrich*', Germany's highest order of the *Pour-le-Merit*. So, like everyone else, Kunze grumbled, and then did what his *Leutnant* told him to do.

That was Kunze, pure product of Frederick of Prussia's school of thought, a king's readiness to countenance losses greater than that of his enemy in pursuit of victory, which had earned the Prussian warrior king the sobriquet of 'Grave Digger'. Yes, Kunze was the ideal German soldier: brave, obedient, never demanding to know the reason why, with a fearlessness bordering on recklessness that showed a lack of imagination. In a way, it was amazing that he was still alive. Perhaps he had had more luck than the others, or perhaps with a farm boy's intelligence, he was shrewd enough to try and foresee his enemies' moves – keeping his head down when it was called for.

At the outbreak of WW1, Feldwebel (Sgt) Kunze was twenty-two, a good age to die for *Kaiser und Vaterland*. Because he was born in Thuringia, he was automatically disqualified from enrolling into one of Prussia's elite infantry formations. However, he showed such an eagerness to die for his Kaiser, that the 24 Infanterie Regiment 'Brandenburg' took him on, not as one of the *Landsers* (attack troopers) marching behind the band, but as a mere *Pionier* (sapper), whose principal task it was to clear barbed wire entanglements and mines in front of the advancing *Sturmtruppen* (storm troops). The 24 Infanterie Regiment Brandenburg, a regiment famous for its iron discipline and perfect drill formation, had been formed as the elite of Prussia's army by none less than the Great Frederick himself, who also bestowed on them their regimental motto: '*Mehr als die Pflicht!* – More than just duty!' After the battle of Jena against Napoleon's armies (1806), *Marschall* Blücher had said of them: 'The Brandenburgers are the greatest. Their only fault is that they are much too brave.' At the outbreak of the First World War, they had been incorporated into General von Lochow's III Prussian Army Corps, and received their baptism by fire when they smashed through the British Expeditionary Force at Mons in the autumn of 1914. They marched all the way to the outskirts of Paris, but were turned around within 'sight of the Eiffel Tower' in the much discussed 'General von Kluck's Turn' at the Marne.

In 1915, the regiment was withdrawn from the Western front and sent to Serbia to bolster a slowly disintegrating Austrian Army. In a series of suicidal attacks, they smashed the Serbs, before they were again put on a train and shipped back to France in order to become part of the planned offensive against Verdun. On their train journey through Germany, the population tried to cheer them at various railway stops: '*Bravo, ihr tapferen Feldgrauen* – Hail to you brave men in field grey, give it to the *poilus* [French soldiers]. The *Vaterland* is eternally grateful to its victorious soldiers.'

The soldiers shrugged their shoulders. Those *Zuhausehocker* (sit-around-at-home-types) had never lived through a *Trommelfeuer* (artillery bombardment), and had not the slightest idea what a machine-gun bullet could do to human flesh. To hell with all that *Hurra-Patriotismus*! After a year and a half in the frontline the troops were worn out; very little was left of the exuberance of the first month of the war, when victory followed upon victory. August 1914 was still a time when Germans laughed at the signs painted by the French on the side of village houses: '*On les aura!* – We shall get them!' For the German soldier it was a great joke to paint the extra word 'pas': '*On ne les aura pas!* – We shall *not* get them!'

During their seemingly unstoppable advance on Paris, even the *poilus* began to murmur: '*On ne les aura pas!*', and, with it, the morale of the French, together with their frontline, collapsed. But that was in August 1914, and this was February 1916, after one and a half years of butchery on a sheer unimaginable scale. Time and again, the *Feldgrauen* (German soldiers) were sent out, with little or no support, straight into the centre of the enemy line, to be mowed down by machine guns. Of the original complement of the Brandenburger Regiment of 5000, barely 500 were still left to fight; the rest lay out in no-man's-land, their bones mouldering in the craters dug by artillery shells.

For almost a year, the Western Front had lain frozen in sleep. Sure, a few hundred thousand had died, victims of artillery duels and trench-line disease, of mud, infection and gangrene. But, other than such 'minor details', the daily bulletin issued by the German high command called it: '*Im Westen nichts Neues* – All quiet on the Western front.' This quietness was to be shattered with an earth-shaking bang. It started with a harebrained idea, never before tried in warfare: not to defeat the enemy in battle, but to bleed him white! In December 1915, the chief of Germany's General Staff, General Erich von Falkenhayn, laid this plan before the Kaiser. 'There are objectives within reach . . . for the retention of which the French General Staff would be forced to throw in every man they have. If they do so the forces of France will be bled to death, since there can be no question of voluntary withdrawal, whether or not we reach our goal . . . this objective is Verdun.'

For the last two months, General von Falkenhayn had

been pumping seventy-two battalions, their artillery and support units into a narrow frontline facing Verdun. The plan was to achieve a breakthrough and, with the German superior firepower of long-range artillery, cause an avalanche of casualties. The Kaiser had readily accepted the plan because he needed a major battle to keep the hungry masses at home from thinking about their problems. In Falkenhayn's plan he could see a solution; he accepted the idea and with it, he turned Verdun into a monstrous graveyard.

The Germans called it '*Operation Gericht* – Operation Judgment', and the French: '*Les champs de carnage* – The Fields of Slaughter'. And in the middle of it all: Fort Douaumont, *mot magique* for the French, and the biggest fortress in the French Rivières Line. The Germans called it the '*Sargdeckel*' (coffin lid). General Philippe Petain, the eventual commander of Verdun, called Douaumont 'the queen buttress in the entire French defence system'. With its carapace of steel and concrete, sitting squat astride a commanding 388-metre-high ridge, it controlled the approaches to Verdun. It was an indestructible hump, shaped like a turtle and bristling with heavy guns. An ingenious system of counter-weights pulled up its gun turrets, forged of 1-metre thick steel; in case of a bombardment, the turrets could recede flush into the 3-metre concrete shell, and not even a direct hit from one of the much-feared 42cm German mortars could put a dent into them – unless a lucky shot struck one of the few vulnerable spots, such as a gun port.

The fortress was protected by a wide *glacis* (field of fire), fronted by an 8-metre deep moat. If – and that was the most improbable *if* – anybody should ever manage to cut their way through the triple entanglements of barbed wire, the attackers could be swept from the field by turret-mounted machine guns firing in every direction. The interior of the fort was a rabbit warren of barrack rooms, hospital, ammunition storage, communication centre, and look-out posts, protected by steel shutters at each individual level. The air-lock doors and pillboxes were considered an unnecessary luxury as no enemy would ever get inside this magnificent fortress. Its main armament were the latest 155mm rapid-fire guns, capable of firing a shell every twenty seconds. Targets had been pre-sighted and the guns could be blind-fired in fog or at night.

In 1915 an event occurred that put the entire layout of France's string of fortresses in question. *Maréchal* Joffre took command of the French Army. This 62-year-old engineer had no use for static defences; he wanted all his men in the forward trenches, backed up by mobile artillery. The problem was that France had no artillery capable standing up to the German long-range pieces. Still, the order went out to strip Douaumont of most of its guns. But even more insane was the order pulling out its 600-strong garrison of experienced gunners in a move that was missed by the Kaiser's military intelligence. In departing, the *poilus* wrote – as a reminder of their presence – a phrase on the walls of the casemate: '*Il vaut mieux être sous les ruines.* – Bury yourself beneath the ruins of the fort rather than surrender!' Later, this slogan was to take on great significance – for the Germans!

While the pulled-out defenders of Douaumont were dig-ging trenches ahead of the fortress line, their battalion was hit by heavy German siege mortars and long-range artillery and all five hundred died, including the fort's comman-dant. The defence of the mightiest fortress in the French line was handed to a 65-year-old civilian without prior military experience who, for the occasion, was promoted to *sergeant chef*; Monsieur Chenot took his promotion very seriously and had a uniform tailored to befit his rank. With a skeleton crew of fifty-six men he was to service the three guns – two 75mm and one 155mm, all that was left after the rest had been stripped.

An incident in late 1915 showed the lunacy of the new French order. In a reshuffle of its army command, the fortress line was put under orders of the Governor of Verdun, General Herr, while the sector in which the main fortress was located was placed under another commander, General Chrétien. Since Chrétien and Herr, going back a long time, had little to say to each other, nothing much was done to coordinate a defensive strategy. Therefore, it happened that in December 1915, the Corps Commander General Chrétien went on an inspection tour of all defences in his sector. When he arrived before the tightly shut gate of Douaumont, Monsieur Chenot, infused with his importance as the commandant of the nation's biggest fortress, refused to open the door to the general. The reply, which was given by a sergeant to a general, must remain unique in the annals of warfare: 'This fort opens only to the Monsieur le Gouverneur de Verdun, and I will not allow you to enter without his explicit order.' To add insult to injury, Monsieur Chenot next yelled down from an open gun turret: 'I should have you arrested as a spy!'

This insult may have played a role in the forthcoming drama.

The Germans launched their Verdun offensive, 'Operation Gericht', at 09.00 hours on 22 February 1916. In a final vestige of military romantics in modern warfare, their III Army Corps, mainly Brandenburgers, marched in formation behind a military band playing 'Preussen's Gloria' into the concentrated fire of French machine guns. Despite their horrendous casualties, they continued to advance with cries of: '*Vorwärts mit Gott für Kaiser und Vaterland!*' That same morning, Lt Colonel Driant, with his regiment of Chasseurs, was lying in wait ahead and slightly to the flank of Douaumont in the Caures Woods. Driant tried desperately to get through to General Chrétien and warn him of the danger by leaving the cornerstone fortress of the entire French frontline stripped of its defences. Nobody at Corps level cared to listen and his message never reached General Herr until it was much too late to stave off the disaster. On the night of the 22nd, Colonel Driant visited the position of Lt Robin, who was placed slightly in advance of the Caures Woods. '*Mon Colonel*, what am I to do with my eighty soldiers?'

'My poor Robin, I cannot help you,' replied the harassed colonel. 'Our order is to hold out to the last man.'

'But there is at least a full regiment coming down on us.' Lt Robin was wrong in his estimate. They weren't facing a regiment, but the entire German XVIII Army Corps. The Germans launched their attack with the 81, 87, 115 and 117 Regiments and in record time overran the position to the east of Driant's battalion. During this battle the French 362me Régiment lost 1800 men.

The German breakthrough opened the gate towards the twin pillars of Douaumont and Vaux. To stem that onslaught on his position in the Caures Woods, Lt-Col. Driant sacrificed his 1200 chasseurs. The brave colonel fought on until there was no more hope, before he gave the order to withdraw. One of his soldiers, Chasseur Papin, was wounded in the shoulder and bleeding profusely. Driant dragged him into a shell crater and applied a bandage, when the first Germans appeared on the crater's rim. A bullet struck Driant. 'Oh! Mon Dieu!' he cried out before he fell face down on to the wounded chasseur. But the Germans also suffered heavily; in the attack, their XVIII Army Corps lost 2350 soldiers. The official French war diary vindicated Driant's heroic stand. 'The Chasseurs of Lt-Col. Driant fought a valiant holding action, while nobody heard their call for assistance. What they accepted, accomplished and suffered is beyond description.'

All along the line the picture was very much the same; the defenders fought to the last bullet, but could do nothing against the German artillery. The long-range 250mm Krupp cannons with their 300kg shells flattened the French trenches and the *poilus* in them: '*Toute personne qui n'aura pas vu* – Anyone who hasn't seen the fields of carnage will never be able to get an idea. When you advance, the shells rain down at every single step, and still we must advance. We have to be careful not to step on all the horribly mutilated bodies that lie in the mud. Further ahead are a few wounded that are being bandaged, others are being carried back on stretchers. Some cry, some just lie there. We see some that have no more legs, others no head and which have been lying for weeks in the field.'[1]

With Driant's regiment wiped out, nothing was to halt the German advance.

Another calamity most certainly added to the drama. On 24 February 1916, General Chrétien, whose pride had been so greatly hurt at Douaumont, was reassigned in the middle of a battle and had to hand the command of his XXme Corps to General Balfourier, a man who arrived at Verdun after a long drive that left him utterly exhausted, having passed through an artillery barrage where his car had been smashed and his driver killed.

'What's the situation?' Balfourier enquired.

'There's nothing to worry about, the forts[2] are all properly manned,' Chrétien told him, and Balfourier had no reason to believe that it wasn't so. While he left to take a

---

[1] Letter found on a dead *poilu* in the Caures Woods.
[2] There were two major forts, both intended to protect each other, Douaumont and Vaux.

nap, the commander of the two brigades covering the flanks
of Fort Douaumont, General Deligny, urgently suggested
shifting his headquarters into the fort. Chrétien assured him
that this wasn't advisable as it would cut him off from his
troops, when a frantic call from the Governor of Verdun,
General Herr, was patched through to Chrétien. '. . . *Les
boches ont brisé la ligne de Driant . . . Géneral, prennez
immediatement toutes les dispositions* – The boches have
broken through Driant at Caures . . . take *immediately* all
dispositions to re-occupy the fortress line and hold it to
the last.'

'*Immediatement!*' was the word General Herr had used –
ordering Chrétien who, at this precise moment, was still the
general-in-command of the fortress sector, to tell General
Deligny to get himself *into* Douaumont. And so, on the
evening of 24 February, General Chrétien signed an order
in the presence of his ADC, Commandant Douare, to
dispatch immediately substantial regular infantry units to
man the fortress. Next morning, on the fateful 25th, when
Chrétien was about to hand over command to General
Balfourier, he received a shock. 'General Balfourier came
at 10.00 hrs into my HQ. We had known each other before
and I informed him of the situation. Then I saw on my desk
two slips of paper. One was the order of engagement for the
25th. The other was my order from the previous night to the
division commanders to immediately occupy the fortresses.
I stressed the importance of the second order and General
Balfourier studied both papers, and he said: "Those orders
still stand".'[3]

But the crucial error had been committed; whatever the
reason, the order that was to go out on the 24th in the
evening was still lying on the general's desk by 10.00 hrs
next morning. Who was guilty of failing to have passed

[3] Archives Nationales, Paris

on the crucial order was never identified, or perhaps, in order to preserve the honour of a general, the affair was buried in silence. If Chrétien did indeed delegate one of his staff officers to pass it on, the order to staff Douaumont with regular troops didn't reach the divisional commander Deligny until 18 hours later, by which time it was much too late. This blunder was to cost France 100,000 men!

And still the series of mistakes didn't end. Deligny had followed his previous orders from General Chrétien 'to anchor your two brigades on both sides of the buttress . . .' As Deligny's two brigades were being moved up to take up positions with Douaumont as its central buttress, one-ton 420mm mortar shells began slamming into the '*Sargdeckel*'. Deligny's brigade commanders wisely gave the fortress a wide berth, fearing losses from German long-range guns concentrating their fire on the fortress. Their bombardment had already proven its disastrous effect on the French. In only two days, between the 22nd and 24th, the French XXXme Corps had lost 65 per cent of its officers and men, all in all 413 officers and 15,892 men.

General Petain eventually came out in defence of the general: 'Chrétien saw our front collapse. Who could hold it? No more troops were available to him; since the night before (23rd) there were a mere 500 per unit left, the rest of their regiments' bloody remains lay scattered in the trenches . . .'

Deligny's move left an undefended corridor of over 500 metres on either flank of the fortress. He felt relatively certain that Douaumont's machine guns, its 155mm and 75mm shells, would take care of that strip of no-man's-land and stop the enemy from breaking through. This assumption was based on the final, yet most fatal breakdown in the chain of command, starting with *Maréchal* Joffre through General Herr, and from there to the frontline units: the covering brigades had never been informed that the fortress was stripped of its guns and virtually unmanned! And so it came about that on the fateful 25 February 1916, the biggest fortress in the world was left to fight on its own, defended by a skeleton crew of fifty-six men, of which only 12 were regular soldiers; the rest were ageing mechanics, left behind to grease guns and door hinges. To put no finer point to it, their commander, Monsieur Chenot, was not only the oldest man in the field, a man who had never heard a bullet whistle past him; still worse, he had always been a lowly employee, never in a position to take any decision of his own. That was the man in charge of the fortress, and about to be hit by the pride of Prussia's army.

Of course, the Germans were not aware of the series of French blunders. In any case, they had no intention of attacking this fortress, something they considered so hopeless an undertaking that it would only waste valuable manpower trying to take what couldn't be taken. The *Oberkommando's* (high command) plan called for leaving the '*Sargdeckel*' untouched and striking around its flanks, scoring a decisive breakthrough to the fortress chain in by-passing its main twin buttresses of Fort Douaumont and Fort Vaux. To do this, both fortresses would be hammered into silence by heavy artillery. The Crown Prince thereby adhered to a patent principle of warfare: by-pass any stout burgh that is too expensive to take, enclose it, and pound it to pieces. He had brought up a battery of 380mm mortars and some of the huge 420mm Big Bertha mortars to lob their one-ton monster shells at the fortress and keep it from reacting; sixty-two of these monsters scored direct hits – and produced no result. On the 25th, the German bombardment continued from 09.00 hrs until noon. The impacts sent up fountains of earth and dug huge craters; it turned the ground in front of the German starting positions into a moonscape. At 15.45 hrs, Major Kurt von Klüfer of the 2 Battalion, 24 Regiment Brandenburg, received his orders: 'Sweep around to the right of Douaumont. Under no circumstances attempt a direct assault.'

It was a cold, snowy winter's day, with a thick cloudy overcast; at 16.00 hrs, the troops went over the trench to launch their attack. While the battalion advanced through the churned-up field, a pioneer unit of a dozen men under the 24-year-old Feldwebel Kunze preceded the infantry. Kunze's men were armed with nothing more lethal than rifles and wire cutters. They were to clear a path through barbed wire entanglements to the right of the fortress for Klüfer's storm companies. Their order was to advance steadily, behind a creeping barrage of heavy artillery shells,[4] impacting as little as 50 metres ahead. They knew that in war, and especially in the precision of artillery fire, nothing ever went according to plan. Kunze's troop didn't trust their own gunners and began to move at a pace directed mostly by their own instinct, dictating both timing as well as the direction of their advance. They moved to wherever the shells had already fallen. The higher they climbed, the less they could see ahead or behind, losing all contact with their battalion.

And now occurred one of these unexplainable sets of circumstances every war is known for, and which often decides history. Obeying their orders, Kunze's lot kept stumbling on, following behind the impacts of the creeping advance of the artillery bombardment. They didn't encounter any enemy, though they could hear the rattle of machine guns from their flank. It was there that Major von Klüfer's 2 Battalion had run into resistance from a machine-gun company under Captain Delarue. Another Brandenburg battalion, the 3rd, ran into a contingent of colonial Zouaves from North Africa. After a brief but

---

[4] An invention, first tried out at Verdun, where shells crept slightly ahead of the advancing units.

bloody fight, the Zouaves turned and ran, chased up the hillside by Brandenburgers.

In what must be a First World War speed record for an advance, a company of Germans under *Oberleutnant* Cordt von Brandis, pursuing their fleeing enemy, stormed in twenty-five minutes the 1000m to the top of the ridge and halted on the crest, a kilometre from the '*Sargdeckel*' fortress.

Their speed was also to be their downfall. No sooner had they reached the top of the hill than a German artillery spotter saw silhouettes on the ridgeline and took these for a French formation preparing a counter-attack. He swung his guns away from Douaumont, bringing a frightful artillery barrage on his own units. *Oberleutnant* von Brandis fired white phosphorous flares, but the signal rockets were snuffed out by the snow flurries; it left him with no choice but to pull his company back from the exposed ridgeline, before 'friendly fire' wiped them all out. Finally, the artillery spotter, having realised his error, aligned the guns back on to their original mission, the barrage creeping up the hill of Douaumont. While this confusion went on, with the guns momentarily diverted from Douaumont, and von Klüfer's 2 Battalion enfiladed by heavy machine-gun fire from the church steeple of the village of Douaumont, Feldwebel Kunze and his men had kept marching through snow flurries in a straight line up the hill. They came upon a single *poilu* with a leg wound hiding out in a crater.

Kunze stopped briefly to slap a bandage over the man's wound to stop the bleeding; as he walked off, and looked over his shoulder, he saw the *poilu* picking up his gun, most likely to use it as his crutch. Kunze shot him dead. They thought that the creeping artillery barrage had been halted when, all of a sudden, the German guns swung back from their faulty ridgeline target to pound once more the hill leading up to the fortress.

Kunze, with his handful of sappers, suddenly found to their horror that they were actually *ahead* of the German artillery halt line, with impacts moving steadily up on them. They were caught in a deadly trap: an enemy fortress ahead and the fire-roller moving in from their back. They couldn't go back, or most assuredly they'd be blown to bits, and they couldn't move ahead, because somewhere beyond the curtain of snow flurries lay the formidable *Sargdeckel*, sprouting machine guns as thickly as a porcupine has needles. What was amazing, was that until this moment the fort's machine guns had remained silent. Kunze followed his survival instinct: the only chance for them to survive the creeping barrage of shells lay up ahead, in the lee of the walls of the fortress, or perhaps down in the moat which surrounded the fortress, and was out-of-reach to the shallow trajectory of the German guns. Kunze, who had been separated from his men, each cowering in his own, private shell crater, managed to round them all up: '*Auf marsch-marsch!*' he yelled over the din, stumbling through the snow flurries towards the fort.

At that moment all hell broke loose in front of them. Kunze was certain that they had been spotted. The men threw themselves to the ground and clutched the earth with their fingers, as the fortress's lone 155mm began belching flame and smoke – firing over their heads at the following storm troopers, or so it seemed. No sooner had the French fired their first shot than the German heavy guns took the fortress for their aim, while their medium calibres continued pounding the approach. The intensity of fire that rained down on Douaumont was near unimaginable. In the three and a half hours since the bombardment began, the eight 210mm mortars of I/Fuss Artillery 12, lobbing its bombs of 600kg, fired 860 shells at the fortress.

Kunze's sappers were caught between French guns, blazing away over their heads, and impacts from German guns both in front and behind. After a nearby explosion, one of his men threw up his hands, struck in the chest by shrapnel. He stumbled forward, cried upon God, and cursed his country. Another clutched the earth and wept quietly for his mother. The rest wearily fought their way through the tangled barbed wire. The ground shook, flames shot from new craters. Yet what every German soldier feared the most, the death-spitting French *mitraillettes*, remained strangely silent. Only one explanation was possible. Since they had moved out into the open *glacis*, the French must have seen them and didn't dream that these men in front could possibly be Germans; they took them as retreating French.

'*Vorwärts!*' Kunze shouted from the top of his lungs between gulps of air. His men could just about hear his cry above the din of impacts. Around them the world had gone completely mad. The sappers followed close on his heels, stiff with fright in case the machine guns started to fire. Actually, what had happened was that an ageing Monsieur Chenot, suffering from shell-shock from the incessant pounding, had simply failed to put look-outs into the fort's towers and the half-dozen professional gunners, manning the 155mm, were too busy staring out into the blinding snow to look down to the nearby *glacis*.

The barbed wire entanglement had been shredded by impacts, and Kunze's men stumbled on. Suddenly they came upon a two-and-a-half-metre-high spike fence. And beyond it rose a grey-walled monster – like a sleeping sphinx lay the massive complex of Fort Douaumont! What to do? A dozen Germans against Douaumont: the equation was not only uneven, it was downright ludicrous. The silence of the machine guns encouraged Kunze to push on; but how was he to get over the spike fence? There was no visible route and their wire-cutters were of no help against steel bars. Suddenly came the chatter of a machine gun. Kunze heard the cupola ring sharply and he spun around. Bullets slammed into the steel gun turret above him, whizzing off into the sky like angry fireflies. The stream of fire was coming from one of the nearby hills, or perhaps from the village of Douaumont.

Kunze lunged into a shell crater, sliding down into a puddle of mud. He huddled against the side, down for the count from fatigue. A yell overhead made him look up, and he saw his friend Karl Stallwart tumbling towards him. Instinctively, he grabbed him before he fell headlong into his crater to drown in the mud. His friend landed on top of him, shrieking with pain. A bullet had shattered his elbow and gone into his side; another one had grazed his forehead. Kunze used his bayonet as a splint and wrapped a bandage around his friend's arm: '*Bleib liegen, wir bringen dich runter* – Stay put, we'll get you down.' He had no idea how. Bullets from the side, shells from the back and a tall spike fence in front. That's when the god of war lent a helping hand. A German 210mm shell landed nearby, ripped a hole in the fence and, at the same time, its blast lifted Kunze through it, or over it, and he landed in the deep mud of the moat, leaving him dazed but unhurt. He waved to his men, peeking over a crater's edge on the other side of the fence. Only one, his friend Heinrich Stieglitz, wriggled through the hole and slid down into the moat, hanging on to a string of telephone wires. '*Wir müssen Karl runterschaffen* – We have to get Karl down,' said Kunze.

Stieglitz shook his head and screamed to be heard over the noise of explosions: *Den Karl hat's erwischt . . . er ist tot.* – Karl's got it . . . he is dead.'

'*Scheisse*,' said Kunze, trying to comprehend the curious fate of war. The shell that had lifted him to relative safety had also killed his friend. He had seen men die before, but this had been his friend. Scenes passed before his eyes. He blinked several times and stared up at the rim of the moat, imagining the crater with the body of his friend in it. And then a shell exploded a few yards off and his own perilous situation came back to his mind: a sergeant with wire-cutters, leaning against the wall of the biggest fortress on earth, with German shells smashing into the cupola, and steel shrapnel whizzing crazily all around. Instinctively Kunze raised his rifle and drew a bead on a gun port, but couldn't detect movement behind it. Slowly he backed away from the wall to look for the rest of his squad. He called out to them, still cowering in shell craters up on the lip of the moat, telling them to slide down along the same wire Heinrich had used and to join him and a voice answered: '*Feldwebel, du bist vollkommen verrückt* – You are absolutely mad.' But they had to follow him down into the ditch, because up there they would be blown to smithereens by German shells or be seen from the machine-gun turrets of the fortress.

'*Scheisskerls* – Shitheads – obey!' and they came sliding down the wire to join him, because an order was an order in the German Army.

'*Mir nach* – Follow me,' Kunze yelled, and ten scared men dashed along the bottom of the moat towards the rear of the fortress, to get out of the direct artillery fire. By no means did that put them out of danger; artillery shells hit the fortress with increasing accuracy. Inexplicably, the fort's *mitraillettes* remained silent and the *Feldwebel* failed to understand how the look-outs could miss a bunch of steel-helmeted soldiers running around their walls. The German bombardment increased in intensity and they had to get *inside* the walls of concrete. That was their slim, but only chance of survival. Kunze checked for an opening, a gate, a shell hole, but all he saw were walls rising vertically from the ground. Then he spotted an open gun-slit in one of the high cupolas. He was much too exhausted to think and wonder why the hole didn't have a gun sticking out from it! In fact, it was one of the turrets where a 155mm gun had been removed. The hole was some three metres up a sheer cliff.

In a flash of genius, brought on by the urgency of survival he recalled how as boys, on the first day of spring, they had built human pyramids to get at the sausages on the village's May tree. Granted, this wasn't a spring festival with fat sausages as its prize, but a pyramid was a pyramid and it was the only way to get him up near the opening. The sappers, with their backs pressed against the wall, built a human pyramid, which collapsed three times before Kunze managed to haul himself up and grab the ledge of the gun embrasure. He pulled, until his head and shoulders were through the hole. Before him was only darkness and he expected to be shot at any moment. Nothing happened, nothing moved. With a final push he wriggled through the gun slit.

He found himself in an abandoned gunroom, with a hole in the floor through which the ammunition elevator's cables dangled. For the first time in well over an hour he stopped to catch his breath, blowing into his cold hands, his rifle in the crook of his arm. Through the hole came the blue flashes of explosions along the *glacis*; shrapnel from a shell came flying through the turret's opening. Kunze dropped to the floor and clamped his arms over his head, while the steel cupola above him echoed with a metallic clatter like a church bell. He crawled to the hole in the floor and the smell of stale air hit him from the dark. He lowered his legs into the hole, hanging on to the elevator's cable until his feet found an iron rung. After ten rungs he ended up in a pitch-black tunnel. He was sidling along the wall with a probing rifle barrel held before him, when he struck an obstacle. With trembling fingers he struck a match and took a quick look. He found a door barred by heavy bolts, which could be operated by a central wheel. He turned it, the door opened and cold air struck his face. He was back out in the open, just above the moat where he had left his men. He called out, but they told him in no uncertain terms that he was out of his bloody mind to walk into the lion's den, armed with a rifle. They'd just as happily wait out in the open, crouching down in the cover of the deep moat until the war was over.

Only Heinrich was ready to join him, the rest slunk away and were eventually killed by shrapnel. Kunze quickly pulled Heinrich through the open door, telling him to keep guard and shoot anyone trying to get in or out who didn't wear a German helmet, before he set off all on his own back down the long, dark tunnel. He stumbled along in complete darkness, feeling his way along the humid wall. Way out front was a circle of yellow light; it came from a hurricane lamp hanging on a nail, throwing a yellow glow into the foetid darkness. At least he had a light.

The first tunnel branched into a second, equally dark and narrow, before he reached a stairwell with the thumping of regularly spaced explosions especially dominant. These stairs must lead to the gun tower and the booming sound be that of a firing 155mm. Slowly, in one hand the hurricane lamp, in the other his rifle, he climbed up. His hobnailed boots skittered on the humid stone steps. It felt eerie, creeping around, deep in the bowels of an enemy fortress.

Mentally, the *Feldwebel* was like a man who can never fully wake up. His body made the motions, but it was as if his eyes never focused, or all his limbs were numb. Each of his actions had a dreamy, ineffectual quality, almost as if he no longer believed in his own existence. The stairs ended in a box, with shell casings stacked against the walls and a black iron door. It looked solid, no bullet or shell would ever go through this one. It was meant to protect the stacked, live ammunition from exploding. And there he was, a simple sergeant, who, with one well-aimed bullet, could send France's biggest fortress sky-high! But that would kill him, too, and he didn't feel suicidal at all. The door had a metal wheel, like a bank vault. The *Feldwebel* squeezed himself against the wall, stared fixedly at the wheel, and waited for it to turn. He waited, one minute, two . . . to him it seemed a lifetime. He had to act before someone came for more ammunition, so he listened for the next explosion to dampen the sound of the wheel. *Boom!!* went the cannon, and he quickly turned the wheel, before he pushed on the door. It opened silently, riding on well-greased hinges. He eased his head through the door; a quick glance told him that the *Stollen* (tunnel) led into the bowels of the fortress. Nothing stirred. So where was the enemy? There should have been hundreds of them, and yet everything had an abandoned look. There were no voices, no kitchen smell, just silence – except for the explosions, striking the fort's shell like a drum. The only valid explanation – that there was no garrison – was, for a German soldier, too outrageous to contemplate.

Here began a series of such odd coincidences that is so uniquely special to mortal combat and sometimes turns war into a pantomime of heroism – a farce in the face of impossible odds, the clown with his head stuck in the lion's jaw. Only, this wasn't a circus, this was an impregnable fortress with lethal bullets and men ready to kill. There was a loud report from close by. It had Kunze jump back, until a metal knob from another door jabbed him in the pelvis. He sucked on his teeth so hard that blood popped from his gums on to his dry tongue. Another bang, and this time he was sure that the explosions had come from behind the door. This had to be the access to the gun turret. Carefully he pushed the door open and was momentarily blinded by the strong light from an electric bulb. A quick glance showed him four gunners inside the room, feeding and firing an awesome short-barrelled 155mm gun.

It was difficult to say who was more surprised; Kunze did the only thing that came to his mind, he pointed his rifle and yelled: '*Hände hoch!*' And, with it, Feldwebel Kunze captured the fort's only operational field gun. The surprised gunners didn't put up any resistance when Kunze ordered them to march out of the gallery in front of his rifle; he let them lead him down another dark tunnel that ended up in front of another steel door. He ordered his prisoners to operate the wheel, which they did quite eagerly. The door opened into an interior courtyard. That moment a shell struck a cupola, the air blast whirled debris and dust in his face, while his four captives bolted across the courtyard to make for another door and slid back into the fortress. He felt trapped!

The gunners would certainly raise the rest of the *poilus*, and they would come gunning for him. Then he would die – or perhaps not. Because, like many soldiers, he held on to the primitive belief that if one anticipated the worst it would never happen. But he was so pumped up with adrenaline that he threw out all precaution while diving after them into the same hole. He cursed himself for his madness, armed with a rifle and two hand grenades, running about inside a fortress. He was alone, tired, thirsty and hungry and in pain from a bruised knee. He was trained to receive orders, but there was no one to give him any. Kunze was on his own and he had to act on his own; come to think of it, his action might even earn him the Iron Cross – if he wasn't dead by then.

He found himself before yet another door. Muttering a prayer, he slowly gave it a shove with his rifle, wondering if this time he was going to be blown to bits. This one squeaked on its hinges when opening on to a long, wide corridor dimly lit by candles, with dozens of men lying on bunks; despite the racket of the guns and the impact of shells, they had succumbed to exhausted sleep. What had worked before would perhaps work again. They were asleep, he was wide awake; they were in the light and he was in darkness. They might not notice that he was all alone.

'*Hände hoch!*' he screamed, and they tumbled from their bunks, drowsy with sleep. That's when a shell burst out in the courtyard. The air blast carried in through the tunnel and through the door he had left open, snuffing the candles. Before they could gather their wits and come rushing at him, Kunze slammed the door shut and wedged a metal bar across it. He stumbled along the dark corridor, having just captured thirty men with a bolt-action rifle and without firing a shot. He sat down on the wet floor and searched his pockets for a smoke.

With shaking hands, he fished the stubble of a cigarette from his pocket and lit it with his last match. He was aware of his aching face, his exhaustion. Nothing moved, no sound except the pounding of his heart. He had fought in the trenches and attacked across open fields, and there he was scared. But this dark, damp fortress was like being buried alive inside a tomb. Fear welled up inside, something sinister, like moon eclipses or two-headed calves were for his villagers the omen of an unknown universe. The tunnels closed in on him, he was beset by an understandable panic of claustrophobia, and he fought for air in the foul dampness. Panic overcame him; he tightened his grip on his rifle.

He had an overwhelming impulse to run out of this rabbit warren and into the open, shells or no shells. The width of the abyss that now separated him from other mortals, his comrades, grew more evident, and it was some minutes before he tiptoed forward; his feet moved faster than his mind. He had to get out of here, run away, anywhere. Above this dark tunnel there was fire and death, but down here in the bowels of the fortress it was dark, stifling and frightening. Some god had shown him a way to get in, now he prayed that the same deity would show him the way out. Then he heard shuffling feet further up the dark tunnel. They were coming after him! Or were they? He made out a dim outline of someone walking with a candle. It was a *poilu* without a weapon.

'*Hände hoch!*' Kunze yelled for the third time within twenty minutes. The Frenchman froze, flung his arms into the air and yelped in pain as hot candle wax dripped on to his hands.

'*Ne tirez pas* – Don't shoot!' he screeched in a thin voice; it was a boy, seventeen at the most, hands shaking and his eyes and lips twitching. It occurred to Kunze that shooting this boy was not going to make any difference to the outcome of the war. The *Feldwebel* who, other than his Thuringia dialect spoke no known language, yelled: '*Offizier?*'

The boy didn't understand what the German wanted; all he saw was the wrong end of a pointed rifle.

'*Ne tirez pas, mon Capitaine . . .*' he mumbled. The *Feldwebel* was no *capitaine*, he just jabbed the kid with the barrel of his gun:

'*Wo Offizier?*' Between a thoroughly frightened French teenager and a worried German sergeant, this conversation was more a dialogue of the deaf.

'*Ja, ja, officier,*' stuttered the Frenchman and made a sign with his hand to follow him. He brought Kunze to a room that was abandoned. '*Voici la cantine des officiers* – the dining room of the officers,' stuttered his prisoner. It wasn't entirely empty – in the light of the boy's flickering candle was a table holding a treasure, a basket of farm eggs and a bottle of wine! So what did the good *Feldwebel* do in the midst of a *Trommelfeuer* inside an enemy fortress with probably its entire garrison out searching for him? He sat down at the table and began to crack open eggs and wash them down with generous gulps of *vin rouge*. After weeks of a rancid *Stacheldraht* diet, this was indeed a memorable feast. Soon he was so content with himself that he smacked his lips and offered the bottle to his French captive, who grinned and took a hefty swig. Kunze gulped and he burped and soon warmth was flooding through him, especially after his teenage prisoner had produced a large slice of cheese, bread, and another bottle from behind a munitions shelf.

'Hmm,' marvelled Kunze, '*französischer Wein.*' Such delicacy was ordinarily reserved for colonels and generals. His gluttony took him the better part of half an hour. He was feeling no pain when he heard the distinctive sound of the 155mm gun firing again, the one that he had conquered and silenced. It was time to get out. While the good *Feldwebel* was stuffing himself with eggs and cheese and wine, a gun relief crew had shown up in the turret to find nobody manning the big gun.

'*Quel bordel,*' cursed one of the gunners. 'Those bastards have gone to sleep.' He shoved a shell into the breach, and the gun was back in operation after half an hour's silence, lobbing shells into the heavy snow flurries.

With Kunze inside the fortress now for almost an hour, where was the rest of the Brandenburger's 2 Battalion under Major von Klüfer? The explanation for their delay can be found in a report by French Lt Péricard of the 12me Companie de Chasseurs:

My company was somewhat luckier than the rest, who could only find cover in the many craters while the *boche* shelled our trench line, running in a right angle from Douaumont village towards the fortress. As the only surviving officer of 12me Companie, I held command over the sector. To my left was *Adjudant* Debard with 2me Section (Platoon), Sergeant Durassié and 3me Section held the centre and my 4me Section was the one closest to the fortress. Capitaine Delarue of the 3me Companie Mitraillettes had dug in his machine guns ahead of us on the edge of a wood to cover the approach to Douaumont village.

After heavy shelling, which lasted throughout the morning, the Germans halted their bombardment at 13.00 hrs. It was a pleasant reprieve for my men. It didn't last long; by 15.30 hrs, their guns began shelling the fortress; that's when we noticed white signal rockets some 600 metres from the fortress, but since the enemy's position was covered by a ridge we couldn't make out if they had halted, or were advancing. It was at this time that we began having doubts about the way that the men inside the fortress behaved. There was no counter-fire and Douaumont remained strangely silent. What had happened to their machine guns, why did they not react to the German signal rockets? Their behaviour was incredibly passive.

It must be remembered that none of the French units was aware that only a skeleton crew, commanded by an old civilian, manned the fortress.

Sgt Durassié and myself discussed the situation and we decided that he was to get up to the fortress to see what was going on. He was about to leave, when four or five groups of soldiers appeared 200 metres in front of our lines, walking unconcerned, with their guns slung over their shoulders. These men *came from the German lines*, and were now well within the reach of our fire, and yet they seemed utterly unconcerned. What in the world was going on? That's when we saw their headgear and we understood: they wore the *chéchias* of our Zouaves! These were our soldiers, and we had almost fired on them! We knew that their unit was in our sector because only a few hours before we had taken into our trenches some survivors of the 9me Regiment des Zouaves that had managed to escape from a German attack.

If there was any doubt remaining that those were ours, we called out to a troop that passed our flank, moving up towards the fortress; the last three turned around and waved to us. However, Capitaine Delarue had a suspicion, he went forth to check on their identity when a 210mm shell exploded near him, killed three of his patrol and sent him flying through the air. He tried to get up but felt a pain in his shoulder. Still he managed to crawl back to give orders to his machine gun to open fire on the Zouaves! I ran over to him to ask him to stop the fire, when he yelled at me: 'You've allowed them to pass – they came from the *boche* lines. *Those are boches!*'

That moment we got orders from Colonel de Bénelet: 'Free fire at the Germans!' The Zouaves had quickly disappeared into shell holes. I was still convinced that we were shooting at fellow Frenchmen, and Sgt Durassié offered to crawl ahead to look for himself. He was only a few metres from the Zouaves, when a heavily accented voice called out to him:

'*Posse fusil . . . hierher* – Drop your gun . . . come here!'

Durassié kept yelling: '*Feu! Feu!* – Fire! Fire!' and then immediately threw himself into a shell hole while our machine guns began to chatter, and cut into the advancing Zouaves, which weren't French, but Germans. During the night, Durassie made it back into our lines.'[5]

The action engaged by Capitaine Delarue's machine gunners, and the bravery of Sgt Durassié, had delayed by a full hour Major von Klüfer's 2 Battalion from reaching the fortress in the wake of Kunze's sapper group. The appearance of Germans wearing red Zouave caps remains one of the many unexplained mysteries of the war.

Something else delayed the German main advance. The 6 Kompanie of Lt Müller, with its two platoon leaders, Lt Morgenroth and Lt Radtke, were using the deep valley of the Hassoule to move around the embrasure of the mighty fortress. They belonged to Major von Klüfer's battalion but, like Kunze's lot, had lost contact with head-quarters. Their advance was supposed to be supported by the light howitzers of the 39 Feld Artillerie Kompanie of Lt

[5] Péricard, J., *Verdun 1914–1918*, Paris 1933.

Wackerzapp. The storm troopers had just emerged from the relative protection of the ravine and were advancing along the *glacis* by the side of the fortress, when shells rained down on them. Since no order had been given to German troops to move on the fortress, their own artillery spotters mistook them for retreating French units! Looking with binoculars through drifting snow the spotters saw figures moving towards the fortress, and ordered: '*Massenfeuer um Fort Douaumont!*'

The guns opened up – and struck Major von Klüfer's II Battalion of Brandenburgers, ascending the slope towards the *glacis*. While the troops first thought that the firing came from the fort, this thought was quickly dispelled when more shells fell around them than they counted enemy muzzle flashes. To indicate his troop's forward position and stop the German gunners from killing off his entire unit, Radtke fired phosphorous star shells, which were extinguished by the snow flurries. Lt Radtke, as Kunze had done before him, realised that their single hope for survival was reaching the protection of the deep moat around the fortress. Despite the heavy bombardment, he and his men slithered through craters towards the barbed wire entanglement and the pike fence. Through holes, blasted by the artillery, those who had made it through the bombardment, slid exhausted down into the moat.

While Lt Radtke operated on the left side of the fort, another unit, the 7 Kompanie of Hauptmann's Hans Joachim Haupt also managed to get close to the fortress. When a lieutenant dared to point out to his captain that they had exceeded their artillery's halt-line by several hundred yards, Haupt shouted: 'Damn the halt-line, we're going to storm Douaumont!' And when his men still hesitated, he yelled: '*Vorwärts! Wer fällt, fällt!* – Onwards, who falls, falls!' It was never established which of the two officers crossed first into the ditch to reach the fortress,

Radtke or Haupt; afterwards both claimed the honour and an awkward argument broke out'[6] which was to cast a deep shadow of human weakness over one of the most extraordinary events of the First World War. It is only known that somewhere outside the wire entanglement, creeping up in growing darkness from different directions by using the protection of shell craters, the men of Capt. Haupt met those of Lt Radtke, when a voice cried out: '*Hauptmann Haupt ist gefallen* – Captain Haupt has been killed.' Radtke, as the officer next in rank, took over. But Haupt wasn't dead; a 210mm shell had landed close to him and killed two soldiers next to him, but the captain was merely dazed; the concussion had knocked him down and he lay stunned on the ground.

By this time, Feldwebel Kunze, the 'hero despite himself', had been *inside* Fort Douaumont for well over three-quarters of an hour; he had silenced the only operational cannon, locked up its garrison, and enjoyed a memorable feast. But now he faced a problem – and not a minor one in the Kaiser's army: the good Feldwebel Kunze was quite drunk and drunkenness in war was punishable by execution in the field.

From here on, the accounts differ greatly. One thing is certain: Lt Radtke, either on orders from Capt. Haupt, or on his own initiative, took sixteen men[7] and, with Lt Neumann, penetrated through the moat into the fortress. They came to the door that had been guarded by Heinrich Stieglitz. Radtke found the corpse of a German sapper (probably Stieglitz) across the entrance, killed by fragments from a shell, which had impacted on the

---

[6] According to the official German account.

[7] *Soldaten*, Klein, Kühn, Steiling, Zaeschke, Blankenstein, Reiche, corporals Back, Esner, Zablitzki, Hartung, Haefke, Hempel, Sgts Heyder and Ewald, and Lts Bartsch and Nürnberg (both of 10th Company).

chiselled 'Fort de Douaumont' sign above the door. If it needed proof, the body was a sure indication that some Germans had reached the fortress *before* Radtke and Haupt.

Radtke shouted over his shoulder: '*Mir nach!* – Follow me!' There was no holding them back. Radtke's men stormed into the dark tunnel stretching out into darkness in front of them. In the light of flares, sweat could be seen glistening on brows and upper lips; muscles tensed at strange sounds. One can well imagine their surprise when they saw movement at the end of the corridor and Radtke yelled in heavily accented French: '*Prisonniers, Messieurs!*' and he was answered by a slurred voice: '*Schiesst nicht, ihr Scheisser, ich bins, der Kunze* – Don't shoot, you shitheads, it's me, Kunze.' With the better part of two bottles of delicious burgundy in his belly, Kunze was quite wobbly, and so was his captive who had shared the wine with him. Radtke's men stared at him with gaping mouths, stumbling past them and out the door.

'*Kunze, von wo in der Welt kommst du denn her* – Where in the world are you coming from?' asked *Leutnant* Voigt, the commander of Pionier-Zug 4/22 Sächsische Pioniere. *Leutnant der Landjäger* Voigt was Kunze's Pionier-Zug commander and direct superior. Taking photographs on the way, Lt Voigt, accompanied by *Pionier* Hempel, reached the moat by its '*rue de rempart*', the North Court.[8] So when Voigt asked him where he had just come from, Kunze, bearing a silly grin, pointed with his thumb over the shoulder. '*Von da hinten, Herr Leutnant, und dort*

[8] In civilian life, Lt Voigt was not only an engineer, but – what in this case made him so valuable – an accomplished amateur photographer, who went nowhere without his photo apparatus. It was because of this hobby, and the pictures he took on the afternoon of 25 February 1916, including marking down the times he took them, that a precise account of the taking of Douaumont could be established.

sitzen noch mehr von denen – From back there, and there sit more of those,' and with it he pushed his rifle barrel into his boy prisoner and strolled on.

The moat outside the walls began to look like a Sunday meeting place before church, with Germans congregating from all directions. All had been chased up the hill by their own artillery, and all had the same thought: to find shelter from the bombardment in the moat. While Lt Radtke and his nineteen men began to scour the rabbit warren for the French garrison that had been locked up by Kunze, *Hauptmann* Haupt had also entered the fortress compound. It gave rise to the quarrel about who had been the first inside the fortress. Both seemed to forget that Feldwebel Kunze had preceded them by well over an hour. *Hauptmann* Haupt penetrated into the moat complex by a monster crater from a 420mm shell, which had ripped a huge hole through the pike fence and caved in part of the moat; it had been discovered by Haupt's *Unteroffizier* (Cpl) Huschke.

'*Herr Hauptmann* . . . Over here.' Another officer got in on the act; it was the 27-year-old commander of 8 Kompanie, 3 Battalion, *Oberleutnant* (1st Lt) Cordt von Brandis, who had raced across the *glacis* and slid down the crater into the moat, when out of the opening of the fortress gate emerged the figure of a Frenchman with his hands in the air, followed by a gun-toting Feldwebel Kunze. Brandt managed to join up with Haupt before Kunze came up to them. The artillery was still as furious as ever and the Germans huddled against the wall, staring at Kunze like a creature who had stepped from Mars.

'*Wo . . . woher kommen Sie?*' *Hauptmann* Haupt asked incredulously.

'*Von da drinnen, Herr Hauptmann?*' Kunze pointed behind him, into the tunnel, when he realised that once again someone had asked him the same question: '*Warum*

– why?' Why indeed was everybody so interested in his recent whereabouts?

The captain raised his voice authoritatively. 'Why? Since when does a soldier ask of his officer an explanation?'

Von Brandis, who hadn't interfered up to this point, yelled at Kunze: '*Mein Gott, Mann, hast du deinen Verstand verloren* – Have you lost your reason? You answer when you are asked, *verstanden*?'

But it was Haupt who seemed most excited and flustered; here he was, a professional soldier at the twilight of his career, forty years old and still only a captain with no distinguished accomplishment, suddenly finding himself on the verge of turning into Germany's national hero as the conqueror of the enemy's most impregnable fortress, and there stood this dumb *Feldwebel* about to steal his halo. 'You sound like . . .' and then he suddenly stopped, as a thought came to him. The soldiers who had been watching the scene knew the captain's tone of voice and mannerisms, and they felt something coming that would not be pleasant. How surprised they were when Haupt turned to the *Oberleutnant* of 8 Kompanie, and said: '*Er hat viel mitgemacht* – He's been through a lot. This man looks . . . exhausted.'

He knew, and von Brandis knew, Kunze wasn't exhausted, Kunze was plain drunk. Yet Haupt had momentarily decided to rid himself of 'that dumb soldier' and not charge him with drunkenness, or the true story of who conquered the fortress might come out. Historic truth paled when faced with personal motivations and ambitions. Haupt knew it, and so did von Brandis, whose eyes focused on Kunze. 'Courageous fellow, this *Pionier*. What's your name, soldier?'

'Kunze, *Herr Oberleutnant*.'

Von Brandis knew, should it ever become known what had really occurred, they'd promote the dumb farm boy and turn him into a national hero. He also knew that Haupt would make quite certain that this wouldn't happen. And, indeed, Haupt took Kunze to one side: '*F'webl*, once we have the fortress secured, you shall have two weeks' home leave. Now take a rest.'

Kunze couldn't believe his good fortune; no charge plus two weeks out of the inferno was all he could think of. '*Jawohl . . . Herr Hauptmann . . .*' he stuttered, his brain numb from physical exhaustion and fogged by too much wine. The promise of home leave was the last he remembered before he staggered back into a tunnel and fell asleep.

Lt Radtke, by now deep inside the *Stollen*, needed to silence (once again) the 155mm cannon before it decimated the rest of the battalion, moving up on the *glacis*. He dispatched Lt Neumann, who tried to enter the gun turret from the parapet, but was instantly struck down by a bullet. *Gefreiter* Hartung, trying to pull the mortally wounded lieutenant to safety, was also killed. Meanwhile, Radtke, with only a handful of men, had found a casemate with four dozen utterly confused, unarmed French. This was the same batch that Kunze had locked up and who had been freed by one of the escaping gun crew; they had gone to ground in a deep tunnel, still not knowing what was going on above them. *Soldat* Zaeschke, who had before the war been a waiter in Strasbourg and spoke some French, yelled at them: '*Haut les mains, vous êtes nos prisoniers!*'

Lt Radtke, convinced that the fortress was booby-trapped and that any moment they would all be blown to smithereens, yelled at the shaking French: '*Ou sont les explosives* – Where are the explosive charges?' to which they all shook their heads in confusion. Radtke ordered to have the men, including *Monsieur-Sergeant* Chenot, brought into a room directly above the powder magazine. If the fortress was indeed wired, the French would be the first to die and therefore tell him where the charges were located. Radtke asked Voigt, the sapper lieutenant who had followed him into the *Stollen*, to check for fuse wire. Nothing was found. Radtke couldn't believe that the French hadn't taken the precaution to prepare the fortress for destruction. (Actually, General Herr had ordered it, but his order was not passed on!)

'*Kühn, rauf auf die Panzerkuppel mit unserer Flagge . . .*' With that order, Radtke ordered *Soldat* Kühn[9] to the top of the fortress's cupola, to make the German artillery cease their fire. This incredibly brave soldier undertook a suicidal mission; in mortal peril from impacting shells, he climbed to the top of the fortress and tied an artillery signal flag to a twisted metal tube that had been ripped from the wall by an explosion; he waved it furiously, hoping that the German spotters would see him before he was smashed to pulp. Despite the fountains of earth rising in the air and the heavy snow flurries, the flag was spotted and the shelling stopped! With Kühn's flag flying over the fortress, Fort Douaumont was officially in German hands. It had taken one hour and twenty-five minutes. Its capture was achieved without a single shot being fired.

Shortly before 18.00 hrs *Hauptmann* Haupt, being the senior officer in place, ordered all of his available forces to stand to order. A quick head count of the victorious company came to seventy-nine soldiers and nineteen officers and subalterns, lined up in perfect Prussian order in the interior courtyard. There should have been eighty, but one, a certain *Pionier Feldwebel*, was fast asleep in a tunnel.

'*Männer, wir habe soeben die stärkste Festung Frankreich's erobert* – Men, we've just conquered the strongest fortress of France,' and Haupt's men answered him with a rousing

[9] By a curious coincidence, *Kühn* (in German) stands for courageous.

cheer: '*Für Kaiser und Vaterland!*' While Haupt was busy clearing out the rest of the tunnels, he dispatched the officer junior in rank to him, *Oberleutnant* von Brandis, accompanied by a soldier, to bring news of the fall of Douaumont to regimental HQ, located in the forest of Caurières.

At 18.30 hrs, Major Kurt von Klüfer,[10] the commander of 2 Battalion, which had been delayed by *Capitaine* Delarue's machine guns in the village of Douaumont, finally showed up to take overall command to secure the fortress.

At 19.00 hrs. *Oberleutnant* von Brandis reached regimental HQ and found most of the senior officers bent over a table map, studying a plan that had been overtaken by the event he was about to announce. '*Wie zwei dem Grabe entstiegene Geister* – Like two ghosts, emerging from a grave, they [Brandis and the soldier] appeared in our dug-out.'[11] *Oberstleutnant* von Oven, alerted by the sudden commotion their arrival had caused, jumped up and embraced him. '*Von Brandis, Mann, Mein Gott, wo kommen Sie her* – Where have you come from?'

'From Fort Douaumont, *Herr Oberstleutnant.*'

'Come on, Brandis, no silly jokes.'

Brandis, a man known for his bombast, replied with a grandiose gesture, pointing up the hill. '*Herr Oberstleutnant, ich melde Douaumont ist fest in unserer Hand* – I report, Douaumont is secure in our hands!'

'*Das kann doch nicht wahr sein* – But how can that be, you've passed it on your left! Tell me the truth. How is Haupt, is he still alive? Can I talk to him?' And von Brandis described most skilfully his part in the *Handstreich* (surprise action) to capture the fortress, crossing the barbed wires, overcoming the palisades, down to the last detail

[10] Klüfer, the author of the work much of this account is based on.
[11] From the original regimental report.

of the half shot-off name 'Douaumont' over the main entrance. Kunze's name was mentioned nowhere. Col. von Oven grabbed the field telephone to pass on the momentous news to Corps HQ.

The initial message from regimental HQ, signed by the regimental commander of IR 24, and dispatched by his ADC, Lt Kluge, went out on 25 February 1916, at 22.00 hrs. Its text reflected the jubilation that *Oberleutnant* von Brandis's report had caused at HQ. Given the confusion that reigned, it reported the situation as the regimental staff perceived it to be:

MELDUNG VOM IR 24: FORT DOUAUMONT FEST IN UNSERER HAND, GESTÜRMT DURCH 7/24 UND 8/24 DURCH HAUPT-MANN HAUPT UND OBERLEUTNANT VON BRANDIS. BEIDE FÜHRER GANZ BESONDERS AUSGEZEICHNET – REPORT FROM I.R.24: FORT DOUAUMONT SOLIDLY IN OUR HANDS, STORMED BY THE 7/24 AND 8/24 OF *HAUPTMANN* HAUPT AND *OBERLEUT-NANT* VON BRANDIS. BOTH LEADERS SPECIALLY COURAGEOUS.

It was from the initial encounter between *Oberstleutnant* von Oven, the IR 24th's regimental commander, and *Oberleutnant* von Brandis's version of the action, that the tale emerged of how von Brandis and, to a lesser extent, *Hauptmann* Haupt, in a feat of individual brilliance had stormed the 'invincible' Fort Douaumont – to be transmitted from regiment to Corps, from there on to the German Crown Prince at Army HQ and then directly to the Kaiser. The official German communiqué of 26 February 1916 stated: '*Die Panzerfeste Douaumont, der nordöstliche Eckpfeiler der Festung Verdun* – The Fortress of Douaumont, north-eastern buttress of Fortress Verdun, was captured yesterday by units of the 24th Brandenburg Regiment and is in German hands.' The news shocked countries as far afield as India and the United States. Church bells rang throughout

Germany, and newspapers across the country ran the headline: '*Sieg in Verdun* – Victory in Verdun. The Collapse of France.' And while all this excitement took place, and *Oberstleutnant* von Oven, accompanied by *Oberleutnant* von Brandis rushed up the long slope to congratulate the victors on their momentous achievement, a certain *Feldwebel* Kunze was peacefully snoring off his drink in a corner of the fortress he had conquered.

The French refused to accept that their biggest fortress was gone. It couldn't be, it simply couldn't; Douaumont could not have been lost! Lieutenant Péricard was sent forth to determine the situation, when he stumbled upon the carnage in the Bois de Caures, the smashed remains of Driant's valiant battalion. Before him lay a confused vision of violent death. Lieutenant Péricard finally understood the meaning of ultimate sacrifice, the sanctification. But also its darker meaning – that of ultimate loss. He felt his own mortality. That moment a young French lieutenant spoke what became one of war's immortal phrases: '*Debout les morts!* – Stand up the dead!'

The commander of France's elite 37me Division, General de Bonneval, saw the German signal rockets climb into the sky over Douaumont. His men had lived for forty-eight hours under the explosive rain from German long-range guns, which had subjected them to appalling losses; rather than having his entire division blown to pieces by what must have now been a decisive German breakthrough to his flank, he ordered an immediate withdrawal. With this order two more divisional commanders, those of the 51me and 72me Division, followed suit and every strong point of the formidable 'fortress line', rimming the heights on the right bank of the Meuse River, was abandoned. Dubrulle, a sergeant in the 8me Regiment noted: '*Nous sommes perdu. Ils nous ont jeté dans la fournaise* – We are lost. They have thrown us into the furnace. We were the last resources; they have sacrificed us and our sacrifice will be in vain.' Of course, his generals did not see it in the same way.

'*Heureuses, malgré leur deuil dont le sang coule pour la patrie!* – Lucky, despite their great pain, are the families whose blood has been spilled for *la patrie*!' had declared General Rebillot in *Libre Parole*.

With the fall of Douaumont, French morale cracked, Verdun was virtually left without defence, and some German light units actually managed to get within machine-gun range of the city. And then the unimaginable happened: the German generals wouldn't believe in the reports by their scout patrols that the road to Verdun was open and that the French had withdrawn without putting up a fight. While thousands of civilians were observed by the German look-outs pushing prams and carts piled high with their belonging from the beleaguered city and French sappers were attaching explosive charges to the Meuse bridges, the German general staff was looking for the 'Gallic trap'. They were so convinced it must be a trap that they failed to act, or the war might have been over. The French sent in a new commander, who finally stabilised the line. And so the slaughter continued for another two and a half terrible years. 'A few shell-shocked survivors without contact with their unit, cowering in a muddy shell hole, covered by rusted cans and mangled weapons, shreds of uniforms and unexploded shells, rimmed with rotting corpses, that was the image that endless hundreds of thousands saw and lived at Verdun.'

At Verdun, just as for the rest of the First World War, killing was on a scale wholly disproportionate to any military objective attainable by either side. The German Crown Prince was to note in his memoirs: 'That 25th of February, we were within a stone's throw of ultimate victory.'

*   *   *

French propaganda tried to play down the loss as 'the Germans have occupied a useless ruin'. That night, General Herr was relieved and a new general, General Philippe Pétain, took charge of the Verdun sector. When he took command, he called together his officers: '*Messieurs*, the fall of Douaumont is a stain on the honour of France. We shall not rest until it is once again in our hands.' Throughout the spring and summer of 1916, French generals planned one futile attack after another, and the *poilu*, the common soldier, had to carry them out. Without let-up the French generals attacked a fortress that had been turned into the symbol for *honneur*, moral glory of transcending significance for *la Grande Nation*. '*Pendant les journées* – Day after day, the suffering endured by the soldiers surpasses the imagination. The dust whirled up by the endless shells, the summer heat, the acid air of exploding shells, has brought on an unsupportable thirst. All our canteens are empty, we've been forced to drink our urine.'[12] The Germans hung on equally stubbornly and turned Douaumont into a real *Sargdeckel*, coffin's lid. Neither side would give in, advance could be measured in metres. The Germans took Fort Douaumont without cost, and the French retook it at a staggering price.[13] To recover Fort Douaumont from the Germans, French heavy artillery fired 790,000 shells and their infantry lost two entire armies storming the bastion.

For the third time in forty-eight hours, an attack on the fortress had failed. Demoralised and haggard, revolted by the order to go over the top, again and again, into the fire from Spandau machine guns, the few that were left cowered exhausted in a shell hole in no-man's-land. '*Salauds!*

[12] *Historique du 67me Régiment d'Infantrie.*
[13] During the ten-month battle, losses by both French and Germans were between 800,000 and 1,000,000.

Ordures de merde – Scoundrels! Pieces of shit . . .' they cursed their own officers. That was before those terrible Krupps opened up on them. The dead from the last attack, who they had buried the night before, were flung up and impaled on torn branches of shredded trees. '*Va petit soldat! Ta fatigue, tes blessures* – Go on, little soldier, who cares about your exhaustion, your wounds . . .' wrote the Abbé Sertillanges:

Our *bataillon* set out for the assault on that cursed hill. No sooner had we come out into the open, than we were met by a murderous crossfire from concealed machine guns. All around us the ground burst in great fountains of earth; it was as if hell had been let loose. Only slowly, step for painful step could we advance across the cratered field. Our losses were murderous. It was desperate. All examples of heroic endeavour were useless and our artillery fired without noticeable result. We were hoping to get some relief from another reserve *bataillon*, attacking from the flank, because our frontal assault was a march into annihilation. From the ridgeline, machine guns sprayed us with death. Our orders were as always: *En avant!* It was a race with death. By 6pm, death had won. Our *bataillon* was decimated and we were ordered to retreat. From the 750 that had set off, we counted forty-two survivors. I guess, we were the lucky ones.'

The French soldier who wrote this account in a letter to his wife was killed a week later, on 24 October 1916, in the assault on Douaumont that finally proved successful.

'*La chute de Douaumont a côûté cent mille hommes à la France* – The fall of Douaumont has cost France one hundred thousand men,' wrote Philippe Petain, *Maréchal de France*.

An entire generation of French and Germans passed through Verdun before it was finally over. Verdun decided nothing. At Verdun, there were only losers. One of the

German defenders, *Leutnant* Werner Beumelburg, who fell in the defence of the fortress, wrote shortly before his death a poem that he called *Douaumont 1916*:

> *Sie klagten nicht als sie sterben mussten.*
> *Leiden und Sterben für eine grosse Idee ist ehrenvoll.*
> *Leiden und Sterben fürs Vaterland ist heilig . . .*

> They did not complain when they had to die.
> To suffer and die for a great ideal is honourable.
> To suffer and die for the Vaterland is sacred.

Oberleutnant von Brandis was lionised as was, to a lesser extent, *Hauptmann* Haupt; their pictures appeared in newspapers as '*Die Erstürmer von Douaumont*'. Both were decorated with Germany's highest medal, the *Pour-le-Merit*.

Leutnant Radtke, who deserved at least as much, was denied the honour.

As for *Feldwebel* Kunze, he was not even mentioned.

After the war, the official German war report of the fight for Panzerfeste Douaumont contained a single line: '*Ein Häufchen von Pionieren unter dem Vfb Kunze, das von links her auch schon ins Fort eingedrungen war* – A small group of sappers under a Sergeant Kunze had also already entered the fortress from the left . . .' Nothing more.

The part that Lt Radtke played was at first not written up; within hours of his exploit he was struck down by shrapnel, seriously wounded and evacuated. It was only weeks later in hospital when he heard that the Kaiser had decorated Haupt and von Brandis with the '*Blaue Heinrich*', the *Pour-le-Merit*. Haupt soon slipped into anonymity; not so von Brandis, who turned into the Crown Prince's favourite 'right stuff'. His nationwide fame was such that the burghers of a Pomeranian village changed its name to Brandis. In his book, *Die Stürmer von*

Douaumont, Oberleutnant von Brandis gave little account of the role anyone but himself had played in the capture of the fortress, although he wrote rather carelessly that he had 'seen the artillery flag being waved from the top of the cupola'. This implied that Lt Radtke or Capt. Haupt (considering the ensuing quarrel as to who had ordered the flag bearer to the top) must have been inside the fortress before him. Until 1927, the von Brandis account was never disputed; then, the published official *Reichs Archive* version established Lt Radtke's part in the fall of the fortress. But there was nothing about a *VFb* Kunze.

Following the end of the Great War, Major Kurt von Klüfer, the commanding officer of 2 Battalion of the 24th Infanterie Regiment Brandenburg, became obsessed with establishing the truth of what really had taken place on 25 February 1916. His first and only indication was based on a note in the German army archives, which recorded a call between *Oblt* Van Brandis, 8/24, and Lt Kluge, a call that was eventually confirmed by Kluge, who remembered quite clearly the text of their conversation.[14] Von Brandis, using the field telephone of the advanced 6/24 *Meldertruppe* (signal troop) reported: '*Das Fort ist fest in unserer Hand . . . Haupt soll gefallen sein . . . Ich gehe jetzt ins Fort.*' The fact that Brandis told Kluge at that moment that the fort 'is secure in our hands', followed by, 'Haupt is reported to have fallen' showed that von Brandis hadn't as yet caught up with Haupt, who was very much alive and advancing on Douaumont. But the final phrase was the clincher; having previously said that 'the fortress is solidly in our hands', he then added: '*I'm going in now.*' This established without any doubt that von Brandis went in *after* someone else had already taken the fortress. But

---

[14] Declaration by Lt Kluge, made on 8 March 1937.

who? At the time of the Brandis call, Haupt and Radtke were still *outside* the moat fence, and Brandis was on his way up the *glacis*. Klüfer had nothing else to go on than a single line in the official report about a sapper team 'that had also entered the fortress'. He spent years trying to locate the leader of the *Pioniere*, but he had vanished, probably died in the trenches during later action.

Twenty years were to pass when, in December of 1936, the same Kunze, an ageing police constable in Thuringia, sent a letter to his former battalion commander Kurt von Klüfer. They arranged to meet and Kunze told him the full story.

'*Mein Gott, Kunze, warum Ihr langes Schweigen* – Why your long silence?'

'*Herr Major, an dem Tag von Douaumont war ich besoffen* – I was drunk that day, and I was frightened about having to face the firing squad.'

With this new information, Klüfer went to work; he located and interviewed others to check on Kunze's story, and finally published the results in a book in 1938. None of the many books published on that extraordinary event, prior to Klüfer's work,[15] even mentioned Kunze. Klüfer's account gives precise details of names and times of entry:

1. **16.07 hrs.** Kunze entered first the outer fortress, and penetrated into the fort's interior at 16.50 hrs; at 17.33 hrs Kunze left ('in an excited state') the officers' mess.
2. **17.40 hrs.** Lt Radtke and Capt Haupt penetrated into the interior
3. **17.44 hrs.** Kunze met Lt Voigt, followed by three comrades from his own 4/22, the soldiers Beyer, Leube and Münch. He led his three buddies into

[15] Klüfer, Kurt v, *Seelenkräfte im Kampf um Douaumont*, Berlin, 1938.

the officers' mess to partake of his find of French burgundy.

4. **17.53 hrs.** A 'highly agitated' Kunze met Capt Haupt inside the fortress to report.

5. **17.55 hrs.** Capt Haupt met von Brandis in the main tunnel (von Brandis became thus only the 64th German to enter the fortress). Haupt ordered von Brandis to collect enough men to safeguard the exterior surrounding the fortress, while he, Haupt, would look after the interior.

6. **18.05 hrs.** Von Brandis managed to collect ninety-eight men plus four other ranks for the task. [There is no further mention of Kunze, who had by now disappeared from the scene.]

'. . . FORT DOUAUMONT SECURE IN OUR HANDS, STORMED BY THE 7/24 AND 8/24 OF HAUPTMANN HAUPT AND OBER-LEUTNANT VON BRANDIS . . .' One message, sent in a moment of jubilation over an unimaginable feat, set in motion the 'Douaumont myth' that lasted twenty-two years. The soldiers who had shared Kunze's walk up the long hill, *Unteroffizier* (Lance-Corporal) Sachse, *Gefreiter* (Cpl) Behrend, *Gefreiter* Baack, and Private Schramm, were killed in the Great War. Major von Klüfer's book, containing Kunze's account, was published too late to make any difference. By 1938, the attention of Germany and, with it, that of the world, was focused on the approaching thunder clouds of another world war. In 1938, Adolf Hitler addressed a huge gathering of German soldiers. As a shining example, he held up the bravery of the men of Douaumont as the ideal of the future German soldier:

'Gewonnen aber in aller Zukunft wird ein Kampf – wie jener um Douaumont – trotz allem Soldatenglücks und trotz hochrageneder Einzeltaten nur dann, wenn jeder einzelne nach seinen Gaben an der Stelle seine Schuldigkeit getan haben wird,

an die das Schicksal ihn gestellt hat – We shall win a future battle – as did those at Douaumont – despite *Soldatenglück* [soldier's good fortune] and exceptional individual performance only when every single one according to his ability performs the duty which fate has put before him.'

The German *Reichs Archive* contains a note of that historic 25 February 1916:

Dieser Tag ist ein neues unwiderlegliches Zeugnis für das historische Gesetz, dass Männer Geschichte machen – This day provides unquestionable proof of the historic law that it is men who make history.

Yes, it is men who make history, but where then was the hero who blundered into an impregnable fortress and single-handedly conquered it, then didn't dare tell about it, afraid of being court-martialled for drunkenness in face of the enemy? A farm boy from Thuringia had been asked to commit patriotic suicide; he never received a medal, he was not given a soldier's pension. A brave man did not benefit from his truly amazing exploit. Others got the credit and were honoured.

A simple Feldwebel was dumped into history's *oubliettes*. Kunze? *Kunze who?*

Kunze's motivation was the basic instinct for survival when physical dangers threaten a soldier. He was caught in a deadly trap. From behind, a creeping artillery barrage rolling up on him, and before him, the world's biggest enemy fortress, bristling with machine guns, but also offering the protection of a shellproof wall – his only chance to make it through the rain of explosives. The rest came about by pure accident, a simple soldier pushed into a feat of heroism by mortal danger. Kunze's initiative at the critical moment paid off. After which, being too drunk, he let others take his honours.

It was one of the aspects of the vanity of Prussia's officer caste, and the manner in which awards were distributed by, and to them, that Kunze never did receive the unstinted praise he so richly deserved.

Boy Jack Cornwell, A return to the land fit for heroes

'Fate set his name in honour grim
And even death is proud of him.'
Eulogy for John Travers Cornwell, July 1916

'What is our task? To make Britain a fit country for heroes to live.'
Prime Minister Lloyd George, 24 November 1918

The Secretary of the Admiralty made the following announcement last night:

The Grand Fleet came in touch with the German High Seas Fleet at 3.30 on the afternoon of May 31. The leading ships of the two fleets carried on a vigorous fight, in which battle cruisers, fast battleships, and subsidiary craft all took active part. There were great losses on both sides.

The ships can be replaced; it is the courageous and dauntless men who formed their companies that we mourn. Assuredly our first thoughts will be for the gallant fellows who died bravely facing great odds.[1]

'Of all the great heroes . . .' We speak of those honoured

[1] *The Times*, 5 June 1916.

with medals and celebrated in song. But what about their loved ones, their fathers, their mothers? Those who were left to weep? A story of 'unsung heroes' would be incomplete without giving some thought to them. Such is the story of a much-celebrated hero, the youngest in His Majesty's Service ever to be awarded the Victoria Cross, and the family he left behind.

At the beginning of the Great War, the belligerent nations possessed two huge battle fleets, the British Grand Fleet and the Kaiser's *Hochseeflotte*. Both were truly formidable forces. Although the British Navy had more capital ships, the fleets' firepower matched each other, but not their radius of operation. While Britain, with its vast colonial empire, could re-coal and supply its navy in distant lands, the German fleet was dependent upon the proximity of home bases to be capable of matching British firepower and manoeuvrability. Thereby, the 'Kaiser's pride' could never wage a war at sea far from their home bases, which were located on the North Sea. For this reason, the British Grand Fleet was kept at anchor in their Scottish bases, in order to bottle up German capital ships, in case their admirals decided to sally forth. It was feared, should the Germans manage to achieve a surprise sortie, they could inflict a great deal of damage, and very quickly. Curiously, in the first years of war, a certain reluctance to use the initiative seemed to be prevalent in both naval commands.

While the Germans relied on their submarine screen to keep sea lanes clear of enemy war ships, England launched a series of fast cruisers to patrol the waters of the North Sea. One of these new vessels was *HMS Chester*, a fast scout cruiser in the Royal Navy's Battlecruiser Squadron of Vice Admiral David Beatty. At mid-morning, on this 31 May 1916, the vice admiral had broken wireless silence and ordered the captain of the *Chester* to check the situation off the west coast of Jutland, from where heavy smoke had been reported. It was known that Danish farmers were used to burning fields after harvest, but, first of all, smoke from straw was white and late May wasn't harvest time. This could mean only one thing: a German naval unit was out somewhere to their east and must be found and sunk before it did any damage.

The bow gun crew of the *Chester*, on battle stations for over two hours, had watched the smoke clouds for the last hour, when the first in the line of huge warships crawled over the horizon.

'Holy cow, it's the Kaiser's blinkin' *Flotte*!' They knew only too well that their light cruiser was out-ranged and out-gunned against the huge monsters of the German Kaiser. The voicepipe squeaked: 'Main armaments close up!'

The ten members of the forward gun turret of HMS *Chester* were all seasoned mariners – all but one, that is. 'The boy' was sixteen-year-old John Travers Cornwell who had joined England's most modern light cruiser on 1 May 1916. Thirty-one days later he was a hero, with his picture everywhere. The founder of the Boy Scouts, Sir Robert Baden-Powell, created a special Cornwell medal as highest reward for 'scout's honour', given for outstanding duty and bravery. And yet, in the beginning, 'Boy' Cornwell had none of that; he was just an ordinary lad from Leyton in Essex; of modest background, he left school at an early age to earn money for the family's support, and got caught up in the prevailing wave of German-phobia: 'I want to do my thing for King and country.' His older stepbrother was already in the service with an infantry regiment in Flanders; that's why his father, Eli Cornwell, a tram driver, and a reserve private in the Royal Defence Corps, refused Boy permission to join the Navy: 'You help your mother keep house.' Teenage Jack took a job as milk-van delivery boy.

On 27 July 1915, and after the refusal by his father, he went secretly to a Royal Navy recruitment centre. By changing his birth date, he was accepted for a gunnery-training programme aboard the HMS *Vivid*. The standard of combat readiness and weapon training was high, the training was competitive, and young Jack found himself subjected to the rigours of navy discipline, which instilled in him a sacred sense of duty for King and country. Like any teenager of his time, he itched to do honourable battle; the impatience to get into action was natural enough in a sixteen-year-old at the moment his country was at war. Although he could not have known, the action he so fervently prayed for was to involve him in the greatest sea battle of modern times, and win him nationwide acclaim.

At 15.49 pm on 31 May 1916, in the North Sea off the coast of Jutland (Skagerrak), Boy First Class Cornwell and thousands of English seamen of Sir John Jellicoe's British Grand Fleet, met up with the might of the Kaiser's *Hochseeflotte* (High Sea Fleet) under Admiral Reinhard Scheer, in an engagement of such might that the world had never before witnessed, and probably never will again.[2] Fifty ships with 15-inch monster guns, shooting it out with one-ton shells like in some Western gunfight.

The initial encounter was fought between the Royal Navy's Battlecruiser Squadron of Vice Admiral David Beatty and the *schweren Kreuzer* (heavy cruisers) of *Vize-Admiral* Franz von Hipper. The sides were pretty evenly matched, but not their gunnery. The accuracy of the German guns proved devastating. Struck by three shells, the battlecruiser *HMS Indefatigable* virtually disintegrated. A

[2] Strength: British Grand Fleet (Jellicoe and Beatty): 148 ships, including 28 battleships; German *Hochseeflotte* (Scheer and Hipper): 99 ships, including 22 battleships.

few minutes later, *HMS Queen Mary* and *HMS Invincible* also disappeared beneath the waves as internal explosions ripped them apart, causing Vice Admiral Sir David Beatty[3] sailing in *HMS Lion* to remark: 'There seems to be something wrong with our bloody ships today.' There was indeed, but it had nothing to do with the shipbuilders. In battle, it was vital to provide shells and powder propellant for the various gun turrets as fast as supply crews could handle it. Working in the powder magazines in the bowels of the ships, sweaty men removed cordite charges from their protective canisters and pre-stacked them on trolleys, while others pushed the bags with propellant on their carts to the lifts. Harried for speed to supply the guns with readied, but now-unprotected cotton bags with highly volatile cordite, the crews left the connecting doors between powder magazine, lift, and gun turret open. A flash from an impacting shell, regardless of calibre, could set off the spark on the trail of spilled cordite right down into the belly of the vessel. And that's precisely what happened when German shells struck. The explosion lifted the *Indefatigable*'s bow high into the air, the stern dipped into the sea. In two minutes she was gone. Of the *Indefatigable*'s crew of 1017, only two survived; aboard the *Queen Mary* it was no different: of its 1266 sailors, a mere twenty lived. The *Invincible* counted six survivors out of 1206. Beatty's *Lion* received a hit on Q-turret and only the quick reaction by Major Harvey of the Royal Marines saved the ship. Though mortally wounded, Harvey and his men opened the shuttlecocks and flooded the powder magazine.

HMS Chester, as part of Rear-Admiral Hood's 3rd Battle-cruiser Squadron, had been sent out earlier to scout

---

[3] Beatty's *HM* Battlecruiser Fleet consisted of six battlecruisers, four dreadnoughts, fourteen light cruisers, including *HMS Chester*, twenty-seven destroyers, and one seaplane carrier.

the starboard flank of Beatty's cruiser squadrons, when they came face to face with four heavy cruisers of Admiral Hipper's 2 *Kreuzerflotte*. Each minute brought the two formations closer together.

'Flagship's signalling, sir. Engage enemy.'

'Hoist battle ensign!' Captain Robert Lawson of the *Chester* gave his instructions. 'I want maximum revolutions. Range nine-five-oh.' Fire control passed the order to the three gun-turret controls. The sight-setter in the forward turret, Boy Seaman Cornwell, repeated the order. 'Range nine-five-oh.' The ship jolted violently under the shock of several near misses. Boy Cornwell stared through his finder, when in front of his glass bloomed a black cloud with a heart of flame and he staggered as the deck suddenly canted beneath him. Boy found himself on the ground, not knowing how he got there. His chief gunner called out: 'The bloody Fritz has hit us!'

Chester, with its six 5.5-inch guns, was hopelessly outgunned against the thirty 5.9-inch cannons of Hipper's squadron. At 16.40 hrs, *HMS Chester* was hit seventeen times. The cruiser staggered under the impacting salvoes, its upperworks burst apart with a roar, but its battle flag was still flying. Suddenly, Boy was stunned by a deafening blow, and thrown hard against the steel plating. In his ears sounded a gigantic clang. The blast from the shell that struck the forward 5.5-inch gun turret was like a thunderclap; the great searing tongue of flame peeled back the turret's steel like a can of sardines. Bits of bodies were scattered among the wreckage, everyone inside the turret was dead; everyone except the gun's sixteen-year-old sight-setter. His drill jacket was ripped open to the waist and he was bleeding from multiple wounds to his chest and abdomen. Boy groped his way back on to his feet, crawled with gasping lungs to his assigned post, and then hung on stubbornly to his gun-sight to keep him from falling over, waiting for further orders.

The *Chester* disappeared in a forest of splashes. Her engines roared frantically as she dodged the clusters of impacts. Near misses burst around her. Then she was hit again; an explosion wrecked her hull. Heavy shocks sheared rivets in the armour plating, flames were soaring, ammunition exploding, water from shell geysers lapped over bloodstained scuppers. Somehow, Boy Cornwell felt completely detached from the surrounding mayhem. For what seemed like an eternity, there were no more guns firing, no more shells exploding, only deep silence. In the thickening smoke, he cursed the sweat that ran into his eyes. For a moment he tore his eyes from the rubber-cup sight and saw nearby a ship explode; its great bulk seemed to rise from the water, squirming in agony. Through the deckplates he felt the *Chester* shudder and vibrate around him, followed by another concussion from a heavy shell near the bridge, carrying in its hot blast shards of metal and debris of bodies. The impact had cured Boy of his creeping numbness.

From somewhere appeared a deck officer on a round of damage control. Corpses cluttered his path. He saw a pall of smoke rising from the forward 5.5-inch gun, staved in by some giant hammer. There was no sign of life from the dented turret, gashed and opened by splinters. Then he noticed the boy; he smiled bravely as the officer tried to help him. 'Get down to the infirmary and have that looked after.'

'Yessir,' answered Boy Cornwell, and then stuck by his post. Despite the devastation and death around him, his gun-sight and voicepipe curiously functioned exactly as it had so many times before while practising in the months past. The pain in his chest became nearly unbearable, but he forced himself not to pass out. With a black hatred and an ingrained sense of duty he followed the enemy vessels in the crosshairs. It felt good to hit back when his *Chester* was being hit so hard. Even if his own gun no longer existed and his buddies were all dead, he had been given

an assignment, to man fire control, and most valiantly he
did; if asked, he could pass on firing positions to the still
working turrets. Blood was running down his legs, flowing
into his punctured lungs. With his life ebbing away, Boy
stuck to his post as if that was another sea exercise. He
kept reciting poems he had learned in school and thought
of his family, until the pain was eating not only into his
muscles, but into his mind, and he just hung there, with
his hands clutched around his gun-sight.

Meanwhile, the sea battle increased in fury. Ships were
struck and ships sank. Gun barrels were overheating, then
again cooled down by the many near misses that dumped
tons of water over them. The *Chester* was a shell-blasted
wreck defying more explosions; equally death-defying was
a mortally wounded teenager, hanging on to his gun-sight
with bleeding arms, defiantly holding out in the most
exposed position despite the volleys of incoming shells,
willing himself to remain at his post in case he was needed.
If he stayed at his gun, with his life's blood running down
his legs, this was not for personal glory, but because he
considered abandoning his position to be an unthinkable
dereliction of a sailor's duty.

As dusk settled, Admiral Jellicoe crossed the German line
and then ordered his ships to avoid further combat, with a
dry: 'I don't want to lose the war in one afternoon.' Later
that night, in more confused action where ships had to set
their gunnery distance by the enemy's muzzle flashes, more
ships were lost. Both sides called it a victory. But since the
Germans had sunk twice as much tonnage as the British,
and killed 6748 British seamen to a loss of 3058 Germans,
the pride of the Royal Navy was hurt. The Navy, and the
country, looked for a hero.

At the end of their engagement, hands had to undo Boy's
wrists, clasped around his gun-sight, and carry him into the

belly of the ship. The ship's doctor, in his blood-splattered rubber apron, took one look and shook his head. Despite the many shell holes that had ripped her decks open, *HMS Chester* was able to make enough steam to disengage and limp back into harbour. One of the first to be taken off was Boy Seaman Cornwell. He was brought to Grimsby Hospital, where he died of his terrible wounds on 2 June 1916. Captain Robert Lawson of the *Chester* wrote to his mother:

His devotion to duty was an example to all of us. The wounds, which resulted in his death, were received in the first few minutes of the action. He remained steadily at his most exposed post on the gun, waiting for orders. His gun would not bear on the enemy; all of the crew had been killed and he was the only one who was in such an exposed position. But he felt he might be needed and indeed he might have been; so he stayed there, standing and waiting, under heavy fire, with just his brave heart, and God's help to support him.[4]

Capt. Lawson sent a similar report to his cruiser squadron commander, Vice Admiral Beatty, who mentioned the boy's bravery in his official dispatch: '. . . standing alone at a most exposed post, quietly awaiting orders, until the end of the action, with the gun's crew dead around him . . .'

The English had their hero! Jack Cornwell's image of the never-to-be-vanquished rose like a magnificent meteor, the incarnation, and symbol of one who refused to give in. In its desperate search for patriotic glory after a battle that was not lost, but certainly not won,[5] the press quickly picked up on the heroic tale of Boy Cornwell. The picture of a smiling young boy in navy blues was splashed across the nation's front pages, until the day it was replaced by another, much

[4] Winton, J., *The Victoria Cross at Sea*, London, 1978.
[5] The German Fleet lost eleven ships and 2551 men; the British Grand Fleet lost fourteen ships and 6097 men were killed.

more dramatic photograph. It showed a common grave, subtitled: 'JUTLAND HERO'S FINAL RESTING PLACE'. The Navy hadn't done anything to provide the boy's family with a decent gravesite for its hero and his mother, Lily Cornwell, had collected his body from the Grimsby infirmary; being without means, she had the nation's youngest hero buried in a common grave in Grimsby, Lincolnshire. London's *Daily Sketch* wrote in its lead article:

England will be shocked today to learn that the boy-hero of the naval victory has been buried in a common grave. The flowers were sent by his schoolmates – they in their humble way paid honour that the Admiralty failed to give the young hero.

From that moment on, the Boy Cornwell Saga took on 'a convulsive spasm of collective commemoration'.[6] A spate of articles and editorials followed, the Boy's photo was plastered on school walls throughout the country, and a famous court painter, Frank Salisbury, portrayed him for the Admiralty, using his younger brother Ernest as his model. The picture of a grim-looking Boy Cornwell, standing next to his gun aboard the *Chester*, became a Royal Navy recruitment poster. The ward where he died in Grimsby Hospital was named the 'Boy Cornwell Room'. With daily headlines and public outcry reaching a veritable crescendo, Lord Beresford rose in the House of Lords and demanded to call upon the Admiralty, to insist that the heroic boy be awarded a posthumous Victoria Cross. The VC's committee chairman, the Duke of Devonshire, replied that no such recommendation had been presented, nor was one expected. Three naval commanders had already received their VCs for outstanding conduct in the Battle of Jutland,[7] but in the case of Boy Cornwell, the award board

[6] Winton, J., *The Victoria Cross at Sea*, London, 1978.
[7] Edward Barry, Stewart Bingham, Loftus William Jones and Francis John William Harvey

proved most reluctant, because Boy was a teenager, and not a fully fledged sailor, only an apprentice boy seaman and therefore not eligible for a Victoria Cross. Once journalists hungering for sensational stories brought this unfortunate reply to public knowledge, it had the Royal Navy's mailboxes flooded with injurious letters from across the land, and the popular press had its field day. The Navy tried to defend itself against the press's accusations with an unfortunate statement: 'Many of his shipmates were more fortunate in resting in the North Sea where not even a ghoulish pressman can disturb their mortal remains.'

Indeed, Boy's mortal remains were not allowed to rest in peace. On 29 July 1916, the Admiralty decided that his body was to be exhumed and given a proper state funeral, with all the pomp and pageantry of military bands reserved for such an occasion. Boys from the Crystal Palace Naval Depot drew the gun carriage, followed by his grieving mother, in company with the Bishop of Barking and a high representative from the Admiralty. Thousands lined the funeral route, church bells rang and shops remained closed; throughout the country, school bells rang and children observed a minute of silence. Six comrades, all boy seamen of *HMS Chester*, carried the coffin draped with the White Ensign to its final resting place in Manor Park Cemetery. There were wreaths marked 'with deep respect' from the Lord Mayor of London and Vice Admiral Beatty. Afterwards, it was claimed 'that the press had fabricated its hero'. Newspapers certainly helped in bringing his valiant feat to the public. But the gallant stand was that of a boy, and a boy alone. With public pressure building up, the palace announced on 30 September 1916 that Boy Seaman First Class John Travers Cornwell was to receive posthumously the Victoria Cross.

On 16 November 1916, at a ceremony at Buckingham

Palace, the King presented the coveted medal to Jack's mother: 'Have you heard, ladies, Lily Cornwell's gone to see the king . . .' For a few days, Jack's mother became the talk of the town. Not that she had asked for glory; she would have much preferred to have her son alive by her side. But he was gone, having given his young life for his King and country. The rest was quite sad for this simple, God-fearing woman who worked hard to try and make ends meet for her little family, while her husband and sons had gone to war. Like any other mother or wife with someone in the field, Lily Cornwell had always fretted about the day she would receive a letter from the War Ministry. When the postman came to her house, it was about Jack. She had buried him. There was no one to help a mother giving her fallen son a decent grave; she had taken little Lily and Ernest, dressed them in their Sunday finest, and with a black shawl around her shoulders, the three followed the cart with the coffin. A few weeks later, a man from a London newspaper had shown up, taken a photograph of the grave and suddenly her Jack was famous. The Navy had dug him up and given him a magnificent funeral, with real flowers and a decent resting place. But soon the flowers wilted, and so did the attention the newspapers had shown a boy-hero's mother.

If Jack Cornwell was by no means an 'unsung hero', the rest of the Boy Cornwell Story held nothing ennobling for those who benefited from a sixteen-year-old's heroism. More sadness fell on Lily Cornwell. In October 1916, her husband Eli Cornwell died of bronchial catarrh which, for lack of funds, had been left untreated; shortly thereafter the family's last provider, Jack's older stepbrother Arthur, was killed in Flanders. Mother Lily, with her two small children, was left without financial means, while hundreds of thousands of pounds were raised by selling Boy Cornwell stamps and Boy Cornwell picture postcards for the 'Boy

Cornwell Memorial Fund'. Seven million schoolchildren bought the one-penny stamp with the Boy's image! The benefit was used to create naval scholarships, build cottages for retired seamen, and refurbish the Star and Garter Home in Richmond; none of it reached the hero's mother, living on a minimum subsistence in a shabby walk-up in Stepney. Sometimes she would remove the press clippings from the shoebox, which only helped to stir the wound and revive the hurt. Then she sat for hours in her chair, clutching in her hands a frame with the faded photo of a family of six, happily smiling into the lens. The picture had been taken in a photographer's stand during a village carnival, only months before the guns of August 1914 started to shatter the peace in the world. Those guns had taken everything from her.

With her widow's pension of 6s 6d a week and an occasional hand-out from the Navy League, Mother Lily Cornwell, a brave and simple woman, one who had shaken a king's hand and walked behind a flag-draped coffin; a woman who had given all to her country, who lost a husband and two of her sons in war; a woman suffering the torment of grief every time she saw her boy smiling down at her from one of the thousand recruitment poster; a woman who more and more withdrew into herself and slowly wasted away, was worn out. Three years after her Jack had been given a state funeral, neighbours found her rolled up on her bed. The mother of one of the nation's most celebrated heroes, Lily Cornwell had been quietly forgotten and died in poverty at the age of only forty-eight. A statement by the official author of *The Victoria Cross at Sea* summed it up: 'In retrospect, it seems that much more of the money raised for Jack Cornwell might have been used to help his own immediate family.'[8]

[8] Winton, J., *The Victoria Cross at Sea*.

This hero's mother was an example of official disregard,[9] yet she wasn't the exception. As the war ended victoriously in 1918, England was no longer in need of heroes. Thousands of returning ex-servicemen were overcome with the resentment that nobody seemed to care what they had gone through. They were exhausted by war, depressed and often bitter. The life they discovered on their return seemed trivial and absurd to those who had lived and died in the trenches; they didn't notice the misery of others, they only saw tuxedoed young men and girls in glitzy outfits, tossing back glasses of champagne, tangoing their way out of the ashes of a terrible war. Was that what they had fought for? The list of inconsistencies was endless; 'England back to normal' was a mockery to those who had fought at Jutland or the Somme. Naturally enough, nobody cared to hear about Flanders. The English wanted to forget the past, and much of the present as well. They had their own tragedies and didn't wish to be reminded of other people's misfortunes.

The great dream of a better mankind was gone. 'I pictured civilian life so different,' said a veteran from the slaughter at Ypres. 'We all have,' answered another, who had been at the Dardanelles. The homecomers were condemned to face indifference, the bitter deception of the unwanted, with its lack of housing and no hope for employment. They cried '*betrayal!*' and meant it. With their hard-earned victory, all had collapsed, perverted, forgotten. It left only despair and alcohol. Ex-soldiers stood on street corners with sandwich-boards, begging for any kind of job to feed their families, while others slept rolled up in blankets on the banks of the

---

[9] A small amount of the collected funds was offered to his sister Lily (same name as her mother) shortly after the war to book her passage to Canada.

Thames.[10] On the banks of the Rhine or the Danube, such behaviour seemed normal enough; after all, Germany was the loser. But not in England, they said. And yet, England's great victory was disastrous, because at huge expense in wealth and blood, it had gained nothing in its aftermath that it didn't have before. This much could be safely predicted: the country that had won a war was headed for hard times. And for the millions that had fought and suffered? Those champions of countless, alas unrecorded heroic feats? For four bloody years, the drive for glorious victory had burned deeply in their hearts. That was the homecoming a country reserved for the bravest of brave from the bloodied trenches and the ships of war, to what Prime Minister David Lloyd George had promised them as 'a land fit for heroes'.

Theirs too is a tale of the unsung heroes.

> We've finished up the filthy war
> We've won what we were fighting for . . .
> Or have we? I don't know . . .[11]

Boy Cornwell's honour was concomitant with his *personal courage*; his motivation was to perform his duty for King and country, as any British sailor would. This was something that officialdom sadly failed to respect; in the end, those who benefited from his heroism didn't have much to be proud of – ending as it did with their neglect of the next-of-kin of the nation's youngest war hero.

10 Sydney Chaplin, returning from the war.
11 Poem by Robert Service, 'L'Envoi'.

Cunningham, Devereux & Elrod, The right stuff

SEND US (STOP NOW IS THE TIME FOR ALL GOOD MEN TO
COME TO THE AID OF THEIR PARTY STOP CUNNINGHAM STOP)
MORE JAPS . . .

> Garbled message from Wake Atoll, 11 December 1941

The first thing Major James Devereux, United States
Marine Corps, noticed after his head cleared from the
blast, was a shiny black beetle scurrying across the sand
near his cheek. For a moment he tried to shut his ears
to the roar of the guns, to the desperate cries of men,
and the insistent rattle of a machine gun. A living mass
had come at them; until that mass was broken up into
individual faces and nasty bayonets, and everyone was
fighting for their lives with the desperation of front-line
troops anywhere, blundering through a world of tearing
noise and billowing smoke. Then there was only deep
silence and he was tumbling into a great void. From
somewhere near the water's edge he thought he heard the
thin sound of a bugle and he noticed the enemy's assault
faltering. Through the mist still clouding his eyes, Major
Devereux saw a shattered beach strewn with corpses, a
terrible panorama of death. But what mattered most to

him was that his men had stood and they had held. There might be hope after all.

Long before that bloody encounter took place on a wishbone-shaped strip of sand around its central blue lagoon, and protected by needle-sharp coral reefs, the site was best described as 'a place from practically nowhere'. It was a desolate and hot place, where nothing but gnarled, waist-high scrub grew, the exclusive domain of sea birds, and a unique species of sand rat feeding on birds' eggs. The only visitors to the island were giant turtles. The place wasn't even marked on ancient mariners' maps for a stopover, as it lacked the two necessities vital for ocean-going vessels: a deep-water approach and a fresh-water source. In other words, it was a place definitely not worth the detour.

In the aftermath of the Spanish-American War of 1899, fought principally by Teddy Roosevelt's Roughriders in Cuba, the United States had inherited that coral atoll in the middle of the Pacific Ocean as a by-product of its peace treaty with Spain, and didn't really know what to do with it. But because they had it, the US administration made an effort to send a ship to inspect their newly acquired property. They found an atoll consisting of three separate islands: Wilkes, to the east, Peale to the north, and Wake, the largest of the group – which didn't mean a lot as anyone could walk it in fifteen minutes from end to end. The inspectors charted the atoll's sea approaches, marked reefs and unseen coral barriers so that sea captains running before a storm wouldn't smash into them and drown in the angry waters. As there was no real clear passage from the sea into the interior lagoon, in their view Wake held no a strategic value; the United States of America relied on its mighty Pacific Fleet for its Far East strategy; the fleet was anchored at Pearl Harbor in the Hawaiian Islands chain. In the end, the commission's report on Wake Atoll discouraged all further development. For the next thirty years, a strip of sand in the middle of a gigantic ocean went back to sleep.

In the early 1930s, an upstart airline, Pan American Airways, explored new travel routes. One route, until then ignored because there was no aircraft capable of flying such vast distances, flew directly across the Pacific. The company had developed large, four-engine flying boats called Clippers for their transatlantic traffic and was setting its sights on a direct route to the Far East. Because the Pacific was twice the size of the Atlantic, it created the problem of refuelling midway. The report on Wake, prepared by the first surveying team, had been put to rest in some dusty basement. In his son's school atlas a PanAm planner discovered a speck in the midst of the big blue blob of water, bearing the colours of the United States: 'It seems we own a piece of real estate smack in the middle of the Pacific; this could be a perfect refuelling point.'

Pan American sent out a ship to scout the rediscovered national sand pile. The crew found scorpions, snakes, rats, low scrub, but they also found a sheltered interior lagoon, which was ideal for their purposes. Its water was protected by an outer reef barrier and always calm for a landing, as it was sufficiently deep to take a big flying boat. Then came the question of an infrastructure, fuel storage tanks, piers, a repair hangar, accommodation for ground staff, and a hotel for passengers spending the layover on an atoll. Constructing anything on the island promised to be a major undertaking; at its highest point it rose a mere six feet above high-tide level, and was therefore liable to be swamped by waves during Pacific gales. But where there is a will there is a way, and American ingenuity combined with skilled construction crews began excavating and pouring concrete. A compound was born. In the spring of 1935, the first PanAm Clipper splashed down on the crystal-clear lagoon.

Its passengers deplaned, excitedly stomping around like 20th-century Columbus's making a momentous discovery. To bear witness to their exploit back 'in the real world', they took photographs of each other. This gave the intrepid world traveller endless material for his next Philadelphian or Bostonian cocktail party.

'What, you have never heard of Wake?'

'Isn't that somewhere off the coast of Alaska?'

'It's in the middle between us and the Japanese,' explained the trans-Pacific explorer, producing a conch presented as a memento by the ground staff at Wake.

The days of the pith helmet exploration and silver cutlery meals aboard a Clipper were quickly drawing to an end. By the end of the thirties, the world was headed for a gigantic conflagration. Hitler signed peace-in-our-time deals he never intended to keep. Japan had already overrun a major portion of Manchuria, waging a full-scale mechanised war against a combination of badly armed nationalist and Communist Chinese. To complete its expansionary hold on the Asian hemisphere and fuel its voracious war machine of ships, planes and tanks, Japan was in desperate need of oil; when the United States refused to sell it to them, Japan cast its glance at Dutch Indonesia and its vast oil reserves of Sumatra, Java and Irian Jaya. In order to get to the precious oil fields, Japanese armies had to pass the British crown colonies of Hong Kong and Singapore, and that would bring the Empire of the Rising Sun into conflict with the European powers allied with the United States. With Europe embroiled in a devastating war, and the resources of the United Kingdom stressed to the limit, it could be discounted as a Far Eastern force. That left only the United States, a country increasingly concerned about the danger posed by Japanese armies to its overseas possession in the Philippines. The Japanese ultra-nationalists were willing to take a calculated risk. The single voice of dissent was that of Admiral Yamamoto, chief of Japan's Navy, who dared to warn his emperor: 'Your Imperial Majesty, I may assure you six months of victory. After that, we shall lose the war.'

It is a fact that the Japanese militaries were not out to crush the United States in a war they knew they could never win. They acted on Bismarck's principle to score a quick victory and offer an 'honourable peace with concessions'. If Japan's ultimate aim was to create a Greater Asia Confederation, controlled from Tokyo and incorporating a pacified China, it needed to limit America's ambitions in South East Asia. To achieve this goal a rapid conquest of the designed areas was planned – and that again called for the elimination of the single greatest threat to their expansionist design, the American Pacific Fleet.

On the other side of the Pacific sat America's strategic planners; to them it became clear that their Far East trade was at stake, which must eventually lead to a confrontation with Japan. President Roosevelt warned his nation in a speech: 'The war is approaching the brink of the Western Hemisphere itself. It is coming very close to home . . .' The first memorandum of a possible defence of the Western Pacific was presented to President Roosevelt by the joint chiefs under the code name 'Rainbow': '. . . to prevent the violation of the letter and spirit of the Monroe Doctrine out into the Pacific as far as Hawaii, Wake and Samoa . . .' Significantly, it didn't include Guam or the Philippines, but it was accepted that America would have to go to the defence of European colonial possessions.

For once, the American military planners got it right. Given the enormity of the Pacific Ocean, it was considered that any future battle would be conducted with the latest arms in the arsenal of modern nations – its air power. Aerial attacks would make surface naval forces of the battleship era vulnerable and, probably, even obsolete.

Hitler's *Blitzkrieg* strategy, employing his JU-87 Stuka-force as 'airborne artillery', had pointed in that direction. The US Navy began planning for this eventuality. Fighter aircraft needed a platform to start and land; this could be an aircraft carrier or a strip of land. One such location, which acted as a mid-ocean fixed landing strip and refuelling place was Wake Atoll.

In February 1941, while London was suffering under the Blitz and the drum roll of war approached the United States, the US Department of Defense engaged a work crew of one thousand, under the supervision of a hard-fisted Irish engineer, Dan Teters, who had 'stopped attacks' as linebacker of the University of Washington football squad. For the next ten months, his crews dug and levelled and nothing could interrupt their effort, neither broiling heat nor lashing storms. A landing strip was blasted from coral; fuel storage tanks went up; Quonset huts were riveted together to house a battalion-size force. The atoll's main defences were designed around six 5-inch naval guns, stripped from a First World War cruiser and installed in three strategic locations: Koku Point on Wilkes Island, Peacock Point on Wake Island, and Taki Point on Peale Island. Twelve 3-inch anti-aircraft guns supported this heavy armament.

Eighteen .50-calibre heavy and thirty .30-caliber medium machine guns protected the batteries from possible ground attacks. The coral proved too hard to implant stakes for a barbed wire entanglement; but nature had provided the atoll with its own defence against ship-launched invasions, a reef of flesh-slicing coral heads that wound protectively around the three islands and its inner lagoon. The atoll's principal function was intended as a base for aerial reconnaissance to scout enemy naval movements, and a rapid interception force to launch interrupt-missions of enemy supply lanes. To attack lone raiders and unarmed merchantmen was one thing; to stand up against a full scale invasion was quite another. For such an eventuality, Wake was neither intended nor prepared for.

The first (and only) regular unit to set foot on the island was a contingent of 449 US Marines from the 1st USMC Defense Battalion, Wake Detachment, placed under the command of a 38-year-old professional soldier, Major James Devereux. Born in Cuba, educated in the United States and Switzerland, Devereux had joined the Marine Corps in 1923 and earned his promotion fighting bandits in the jungles of Nicaragua and the Philippines. He was a tall, lanky American with an air of understated strength and power; a hardworking, intelligent, well-organised, efficient aviator. In the inter-war years there wasn't much of a future outlook in the US Navy for a youngster who wanted to get ahead in life; he had received a lucrative offer from a civilian airline. But Devereux had been strongly encouraged to remain in the USMC and, in effect, to accept an American version of the Gulag Archipelago, commanding an air group on forlorn Wake.

The up side was that it gave him a chance to work with fighter pilots and combat aircraft. He accepted the position, even though it was obvious to all that if he wanted to remain in the forces, he had little choice. Always dressed in ordinary fatigues, many of those close to him thought that he felt uncomfortable with the trappings of a major in the Marines, and everyone on the island agreed that at the very least he was the most visible commanding officer anyone had ever known. His men were partly veterans, partly untried recruits; all were US Marines, a title they carried with pride. Wake was considered a good training base because nothing major was expected to happen there. As a matter of fact, Wake was not Hawaii: 'Wake Atoll: no women at all, no beer at all – nuddin' at all.'

Critics in Washington shared their lack of enthusiasm; they felt that 449 Marines, who had to be fed and clothed and were marooned on a desert island, were a definite waste of taxpayer's money. They had nothing to boast about and nothing to look forward to for the next century. At best, the battalion was headed for an unmemorable place in the reserves and the only chance for advancement of their officers was in the proverbial army boneyard. No one at home bothered to ask questions about readiness, training and motivation. The only one who worried about such details was Major Devereux. To keep his men from getting lethargic in a place that virtually called for inactivity, other than running back and forth singing, and saluting officers, Major Devereux kept them working from daybreak to dusk; they were given a shovel and told to fill sandbags. There was no shortage of sand; they worked filling bags, stacking bags, and pushing wheelbarrows heaped with bags. Everything had to be blasted from coral. Fortunately, the civilian work team had an ample supply of dynamite.

Working under the supervision of civilian engineers, the Marines turned the island into a labyrinth of dug-in positions for machine guns with interconnected covered trenches, emergency hospital facilities and storage space for weapons, food and ammunition. Everything was carefully camouflaged with sand. Nothing could be spotted from the air, but on the ground Wake had been turned into a spiky porcupine. Unfortunately Major Devereux still lacked adequate fire-control equipment and artillery range-finders for his heavy guns. This gear had been requested, but the pertinent requisition form was left buried under a pile of papers on the desk of a stateside quartermaster, and the equipment never arrived – nor, for that matter, did the rest of the intended US Marine contingent. Perhaps some military stateside considered Devereux's fortress a waste of time. After all, in November 1941 the Great Pacific was still a calm lake.

On 28 November, US Navy Commander Winfield Scott Cunningham, class of 1921, an expert on naval aviation, took over as Wake's base commander. Cunningham was a softly spoken yet energetic fighter pilot who had risen through the ranks from an officer training school pilot candidate to commander of a military installation defending an island in the middle of nowhere. Major Devereux reverted to his role as chief of ground troops stationed on the atoll. With the war's thunderclouds approaching, a flight of B-17 four-engine 'Flying Fortress' bombers was ferried from California to the Philippines; they were the first to inaugurate the new Wake airstrip, long enough for the landing, but not equipped with motorised pumps to handle the refuelling operation for the 3000-gallon capacity of each of the four-engine planes. Having finished with their sandbags, the Marines were now ordered to start pumping fuel by hand from 40-gallon drums stacked alongside the strip. 'Make sure that no sand gets into the tanks,' pilots were quick to caution the sweating refuelling crews. What kind of request was this on an island where the prevailing winds whirled up sand 365 days a year? The grunts sweated, they cursed and they pumped, and they were mighty glad when the last of the B-17s took to the air.[1]

On 4 December came new excitement in their daily routine. Two hundred miles to the northeast of Wake, the carrier *USS Enterprise* turned into the wind and launched twelve Grumman F4F-3 Wildcat fighter aircraft of Marine

---

[1] The entire B-17 fleet, stationed in the Philippines, was wiped out like sitting ducks on the runway on the first day of the war, because of a failure in high command. General MacArthur forgot to inform the US Air Force commander of the attack on Pearl Harbor, which had taken place a few hours before.

Fighter Squadron 211. Within the hour, the planes landed on Wake.[2]

'Bloody hell, look at all that sand, and no hardened shelters,' Major Paul Putnam, squadron commander, complained to his XO (executive officer), Captain Henry T. 'Hank' Elrod. Putnam had good reason to be upset; before taking command of the squadron on 17 November, he had been assured shelters for his precious planes to prevent them from being blown 'into the soup' by a Pacific gale.

'Until they put them up, we just have to do with what we got,' drily remarked his XO, a cool, slow-talking country boy from Georgia, with boyish good looks and a cap sitting at a rakish angle. Henry T. Elrod was no different from all the kids that grew up in the depression years in America's South: Little League baseball, high school football, and chatting up the chicks in dad's Model-T Ford. Until the day a flying circus came to town. Young Hank had stared in fascination at the acts of daredevilry performed by stunt pilots in 'stringbag' double-deckers. He scraped together his economy to be taken up in one of them fancy flying machines. It was the first time he looked down on the world from up above. From that day he knew that he would pilot a plane. His parents sent him to the University of Georgia and then to Yale. The fastest way to get up into the air was to join the budding US Marine Corps flying section. Henry Elrod joined it in 1927, and received his wings in 1931, by which time he had become an early version of *Top Gun*.

Other than what was already stationed on the island in men, armament and supplies, nothing more would be added. The *William Ward Burrows*, a troop vessel carrying a Marine battalion intended to strengthen Wake,

[2] Due to this delivery, the invaluable aircraft carrier was away from its anchoring in Pearl Harbor on the morning of the Japanese attack.

was rerouted to Johnston Island. The only other Yankee presence in the region were two cruising submarines, the *USS Triton* and the *USS Tambor*, but these depended on their orders from Pearl Harbor.

On 7 December,[3] PanAm's Philippine Clipper landed in the lagoon, carrying mail for a string of American possessions in the Pacific, but no passengers. Around noon, Major Devereux called an 'all-man-to-battle-stations', a routine check to test how prepared the island's defences were. As it was a Sunday (Saturday 6 December in Hawaii and the continental US), he gave his battalion the rest of the day off, to laze in the shade, play dice or write home. In their letters they wrote that this day, 7 December 1941, was just another day like the one before, or the one that would follow, and that all they did was watch clouds go by.

Meanwhile, in the continental United States, ever since the Japanese had signed their tri-partite treaty with Hitler's Germany and Mussolini's Italy in 1940, this identified a potential Pacific adversary. Great efforts had been going on to gather as much advance warning as possible about Japan's intentions. A brilliant cryptanalyst of the US Army's Signal Corps, Col. William Friedman, assisted by Harry Lawrence Clark, had put together a code breaker called 'Magic', capable of decoding Japan's secret diplomatic messages. Shortly before noon on Saturday, 6 December 1941, a female code specialist, Dorothy Edgers, working out of the Office of US Naval Intelligence that operated the 'Magic' machine, decoded an ultra-secret message

[3] Wake Atoll lies across the international dateline, and while it was only Saturday, 6 December in Hawaii and America, it was already Sunday, 7 December in Wake and Japan. That date-change was to play a major role within the next twenty-four hours.

from Tokyo to the Japanese Embassy in Washington, which identified Honolulu as a target for a forthcoming attack. She immediately informed her superior; however, as this was a weekend, and since Mrs Edgers was a recent addition to the Navy's decoding section, her excited voice wasn't taken overly seriously. 'This has time until Monday,' she was told, and with it – incredible as it may seem – a vital piece of information was put on the shelf. That wasn't all. At 05.00 hrs on Sunday, the US Army Chief of Staff, General George C. Marshall, was handed yet another signal, which again indicated that a Japanese attack was imminent, although his signal did not contain the precise target identification, as had that of Mrs Edgers. Gen. Marshall, out on a horseback ride, didn't get to his office until 11.30am, at which time he ordered to have a dispatch sent out to all outlying American garrisons. A freak storm centre that ranged across the Pacific wrought havoc with radio reception. A few received the warning clearly, such as the Philippines and the Panama Canal Zone. Others received only part of the message and couldn't make sense of it. But some heard nothing. One of them was Fort Shafter, the US Army's communication centre in Hawaii.

It was now 07.55 hrs (Hawaii time), Sunday 7 December in Pearl Harbor, when Commandant Mitsui Fuchida of His Imperial Majesty's Japanese Navy, leading a wave of 183 airplanes, dropped from the skies on the sleeping US naval base of Pearl Harbor and, with his shout of '*Tora! Tora! Tora!*', launched the world into a conflict to span the globe. Without a declaration of war, waves of carrier-launched Japanese fighter planes sank a major portion of America's Pacific Fleet. By 10.00 hrs (Hawaii time), Japan's surprise attack had sunk or damaged beyond repair the battleships *USS Arizona*, *California*, *West Virginia*, *Oklahoma*, *Tennessee*, *Maryland*, *Pennsylvania*, *Nevada* and *Utah*, the cruisers *USS Honolulu*, *Helena* and *Raleigh*, the destroyers *Cassin*, *Downes*, and *Shaw*, and the seaplane tender *Curtiss*. Furthermore, in simultaneous attacks on Hawaiian airfields, 188 US planes were destroyed on the ground, while another 159 were damaged. In all, 2403 sailors, soldiers, and civilians were killed. Throughout America, the outcry over this unprovoked and undeclared attack raised a cowboy thirst for frontier vengeance.

Across the international dateline to the east of Hawaii, a red sun was rising over the endless Pacific horizon. One moment, the men of the 1st US Marines Defense Battalion on Wake were watching clouds go by, and the next they found themselves at war. Dawn broke over Wake on Monday 8 December 1941 (Sunday 7 December, Hawaiian time zone). At 06.00 hrs (Wake time), a bugle called the duty detachment to the morning flag parade. The only thing that changed the daily routine was the departure of PanAm's Philippine Clipper; at 06.30 hrs, the heavy flying boat cut a wake across the lagoon, skimmed low over the mast with the stars and stripes flapping in the morning breeze, before heading out over the ocean – direction Guam. It was now 06.50 hrs; having watched, like everyone else, the majestic Clipper taking off, the two on-duty members of the US Army Signal Corps went inside their Quonset hut to prepare for their routine daily 07.00 hrs (it was now 10.40 hrs in Pearl Harbor) radio call with US Navy's Pacific Headquarters at Hickham Field in Hawaii. An agitated voice *en clair* blared from the speaker: 'We're under attack . . . we're under attack . . . this is not a drill, I repeat, this is not a drill . . . dive bombers . . . those bastards are all over the place . . .' the speaker was momentarily interrupted by loud explosions, '. . . I can see their red suns on the wings . . . there are fucking Japs everywhere . . . this is not a drill . . .' It came so suddenly that Wake's communication chief, Captain Henry S. Wilson, US Army Signal Corps, sat stunned in front of the radio console, before he ran to Devereux's quarters, where he found the major shaving.

'Major, we're at war.'

'C'mon, captain, cool down.'

'No, it's for real. The Japs are bombing Pearl.'

'Jeezus . . .' Devereux immediately rushed to see the base commander, Cmdr Cunningham, who he found having a leisurely breakfast in the canteen of the construction crew, discussing the work in progress with Dan Teters.

'Commander, I must talk to you.'

Cunningham excused himself, and left Teters finishing his breakfast. When Devereux gave him the news, Cunningham couldn't believe it. But a follow-up message from Pearl Harbor confirmed the attack.

On Wake, as in all outlying US stations across the Pacific, the sirens howled. The entire complement of US Marines lined up under the American flag.

'Battalion, *teeen-HUT*!'

All 449 men in T-shirts and khaki trousers stood smartly as Cmdr Cunningham stepped under the stars and stripes, flapping in the morning breeze.

'Men, I've just received the following message from Pacific Command:

DECEMBER 7, 1941. FROM THE SECRETARY OF THE NAVY.
TO ALL SHIPS AND STATIONS OF THE US PACIFIC FLEET.
THE PRESIDENT OF THE UNITED STATES HAS SIGNED TODAY
AN ACT WHICH DECLARES THAT A STATE OF WAR EXISTS
BETWEEN THE UNITED STATES AND THE EMPIRE OF JAPAN . . .

It didn't need an explanation; they understood what it meant. The United States had become embroiled in this global conflict. And Wake, being one of the US territories closest to the Empire of the Rising Sun, the

1st Defense Battalion, US Marine Corps, had suddenly become America's front line!

Private Harold Borth and Sergeant James Hall were ordered as observers to the highest point, the island's water tower. Their view was limited to under a mile by a rain squall nearing the atoll. The gun crews of the 5-inch naval cannons and 3-inch anti-aircraft guns busied themselves filling their ready cases with fused shells. Until now, the civilian construction crews hadn't been told; they made jokes while Marine units with live ammunition manned their positions.

'Ain't you guys overdoing yer drills,' grinned Eric Lehtola, a bulldozer operator.

'This ain't no drill, buddy,' snapped Sergeant Raymond Gragg from behind his sandbagged machine gun, 'them Japs is coming.'

'Oh jah?' stuttered Lehtola, his mouth agape. As the news raced through camp, trench-diggers dropped their shovels, truckers stopped their trucks, and they all stood around in heated discussion: '. . . Our battleships are already on their way . . . The B-17s are knocking the shit out of the Emperor's palace in Tokyo . . . Nothing to worry about, you'll see, in a day or two, the Japs will be crushed and all is going to be back to normal . . .' Wishful thinking.

Major Putnam briefed his pilots; the ground mechanics prepared the planes for a two-minute take-off. PanAm's Philippine Clipper, on its way to Guam, having been reached over radio by the airline's station manager, John Cooke, was warned of the danger; he turned around and came down on the central lagoon for an emergency landing. Cunningham and Devereux were in conference: 'Until we know what comes at us, we must stick to a routine. There's no sense in setting off a general panic.'

'What are we going to do with the civilians?' Devereux wanted to know.

'Let's give them a choice. They can assist us – or they can watch.'

'Red Irish' Teters solved the civilian problem: 'How can my boys help?'

'Grab a gun and shoot,' said Devereux. He ordered USMC Gunner John Hamas to distribute the spare Browning automatics, Thompson submachine guns, Springfield rifles, gas masks, steel helmets and boxes of pineapple grenades. Many of the construction crews were war veterans who had learned how to shoot in France back in 1917. Only a few looked for their salvation in the bushes. These were the first ones to die.

Putnam ordered two flights of two pairs of Wildcats to take off and patrol the approaches to the atoll. He briefed his pilots: 'I want you out to sea at extreme radio range. Scout only, not engage.'

'How high?'

'As high as possible. They'll come in above the clouds.' He was wrong.

Meanwhile, building activity continued at a feverish pace to get the hardened shelters ready for the Grumman Wildcats. This time it was not to protect them from storm damage. 'Can we move the parked aircraft away from the runway?' Putnam queried.

'Negative,' replied Teters, 'you'd only get them fouled up with our equipment and this could damage your flying machines.'

'Okay. By what time do you expect us to move them?'

'We'll have your first shelters up by 14.00 hours.' It proved to be two hours and twenty-two minutes too late!

Several hours before, a flight of 34 Mitsubishi G3M2 Type 96 Nell land-attack planes of the Chitose Air Group had taken off from Roi-Namur in the Marshalls, 700 miles (1120 km) to the south of Wake. As they neared Wake, they slipped into a cloud formation. That's why the four patrolling Grumman Wildcats failed to see them. At 11.38 hrs, waves of Nells roared out of the cloud at a mere 1500 feet and made straight for the atoll's airstrip.

'Get in the hole!'

Bombs rained down on Wake. Surprised Marines and workers threw themselves flat on the ground. Two Wildcat pilots, Lt Robert Conderman and Lt George Graves, who had been scheduled for take-off as the next scout patrol, had been sitting in their flight gear next to the runway when the first wave of Nells dived in. Grapes of bombs centred on the buildings and the repair shed. They knew that the sensible thing would be to take cover. But they were trained as fighter pilots, and Graves sprinted across the field to his parked aircraft; as he climbed up the ladder into the cockpit, a bomb scored a direct hit on his Wildcat. Lt Graves was Wake's first casualty. The other pilot, Lt Conderman, was running for his life; behind him he sensed rather than heard the next wave of bombers diving in. The pall of smoke from Graves' exploding fuel tank nearly choked him. He fought for breath, zigzagging between bullets down the runway to reach his aircraft. He had almost made it when shrapnel struck him in his leg. As he tried to crawl to safety, his plane blew up and a portion of the torn-off wing pinned him beneath the wreckage. Corporal Robert Page and Lt Frank Holden, hearing Conderman call out for help, ran to the burning wreck, when the next wave of attackers raced low over the runway, strafing and bombing. A projectile ricocheted off a coral head and mortally struck Lt Holden. Bomb fragments wounded Lt Webb, who took Holden's place to pull Conderman from the fire.

Men tried to run for cover behind coral outcrops and were plucked off by the planes' raking machine guns. Dan Teters saw a Nell coming in straight and low, the yellow flames from Wake's burning oil tank reflecting from its propeller blades. More explosions made the ground shake; there was a whine of flying metal fragments and Teters heard someone scream. Suddenly, right above him was a bright flare. A 3-inch shell had hit a plane in its wing tanks, and six tons of hydraulic fluid, human flesh, and magnesium alloy flared up in a green light. Where it fell into the sea, the water sizzled.

For those not directly hit on the islands of Wilkes and Peale, the attack on neighbouring Wake had been a horrid spectacle to watch. The surprise attack proved utterly devastating; the 3-inch anti-aircraft batteries managed to throw only forty rounds at the dive-bombers. Thirty-four Nell bombers had attacked Wake; of these, twenty-nine bombed within 300 metres of their aiming point. Most of the ground installations were in shambles; the bombing runs wrecked the Pan American facilities, killing nine of its ground staff, plus another twenty-five construction workers.

For all practical purpose, within three minutes VMF-211 Squadron ceased to exist. Of the twelve Wildcats, the eight that had been parked along the runway were total write-offs. Only the four planes in the air escaped destruction. Even greater was the loss in human lives; twenty-three of the squadron's fifty-five pilots and ground crew were killed during those terrible first instants. Major Putnam had received a bullet through his shoulder but continued his role as squadron commander. Lt Graves, in charge of aircraft repair crews, was killed. So were his eighteen ground mechanics, lying buried under the rubble of the maintenance shed. Every single spare was lost. Two 25,000-gallon avgas fuel tanks were shot to pieces. Only the runway was left untouched, which confirmed the enemy's intention to leave the island's airstrip intact to use it for their own planes. And this again meant that an invasion force could be expected momentarily to appear over the horizon.

While the Marines and construction crews licked their wounds, cleared the rubble and buried their dead, a final group managed to quit the island; the civilian ground staff of Pan American Airways jammed aboard the Philippine Clipper, which had miraculously survived, although thirty-two bullets had riddled the fuselage. Weighed down as it was, the Clipper managed to get into the air, but then climbed scarcely at all, its engines howling at maximum power. The captain settled on a course for Midway. Ahead lay the unusually long flight out over the Pacific, the plane riddled with bullet holes and scared passengers. Through the ports the crew's eyes searched the sky for a hostile presence, when suddenly they discovered silvery flashes in the distance. A brace of Japanese fighters had spotted them and raced in for a closer inspection; however the Clipper managed to dive into a cloud. When they exited from the milky grey, the skies before them were clear of enemy aircraft. They landed safely at Midway.

Reserve Lt Gustave Kahn, US Medical Corps, and the physician for the construction party, Dr Lawton Shank, had set up an emergency operating theatre in the damaged construction camp. They cut and patched as fast as the wounded were brought to them. Given the primitive means at their disposal – bomb blasts had shattered glass vials and medicine bottles – they worked wonders and saved a great many. Unfortunately, some were beyond help, including the badly burned pilot Lt Conderman, who died during the night.

The raid had not only decimated the personnel of VMF 211 Fighter Squadron, but equally its fighter strength; Putnam's Flying Circus was reduced to four shrapnel-ventilated Wildcats which, even in prime condition, were inferior in speed and manoeuvrability to the superb Japanese Zero fighters.

Yet when it came to piloting, these duster pilots from the American prairie states had no equal. Maj. Putnam appointed Lt John Kinney[4] to take the place of the fallen Lt Graves as his chief of ground repair crews. 'Keep my four planes flying, and I'll see to it that they'll give you a medal as big as a pizza.'

'Okay, you've got it,' Kinney replied with a savage grin. 'Have the pizza delivered to me in San Francisco.' Kinney did keep the four planes flying. With an air of defiance, he went about working hard and competently at precisely what he should do. He began by stripping the smashed planes of any scrap that was worth keeping. Next morning, four planes, with band-aids on wings, were ready and their pilots could go up to prove their mettle again. Unfortunately, Capt Tharin taxied his Wildcat into an oil drum, and he damaged his plane's propeller. Until it could be repaired, it reduced Wake's air defences to three planes. A patrol with Lt Kliewer and Sgt Hamilton set off on a scout-and-intercept mission; ten miles (16 km) from shore they spotted a sizeable formation of twin-engine Nells on the Wake run.

'Bandits at three o'clock!' called out Hamilton, pointing down at the silvery planes with red sun targets prominently on their wings, skimming low over the sea.

Two against thirty; the odds weren't good. 'Let's get them,' replied Kliewer.

From a position high above the Japanese their dive made up for the difference in airspeed. The first burst from their guns resulted in one enemy plane going down in flames and another turning off, trailing smoke. Then Peale Island's anti-aircraft guns began hammering away and they had to veer off, or risk getting shot down by their own artillery. That day, five enemy aircraft were hit; one plane crashed in

4 He ended his career as brigadier-general in the USMC.

the lagoon. From its fuselage markings, Cmdr Cunningham established that they were under attack by aircraft from the 24th Japanese Air Flotilla.

The following morning's raid was a repeat of the two previous days, only this time the Japanese arrived fifteen minutes earlier. To avoid Wake's anti-aircraft defences, the Nells flew a high approach pattern at 18,000 feet (5400 metres). But then they came down. Wake's gunners were rewarded with several spectacular hits, and planes could be seen splashing down. The enemy had also overlooked the four Wildcats, ready to pounce at them out of the blinding sun. VMF 211's flight leader was Capt. Hank Elrod; his training had prepared him for combat, but nothing was like the real thing. To go with four bullet-riddled planes against an armada of thirty to forty, bristling with machine guns, was madness. But then they were all mad. Putnam had always been amazed by the pilots he encountered in his years of flying, but nothing quite like Hank Elrod; he was the coolest; his expression, his demeanour, his attitude was unshakeable, almost detached from the business of deadly combat.

Lt Kliewer was the first to spot them. He was so excited that he forgot his radio discipline. 'Bandits, bandits all over the place . . .'

'Okay, copy . . . Hang at twenty-thou and then come down on the bastards . . .' The bombers' throttles were now at full thrust. Elrod opted for an attack pouncing with his four planes on the bandits from up high. More reports came in.

'Twelve bandits at three o'clock . . .'

'Three bandits at twelve o'clock . . .'

'Three bandits at six o'clock . . .' Suddenly they were everywhere. *Damn them!* Elrod cursed to himself. There were just too many of them. At least he would get one bandit before they started attacking the island.

Kliewer and Hamilton caught one Jap in a perfect pincer manoeuvre. Tracers lit up the sky as they drove towards the plane ahead of them. Seconds later there was an explosion and whatever was left of the Nell scattered to the ocean below. Elrod saw a Nell pulling from the formation to trail Kliewer's Wildcat, manoeuvring close enough for a gun burst. He called out a warning: 'Bandit on your tail . . . break right . . .'

Kliewer jinked away, not in a predictable pattern but mixing altitude with speed change. Now that Kliewer was safe, Elrod put his mind to 'chasing Japs'. He picked out a straggler and controlled his Wildcat to get in close to his enemy. The Japanese formation was right below him and the sight filled him with an overwhelming red-hot rage. He hit the button when a Nell bomber was directly in front of him. At this range, he couldn't miss.

'. . . Die, sucker, die!' An orange and yellow fireball erupted in the sky ahead of Elrod's Wildcat as his bullets had found their target. The Nell was beginning its death-spiral to the dark waters below.

'Good shooting, Capt'n . . .'

The radio went wild: '. . . Splash 'em . . . two bandits at eleven . . . I'm hit . . .'

In a wild mêlée they raced at each other not more than two thousand feet (600 metres) above the sea and the radio became a blur of incessant noise of men yelling a string of four-letter words, interspersed with gun bursts.

'Knock it off, you guys,' yelled the captain into his throat mike. Elrod strained against his shoulder harness to look out of his cockpit just in time to see a Japanese formation do a bank and swing away, making straight for Wilkes Island.

'Go after them!' Elrod yelled into a channel that was a mass of confused conversation. His attention was now fully concentrated on another Nell in front of him; it tried a desperate evasive manoeuvre. Elrod watched the Nell growing in his gunsight. The next action called for a great degree of judgement, estimating the enemy's speed and course change. He opened fire, letting go of a two-second burst and much of it went into the Nell. It gave an agonising lurch; hit by a burst from his four .50-calibre wing guns the Japanese disintegrated in mid-air. The explosive shells must have struck an armed bomb. The Japanese dived 1500 feet (450 metres) over Wake. Elrod, still in his steep dive, couldn't avoid flying through the cloud of debris, which rattled on his fuselage like hailstones. He was less than three hundred feet (90 metres) above the water and one mile from the atoll.

'Hank! Bandit on your tail! Drop . . . drop . . . !' Kliewer called out, watching a Japanese bomber on his flight leader's tail. Elrod immediately threw his Wildcat into a screaming right bank and held it until the stall-warning horn came on, as he pushed hard on the stick to pull the Wildcat into a 45-degree bank turn, letting the sudden loss of lift over the wings pull the nose down. He rolled wings-level at one hundred feet (30 metres) above the sea – just a few wing-spans above the dark waters below. He could see tracers lashing out at him, whipping up geysers of water in front of his nose. He pulled the nose up. 'C'mon, baby, you can do it . . .'

He gained a thousand feet (300 metres), then banked sharply and found himself behind and slightly below another enemy bomber. He put up his nose, and, like the first one he had splashed, he let it have a three-second burst from his guns that tore off part of the enemy's wing. It threw the Nell into a vicious spiral; the aircraft cartwheeled edge-on across the water for several hundred yards before plunging into the waters and disappearing forever from sight.

By now his luck had run out. 'Bandit on your tail' came the warning again. Elrod pulled in the throttles to near idling power, rolled inverted, and pulled the plane's nose to the ocean, trying to get his tail vertical and away from the Nell; he levelled off at a hundred feet (30 metres) above the dark waters then banked sharply and hit the throttle to make back for the killing zone. If the others missed, then he could get another shot at the Jap. He climbed steeply, but before he could go after the next on his scorecard, a fist slammed into his aircraft and slewed it sideways. The burst from a Nell had gone through his fuselage and a shell penetrated the motor. The windstream peeled back the torn aluminium of his ailerons like a can of sardines; the motor was labouring and he was losing vision with black engine oil mucking up the Plexiglas. With a Nell on his tail, a rudder shot to pieces and a coughing engine, the aricraft dropped hundreds of feet; rivets popped, and the airflow, rushing compressed through the holes in the wings, screamed like a cat on fire, before Elrod regained hold of the plane. The control stick tightened as the hydraulic power bled away.

'I'm going . . . !' He didn't bail out, because down there they needed every airframe that could somehow be patched up. Also, at the speed he was going the windblast would tear him apart. He closed the fuel-cock and pulled the tank lever to dump fuel to avoid a fire on touchdown. Flying by the seat of his pants, he managed to bring his plane down on the strip. That was instants before a gigantic blast shook the atoll, making his tortured Wildcat ground-loop off the runway.

Sgt Hamilton in Number 3 Wildcat had just lined up behind a Nell when his vision was completely wiped out by a blinding burst of light, and he felt as if all the air had been sucked out of his lungs and replaced by a sheet of fire. His plane was buffeted and the low-flying Nell in front disintegrated – without being fired at! The shock wave flung Hamilton's Wildcat sideways and he struck his head on a cockpit strut. Hamilton found himself dazed and tried to clear his vision; from far-away he thought he heard a voice: 'I'm going . . . I'm going . . .' He look down as a spectacular explosion sent flames hundreds of feet into the air. The water was churned into froth by the shock wave. Wilkes Island seemed on fire before an evilly glowing cloud of dust hid the tortured place from view.

Here is what had occurred. Despite the tremendous barrage of gunfire that poured from the 3-inch batteries, the enemy had concentrated its entire effort to knock out Wilkes Island; wave after wave of Nells criss-crossed the sky, approaching the islands from different angles and heights, dropping bombs. Then suddenly a gigantic ball of fire blew up as if the world had come to a sudden end. Wilkes Island skyrocketed like a fountain and then collapsed on itself. A lucky hit from a 250-lb bomb had penetrated the log protection of the construction works' storage depot, setting off 125 tons of dynamite. It ignited a blossom of fire so huge that it created its own shadows on the sea for miles. Thousands of feet up, the Wildcat pilots thought that their eardrums had ruptured. Glancing down from their cockpits, they stared in horror at an island spewing purple fire, turning the sky crimson, then orange and purple as fire engulfed Wilkes and its garrison.

In this deafening cacophony of the blast that tossed their planes about like toys, explosions spurted from all over the island, exploding readied ammunition in flaming rockets streaking the sky, reaching out like enormous firecrackers. A dense cloud of vaporised dust and debris rose high, hiding the torn island from view, until wind currents in high layers dispersed the cloud. The island, smouldering from a thousand fires, was totally denuded; gone was the camouflage, only shards of charred scrub with blackened gun barrels pointing like spears to the sky remained. The force of the blast was such that it had twisted the 5-inch gun mounts and triggered off every round of ammunition stored on Wilkes. Incredible as it may seem, only two gunners of the main guns on Koku Point lost their lives.

This massive explosion had an important psychological effect on the Japanese pilots, also pitched about wildly by the resulting shock wave. Their previous losses in the skies over Wake – fourteen planes had already gone down in the sea – where little defence had been expected – had the worst effect that a Japanese flight commander could experience, the loss of face. This blast gave them the opportunity to show off their efficiency and this again translated into an exaggerated, non-confirmed version of the damage they had caused. They had a right to be wrong: for them, observing the explosion from their cockpits, Wake had been obliterated.

'WAKE EXPLODED. NO SURVIVORS EXPECTED ON ATOLL,' was the message received by Rear Admiral Sadamichi Kajioka, commanding the Wake Invasion Force. As its consequence, the admiral based his invasion plan on a false assessment. Now his ships could approach far inshore to unload his landing force of elite soldiers to take the atoll's 'obliterated defences'. But there was another fact that pushed Kajioka into a hasty assault without awaiting the results of further reconnaissance missions. The ambitious admiral's vanity had been hurt; he had received a message that the glory, which he had reserved for himself, to be honoured by his emperor as the first Japanese to set foot on American soil, was going to another commander who had overrun the US possession of Guam. Rear Admiral Kajioka swore that he would conquer Wake – the bridge on the Empire's glorious road to victory over America. With Wake, he'd still be the celebrated hero. He scheduled the invasion for 11 December 1941, Pearl Harbor-day plus four. He ordered maximum steam for his

fleet and set out on a northerly course from Kwajalein in
the Marshall Islands.

The first to encounter an element of Kajioka's invasion
force was the submarine *USS Triton*. The sub was riding
on the surface to recharge its depleted batteries, when
a look-out spotted smoke on the horizon. The *Triton*
submerged and fired a spread of four torpedoes at a quickly
approaching destroyer. Then the boat dived to maximum
depth and waited for the tell tale sound of an explosion.

'A hit!' called out the sub's executive officer on hearing a dull bang. What they didn't realise was that their
torpedo had struck (a probable hit because unconfirmed)
the picket of a powerful invasion fleet, sailing 10 nautical
miles behind a destroyer screen. It was made up of the
3,587-ton cruiser *Yubari*, Admiral Kajioka's flagship,
armed with 5.5-inch gun turrets; the cruisers *Tatsuta* and
Tenryu to provide fire support; the destroyers *Mutsuki*,
Kisaragi, *Yayoi*, *Mochizuki*, *Oite*, and *Hayate*; plus two
older destroyers converted to carry a landing force; and
two armed merchantmen for fuel and supplies, the *Kongo
Maru* and *Kinryu Maru*.

Lt Kinney's flight mechanics had slaved all night, rebuilding four airworthy planes with parts stripped from the
wrecked planes on the ground. At 04.00 hrs, the pilots
were ordered on standby. Captains Elrod, Tharin and
Freuler were assigned to the three operational F4F-3s,
while a fourth aircraft was still being armed and readied.
With one 100-lb bomb under each wing, the three machines
were pushed into position for instant take-off. Shortly
before first light, at 05.00 hrs, Kajioka's armada showed
up on the far horizon. Elrod, Tharin and Freuler fired up
their engines and took off to provide air cover against an
anticipated aerial attack by Nells, which they expected to
come simultaneously with a surface invasion.

An orange flicker on the far horizon was followed, moments later, by a howl like an express train passing through a tunnel. At 05.22 hrs, the first salvo of 5.5-inch shells, fired from the *Yubari*, struck Wake. Major Devereux had issued strict orders to his gun officers on Wilkes, Peale and Wake, to hold their fire for his specific command. No use wasting ammunition; the enemy's guns were far superior in range and accuracy to his antiquated 5-inchers. The enemy's shelling zeroed in on the untouched oil tanks in the southwest corner of Wake. Within minutes, the tanks exploded, hiding a large portion of the atoll under a pall of black smoke. The prevailing winds pushed the dense cloud out to sea. Under the cover of smoke, the Japanese troop transports began lowering their landing crafts to ferry Kajioka's Special Naval Landing Force ashore. It wasn't a propitious moment to try for a landing with shallow-bottomed boats. Far-off Pacific storms sent rollers thousands of miles across the sea, increasing steadily in wave height and force before they struck the first natural obstacle, which happened to be Wake. Huge waves rose like glistening black holes from a blue-grey sea before pounding the jagged reef like an aerial bombing; their salt spray reached all the way to the island's gun positions.

Lt Clarence A. Barninger, the gunnery officer of 'A' Battery on Peacock Point, lifted his powerful glasses and took a look across the early-morning sea. From where he was posted, he had a front-seat view of the cruiser *Yubari* sailing in a lordly way parallel to the coastline. She was a sleek-looking vessel, cutting through the heavy seas with an impressive white froth; all her gun turrets were cocked for shore. On either beam of the admiral's flagship, a column of two cruisers and six destroyers fanned into position for an invasion drive. With incredible arrogance, as if to demonstrate the ship's superiority, the *Yubari* wheeled inwards, thereby closing her distance to Barninger's 5-inch

'A' Battery to just about 5000 metres. Lt Barninger watched her pass so close that her high bridge, glittering with binoculars trained on Wake, leapt into his lenses. Why did Major Devereux hold back on permission to fire? With a well-sited 5-inch gun, and a target silhouetted against the orange dawn, a hit would be only a matter of time.

At 06.10 hrs, Lt Barninger's field phone rang. 'Commence firing!'

'Range five-oh-oh!' yelled Barninger.

'Range five-oh-oh!' repeated the chief gunner.

'Fire!'

A blinding light burst over the island, so bright that Marines nearby winced and shut their eyes. 'A' Battery's twin guns belched fire and brown smoke. The blast sound fanned out across the water. Two waterspouts shot into the air. But the salvo had given away Barninger's camouflaged gun position; a broadside of counter-fire instantly replied from *Yubari*'s guns. However, their gunnery was not accurate enough to do any harm other than splinter some coral.

With his eyes pressed to the rubber cups of his glasses, the lieutenant ordered in a cool tone: 'Short! Up two hundred.'

'Distance five-two . . . locked on . . .'

'Fire!'

The gun again belched fire.

'Over! Down one hundred.'

A sweating crew fed more shells into the smoking breeches as a new salvo from the *Yubari* howled in overhead. Much closer, this one; the cloud of sand dust and cordite had the crew retching.

'Distance five-one . . . locked on . . .'

'A' Battery's third round smashed squarely into the *Yubari*. Within minutes the Japanese cruiser turned into a blazing hulk; it slewed around, belching smoke, and disappeared behind its cloud of smoke from fires raging on board.

'L' Battery on Wilkes Island, the twin 5-inch guns that had been reported obliterated by the monumental explosion twenty-four hours before, had one barrel still functioning; cannibalising parts from one gun, Lt John McAlister got the other gun back into operation before first light. His ammunition had burst in the explosion – it was this that had caused the deaths of the two gunners – and he had been given only a few dozen shells. He had no range finder, and his operational gun had a bent mounting. But his men had will, and with their manual training mechanism brought the barrel to bear on the leading destroyer, the *Hayate*, sailing provocatively close to shore.

06.10 hrs: 'Fire!'

The first shell went over the *Hayate*, the second was short, but the next three shells hit the destroyer just below the bridge. One penetrated into the ammunition ready-room and caused an internal explosion. The *Hayate* sank within a minute, taking with her a crew of 167.

'My God.' The gun crew stared open-mouthed across the sea. 'She's gone!'

Platoon Sgt Henry Bedell yelled at them: 'Knock it off, get back to your gun. Wha' d'ya think this is, hitting a home run at a ball game?'

The gun swivelled on to its next targets, the *Oite* and then the *Mochizuki*, both of which suffered impacts, as did a transporter. Then they ran out of shells.

'B' Battery on Toki Point, under Lt Woodrow Kessler, had their work cut out. They shot it out with no less than three destroyers, the *Yayoi*, *Mutsuki* and *Kisaragi*, and two cruisers, the *Tenryu* and the *Tatsuta*. A large piece of shrapnel from an incoming shell damaged one of the gun mounts, but Kessler's crew kept loading and firing with the remaining gun and, at a distance of 10,000 metres, its tenth round set *Yayoi*'s stern on fire.

While this duelling with heavy naval guns was going on, what was going on in the skies over Wake? Four Wildcats were up in the air: Paul Putnam, Hank Elrod, Herbert Freuler and Frank Tharin. To their amazement, the naval assault was launched without an air cover. This freed the American pilots for their secondary role, ship interception. Shortly after 07.00 hrs, the Japanese admiral had had enough; with several ships aflame, he turned off and headed for the open sea. That's when three Wildcats pounced on the enemy's ships with their 100-lb bombs. Putnam, Tharin and Freuler made a combined bombing-strafing run on the *Tenryu*, which suffered superficial damage from near-hits. During this run, Tharin's Wildcat was damaged by anti-aircraft fire from the destroyer screen and he was slightly wounded, but he kept on flying.

The fourth aircraft, that of Captain Elrod, had split off from the formation. He was keen; his idea of fun was dead-reckoning in foul weather. In that he was served, having lost touch with Putnam's flight in the murky overcast. He had dropped yet lower to fly barely above the high-reaching wave tops of an ill-tempered ocean, when he saw in the distance what looked like grey outlines of ships and climbed into a cloud to avoid their gunfire.

He clicked his mike: 'Ships ahead. Going after them,' he said in his calm drawl, his hands on the stick and his eyes unmoving straight ahead. Suddenly he came to a break in the clouds and right below him was a big ship bristling with guns, white water churning at her stern. Elrod took a good look before he climbed on full power into the cloud. Quickly he swung his fighter through a 180-degree turn and tore back towards his target. Moments later he lined up on the heavy destroyer *Kisaragi*. They had also seen him and a tremendous barrage of anti-aircraft gunfire erupted from its decks. The best defence was to point a fighter's nose at the tracers, presenting the smallest possible target.

At 07.31 hrs, almost straight overhead the fire-spitting vessel, he tilted the aircraft on its wing and put it into a steep dive. One wingtip pointed towards the roof of the sky and the plane's nose went straight down. Elrod slid into the stream of tracers racing at him from the destroyer's deck and impacting shrapnel rattled his Wildcat. He was hurtling straight down at a heart-stopping pace, the fuselage screamed and wing rivets popped. He fought the violent vibration and managed to hold on to his dive, aiming for the ship's rear funnel. Frantically he worked the controls, holding true course over the vital seconds it took for an accurate bomb drop. The sea and his target came racing at him through the Plexiglas canopy.

At a mere 500 feet (150 metres), he pulled back on the stick and released his two bombs. Freed of its load, the plane bounced up and then sky was again above him; a crackling clogged his ears and the sudden sense of extreme heat and smoke choked him. His bombs! One had splashed next to the ship. But the other made in a straight line for the rear deck, where anti-submarine depth charges were stored. The destroyer blew up in a gigantic ball of fire, gun barrels, masts, and bits of human flesh raining down on a wild-gone sea. Elrod's ears cleared and in his earphones he thought he heard a voice call out: 'Bingo!'

When the cloud cleared, the *Kisaragi* was gone. The shock wave from the explosion whipped Elrod's tail plane into the air, jamming its tail rudder. A shell from the undulating lines of tracers sweeping the sky in seemingly random patterns from the amphibious assault ship that had accompanied the *Kisaragi* shattered his cockpit's Plexiglas. Another struck his engine; the impact was like a hammer blow, and he banged his head. The windblast hit him in the face; it kept him awake and drove out the acrid smoke that began filling his cockpit. His oil-flow indicator light went to red and the beeper howled; any moment now the engine would seize up. His airspeed dropped, and so did his plane. He had the sensation of weightlessness as his Wildcat started to lose altitude.

'Hank! Get out! Eject!' he could hear in his earphones over the windblast. Elrod reached for the canopy release handle and pulled, but the damned thing was jammed. He couldn't get out and he couldn't make it back to the airstrip; he checked his seat-straps, watched the turn-and-bank indicator and saw that he was flying lopsided due to the large hole in his starboard wing. He aimed for a long stretch of sand along Wake's water's edge. The plane was sinking at the frightening rate of ten metres a second, when the beach came up and slapped him so hard that the breath went out of him. The crazily spinning blades bit into coral, sending off sparks, the undercarriage was ripped out on the razor-sharp coral heads, and the wing-tanks were slashed, gushing volatile aviation gasoline. When his vision cleared, Elrod the Miraculous wriggled out through the hole in his cockpit with nothing more than scratches, burns and bruises. That was instants before the gushing avgas touched the hot engine cowl and his Wildcat blew up.

After quick refuelling and re-arming stops, the remaining three Wildcats went back into the air to confront a formation of thirty bombers, which had finally arrived to assist Kajioka's hard-pressed fleet. The Wildcats pounced on the Nells, downing two and sending off a third trailing flames. During the ensuing aerial combat, Freuler's machine received a bullet through the engine block. Without engine power he brought it down like a top-heavy glider. Sgt Hamilton, who had taken over the aircraft from the wounded Tharin, took it back up, despite holes in its fuselage. He engaged in more dogfights, and when he eventually landed, his Wildcat looked like the proverbial sieve.

That day, Wake's guns and planes had scored the first major American victory.

Humbled by sizeable casualties, Kajioka's invasion fleet made for the Marshall Islands, licking its wounds. The admiral thought it better than to inform Imperial Naval Command immediately; so far he had done nothing noteworthy except get half of his invasion force destroyed or badly damaged. He needed to show a decisive action before announcing the disaster. He was certain to be hauled over the carpet by Admiral Yamamoto for losing several valuable vessels and, in the end, he wrote a justification into his report: 'AMERICANS FIERCELY COUNTERATTACKED. WE WERE TEMPORARILY FORCED TO RETIRE.'

For the loss of two US planes (one could be repaired) and four wounded Marines, the Americans accounted for five enemy aircraft downed, two destroyers sunk, the admiral's flagship *Yubari* damaged, as well as two old cruisers wrecked. Hundreds of seamen were lost in the explosions on the destroyers. That wasn't all. Seven hundred soldiers of the invasion force had been put into their landing crafts in heavy seas; when the attack was cancelled, and while trying to re-embark their ships, waves swamped their unstable landing crafts and they were sucked down into the airless blackness beneath the sea. For Japan's high command, Rear Admiral Kajioka's attack of 11 December was an unmitigated disaster. But more than that, the debacle of Wake was a moral setback. Their 'invincible armada' had suffered its first defeat. America had shown its teeth. The War in the Pacific was now four days old.

The story of Wake's heroic defence was released to an American press desperate for positive news. Cmdr Cunningham went on to make history with the wording of a coded message. US Navy regulations required dispatching a coded message by mixing its text with gibberish to confuse any possible intercept. Thus, Cunningham's message, received by CinCPac (Commander-in-Chief Pacific) in Hawaii, read:

SEND US STOP NOW IS THE TIME FOR ALL GOOD MEN TO COME TO THE AID OF THEIR PARTY STOP CUNNINGHAM MORE JAPS . . .

Once decoded, it asked for US forces to come to their aid as more Japs were on their way. By chance, a psychological warfare specialist and former writer of publicity slogans, got hold of the text. He recognised its propaganda value; by cutting some words he turned it into one of the catchiest slogans of the War in the Pacific: '*SEND US MORE JAPS!*'

Slogans were nothing to amuse the men on Wake; they didn't have use for morale-building phrases. What they needed were shells, supplies and reinforcements, all of which had been promised. Cmdr Cunningham did receive a cable, giving him permission to use 'expensive heavy office stationery to glaze damaged window panes'. There was nothing to glaze; Jap bombs had reduced all windowed structures to rubble. Putnam's 'Wake Atoll Airforce' was now reduced to two operational aircraft, and even these were held together by wire and hope, just as its pilots were taped up and bandaged. On the following day, Captain Tharin took up a plane and shot down a Japanese Mavis flying-boat. The other Wildcat, flown by Lt David Kliewer along the underside of a heavy cloud cover, like a fly on the ceiling, spotted a small Japanese submarine marauding near the island. He pushed his plane into a steep dive, released his two 100-lb bombs. The explosion caused debris from the sub to float to the surface.

For the marooned island force, air raids became the routine. Daily bombing runs by thirty to forty Nell bombers had turned the three atolls into a heap of ruins. With no more targets to destroy, the Japanese dropped their bombs on what they had bombed the day before, or the day before that. Wake hadn't taken it lying down; it had shown its teeth. Its air-defence gunners had shot down a considerable number of flying boats and bombers. At every attack, the flurry of gunfire was as spectacular as it was frightening. Shells exploded in the skies over the island, making it look like a dome of sparklers and black cotton puffs. Some Nells banked sharply before reaching the curtain of fire and their bombs exploded harmlessly in the water. But not all turned off. Many braved the firestorm and came in low over the islands. Those on the ground, who weren't active with a 3-inch gun, sat in their sandbagged foxholes, cursing, praying, and digging their fingers into the sand until the storm passed. For all, war had become the routine of waiting to be bombed and then clearing up the rubble.

On 14 December, Captain Freuler in a Wildcat tried to avoid a worker crossing the runway; he ground-looped his plane into a crane. That same evening, during a raid by thirty Nells, a bomb smashed the last airworthy Wildcat. Lt Kinney's ground mechanics went to work – among them, US Navy Machinist's Mate Hesson, who had suffered a deep gash from a bomb splinter the previous morning. Despite his open wound and doctor's strict orders, Hesson sneaked from the first-aid shelter to report back on duty and then carried on as effectively as ever. For the rest of the exhausted mechanics, his example was a true morale builder. Putnam cited Hesson's service as being 'the very foundation of the entire aerial defence of Wake Island'. In one night, ground crews, ably assisted by civilian mechanics, virtually screwed together two homemade aircraft that somehow would stay in the air.

It was only natural that the media overexposure following Japan's sneak attack on Pearl Harbor and the dramatic sinking of America's Pacific Fleet had pushed all else off the nation's front pages. It was followed by more bad news; Guam fell, the Philippines were invaded, the British battleships, *Prince of Wales* and *Repulse*, sunk off Singapore, Hong Kong fell. The heroic stand on Wake was turning into the nation's morale booster. There were no independent dispatches from the beleaguered island, and the press had to rely on censored official handouts. With Wake grabbing the headlines, something had to be done by the US Navy to show its support of the men of the 1st USMC Defense Battalion. A relief convoy, made up of the heavy cruisers *USS Astoria*, *Minneapolis* and *San Francisco*, was being constituted. They were to accompany the aircraft carrier *USS Saratoga*, as soon as the flat-top reached Hawaiian waters from her refuelling stop off California. In the late hours of 15 December, Task Force 14, consisting of the seaplane tender *Tangier*, the oiler *Neches* and the aircraft carrier *USS Saratoga*, Admiral Frank Fletcher's flagship, protected by four destroyers, left Pearl Harbor. The *Tangier* carried elements of the 4th USMC Defense Battalion, plus vitally needed ammunition and equipment, including ground radar. Aboard the Saratoga was Major Verne McCaul's VMF-221 Squadron of F2A-3 Brewster Buffaloes, an unsuited, slow fighter aircraft, flown by pilots that had never taken off from a carrier. Once at sea the seals on the envelopes were broken and the crews told: 'Destination Wake!'

If Wake was good for American fighting spirit, it was not good for Japanese morale. For Admiral Isoroku Yamamoto, Commander in Chief of Japan's Combined Fleet, and Vice-Admiral Nariyoshi Inouye, Commander Fourth Fleet, Wake turned into a sticky symbol. 'The Americans' defiance must be broken!' came the order down from the top. Allotted for the task were Japan's pride, the giant aircraft carriers *Soryu* and *Hiryu*, plus an escort of six heavy cruisers, put under the command of Rear Admiral Hiroaki Abe. On 16 December, the Wake Island Reinforcement Force of two carriers with a complement of 118 attack aircraft, screened by the heavy cruisers *Tone* and *Chikuma* and the destroyers *Tanikaze* and *Urakaze*, steamed for Wake. For forty-eight hours, they managed to conceal their move from American intelligence, before a US Navy listening post intercepted a coded transmission of a mission by two carrier groups; they were unable to decipher their destination, or present whereabouts.

In the aftershock of Pearl Harbor, CinCPac, US Admiral Kimmel, had devised a solid plan for deploying a strong American carrier force to relieve Wake. But Secretary of the Navy Frank Knox, who had been told by President Roosevelt, in fear of a congressional investigation, to find a scapegoat for the Pearl Harbor debacle, fired Kimmel. His dismissal altered the operational plans of US Pacific Command in Hawaii. Admiral Pye, who temporarily replaced Kimmel, was not willing to risk the *Saratoga* against two of the world's biggest aircraft carriers, whose pilots had proven their efficiency at Pearl Harbor.

Pye's planning officer, McMorris, when asked by his chief what lay off Wake, replied: 'Frankly, sir, we ain't got no more idea'n a billygoat.'

'You got any good news for us?' Admiral Pye asked wryly.

'Sort of. The Japanese have lost the first battle at Wake. We think the enemy wanted to use the airstrip there to stage bombers to support an assault on Midway. Cunningham's men are holding out. They've called for support.'

Admiral Pye let his decision hang in the air; Task Force 14 was allowed to continue, but only after it had been reinforced by another heavy cruiser squadron, Task Force 11.

*   *   *

Aboard the Japanese 8th Cruiser Division (Rear Admiral Hiroaki Abe) an invasion plan was worked out: this time, the attack on Wake would be launched *without* preparatory bombardment. Two old destroyers were converted as troop landing craft and scheduled to be sacrificed; ramming their keels over the coral reefs, they were to be run aground on the atoll and unload 1000 of Japan's elite attack forces, the Maizuru 2nd Special Naval Landing Force, all veterans who had received their baptism by fire in Manchuria. Naval and ground troop commanders were told that failure was not to be contemplated.

A US Navy Catalina flying boat, landing in the lagoon on 20 December, brought news of the relief attempt by Task Force 14, and ordered Commander Cunningham to ready the remaining 350 civilians for evacuation on D-Day, which was set for the morning of 24 December. 'We'll be home for Christmas . . .' became the main conversation piece among the construction workers. Major Putnam handed the Catalina pilot a report to his superior of Marine Aircraft Group 21, which went straight to the point: '. . . Parts and assemblies have been traded back and forth so that no airplane can be identified. Engines have been traded from plane to plane, have been junked, stripped, rebuilt and airframes all but created.' In fact, the last aircraft to fly was a miracle of ingenuity, an airplane built from parts salvaged from twelve wrecked planes. Putnam added one more line: 'All hands have behaved splendidly and held up in a manner of which the US Marine Corps may well tell.'

On 21 December, more Japanese planes struck the atoll. Only this time Val and Kate bombers, escorted by Zero fighters, carried out the raid! Since these planes were carrier launched, it made the defenders of Wake aware that an enemy carrier was in the vicinity. In fact, the aircraft had been launched from the giant *Hiryu*. At 11.35 hrs Lt Carl Davidson, flying to the north of the atoll, radioed Capt. Herbert Freuler in the second patrol air-craft: 'Large formation of Bandits on approach. Am engaging.'

Freuler joined up with Davidson; they went after a flight of six Kates. Freuler dropped one, sending a second off in smoke, before several Zeros got him in their sights. Davidson split off to go after another wave. The last Freuler saw of Lt Davidson was chasing after a Kate while being trailed by at least four Zeros. A Zero on Freuler's tail fired; two bullets went through his parachute and his seat. Freuler, badly wounded and on the point of blacking out, pushed the stick forward, executed a dive and successfully crash-landed. But then his canopy jammed and the plane caught fire. An alert ground crew managed to hack him out of the canopy. Lt Carl Davidson was lost at sea.

On 22 December, Task Force 14 was 425 miles (680 km) off Wake, less than a day's sailing. CinCPac became increasingly concerned over Cunningham's latest report of the attack by carrier-launched aircraft. Until more detailed information was forthcoming, Admiral Pye ordered Admiral Fletcher aboard the *Saratoga* to hold his ships on station.

Shortly after midnight of 23 December 1941, a heavy weather front rolled in on Wake and, in the rain squalls, visibility became virtually nil. 'Another rainy day, not the sort of weather for an invasion,' said one of Barninger's crew of the 5-inch gun on Peacock Point, facing the part of darkness that was the sea.

'It's too bloody quiet,' observed the lieutenant, listening to the sound of waves on the offshore reef. Minutes later, flashes lit up the clouds, which Barninger initially put as distant lightning. However, when the irregular flashes continued he called Major Devereux: 'We've got visuals of flashes way off the windy side of the island.'[5]

'Incoming gunfire?' Devereux wanted to know.

'Negative, probably the weather front moving in.'

Thunder boomed, a beating rain started; but the flashes were not from lightning. Barninger could see the telling suns from the muzzles of big guns. Again he called Devereux. This time the transmission was crackling with static and echoes. Still, Barninger managed to communicate the bad news: 'Something's coming our way . . .'

Devereux woke Cunningham who, after having observed the flashes, radioed CinCPac at 01.45 hrs: 'GUNFIRE BETWEEN SHIPS TO NORTHEAST OF ISLAND.'

The sirens howled and the garrison was put on alert. Captain Platt of 'L' Battery on Wilkes sited a machine-gun crew at the edge of the lagoon to cover the approach to the causeway across the Wilkes Channel. Lt Arthur Poindexter rounded up a composite group of civilians from the camp's administration pool and added eight Marines to guide the unit. He supplied them with four light machine guns and sufficient ammunition, and told them to get instantly over to Peale Island. But before they moved out, Major Devereux intercepted the Poindexter group and held it back as his mobile reserve.

It was 02.35 hrs. The Japanese arrived by stealth. Covered by darkness and the sound of the heavy surf rolling in, the first Japanese landing craft took the American outposts by surprise. Rather than seeing them, Gunner McKinstry, stationed on Wilkes, suddenly had the feeling of a crowded blackness before him. He asked for permission to switch on the searchlight. It came on for a few moments, but that was long enough. Its powerful beam greased everything in sight. Through a curtain of rain and darkness he saw the

---

[5] It was never established what these flashes were.

bow of a landing craft 200 feet (150 metres) from his crew's position.

McKinstry couldn't depress the barrel of his heavy gun far enough to hit the craft, yet something had to be done, and quickly. Platoon Sergeant Henry Bedell grabbed a satchel with grenades and with Marine Willi Buehler, jogged towards the beach. No need to crouch or do a low crawl or do any hiding. Those on the landing craft had to be blind not to spot them. Maybe he could reach the beach before they made it ashore. He saw the bow of the craft straight ahead. The two reached the sandy strip at water's edge and moved out of the scrub, pulling the pins on their grenades. Bedell, splashing across the surf, was within distance to lob his grenade, when a shot rang out, followed instantly by a dozen more reports. He threw up his arms, the grenade dropped from his hand and he pitched dead into the water. Buehler was also struck, but managed to crawl behind the cover of a coral head. Moments later the boat's gunwale came down and out spilled a company from the Takano Unit of the Special Naval Landing Force. McKinstry and another Marine rushed to the .50-calibre machine gun, protecting his 3-inch gun, and their hail of bullets met the invaders. From their flank, another machine gun sent a stream of tracers into the advancing Japanese. Marine Sandy Kay's .50-calibre fire enfiladed the Takano Unit from their flank and bowled them over; the shock stopped their advance from reaching the 3-inch gun position. This brief delay gave the gun crew time to extract the firing pins from the cannon and bury them in the sand.

At 02.50 hrs, Cunningham radioed a follow-up message to the Chief of the 14th US Naval District: 'ISLAND UNDER GUNFIRE. ENEMY APPARENTLY LANDING.'

On the southern tip of Wake, on Peacock Point, Sergeant Raymond Gragg, in charge of a machine-gun squad placed behind sandbags protectively around Lt Barninger's 5-inch gun battery, heard a deep-throated, liquid rumble coming from the darkness. It sounded like the engine of a sizeable ship; but that couldn't be! Between him and 'them' lay the submerged reef of razor-coral to protect the island from naval landings. Of one thing Gragg was certain, it didn't sound like the clug-clug of a two-stroke outboard engine.

'Sarge, I don't like the sound of that mother,' mumbled one of his men.

'Button up, Marine!' growled the veteran sergeant. But the sound kept increasing in intensity. Something big was heading towards shore, followed by the urgent roar of high-revving marine diesels from quite close by. There was no more doubt as to its origin – Sgt Gragg cranked up command centre to report: 'Big enemy landing craft on approach. Estimated distance 1000 yards (900 metres).' He was out by 500 yards (450 metres).

'Hold with what you've got,' Devereux's voice came back. Dammit, hold with what? Whatever was coming towards shore was a heck of a lot too big for his dozen men and two machine guns. 'Orders from the major, we're to hold!' They took cover behind their sandbags. Suddenly came a high-pitched tearing sound.

'Sonofabitch! Here they come . . .' yelled a gunner and pressed the trigger – his heavy machine gun shuddered and belched as the bow of a big ship tore over the reef and roared straight for their position. It buried its bow on the beach, not 50 yards (45 metres) from Sergeant Gragg. Hundreds of Japanese poured overboard on rope ladders. This time, nothing stopped them; they came on in suicidal waves. The night was thick with screaming shells, hissing splinters and unearthly yells.

Lt Robert Hanna, in charge of the machine guns near the airstrip, with Corporal Ralph Holewinski and three civilians, Paul Gay, Eric Lehtola and Bob Bryan in tow, sprinted for the 3-inch cannon beyond the airstrip, which was in a direct line of charge by yelling Japanese. Running tall, with his Thompson submachine gun blazing, he threw back the advancing enemy as they were about to take possession of the gun.

Major Putnam put his crews to chip holes into the runway and plant anti-tank mines on the strip; any Japanese plane attempting a night landing, would detonate them.

The Japanese assault ships began launching wave after wave of small landing craft to beach them. By 03.00 hrs, the enemy had established bridgeheads on the three islands; they had cut the telephone landlines and Major Devereux lost all communication with his outlying gun positions; he didn't know where or how many of the enemy had come ashore. He ordered Lt Poindexter's drummed-together reserve squad of eight Marines and fourteen construction workers, armed with grenades, pistols and four machine guns, to set up a line of defence in the scrub between the construction camp and the airstrip; this way they could also sweep the narrow causeway over the Wilkes Channel, which separated Wake from Wilkes. Across the narrow strip of water flickered the muzzle flashes of a hundred rifles. A Jap machine gun started to stutter. Bullets whizzed over their heads. Not all struck. Only some.

'They've got us pinned down,' called out a construction man, firing his Springfield repeater at shadows. Next to him lay his dead buddy. For all they knew, the Japanese had landed behind them, circling in on them for their final loss. Another construction worker began shrieking and before anyone could stop him, he was over the edge. He swayed backwards and folded up with a dying, inarticulate scream, his chest perforated by bullets. Poindexter had detected two more landing barges trying to float across the coral. While the lieutenant kept the Japanese coxswains' heads down with a stream of fire from a machine gun, two men from his unit sprinted to the beach and hid behind coral heads. No sooner had the barges ground to a halt on the sand, 'Cap' Rutledge, a construction foreman, and First Class Barnes, lobbed grenades into the boats, killing a great number of enemy. Still, the gunwales dropped and a flood of Japanese climbed over their dead and dying to rush ashore.

Poindexter's small group saw the enemy, not as individuals, but as a vast mass of shapes in the dark. They came on with a ferocious yell and flooded across the causeway. By the flames of a fiercely burning landing craft, the thin line of US Marines and civilians clung to their position. They fought with bullets and rifle butts, shovels and bare fists. Locked into brutal individual brawls, Japanese and Americans staggered under the impact of heavy slugs, crying, bleeding, twisting and falling. Despite the great sacrifice by Poindexter's thin line, the Japanese finally made it across the causeway.

On Wake, Lt Hanna's men pushed shell after shell into the fuming, hot breech of the recovered 3-inch gun. At point-blank range, they poured fourteen rounds into a beached warship, stuck on the coral reef, striking the fuel tanks and setting her on fire. The flames found the diesel fuel in the ship's storage tanks, bursting aflame in a ball of fire; internal explosions shook her. The explosions were just as devastating to the men trying to lower themselves into small landing crafts, setting their clothes and hair on fire. In the glare of the fire Hanna's men could see men flinging themselves overboard into the burning oil-covered water. A few of his men stopped to look at the dying ship. Hanna yelled furiously: 'Move it!'

The flames showed a second beached vessel in the vicinity, and Hanna's 'civilian gun crew' switched targets. When a handful of Japanese tried to infiltrate the gun position, Hanna coolly pulled out his .45 Browning pistol and within moments, three dead Japanese lay in front of him. This incident showed the urgent need to reinforce the last operating gun. Hanna couldn't be expected to hold out much longer. Devereux ordered Putnam's aircrews to set up a defensive perimeter around the cannon.

At 06.12 hrs, the giant *Soryu*, 250 miles (400 km) to the south, had turned into the wind and launched twelve attack aircraft. In less than an hour, the planes were strafing Wake's last strongpoint. Fires were burning brightly all over, there was nowhere else to hide. At the site of the construction camp, Lt Poindexter was joined by more stragglers and, with a fifty-five men platoon, held off the attack by a Japanese battalion of eight hundred.

First light made it clear that burning, smoking Wake Atoll was ringed by Japanese naval crafts. The heavy cruisers *Aoba*, *Kinugasa*, *Furutaka* and *Kako* threw shell after shell at the island's defences, a naval bombardment such as cannot be described in its intensity. The three atolls were smothered under a dense cloud of dust, whirled high into the air by the deluge of shells. This time, Admiral Kajioka made sure that this was not a repeat of the surprising American victory of a few days ago. The rate of enemy fire was continuously on the increase, heavy projectiles were bursting in clusters, blasting the sand, trenches and Marines. Long before the sound came the whoosh, which sucked out the air, causing fits of coughing. Marines retched from the nauseating cordite, before sucking in gulps of air. Their mouths, nostrils, and ears were clogged with dust and their eyes blinded by sand. They began to think not of the Japanese in front of them, but of the Japanese behind them. One of the Marines was hanging over the trench with a trail of red running down his trouser leg. Punctuated by explosions and the sound of passing shells, his buddy yelled: 'Talk to me, Chuck!' But Chuck wouldn't talk. He was dead.

Mortar shells burst in the brush, chipping coral. That's

when Devereux heard a swift '*whooz*' and ducked instinctively. A round of mortar shells screamed in and exploded in rapid succession near his unprotected position. A blinding light enveloped him and he was suffused with golden warmth before the concussion knocked him out and he stayed down. His men thought they had lost him, but then he got up again, covered in dust and bleeding from cuts on his forehead. Everywhere, his Marines were hard at work killing Japanese. In many places the enemy was driven back. Waves washed corpses on to the shore, leaving them sprawled out on the sand; corpses floated with their heads and shoulders submerged in the swell between reef and beach. On the sandy beach, one group of Japanese lay clustered around their machine gun; it had fired only twenty rounds before its crew had died from a direct hit by a 3-inch shell. Neither burning ships nor human losses would stop Kajioka. Troop transports disgorged more troops. Waves helped heave small boats over the coral reefs. Surprisingly, Hanna's 3-inch gun was still firing, with Major Putnam's mechanics putting a machine-gun cordon around it. A bullet grazed the major's jaw, soaking his shirt and the picture of his wife and daughters.

'Hell,' he said to his men, 'this is as far as we go.'

He turned to Elrod, 'Cover my ass.' He broke off as cordite fumes billowed around his hole from a cluster of mortar bomb explosions. When the cloud cleared, he saw Elrod strolling off, tall and remote, his features a mask of fierce determination. The fighter ace, who had downed a few planes and sunk a destroyer, and a group of flight mechanics held on to the flank of Putnam's defensive line, anchored on dense undergrowth near the big gun, invisible to any attacker storming up from the sea. Japanese by the hundreds jumped from their boats and waded towards shore. Elrod knew that his dozen men were heavily outnumbered, and that at least two companies were moving in on them, but he didn't consider his situation hopeless; his troops held a superior position, and the enemy's naval guns could no longer interfere, or they'd decimate their own troops. The enemy did exactly what Elrod had anticipated them to do, heading for a concentric assault. This brought them into the fixed fire lane from Elrod's machine guns.

'Free fire,' yelled Elrod, while the first wave of attackers was still ankle-deep in water. The scrub erupted; the vicious clatter of heavy machine guns with their sharp staccato shattered the silence like a bolt from the clear sky. The shoreline flickered spitting out bullets, raking the water. The initial wave of enemy soldiers was slaughtered, but that didn't stop others from hurtling forward, regardless of losses. A searchlight flashed on. The attackers were caught in its beam and stunned by its dazzling brightness. A Japanese officer raised his hand as though requesting the machine gunner to stop. It was his last conscious act because seconds later he was cut down in the withering fire that shredded belts, uniforms and flesh. Another wave of attackers dropped out of sight, collapsing a few yards up on American soil. Elrod hurtled from position to position, shoring up the morale of his men. He didn't stand back when it came to the hand-to-hand carnage, where terror made men claw at each other like wild beasts – that man simply seemed indestructible. As more enemies came storming ashore, they ran into a curtain of bullets and thrashed around in agony. Very few made it to the cover of the scrub, and those who did, howling and brandishing bayonets, were engaged by Marines which jumped to the top of their sandbag barrier and clubbed them with their rifle butts or spades. One group of attackers was close to reaching Hanna's 3-inch gun. Elrod gathered five men, including First Class Hesson, still suffering from his shrapnel wound, which didn't prevent him from firing his Thompson submachine gun. Cursing and screaming they drove into the advancing enemy, killing a great number of Japanese. One of Elrod's five beckoned fiercely with his arm at the many dead, when a single shot rang out. He threw up his arms and dropped with a shoulder wound.

'Get down! There's a goddamned Jap sniper somewhere,' yelled Corporal Holewinski. Another whiplash crack made the coral at the corporal's feet chip with a twang. The bullet must have come straight through the pile of corpses near the shore. Elrod jumped up and motioned with his arm at the big gun.

'C'mon, fellers,' he yelled. 'Don't hang around. We'll take a break when we get there . . .' What it finally came down to was man's animal instinct to survive, to do what he was afraid to do, to know that the only way to overcome danger was to take insane risks. He took a deep breath and did what had to be done. He ran towards the gun. Elrod's remaining foursome scampered bent-over through the scrub in the direction of Hanna's gun. First Class Hesson ran on, his thoughts on the hidden marksman, with a vision of his own body sprawled on top of the dead Japs lying there. Perhaps that sonofabitch sniper was already aiming his rifle at him. They met up with a half-dozen of the enemy; this time there was no shouting, no confusion; it was expert teamwork, which lasted only a few seconds. In hand-to-hand fighting, the burly Marines held the advantage both in weight and muscle power over the smaller Japanese. Then they had done it, the Japs were stopped cold. The blood-smeared Marines grouped under the cover of the dense scrub, breathing hard, mopping their faces.

Crack! At the whiplash bang of a shot, the submachine gun slipped from Elrod's hand; he made a few more erratic steps before he crumpled. A Japanese, playing dead among the heap of casualties, had shot their valiant captain. Hesson pulled the pin on a grenade and threw it into the heap of corpses, then dashed head-down to his fallen leader. There was nothing he could do for him. The hero of Wake had been mortally wounded.

'The captain's bought it . . .' Their faces were grim. They felt the loss of Captain Elrod more than just the loss of a commander; for each of them it became a personal loss, a man they respected, and who had respected them. Two troopers lifted the captain's body and carried him into the shelter of sandbags. It was all they could do for their gallant comrade-in-arms. Perhaps it was an invincible fate that the best must die.

While this carnage took place on a tiny speck in the middle of the ocean, messages streamed into HQ Pearl Harbor from all its outlying Pacific stations. But Wake was the exception, very much in the limelight. Something had to be done. Admiral Pye called a staff conference. His intelligence chief voiced concern over the reported presence of a major Japanese carrier strike force in its vicinity. Time was of the essence, the task force had to reach Wake *before* the Japanese carriers were in close to launch their planes. The choice was simple: slow the *Saratoga* down to let the escorts keep up, but lose the chance to get there in time, or drop the cruiser screen, go on unescorted and risk the carrier to enemy bombers.

'We cannot afford losing one of our flat-tops.' With it, Admiral Pye decided to recall the combined Task Force 11/14. Admiral Fletcher, hurrying to the relief of Wake, received Pye's order 'to return without making contact with the enemy'. When the message was received aboard the *USS Saratoga*, Admiral Fletcher went red in the face, tore off his cap and threw it on the card table. He wasn't the only one outraged; so was his fleet's air commander, Rear Admiral Aubrey W. Fitch, as well as the combat flight crews aboard, itching to unload their bombs on the ships that had killed their buddies in Pearl Harbor. Pye's turn-around order became eventually a much-argued issue, especially once it became known that 'heroic Wake' had been abandoned to its fate.[6] Had Fletcher been allowed to continue, the decisive Battle of Midway might well have been fought many months before. Who knows? Or perhaps the precious *Saratoga* might have been sunk. As it was, she went on to gain her laurels another day – but at Wake, the Japanese had beaten them to the island by one day.

For the defenders on the atoll, no doubt about the outcome was contained in a brief message from CinCPac: 'NO FRIENDLY VESSELS SHOULD BE IN YOUR VICINITY TODAY.' Wake had been cut loose. Devereux's men couldn't expect relief.

Earlier, a company of Japanese had gone straight for Battery 'F' on Wilkes. The gun crew tried in vain to stave off the Japanese from reaching their 3-inch guns.

'How's your situation?' Capt. Wesley Platt, commander on Wilkes, wanted to know.

'Shitty,' came back the dry reply by Sergeant Raymond Coulson.

'Evacuate immediately,' Platt told him. 'Set up a couple of .30-cal to cover your men's withdrawal.'

The handful of Americans who had survived the initial onslaught, were now crawling away in the light of dawn, dragging with them their wounded comrades. Sgt Coulson managed to pin down the enemy with a stream of fire while his comrades made for the safety of the dense scrub.

Major Devereux felt like a fire chief trying to put out a fire with a leaky hose; he rushed his last reinforcements to Capt. Platt and Lt McAlister. To recapture the abandoned

[6] When asked in 1970 if the relief expedition's arrival would have made any difference to the outcome at Wake, Devereux replied: 'I rather doubt that that particular task force, with its size and composition, could have been very effective . . . I think it was wise . . . to pull back.'

3-inch gun of Battery 'F' on Wilkes, Platt, McAllister and a group of Marines stormed across brush and sand with blazing rifles, firing from the hip and lobbing grenades. Yells, curses and explosions, submachine guns belching flame, catching the bunched-up enemy at their focal point in an intermittent line of converging tracers; ten, twenty, a hundred Japanese collapsed in heaps of agonising flesh. McAlister's men retook the gun, along with discarded ammunition crates and bags of rice. The rout of the enemy was complete; the charge, which had lasted less than two minutes, left in its wake ninety-eight dead Japanese for the loss of eleven of their own. It was to be the US Marines' final victory on Wake.

At 06.52 hrs (10.32 hrs, 22 December 1941, in Pearl Harbor), Cunningham radioed to CinCPac: 'ENEMY ON ISLAND. SEVERAL WARSHIPS PLUS TRANSPORTS MOVING IN. ISSUE IN DOUBT.' With this message, Wake radio fell silent.

By 08.00 hrs, Wilkes Island was still holding out and even repulsing consecutive attacks, but the defensive perimeter on Wake had shrunk to the size of two football fields. After a heroic stand of almost six hours, the pressure, the fatigue and the lack of ammunition, was telling. The men, with their powder-blackened faces, had all been wounded. Major Devereux managed to find an uncut landline to Cunningham's HQ. The first thing he asked: 'What's the news on the relief task force?'

'It's been cancelled . . . What's the situation your way?'

'Real bad. The whole place is in shambles; they're crawling around everywhere. My men can't hold out much longer.'

There was a momentary pause, before Cunningham said: 'Okay, we've done all we could. Now we must look after saving lives . . .'

They had made a heroic stand. Nobody could blame

them putting down their arms. Cunningham authorised Devereux to initiate steps for immediate surrender. A few minutes later, a dispatch runner reached Lt Barninger; 'A' Battery's guns had ceased firing long ago, but his heavy machine guns were still operational. 'Destroy your equipment,' was the message. A frustrated lieutenant took his pistol and fired six bullets into the gun's rangefinder; his crew removed the firing pins and smashed them on the coral. Not all units could be reached; it so happened that Lt Poindexter's men kept on firing after Lt Barninger's men had strung up a white sheet on their 5-inch gun barrel pointing skyward.

It was now 10.15 hrs. Major Devereux, with a handkerchief tied to a broom handle, accompanied by USMC Sgt Donald Malleck, set off on his painful walk towards the eastern shore of Wake in order to establish contact with a superior Japanese officer. They were stopped by a soldier with his rifle levelled at them. Devereux pointed to his flag of truce, and the soldier brought them at rifle-point to the workers' camp where Devereux found a Japanese captain who understood some English. Within ten minutes, their group was joined by a Japanese colonel as well by Cmdr Cunningham, who, for the surrender ceremony, had put on his beribboned navy blue parade jacket. All of a sudden a series of explosions rocked the island. The Japanese officers jumped up and pulled out their pistols; for the three Americans the situation became downright nasty. The Japanese colonel yelled an order and his guards rushed in with their fingers on the trigger. In fact, when Lt Kliewer's men saw the white flags, they refused to believe it. 'It's a dirty Jap trick, lioot. US Marines never surrender.' But Kliewer, looking over a forest of red-sun flags strung up along the beach, knew that this was indeed the end. He pushed the plunger that set off the mines placed on the airfield to turn 'his airstrip' into a series of deep craters. Those were the bangs the negotiators heard. Within minutes, the last Americans put down their weapons and came out. The final image of Wake that accompanied Major Devereux on his way into prison camp was that of a Japanese sailor scaling the twisted beams of the wrecked water tower to cut down the stars and stripes that had been flying throughout the siege. It was now 13.00 hrs, 23 December 1941. Wake Atoll was no longer American.

For sixteen heroic days, 449 US Marines of the 1st USMC Defense Battalion and the crews of Marine Fighter Squadron VMF-211, valiantly assisted by 1146 civilians, had done battle with an enemy many times their size. They had stood up to the ineffable storm of blood and violent death that had come up from the sea and invaded the island that was, in fact, America's outer frontier.

Wake was never a prize. For the remainder of the war, it served no useful purpose. Americans, who began to rely on their massive fleets of aircraft carriers, bypassed it. Nor did the Japanese launch planes from its runway; for that, the fuel economy of their land-based planes was too limited. Time and again, the runway was bombed by American planes and then put back into shape by the original construction crew, which was kept prisoner on the island. On the morning of 7 October 1943, the last one hundred civilians were lined up in front of their barracks, and cold-bloodedly executed.

Major Devereux attempted two escapes from a Japanese PoW camp, was twice caught, and severely punished. He never gave up hope that one day he could rejoin the USMC and fight against the nation's enemy.[7] For the Japanese, Wake ceased to have any military significance and its

---

[7] After the war, Devereux remained in the Marine Corps and rose to the rank of USMC Brigadier-General.

garrison was all but forgotten. Only their submarines could undertake the perilous voyage to bring supplies. Over the next years, 1288 Japanese perished from hunger and untreated diseases. On 4 September 1945, without ever having fired a shot during his tenure, Rear Admiral Shigematsu Sakaibara surrendered Wake to US Navy Commander William Masek.[8]

So, 1221 days after it was cut down by a victorious Japanese soldier, the stars and stripes went back up the rusting, twisted remains of the old water tower. 'It was here,' declared Cmdr Masek during the takeover ceremony, 'that the Marines showed us how.'

'The courageous conduct of the officers and men who defended Wake Island against an overwhelming superiority of enemy air, sea, and land attacks from December 8 to 22, 1941, has been noted with admiration by their fellow countrymen and the civilised world, and will not be forgotten so long as gallantry and heroism are respected and honoured. They are commended for their devotion to duty and splendid conduct at their battle stations under most adverse conditions. With limited defensive means against attacks in great force, they manned their shore installations and flew their aircraft so well that five enemy warships were either sunk or severely damaged, many hostile planes shot down, and an unknown number of land troops destroyed.' US President Franklin D. Roosevelt signed this citation on 5 January 1942.

The Pacific Clipper belongs to a bygone era. Modern planes, capable of crossing wide oceans without refuelling, soar high over the Pacific with their load of American businessmen to conduct affairs in the land of their erstwhile

---

[8] Sakaibara and eleven officers were charged with a war crime – the murder of the work crew – and hung.

enemy. When they glance down from the windows of their plane, they will see, ten miles (16 km) below, a triangular atoll in the midst of a deep blue ocean. Nothing more. Fifty years of tides and storms have covered the wounds of a murderous war.

Wake became one of the many episodes of America's War in the Pacific; its heroic stand was quickly pushed from the headlines by other battles: Midway, Guadalcanal, Tarawa, Iwo Jima and Okinawa. But for one fleeting moment in America's history, Wake captured a nation's attention. Fearing reprisals by their jailers in Japanese PoW camps, the US Navy never released the names of Cunningham, Devereux, Elrod[9] or any others until after the war. And after all was over and an atomic bomb had written *finis* to Japanese ambitions, giving out names served no further purpose; the heroes of Wake became a forgotten detail of history, finding their resting place in a dusty archival niche.

Today, a single monument stands near the runway on Wake Atoll. It is a pillar with the rusting remains of the engine and twisted propeller of Captain Henry T. Elrod's Wildcat fighter aircraft.

Cunningham and Devereux had resolution and determination; they stood firm when the issue hung in the balance. Cut off on an island, with no hope of outside assistance, they fought it out. The intensity of combat became the chief determinant of what firm resolution can accomplish. As the first battle in the war, their heroic stand helped to raise the fighting spirit of a downhearted America.

Elrod's attribute was one of visible bravery in action,

[9] Today, a sleek missile frigate, the *USS Elrod*, named after the pilot who was awarded the Medal of Honor posthumously, sails the Seven Seas.

the exposure of the body to the wounds of war. He was a good pilot doing his job, which was blowing Japanese out of the air and sinking enemy ships; he became America's first fighter ace in the Second World War. By the time the full story came to be known, the war was over and the average American was back to what Americans are so good at, running their business, looking ahead and forgetting all about war.

Die Weisse Rose,
'Calling all Germans . . .'

Aufruf an alle Deutsche! – Calling all Germans!

Hitler leads our nation with mathematical certainty into the abyss. Hitler can no longer win the war, only prolong it. His, and the guilt of his assistants, has long passed all decent measure. The time for his just punishment moves ever closer, the day to settle accounts has come. Our youth will end this abominable tyranny, and the worst our German nation ever had to suffer. Do we want to sacrifice what is still left of Germany's youth to the lowest instincts of a party clique? Never! *Niemals!*[1]

The 5th tract of the Weisse Rose, 27 January 1943

Any man who feels morally responsible must join his voice to ours and rise against the menacing domination by a brutal force . . .

Professor Kurt Huber, 19 April 1943

---

[1] The original text: *Aufruf an alle Deutsche! Mit mathematischer Sicherheit führt Hitler das deutsche Volk in den Abgrund. Hitler kann den Krieg nicht gewinnen, nur noch verlängern! Seine und seiner Helfer Schuld hat jedes Mass unendlich überschritten. Die gerechte Strafe rückt näher und näher. Der Tag der Abrechnung ist gekommen, der Abrechnung unserer deutschen Jugend mit scheuungswürdigsten Tyrannis, die unser Volk je erduldet hat.*

'*Ist es Zeit?* – Is it time?' asked the girl. The woman in the drab uniform handed the slim figure a lit cigarette and nodded: '*Zwei Minuten* – Two minutes!' The prison warden respected the girl's moral fortitude. It was in the first days of a timid thaw that had finally driven off the bitter cold of a precocious winter. In the streets, whatever remained of its former splendour, nothing helped to hide the picture of desolation of a town reduced to rubble. Inside the plain, whitewashed room it was chilly. A ray of afternoon sun came through a high, barred window and fell squarely on to the girl's face. It was a pretty face, framed by cropped hair the colour of aged honey. Yet the most remarkable feature were her eyes, aglow with holy fire. The door opened and two young men were led in. The three youngsters fell into each other's arms. One cried, '*Wir haben das Unmögliche begonnen* – We've set out on the impossible.' By 1943 there was little hope for 'the impossible' to succeed. A vicious party organisation was in effective control of the country, the product of a war psychosis holding all of Germany in its grip. Fanatics of brutal repression were using drastic despotic measures against autonomous-thinking young Germans. Death was only one.

'It is enough if we've raised the conscience of only some of our people. We're the first, but others will take up our banner.' The girl inhaled deeply on her cigarette, before she passed it to one of the young men. The door opened to a priest who turned towards the girl.

'*Niemand hat grössere Liebe* – Nobody has greater love than he who offers his life for the sake of his friends,' he said, before he pointed at the last rays of the sun, slanting through the barred window: 'Life is like the sun; she will rise again.'

The female guard said: 'It is time.'

Handcuffs snapped around the girl's wrists.

'My friends, we shall soon meet again in eternity.'

'*Freiheit!*' spoke the young men quietly, trying to hold back their emotion.

'*Freiheit!*' the girl replied, holding her head high.

With a sound that echoed along the hallways, the heavy door closed behind her.

When the people of Munich went to work, that 23 February 1943, they found walls plastered with red posters.

Im Namen des Volkes. Wegen Hochverrats wurden zum Tode verurteilt – Sentenced to death for high treason:

   der 25-jährige Hans Scholl

   seine 22-jährige Schwester, Sophie Scholl

   und der 24-jährige Christoph Probst.

   Das Urteil wurde bereits vollstreckt – Sentence has been executed.

In the Germany of Adolf Hitler, everything was done *Im Namen des Volkes*. People were arrested 'in the name of the people' and wars were started 'by the will of the people'. Yet the people were never consulted. Opponents of the regime had to flee the country (if they could!) to continue their political activities from exile. Propaganda from abroad by political exiles seemed the only way open to undermine Nazi rule. But in a land where all means of communication were tightly controlled and all unfavourable news suppressed, this had no effect on the German nation. What happened under Hitler could never be understood or estimated in any commonsensical fashion that would sound reasonable and natural to the average democratic Westerner, nor could he imagine that a civilised state could really perpetrate such a cheap system of falsehood. In *Mein Kampf*, his political bible, Hitler had spelled it out: '*Die breite Masse eines Volkes fällt leichter zum Opfer einer grossen Lüge als einer kleinen* – The wide mass of a nation will more easily fall victim to a big lie than to a small one.' Hitler wasn't the only one who lied – Goebbels did, Göring did, everybody did, from the party bosses, to the provincial *gauleiter* all the way down to the neighbourhood block warden. Journalists gave themselves to propagate the lie, as did schoolteachers: A reign of the collective lie.

Inside Germany, unlike in the countries of Europe under the German jackboot, the formation of a single, unified resistance movement never came about; opposition parties were outlawed and its leaders arrested; there were no religious sanctuaries and no forest *maquis* to hide in and fight from. The burden of resistance fell primarily on individuals relying on their conscience, perhaps counting on help from some who thought alike. Such small groups did exist. They emerged from all social strata and their resistance took on varied forms, but always with limited means. Their weakness lay in the divergence of causes and the Nazis cleverly exploited this flaw. There were the Communists who had escaped the fascist dragnet and held comradely ties with the Soviet Union; there were members of the Lutheran clergy out for a religious revival; there were the aristocratic Junkers of the officer class who refused to follow the military whims of a 'corporal', and his clique of political upstarts; there were the traditional elitists and liberal intelligentsia, who had nothing in common with beer-hall brawlers, and were striving for the moral restoration of Germany. And finally, there was a 'revolt of conscience', ready to pay the ultimate price for standing up to Nazi barbarity.

In the beginning, those who voiced scruples about Hitler's brutal designs most forcefully were a group of youngsters. Called into being by a half-dozen Munich university students, they hoped to form the unifying nucleus for a youth revolt to prevent a ruthless man from wasting their generation. They didn't ask for something outrageous, just for *Freiheit* – freedom to express their thoughts, to be given a say in choosing the path into their future, and the right to say 'no'. It was left to the suppressive control by a totalitarian regime over the means of broad communication that very few inside Germany ever got to hear of the *Weisse Rose*.

Germany in the summer of 1942: things were not going well. Not as the *Führer* had promised. The *Blitzkrieg* had run headlong into a human shield at Stalingrad, and losses to the *Wehrmacht* were growing out of all proportions. Already the year before, in a fit of dictator's megalomania, Adolf Hitler had sealed the nation's demise when he declared war on the United States;[2] simple arithmetic said that America's population was almost three times that of Germany, and its industrial potential was enormous. With the entry of the United States into the war, Germany's position took a turn for the worse. Allied bombers dumped tons of explosives on German cities, food rationing was tightening the nation's belts; and yet, the majority of Germans continued acting in strict conformity with Hitler's dictates, because they had no choice. For a good reason.

In Bavaria, SS uniforms may not have been quite as visible as in Poland and Russia, but plainclothes enforcers were everywhere. The Gestapo had spread its net of informers throughout southern Germany, a traditionally religious bastion. They were so obsessed with obtaining information that some of the replacement preachers, coming new to Bavarian and Austrian parishes, were not priests at all.

[2] It must be remembered that Japan – though a member of the tri-partite agreement with Nazi Germany – never did declare war on the Soviet Union. Therefore, Japan's attack on Pearl Harbor was never a *causus belli* for Germany.

Therefore, very few were suicidal enough to speak out and face arrest, which was commonly followed by a speedy execution. Into this situation emerged a handful of students from the University of Munich. In age they represented what the Nazi leader had called: '*Deutschland's Zukunft*' (the future).

'On our youth depends the future of the German nation. We must remould the souls of our young and prepare them for their duties,' Hitler had ordered.[3] Yet, in Hitler's book, youth held no political power; it was ignored, its basic rights trampled, its education solely directed towards the ultimate sacrifice for the *Führer*. For years, millions of young boys and girls had been carefully indoctrinated and prepared to envelop Europe in a devastating hurricane; the youngsters were sworn in as the storm troopers of a fascist tidal wave. The slightest opposition to the continuation of a murderous war was strangled by the ruthless secret police of the Third Reich. Now that the champion of repression had ordered them them to push the war to its bitter end and sacrifice an entire generation, five young people dared to give warning.

From early summer 1942 to mid-February 1943, a series of mimeographed letters appeared in mailboxes across southern Germany and the Ostmark (the name for annexed Austria): '*Aufruf an alle Deutschen!*' – calling on all Germans to react against the inhuman methods of the Nazi regime, not in the occupied territories, but in the very heart of Germany itself. Hitler was told. He went red in the face. 'Find them!' ranted the dictator. His order to 'find them' went down the official ladder; his rage reverberated across the land. SS-boss Heinrich Himmler passed it over to the notorious *Sicherheitsdienst* and the affair came to a

[3] By 1938, 8.7 million boys and girls were members of the *Hitlerjugend*.

vibrating halt in Berlin's Prinz-Albrechtstrasse on the desk of Heinrich Müller, boss of the *Geheime Staatspolizei* (Gestapo).[4] Müller, a square-headed man in ruthless pursuit of personal power, with the outward expression of an innocent, gentle Bavarian peasant, barked: 'Bring them to me – alive.'

The Scholl family of Forchtenberg was no different to its neighbours. Devout Lutherans, they had seen their church emasculated by the Nazis and the Word of God abused. Worse, they had watched a great number of Lutherans and Catholics join the party, viewing Hitler as their saviour when he promised a job for every good Aryan. The foolish masses had cheered and waved when a dictator's legions trampled across Austria and Czechoslovakia, Poland, France and Russia. The initial successes legitimised everything. For a long time the young Scholls hesitated, plagued by the feeling that they would be traitors to their country at war if they were to speak out. Yet, their Christian conscience drove them to stand up against the lies of a man and his party, out to conquer the world at the price of sacrificing Germany's youth.

Sophie Scholl, a tousled-haired girl with a pug nose and a healthy complexion, was born on 9 May 1921, the fourth of five children to the burgomaster of Forchtenberg. In 1933, shortly after Hitler's rise to power, she joined the *Bund Deutscher Mädchen* (BDM), the girl's sector of the *Hitlerjugend* (HJ) at a time when the impression that Hitler made on Germany's youth was best expressed by a ten-year-old before a newsreel camera: 'We will fight and die for our Führer. *Heil Hitler!*' Sophie's enthusiasm for slogans like '*ein Volk, ein Reich, ein Führer*' (one people,

---

[4] Müller had become *Gestapo* head after Heydrich's assassination in Prague.

one nation, one leader) soon turned to criticism, especially after her brother Hans was denounced by a friend, who had felt it his duty to inform local authorities of a despairing remark the young Scholl had made about the sacred duty of every boy of Aryan extraction to lay down his life for the Führer. Her brother was picked up, since in Germany everyone was either a good Nazi, or nothing at all. Hans was lucky; they only slapped his fingers and let him go with a promise that from now on he would be a good boy. This was a shock to Sophie who simply worshipped her older brother and she became careful about choosing her friends. In May 1942, her excellent high-school notes got her into Munich University, where she registered for courses in biology and philosophy.

Hans Scholl, Sophie's brother, was born on 22 September 1918 in Ingersheim. As most young boys of the early thirties, he was enthusiastic about Hitler's promises for a renascent Germany after the Depression following a devastating world war. Soon the Nazi hydra reared its ugly head.[5] Father Scholl, who referred to Hitler as a '*Rattenfänger*' (Pied Piper), was not overjoyed when his son joined the *Hitlerjugend*. Hans proved his leadership qualities and was appointed *Fähnleinführer* (junior company commander). He was invited to participate at the '*Macht des Willens*' monster-rally at Nürnberg in September 1935. He returned from it with the deepening feeling that Hitler was using Germany's youth for his political machination. Shortly before the outbreak of war, Hans moved from his family's residence at Ulm to the Bavarian capital.

Munich was Hitler's town. It was here, in 1920, that the

[5] In 1934, Hitler used his newly formed SS squads (SS for *Schutz Staffel* or protection squad) to murder hundreds of his old party comrades of the SA *(Sturm Abteilung)* in order to usurp unrestrained power.

Sozialistische Arbeiter Partei was founded. Neither socialist nor nationalist, it was more a gathering of two dozen
beer-drinking war veterans starting one of the numerous
parties after the First World War. It was in Munich that an
Austrian-born corporal in the Kaiser's army, Adolf Hitler,
joined a gathering of twenty men, and shrewdly discovered
in the total absence of a political programme an easy way
to take charge. He added *National* and *Deutsche* to their
party logo and turned it into a small, but politically active
Nazional Sozialistische Deutsche Arbeiter Partei (NSDAP)
– the Nazis.

During the night of 8 to 9 November 1923, he gathered
around him several hundred of his faithful *Parteigenossen*
in Munich's *Bürgerbräukeller*, a huge beer cellar. His
opening remarks were about daily truths that everybody
knew, misery and unemployment. His voice was climbing
higher and higher, sweeping his listeners along with him
till he smashed out, '*So kann es nicht weitergehen* – This
cannot go on . . .' The audience roared, as if that had
already changed everything. The man at the head of the
hall waited. His face shone. And then it came – broad,
persuasive, irresistible – promise after promise; it simply
rained promises; a paradise was built up over the assembled
heads; a lottery where every loser was a winner, and in
which every man found his own happiness and his settling
of private scores.

Hitler climbed on a stein-covered table, pulled out his
pistol, fired a shot into the ceiling and, to the ecstatic howl
of his followers, proclaimed '*Die nazionale Revolution*'. He
tried to imitate his idol Mussolini, who had marched at the
head of his blackshirts on Rome, overthrown a tottering
Italian government, and taken control of the country. Now
was to be his moment. After a copious intake of Munich
brew, Hitler and his *Genossen* marched from the beer
hall to the *Feldherrnhalle* to call for the dissolution of

the Bavarian government. The *Bayerische Landespolizei* (Bavarian police) refused to play his game and fired into the flag-waving marchers. Hitler managed to escape, but sixteen of his followers lay dead. Hitler was arrested and condemned to a prison sentence of nine months, which he spent dictating his political bible *Mein Kampf* to his cell mate, Rudolf Hess. On 30 January 1933, Hitler came to power through triangular elections, when the leading Socialists and Communists knocked each other out. He raised Munich to '*Hauptstadt der Bewegung*' (Capital of the Party, 2 August 1935).

With the new title came a new local government, headed by a *Gauleiter*. Munich's university did not escape the shake-up. Learned professors were put out to pasture, Jewish scientists fled to England or America, among them some Nobel-Prize laureates researching in the revolutionary field of nuclear physics. A new rector arrived, *SS-Oberführer* Wüst, who took over the chair of Aryan race science, and the university's educational programme was made to fit Nazi ideology. Everything became pristine-Aryan, down to its janitor, *Hausmeister* Schmied, a man with a beer pouch and an unquestionable loyalty to the party. He considered himself of officer rank, since he commanded a battalion of charwomen. But his main function was to spy on the student body and to report anti-party remarks to his superiors.

In mid-summer of 1939, Propaganda Minister Dr Josef Goebbels came to town. The streets were festively decorated with Nazi bunting and crawling with police. Inside the vast festival hall, swastika banners were draped over the speaker platform. And a giant banderole: *Mit dem Führer und der Partei* – With Hitler and the Party. Crammed into the hall were a huge number of people; the front rows had been taken up by dignitaries in brown and black uniforms, with a sprinkling of army-grey generals. A small section was reserved 'for the people', workers and minor officials. The greatest part was made up by the propaganda minister's 'cheering section', all young: the nation's future. A medical student, Hans Scholl was among them.

'*Sieg Heil!*' The speaker on the platform was not overly tall, but his amplified voice carried without difficulty to the remotest corner of the great hall, and by loudspeaker to the immense crowd gathered outside. He began the build-up in a voice that carried conviction without heeding much of what it said, about the party having fulfilled their promise to build roads (true, but all seemed to lead to the French and Polish borders) and motor vehicles (again true, but somehow they were tracked and carried a gun turret). When the hall was 'heated up', he turned it full on the audience, and in a changed, shrill tone whipped out sentence after sentence, about how their Führer had tried to talk peace with the leaders of the European powers, and how they had denied Germany its justified demands to regain its former national borders: '. . . *Danzig heim ins Reich*'[6] was his key phrase. And now that a new Germany had risen from the shameful ashes of a lost war, and was stronger than ever before, never again would *he*, their Führer, allow his nation to live in dishonour. '*Wollt ihr ewig in Schmach und Schande leben* – Do you want to live forever in disgrace and shame?' The crowd screamed: '*Nein!*' and four weeks later, German armies marched into Poland.

In the autumn of 1939, together with three others – Alexander Schmorell, Christoph Probst and Willi Graf, all of whom were destined to take a prominent part in his life – the 21-year-old Hans Schol was admitted into the medical faculty of Munich's university. Shortly before

6 The return of Danzig to Germany became the key to declaring war on Poland.

Hitler's invasion of the Soviet Union, Scholl was called up into the army, but in the beginning of 1942, following seven months on the Russian front, he received a special dispensation, which allowed him to return home in order to further his medical studies. More than shoot-them-up soldiers, the army needed qualified surgeons to patch up its growing number of war casualties. Hans Scholl reached Munich at about the same time that his sister Sophie was to begin her first-year courses in biology and philosophy. The young students that the Scholls met in class were the sons and daughters of upright burghers, loyal members of the party; class origin and unquestioned loyalty was the Nazi regime's chief criteria for admission into a place of higher learning.

Hans and Sophie could have lived a relatively undemanding student life in wartime Germany, but fate wanted it otherwise. Munich, the hub of the Nazi movement, was a dangerous place to live for anyone with anti-Hitler sentiments, and nobody was prepared to express such feelings openly. News was hard to come by. Listening to a foreign radio station was punishable by death. Telling political jokes, deriding the Nazi leadership, was punishable by death. Failing to join in exuberant outbursts during the Führer's speech, at words flowing from the lips of 'the nation's greatest genius', was dangerous.

Until the third war year, there had been little opposition to Hitler, certainly none from the age group that always produces the pole of opposition to the bourgeois, capitalist world of adults and causes political uproar, the university students; most of them were in uniform somewhere in Russia or North Africa, trying to stay alive. Hans Scholl, Alexander Schmorell, and Christoph Probst had come back from the Russian front with tales of the devastation caused by war and the atrocities committed by the dreaded *SS-Einsatzkommandos* (killer squads). Hans Scholl had a particularly harrying experience. 'It happened in early morning. There was heavy fog, so the SS detachment couldn't see me; I saw a line of lorries with people getting off – families, men, women, children, all mixed together. A SS officer was standing nearby with a riding whip and made them undress. Being thorough, he had them stack their clothes in neat piles according to sex. There must have been a few hundred. When they were all naked the SS guards marched them off and I heard the rattle of a machine gun. After the SS drove off, I went around to discover a pit with bodies wedged together, some still twitching . . .'

Christoph Probst told stories of suffering by the ordinary soldier ordered around by party hacks which had been appointed as their commanders and lacked military experience. He had been attached as medic to an infantry unit. When their seasoned sergeant suggested that an attack into a five-to-one Russian superiority in men and firepower was wasteful, his SS commander told him not to question his orders. His unit attacked and was cut off before most of it was destroyed piecemeal. To which Alexander Schmorell remarked: 'I'm beginning to get mighty tired of this war and the men who lead us.'

It was during this spring that the pretty Sophie fell madly in love with a dashing young lieutenant on home leave, Fritz Hartnagel. But she wasn't so befuddled by her infatuation that it prevented her from giving a good argument, especially when Fritz told her about the victories by German armies in Poland and France.

'How can you talk about victories when you go out there to kill the innocent?'

'I don't shoot anybody,' Fritz held his ground.

'But the Nazis do.'

'Calm yourself, Sophie; it doesn't make sense to take on the Nazis.'

'It is you that has taken an oath to the Führer, not I.

Explain to me please why it is necessary for a man such as Hitler to put many into danger of death – don't tell me it is for the good of the *Vaterland*.'

Fritz, at the time still convinced of Germany's final victory, had little to say in reply. A few weeks later, she wrote to him at the front. 'We mustn't live in the vain hope that this war will soon be over, even if a naïve opinion is propagated throughout our country that England will soon be brought to its knees by our *U-Boote* blockade.'

Sophie and Hans had found lodgings in an abandoned flat, making to do with whatever was available. Sophie's daily task was to figure out what she could produce with a slice of bread and fish paste that didn't taste like fish. Sometimes she left the flat to take long walks. Munich was no longer the Munich of her childhood memories, when their parents had first taken them to the city with its wide, tree-line boulevards. The construction of man, Bavarian man, German man, for home, work and worship, had come down in a pile of its material, a bombed-out rubble of brick and beams. Burst water pipes were hastily patched up to be ready for the next attack with incendiary bombs. Swastika flags trying to prop up a sinking morale, flew from chimneys sticking out of the rubble, and rousing banners strung across the street: '*Mit dem Führer zum Endsieg* – Onward with the Führer to final victory'.

The biggest change was in the people, silently slinking along walls in their worn clothes. War cripples hobbled around on crutches. Nazi *Blockwärte* (section bosses) walked over the junk piles of people's homes to assume authority. A small boy in HJ uniform rattled his penny-collection box for the *Winterhilfe*. And the endless queues going around city blocks, queues for ration cards, and queues for those with ration cards to get whatever was available at the local food store. It so depressed her that she gave up walking in the streets. In the evenings Hans and Sophie sat together in their blacked-out flat and remembered their childhood days, but talked even more frequently about the future, stretching out before them into some opaque haze. Once they went to a party at Alex Schmorell's flat. Someone put on a gramophone record, but nobody danced. Because, by now, the war had reached home.

In the *Flugwachtkommando* Duisburg, a warning had come in about a large formation of B-17's approaching Noordwijk. Until the *Fluko Warnzentrale* knew the formation's precise targeting, they wouldn't warn the specific district. It was senseless to panic the wrong place in this third year of a brutal war, stop work in the factories and have workers rush into shelters. *'Flugrichting des Feindverbandes auf Bayer'*: a warning went out to Munich. A city prepared. Flak barrels were elevated, shells fused, fire engines, and surgical theatres readied, and shelters opened their doors.

It was on a day that Sophie had managed a ride into the countryside. The first colours of autumn, the gold, the brown and the rusty glorified the passage of time. Away from the city, an air of freedom floated over the landscape. She took in deep gulps of breath and looked around her. How nature could be beautiful in peaceful surroundings, sitting in a meadow, with her knees drawn to her chest, reading Spinoza's *L'Ethique*, trying to understand humanity. Was there still some to be found in these mad times when countries headed towards mutual destruction? Her mind wandered to her much beloved Fritz. She was reliving his last home leave, how he had come close to her and gently kissed her, and she had held her breath. How he had held her close and exhorted her to survive, no matter what, and how they swore to find each other after the violence had passed. That had taken place in a meadow like this one, and now he was two thousand kilometres from Bavaria, in a city called Stalingrad. Her thoughts were interrupted by a distinctive rumble; high up in the blue she saw vapour trails of the mighty bomber fleets of the US Air Force, on their way to unload their deadly cargo on some German city. 'This is insanity,' the girl screamed out her anguish to some cows munching on tufts of grass. 'Civilisation has gone mad.'

'*Grosser Feindverband im Anflug auf München* ...' interrupted a radio announcer on the Wunschkonzert (musical request programme).

'Air raid!' yelled *Universitäts Hausmeister* Schmied in his moment of importance, waddling from his janitor's lodge along the university's corridor. '*Alles in den Lufschutzkeller* – Everyone into the air-raid shelter. Hurry.' The sirens kept on howling like banshees; students jostled down the wide stone stairs, running for one of the entrances into the bomb shelter. The siren on the university roof was now screaming hysterically. Hans Scholl, caught up in this madly pushing crowd, made it into the shelter; no sooner had the heavy steel door closed behind them, than the first guns fired; their rumble sounded like distant thunder to the jammed bodies with their phobic stench of body odour and heat of fear. Outside, the siren was still howling, its sound gagged by the closed door. Girls were looking anxiously at the ceiling, as if expecting any moment a bomb to come crashing through the ventilation slits. That was moments before the horrid sound, as if a train whistle was coming down from the heavens, followed by a sickening crash. The huge air-mines lifted whole city blocks into the air, to bring them crashing down over those in the basements. The ultimate in horror was to be buried alive. The students, jammed into the safety of the deepest cellar, could no longer pretend that they didn't know what lay behind the odour of sulphur and charred flesh that was sucked in through the ventilation shafts. Their tongues stuck to their palates, their eyes stung and burned. That stench came from others out there beyond the safety of the shelter, perhaps their mothers and sisters, being fried by the deluge of incendiary bombs. They could feel the immense heat. The cellar looked hopeless in the extreme.

Herr Schmied, the university janitor, cowered next to Hans, trying to behave fearlessly, but in fact searching for assurance in the only male presence nearby. 'Those girls are all afraid,' he said in a high-pitched voice, with a flushed face and eyes dilated, clearly showing his own hysteria. 'What is there to be afraid of? The *Amis* have no fighter protection and our *Luftwaffe* pilots will blow them out of the skies, you just wait and see . . .' Hans knew the stench of fear, and this janitor was terrified. Sitting in the basement they saw nothing of the horror outside, but they felt it; the ground shook and vibrated violently, from a deep rumble it rose to an ear-splitting roar. Above their shelter rose an enormous red flame, followed by the crunching of beams and brick as if the world was coming down on top of them.

Flaming phosphorus poured over the ruins like a cloud-burst. The city was turned into a furnace. People ran shrieking from their ruins, their hair and clothes on fire, in a macabre dance running through banks of flame before they turned into grotesquely curled-up forms in the molten asphalt. Innocent victims, all, in a war that their leaders had brought upon them. Was it therefore so strange that many were no longer firm believers of the propaganda, dished out daily, of the super-race's invincibility and final victory? Believers or not, falling bombs and burning sulphur made no distinction; it only brought people together. All it needed was the igniting spark to set off a popular explosion, thought Hans. That germ of an idea had been planted in the young Scholl by a chance encounter.

In the autumn of 1941, while on a short home leave, Hans had met up with Carl Muth, the creator of the

Christian revue *Hochland*, outlawed by the Nazis. Muth again put Scholl in touch with other 'internal immigrants', a close circle that was not directly engaged in open resistance, but represented more of an intellectual *Widerstand*, men such as Werner Bergengruen, author of *The Tyrant and his Tribunal* (1935), or Ernst Jünger's *The Cliffs of Marble* (1939). In their works, they criticised the idea of a totalitarian regime and their thoughts influenced the young Scholl. Hans also assisted at a lecture by a professor of music and philosophy, Kurt Huber, who stressed the political responsibility of the intellectual. Afterwards he wrote to a friend: 'Nihilistic spiritualism has always presented a great danger to European culture. Once it reaches its ultimate consequence, the kind of total war with which we are now confronted, it opens merely a great void from which nothing can be produced constructively. We are made to believe that, from it, some great national renaissance will result.' Seen from this perspective, Hans saw war, looked upon by the masses, as the great purifying fire. But he could never forget what their father had instilled in them: *politics cannot survive without a strong sense of morals*.

In 1942 the lives of Hans and Sophie Scholl had entered a new and decisive phase. In January a meeting had taken place in a villa in the Berlin suburb of Wannsee, where SS bosses under the guidance of Reinhard Heydrich hammered out details of the 'final solution'. The brutality of a repressive regime came to the fore; people of Jewish faith began to disappear and massacres took place in all the occupied countries of the East. The German armies had reached the Volga and were brought to a halt. At Hitler's insistence, battalion after battalion was fed into the battle and turned the ruins of Stalingrad into a monstrous cemetery for Russians and Germans alike. Allied fleets sank more U-boats than U-boats sank Allied ships.

General Montgomery was about to send Rommel's famed *Afrikakorps* in full retreat across North Africa.

Thousand-bomber raids on German cities became the daily routine. The civilian population suffered greatly. If that wasn't enough to drive home the reality, what made the difference were the thousands of brief announcements that appeared day after day in local papers, or were pinned to church doors and house walls: '. . . *Died for Führer und Vaterland*'. Even though the authorities managed to suppress the true extent of the debacle, a hundred thousand wooden crosses told the true story.

That was the moment when Hans Scholl decided on the *aktiven Widerstand* (active resistance) to a regime that was as dishonest as it was repressive. Every sacrifice of the basic human principles was made in the name of *Führer* and *Vaterland*. With German armies suffering their initial setbacks, terror began to reign with unprecedented fury throughout Germany, and for those who dared to discuss the most profound moral issues waited the guillotine. Hitler's hold over a nation was by its method of terror hidden by a reign of the lie. While the majority of the population cowered in silence before the terror, a 22-year old decided to stand up and expose that lie; for Hans Scholl it became imperative to give a sign that there was still a moral resistance, with someone daring to speak out. He knew that he would be up against the Gestapo, an organisation originally called into being to use its operatives to infiltrate anti-Hitlerian groups, thwarting their plans and coldly eliminating their leaders. The Gestapo had been modelled on Stalin's infamous CHEKA,[7] which was founded by Felix Dzherzhinsky, a complete psychopath who saw a plot on every street corner. Like the CHEKA,

[7] For *Chrezvychainaia kommissia po borbe s kontr-revoliutsiei I sabotazhem*, or: CHK, the later NKVD and KGB.

the Gestapo had rapidly grown into an unwieldy Moloch, run by bureaucrats. This led to a drop in its overall efficiency, but it remained lethal, as the Gestapo faced no restrictions in its way to conduct investigations and carry out reprisals on individuals or groups that were suspected of being dangerous. To meet this end, Gestapo agents acted brutally and were utterly inhuman. Suspicion was equal to arrest or worse. Victims became mere statistics. And now, half a dozen medical students were getting ready to take on this monster.

'Sophie, go back home,' said Hans, wishing to protect his sister.

'Leaving you here?' she asked.

'It's for the best.' He looked out of the tape-covered window, a necessary prevention against breakage from the air blast of a distant bomb.

'I've been watching you for the past weeks and I don't know what's on your mind,' Sophie looked at her brother with glistening eyes. 'But I stay with you. Whatever you decide we must do, I'll be by your side.'

'At the end of this war, we might well find ourselves standing around with empty hands and the world will demand of us: What have you done to stand up to injustice? We must do something to free ourselves of this terrible guilt, committed by a few in the name of a nation.' In his decision to 'rouse the nation' he found full support from his sister.

'We must end this autocracy of one man before we're all dead. Germany's youth is told to die without allowing them a say in the matter. We must raise in them the will to resist this abject tyranny.'

Such were Hans Scholl's guiding thoughts, with which he founded and then inspired his group. Its driving motor were three students in their early twenties: Hans and Sophie Scholl, and their friend Alexander Schmorell. What began as a philosophical discussion between brother and sister was soon joined by a number of equal-thinking students from within the University of Munich: Christoph Probst, Willi Graf, Traute Lafrentz, Hubert Furtwängler, Katherina Schüddekopf and Gisela Scherting. All came from a religious, bourgeois milieu, the type of Lutheranism or Catholicism hostile to the idea of a new theology called National Socialism with its godlike Führer figure. The Scholls were of Lutheran stock, Willi Graf was a Roman Catholic, Schmorell was brought up as an Orthodox Catholic.

Alexander Schmorell, 'Schurik' to his friends, was born on 16 September 1917 in the Russian town of Orenburg to a German father and a Russian mother; he had met Hans Scholl in boot camp of the 2 *Studentenkompanie*.

Christoph Probst was born on 6 November 1919 in Murnau. He was the son of an intellectual who thought nothing of Hitler's promises. Christoph was assigned as gunner to the same Luftwaffe anti-aircraft battery as Hans Scholl.

Willi Graf was born 2 January 1918 in Kuchenheim, and grew up in Saarbrücken and the Rhineland. He was a devout believer in the goodness and morality of Christianity.

By early summer they added one more important member to their group, their academic tutor, Professor Kurt Huber, Swiss by birth (24 October 1893) and with an astounding musical talent. He conducted symphony orchestras before the University of Munich offered him the chair for music and philosophy. In the spring of 1942, he had received a visit from one of his former students, returning from Russia. 'Professor, I have always believed that Germans were decent people, but in the East they're behaving like animals . . .' and then went on to give a description of the crimes perpetrated by the SS. Professor Huber was shaken by the account; his lectures became increasingly politicised, stressing the human over the musical factor. Hans and Sophie listened to the teacher discussing the ills of society in wartime, and took the daring step to win him over to their cause. In that way Kurt Huber became an integral part of Scholl's resistance movement.

Hans Scholl, their uncontested leader, picked their *nom de guerre* from R. Marut Traven's *Die Weisse Rose*. In the beginning, their circle was disorganised and acted naïvely. They had no money and couldn't count on outside help; they were under constant threat of discovery by the Gestapo. As long as their resistance was verbal and limited to those they could trust, the danger wasn't too great. But to prove effective, they would have to widen their activities and make contact with a widespread public – and that would lead them into jeopardy. After many evenings of discussing means of propagating their idea, and because of their financial stress, they came up with a simple way. It happened by accident when Alexander Schmorell mentioned that he had seen a duplicating machine in the window of a second-hand shop. It would be ideally suited to print underground *Flugblätter* (fly leaves). As Schmorell was the only one with financial means, he bought the *Hektographierapparat* (duplicator). They didn't realise that it was the simplicity of their operation which represented their best cover, since the Gestapo was trained to combat well-organised spy networks with highly sophisticated means.

The first of such fly leaves, known as *1 Flugblatt der Weissen Rose* (1st tract) and mailed from central Munich, appeared on 27 June 1942. Written by Hans Scholl and Alexander Schmorell, the tracts were typed by Traute Lafrentz on a portable Remington. Those involved in the duplicating and distribution were Sophie and Inge Scholl, and Christoph Probst. Their first dispatch, printed out in one hundred examples, went by mail to writers, journalists, and intellectuals they hoped could be made to sympathise with their cause. To make sure that the postal service actually delivered the letters to their destination, Hans addressed one letter to himself. Unfortunately, the student-resistant group failed to appreciate the capacity to mobilise German masses, still under the influence of their charismatic Führer. Fearful of possible reprisals, thirty-five of the initial recipients carried their letters to the Gestapo in Munich. That was the first they heard of it.

Three more tracts followed before 12 July 1942. Citing Goethe and Schiller, Aristotle, Novalis and the Bible, they called upon Munich's liberal bourgeoisie to realise that the fundamental right of the individual citizen was betrayed. How could a German nation, proud of their cultural heritage, accept the dictatorship of a gang of criminals and liars? Their first three tracts did not present a clear and circumstantial political option. It was only from the fourth tract on that they pointed out the probability of a German defeat, using as example the setback against the Red Army at the gates of Moscow in the winter of 1941–2. Furthermore, it referred to the unchecked bombardment of German population centres by waves of Allied bombers, which *Reichsmarschall* Goering had assured would never be allowed to happen, or the people could call him 'Maier'! The tract went on to recall the long list of German casualties on the Eastern Front. It finally urged the ordinary citizen to face up to his individual responsibility as a member of Christian culture and Western civilisation, and it ended by giving examples of how their false god Hitler, in his *Mein Kampf*, had deceived the nation.

For this dispatch the students mimeographed several hundred fly leaves and picked addresses from telephone directories. One of the main risks for detection lay in the purchase of the hundreds of stamps necessary for the letters. Sophie volunteered for the chore. She slipped a black armband over her jacket with a swastika prominently displayed in the lapel. Sophie handed an envelope over the counter. 'How much do I have to stick on the envelope?'

'What's in it?' asked the postal clerk.

'A printed form.'

He weighed the letter. '*Drei Pfennige* – Three pennies, but you mustn't add anything written by hand.'

'Can I please have four hundred.'

The clerk eyed her with suspicion. 'Four hundred? What are you going to do with four hundred stamps?'

Sophie put on a sad face. 'My brother fell in Russia . . .'

'I'm so sorry,' said the clerk with an embarrassed smile while he handed her eight sheets of fifty 3-Pfennig stamps.

The first four tracts were all sent out from Munich. But Hans knew that mailing all letters from the same city was too dangerous. The girls volunteered to travel to Köln and Stuttgart with suitcases stuffed with tracts. Like everything they undertook, that too was fraught with danger; railway police were on the permanent look-out for *Speckjäger* with oversized suitcases, black marketeers who smuggled *Speck* (bacon), vegetables and other rationed items into the cities. On her first trip to Freiburg, a police patrol entered Sophie's compartment, but fortunately, a fat woman diverted their attention with her suitcase stuffed with potatoes and lard. While Sophie sat trembling on her suitcase, stashed beneath her bench, the fat woman was led off, calling out her innocence. Traute Lafrenz went to Berlin to establish contact with Jürgen Witgenstein, a friend of Alex Schmorell. Sophie found help in Hans Hirzel, an eighteen-year-old high-school student from Stuttgart, thrilled by the idea of distributing illegal pamphlets throughout Swabia. With a youth network building up, tracts began to appear in private mailboxes all over the country.

Gestapo-Müller was livid. His agents had been unable

to come up with the slightest clue about the mysterious flyleaves. These tracts, mailed out throughout the summer of 1942, suddenly dried up. Gestapo Chief Müller had another problem: he was not SS and had never been a convinced member of the party. He was a Bavarian police inspector who had played his cards right; in the early thirties, just before the Weimar Republic was about to collapse, he had switched to Hitler. Now he was about to play a new game and the stake was enormous.[8] He was one of the many leaders, civilian or military, who thought that their country was headed for disaster. Soon the Allies would invade continental Europe – and Germany had never won a war fought on two fronts. It was time to negotiate. But to suggest such a thing was equal to committing suicide, especially if this suggestion came from the head of the organ that was supposed to fight treachery. He decided it was far better to march along towards the precipice, but, at the same time, start making certain private arrangements. For that it took a cover. He found the ingenious solution: what better cover was there than to display his loyalty to the Führer by smashing an important anti-Nazi network?

By now, just as all of the others involved in the investigation, Müller was convinced that they had to do with a huge organisation, possibly seasoned Communists, aided by funds parachuted to them from outside the country. In 1942, the Gestapo had scored a smashing success when its agents brought down the notorious '*Rote Kapelle*', and then used its radio transmitter and its operator to dispatch fake messages back to Moscow.

They called this operation the *Funkspiel* – 'a game with the radio'. In the 'Red Orchestra' affair it was found that,

---

[8] Müller wasn't the only one. In December 1942, *SS-Reichsführer* Heinrich Himmler dispatched his friend, the lawyer Dr Langbehn, to Zurich to open secret negotiations with US and English officials.

however well organised and extensive, once the foundation of a network had collapsed, and its leader nabbed, the entire structure came tumbling down with the rest. But this time Müller ran into a dead-end. His agents rounded up all known suspects, leftists, intellectuals, writers and priests, and grilled them. Soon it became apparent that they were faced with a totally unknown, well-isolated, highly sophisticated organisation. That the *Weisse Rose* operation was run by five students in their early twenties, using their food money to buy printer's ink, postage stamps and envelopes, never occurred to Gestapo-Müller. He called for his chief investigator, a *Piefke* (a Prussian). It was the Gestapo's standard procedure not to leave an 'in-depth interrogation' to a man from the same region as his victim, or they might just get to like each other.

Müller stared up from his desk with a nasty glint in his eye. 'We must smash that *Weisse Rose* network. Find them,' he said with his thick Bavarian accent. He didn't need to add: or you'll be for the high jump. His investigator went to work. Methodical as he was, he began by checking through the Gestapo archives; every station was adding weekly to 'the list' and central headquarters was crammed with records of names of suspects and undesirables. The name of a Scholl family wasn't on this list; they were a good Lutheran family without a past.

For three months, the *Weisse Rose* remained silent, uncertain of the direction to take. Their initial appeal had remained without response. But that could suddenly change – if the battle for Stalingrad was lost and people began doubting Hitler's military genius. Hans Scholl and Christoph Probst worked on the draft of a new tract. One night in late November, they were deep into their work and their kitchen table was covered with scribbled notes, when somebody knocked on their door. Panic! They didn't expect anyone that night. Papers were shoved into drawers and replaced by schoolbooks. Sophie's shock lasted long enough to be noticed by Schmorell, because it was he – and not the Gestapo – who was knocking on their door. Alex seemed flustered as he rushed past her into the room. 'Hans, I've just heard on the BBC that the Russians have enclosed our entire 6th Army at Stalingrad.'

'That's the beginning of the end,' said Hans.

'Precisely my thought. This is why I thought you should know right away.'

Sophie realised that they had been taking frightful risks and that they existed on borrowed time. Why should she feel so strongly that she should tell her people that they were being led like a bleating herd towards the precipice? But she did, and her will to continue was only reinforced after she had received a letter from her beloved Fritz. It had been written by one of his comrades:

Mein Liebstes! We are near Stalingard. Our battalion has been annihilated. Both my hands are frozen. For weeks, by day as by night, we have been standing guard out in the open, by minus 30°C. This may well be the last letter you shall ever receive from me . . .

Sophie's private world was shattered by the news. His precious hands, trained to soothe pain and heal people, those hands now useless? For her it became a sacred cause to save others suffering a similar fate as her beloved lieutenant. Damn the danger! If, at the beginning, the young people may have had some illusions about the seriousness of their endeavour, they soon could no longer doubt the deadly risks that they incurred, but they never faltered.

One last time, fate was to play into their hands. What they had tried to achieve, raising Germany's youth to an anti-regime reaction, was achieved by a Nazi! Paul Giesler was *Gauleiter* of Munich, a party hack who had used a politician's strongest weapon – his elbows – to come to

Hitler's attention. But Giesler's political acumen matched
that of a ten-year-old. In early January 1943, he proved
this by insisting on putting himself prominently on display
by delivering the key speech at the 470th Anniversary of
Munich's Maximilian University. It was planned as an
expression of loyalty to *Führer und Reich*, a must-attend
event for every Munich student. The great hall of the
Deutsche Museum was festively decorated with a giant
banner draped over the speaker's podium: *Mit unserem
Führer zum Endsieg* (With our Führer to final victory).
The predominantly female student audience was kept in
the back of the hall. The first rows were taken up by a bevy
of SS-men in black uniforms and highly polished boots; for
visual effect, wounded in wheelchairs had been added to
show the nation's resolve to fight on to the bitter end.
Even the *Deutsche Wochenschau* (German Newsreel) was
present to record the august event. Gauleiter Paul Giesler
stepped up to the microphone and raised his hand in the
party salute: '*Sieg Heil!*' And the crowd dutifully returned
the greeting, as was expected of them.

'*Mit unserem, Führer bis zum Endsieg* – With our *Führer*
to final victory.' The crowd responded again, albeit with
somewhat less enthusiasm. Giesler was so encouraged by
the reception of his salutation that he failed to notice the
slight change in tone. He launched into a tirade, which
was as politically banal as it was predictable. '*Sie, meine
Herren Studenten,*' he began, despite the fact that there
were almost no male students present, they were all at
the front. '*Stehen inmitten der Brandung und spüren den
Wellenschlag einer grossen Zeit* – You stand amid the surf,
feeling the waves' pounding of a great time before you. As
the nation's intellectual vanguard your sacred duty is to
fight along the frontlines of our *Vaterland* . . .' So far, so
good. Gauleiter Giesler hadn't said anything exceptional,
only thrashed out the standard party phrases. Taken in

by the attention of the audience, which he attributed to his charisma and oratory power, he then pointed at the back of the hall and pronounced something which was so outrageous that the female students – among them Sophie Scholl – couldn't believe their ears: '*Die Deutsche Universitat ist keine Rettungsanstalt fur höhere Töchter, die sich den Pflichten des Krieges entziehen wollen* – The German University is not a salvation station for daughters of higher standing who wish to escape the duties of this war. It would be much preferable if these same students would think about their duties as a woman and present the Führer, each and every university year, with proof of their loyalty in the form of an upright German son.'

A hush went through the house, followed by a growl. But Gauleiter Giesler was not to be stopped; if that hadn't been enough to upset the female audience, he added a phrase, this one even more stupid: '. . . and for those maidens, who feel themselves too ugly to attract passionate attention, let me assure you, I have enough strong men to provide you with that service!'

If he counted on laughter, what he got was bedlam as enraged female students climbed over the seated SS dignitaries and stormed on to the dais to scream insults and pummel the hapless Gauleiter. In their outrage, the young students displayed astounding courage in face of the highest party authority in Bavaria.

A girl grabbed for the microphone: 'Haven't you done enough . . . dragging out this war, killing our men . . . Damn you.' That's when the doors flew open and units of *Staatspolizei* stormed into the hall. The shock of their brutality was so benumbing that the students put up almost no resistance. This encouraged the dazed party bosses in their highly polished boots to shout encouragements to the club-wielding assailants, wading into the crowd, bashing heads. They did not rest until they had bloodied all those who had dared to stand up to them, and then became infuriated when they saw medical students attempting to give first aid to the injured. They grabbed the student doctors by the hair and dragged them towards the exits where the 'potentially dangerous troublemakers' were herded into tarpaulin-covered trucks.

If the *Staatspolizei* thought they had thus eliminated all leaders of this spontaneous student riot, they were wrong; they missed out on half a dozen of the more dangerous kind. Hans and Sophie Scholl and their *Weisse Rose* group had been silent witnesses to a display of political imbecility and state police brutality, and thought that their time to move on a much wider scale had finally come. All it needed was to continue stirring the students' anger. And so they went back to work on their 5th tract.

'*Aufruf an alle Deutsche!* – Calling all Germans! Hitler leads our nation with mathematical certainty into the abyss . . . But the German nation doesn't see and it doesn't hear. Blindly it follows its Pied Piper into ruin. Freedom of speech! Religious freedom for all confessions! Protection of the individual citizen from the arbitrary crimes of a terror state, such are the foundations for a New Europe. Support the resistance, distribute the tracts! *Die Weisse Rose*.'[9]

For two days (27 to 29 January 1943) every member of the group stuffed letters into postboxes. These were collected by mail trucks the following morning and went to addresses they had once again picked at random from a telephone directory. They finally ran out of envelopes and

[9] The original text: *Was aber tut das deutsche Volk? Es sieht nicht und es hört nicht. Blindlings folgt es seinen Verführern ins Verderben. Freiheit der Rede, Freiheit des Bekenntnisses. Schutz des einzelnen Bürgers vor der Willkür verbrecherischer Gewaltstaaten, das sind die Grundlagen des neuen Europa. Unterstützt die Widerstandsbewegung, verbreitet die Flugblätter.*

the girls offered to place loose tracts in waiting rooms of bus depots and railway stations. That day Munich suffered another devastating air raid. Sophie had been caught in the open and looked on in terror as phosphorous bombs threw showers of glowing white sparks 60 feet (18 metres) into the air. She finally found shelter in a coal cellar. When the sirens announced the end of the attack, she passed only fires. Streets were roped off for unexploded bombs. Trucks and trams were in flames. People with blood streaming from their faces cried out for help. Mothers milled about, calling out the names of their children, who had been caught by the raid on their way home from school. A metallic voice from a loudspeaker van called for all of those whose houses had been struck to report to Party HQ for assistance; it also ordered all next of kin to report missing persons.

Everyone was much too preoccupied to take notice of a girl, carrying a shoulder bag stuffed with compromising tracts. For some hours she wandered around until it became dark and the whole town was *verdunkelt* (blacked out); such was the law. It was bitterly cold, Sophie had the collar of her overcoat pulled up; over her shoulder she carried a bag; it held her Aryan identity papers. But that was not all that she carried; there were also one hundred copies of the 5th tract neatly folded and ready to be pushed under doors. Distributing illegal messages was something she did because she had promised it to herself, but at the same time, she was truly frightened; lately there had been signs that suggested the situation was rapidly changing to the group's peril. Secret police were everywhere, patrolling streets, checking papers at cafés, entering cinemas and railway stations, milling around outside the university. That cold evening, only a few people were still out in the street. Sophie had the uneasy feeling that someone was following her.

'*Fräulein,*' suddenly asked a voice from behind her and her heart skipped a beat. '*Haben Sie Feuer* – Do you have a light?' Behind her stood a man in uniform, holding out a cigarette. She had difficulty making out the officer's face.

'*Ja,*' she stammered with a throat so constricted that she felt she couldn't utter another sound. With trembling hands she struck a match, noticing to her relief that his uniform tabs were not black like the feared SS. He lit his cigarette, smiled at her with a '*Danke schön!*', and walked off.

Sophie had to lean against a wall. It took her a while to calm down. All the confidence and daring she'd mustered for the task had momentarily deserted her; she was convinced that 'they' were watching her. Perhaps this soldier's polite demand for a light was a trap. She felt as if she was crossing a mined no-man's-land; she could only think of Hans and Christoph and Alex and all the others. And she longed to be held tightly by Fritz, to feel warmth and safety, to help her find release from a bone-tight terror.

'The Gestapo knows us better than we understand ourselves. I am not a coward, Hans, but I am truly afraid.'

'Fear is the tool of their trade. They may know our methods, but they don't know who we are. They are out chasing the "big red network",'[10] her brother tried to calm her. '*Es ist unsere heilige Pflicht weiterzumachen* – It is our sacred duty to continue.' Indeed, to continue their fight had become a sacred duty as they could see that their *Vaterland* was headed for the abyss.

Sophie was right, the Gestapo hadn't been idle. Gestapo-Müller had lit a roaring fire with a telegram to his outlying departments: '*Alle Mittel sind anzuwenden* – Use every means to effect arrest.' The Bavarian unit was mobilised for the sole purpose of locating and neutralising the *Weisse*

---

[10] This seems to be an indication that Hans did have some contact inside the Bavarian police.

Rose, since by now the Gestapo was certain that the centre of the network must be in or around Munich; the 5th tract was written on the same typewriter as the four previous ones, and those had all been posted from Bavaria. A reward of 1000 *Reichsmark* was offered for information leading to the arrest 'of plotters against the security of the Vaterland'.

'*Russen, Kommunisten, Militärs?* Who runs this *Weisse Rose* network?' Gestapo-Müller demanded of his chief investigator, a man never reluctant to use torture in order to extract information.

'I cannot make them out. In a way, they are clever, but then they act too amateurish to be Soviet backed; and their approach is definitely non-military; I'd say, it's academic, scientists, professors, pastors, that sort of people. To put them down will not only depend on footwork, but chance. I am almost certain the day I meet *Die Weisse Rose* face to face I shall have the surprise of my life.'

The Gestapo got a break. On 27 January 1943, once the 5th tract was printed out, Sophie had undertaken the dangerous day trip to Stuttgart to deliver 500 fly leaves to Hans Hirzel. She returned immediately to Munich while he went about mailing the letters. Having accomplished his task, the teenager bragged to two of his high-school comrades about a secret mission he was involved in; on 29 January, the two friends in whom he had so imprudently confided, loyal members of the *Hitlerjugend*, went to the city police to denounce Hirzel. The local police inspector, whose preoccupation was directed to keeping traffic arteries open after each new bombing raid and who knew nothing of an ongoing investigation by the Gestapo, listened to the duo, took notes, and remarked drily to his assistant: '*Wichtigmachers* – Self-importants.' He felt however obliged to send a brief note about the denunciation to the *Polizeidirektion* in Munich, where his note was duly received and filed away. The chief of the Bavarian police had bigger worries than some teenager's statement from Ulm. And that's why nothing was done about it, since ordinary police and Gestapo seldom talked to each other.

If the *Weisse Rose* wanted to reach a larger audience, Hans Scholl had to widen his circle. The five students couldn't do it on their own. He managed to establish contact with Falk Harnack, whose brother Arvid Harnack had been executed by the Nazis as a leader of the Soviet-run 'Red Orchestra' spy network; Falk stressed that laying the foundation for a wider, universal resistance movement, must be on a solid, political basis, and he proposed himself as intermediary with the Bonhoeffer-Dohnanyi circle. It was Falk's inference of a finely targeted political message, which made Hans decide to call on Professor Kurt Huber as their 'writing expert' and let him draft the 6th tract.

In the meantime, a source inside police HQ warned Willi Graf[11] that the Gestapo had firmly concluded the *Weisse Rose* to be centred in Munich, that they had set up a special anti-*Weisse Rose* team, and that they were concentrating all their efforts on the Munich area. Traute Lafrentz sat behind her typewriter. 'Don't you think it would be better to lie low for a while?' she asked in a timid voice.

'We must go on. The issue is not only facing us, but every young German. We cannot give in just because a crazy psychopath in Berlin says so, and then leads our nation to ruin.'

'But Hans, with Stalingrad almost gone, isn't it too late to tell them the truth?'

'Was it too late for Jesus when they nailed him to the cross? It is never too late for the truth. The naked truth.'

That night they wrote their finest leader; it spoke of

[11] It was never discovered who this source was, but Willi Graf did have an inside contact in the local police.

throwing off the wreckage of a defeated and dishonoured Third Reich. It was an indictment of every living German for never having begun the fight for individual freedom and challenging the nation's citizens not to die for Adolf Hitler in a war that was lost.

Things moved fast. On 31 January 1943 at Stalingrad, Field Marshal von Paulus surrendered his Sixth Army. An army was sacrificed by a megalomaniac, who refused to allow his beleaguered troops to effect a break-out while there was still time. Some 230,000 German soldiers paid with their lives for one man's folly.

On the 3rd, 8th and again 15th February 1943, students discovered battalions of *Hausmeister* Schmied's charwomen hard at work to scrape 3-foot (90-cm) tall graffiti from the walls near the main entrance of Munich's University: '*Nieder mit Hitler*' (Down with Hitler) and '*Freiheit*' (Freedom) were the slogans that had been written with indelible tar paint by Hans Scholl, Alexander Schmorell und Willi Graf during the night. Elisabeth Hartnagel-Scholl remembered that, together with Sophie and Hans, she walked to the university where they saw a great number of students studying the graffiti.

Sophie giggled: 'They can scrub until their fingers fall off, that's pure tar.'

Hans nudged Elisabeth: 'Let's go on, we don't want to be noticed when the police come around.' He felt let down when he saw a student spit on the '*Freiheit*' graffiti, yelling: '*Schweinehunde!*' (pig dogs), while another cursed: '*Vaterlandsverräter!*' (traitor to the fatherland), and the rest of the student crowd remained silent.

On 3 February, the group began the draft of their 6th tract. They confided its final composition to their professor of philosophy. No question, Prof. Kurt Huber was a first-class recruit. The horrendous losses suffered recently by the German *Wehrmacht* in Stalingrad pushed the professor to stress what the Scholls had badly formulated in their 3 *Flugblatt*:

Nicht der militärische Sieg über den Bolschewismus darf die erste Sorge für jeden Deutschen sein, sondern die Niederlage der Nationalsozialisten – The destruction of Bolshevism mustn't be the principal occupation for Germans, but the downfall of National-Socialism.

With this as his guiding thought, Prof. Huber wrote the *Weisse Rose Flugblatt Nummer 6*:

Kommilitoninnen! Kommilitonen! The entire German nation is looking to us. It expects us to become its leaders once more – as we were already in 1813, rising against Napoleon's terror – so it must be now, in order to break the Nationalist-Socialist terror by the power of our spirit. The ghosts of the Beresina (1812) and Stalingrad (1943) blaze in the East, the fallen cry out to us. *Unser Volk steht im Aufbruch gegen die Verknechtung Europas durch den Nationalsozialismus, im neuen glaubigen Durchbruch von Freiheit und Ehre!* – Our people must rise against the enslaving of Europe by National-Socialism in a decisive breakthrough of our freedom and honour! *Mein Führer*, we thank you for the 300,000 dead of Stalingrad!

On 12 February, a first batch of 200 letters was posted;[12] most did arrive at their intended destination. They were not nearly as successful with their second batch. On 15 February, the girls shoved another 1200 envelopes into postboxes in and around the centre of Munich. Even for a dedicated Nazi, the party organ *Völkischer Beobachter*, printed in Gothic type and thrashing out the daily statements from Dr Goebbels' propaganda machine, made for grim reading.

[12] The letters were addressed to people in Hamburg, Berlin, Chemnitz, Köln, Bonn, Frankfurt, Saarbrücken, Heilbronn, Stuttgart, Ulm, Freiburg, Munich, Innsbruck, Salzburg, Linz and Vienna.

There was something else the citizens of Germany could read on their train to work. The text of the *Weisse Rose Flugblätter*.

'*Erschüttert steht unser Volk vor dem Untergang der Männer von Stalingrad!*[13] – Devastated stands our nation before the fate of the men of Stalingrad. Three hundred and fifty thousand German men have been driven into death and ruin by the strategic genius of a First World War corporal. Do we want to sacrifice what is still left of Germany's youth to the lowest instincts of a party clique? Never! In the name of the German youth we demand from Adolf Hitler's state to return to us our most precious possession, the personal freedom, of which he has deprived us in the shabbiest manner.'

Their end was rapidly approaching. Graf tried to alert the Scholls to the worrisome build-up of Gestapo agents near the centre of town, checking passers-by for suspicious parcels. The leader of the student resistance group accepted their presence as a fact. Hans and Sophie showed an incredible calm throughout these days of stress. Now that the Gestapo was certain that the *Weisse Rose* was located in the Bavarian capital, they checked Munich's central post office for all suspicious mail and pulled 800 letters before these could be sent out. During the night of 15 February, Hans and Alexander made another daring nocturnal sortie with their tar-paint can, to strike where least expected, at the very heart of Bavaria's government. On the following

[13] The original text: *Dreihundertfünfzigtausend deutsche Männer hat die geniale Strategie des Weltkriegsgefreiten sinn- und verantwort- ungslos in Tod und Verderben gehetzt. Wollen wir den niederen Machtinstinkten einer Parteiclique den Rest der deutschen Jugend opfern? Nimmermehr! Im Namen der Deutschen Jugend fordern wir vom Staat Adolf Hitlers die persönliche Freiheit, das kostbarste Gut des Deutschen zurück, um das er uns in der erbärmlichsten Weise betrogen hat.*

morning, the people of Munich were stunned to see written on its walls in man-high letters: *Hitler = Massenmörder* (Hitler = guilty of genocide).

Gestapo-Müller went red in the face. A bad sign. The initial four tracts heralded a problem; but the 5th and 6th tracts, together with the wall-sign campaign, turned it into a nightmare. The Gestapo worked overtime and their work paid off. An agent stumbled on the report that a local police inspector in Ulm had made of a *Wichtigmacher* some three weeks earlier. On 17 February, the Ulm Gestapo pulled in young Hirzel for questioning. His explanations sounded too mad to be true; but he also dropped the name of 'my girlfriend Sophie Scholl' – overlooked at first by the investigator, but not by the stenographer, who put it into her report. The Ulm Gestapo decided to let him loose and then follow him discreetly. The Hirzel boy managed to slip his tail and immediately contacted the Scholl parents in Ulm to get a warning to Hans and Sophie. By now it was quite late, and no night trains were running between Ulm and Munich. In the meantime, a copy of the Hirzel interview was already on its way by special car from Ulm to the Wittelsbacher Palast in Munich, the headquarters of the Gestapo. Müller's special agent, a product of a cumbersome secret intelligence apparatus, was used to dealing with big underground networks that were equipped with radio transmitters and secret inks, and his mind couldn't focus immediately on a story about heroic teenagers and their girlfriends. Yet, reading through the Hirzel report, he stumbled on the name of Sophie Scholl. He decided to take a closer look at the girl the following day, 18 February 1943.

By now, the *Weisse Rose* was pushed to take outrageous risks. They had found out that most of their mail had been intercepted, because the letter they had addressed to themselves had failed to be delivered. They did not know that Sophie's name was already on a Gestapo file, and that an agent, checking the addresses on the 800 confiscated envelopes, was bound to make a cross-reference between the Scholl from the Hirzel interrogation and the Scholl on the suspicious envelope. Despite the tightening noose, they were too deeply involved to stop now; they decided to use all possible means to rouse the people. The Scholls met with Alex and told him that, come morning, they were going to distribute tracts inside the university. Alex tried to talk them out of it. They wouldn't listen. Hans must have known that the Gestapo was on to them. There was still time to put distance between themselves and their pursuers. They had every opportunity to escape; from Munich it was only four hours by car to the Swiss border, or perhaps two days by bicycle, using a trail of forests and deep valleys. Families with small children had managed to take this escape route. The Scholls could have stopped everything and walked away. Providing proof of their integrity and courage, they continued, knowingly heading for disaster. Hans shrugged his shoulders, but it was Sophie who said: 'We must remain true to our combat and this leaves us with no choice.' They worked all night to run off 1000 copies of their 6th tract.

It was 18 February 1943, 07.55 hrs. Hans and Sophie merged into the morning rush to classes, passing Gestapo agents hovering around the university entrance; like many other students, Hans carried a suitcase. They didn't proceed to their classroom, but locked themselves in a toilet and waited for the bell which called students into their laboratories and lecture theatres. Sophie waited another ten minutes before she carefully pushed her head round the door; the corridor was empty. Light came from a window down the long hallway. There was no sound, nothing that would indicate that anyone was patrolling the corridors. She waved to her brother. Light streamed through the rosette window of the interior courtyard. That would make them clearly visible should anyone step from one of the classrooms to go to the toilet. For a moment Sophie hesitated, a deep fear was nudging her; while Hans handed her small piles of tracts from the suitcase, she began placing them throughout the hallways, in toilet cubicles and along the main staircase. They had done the first floor and moved up to the second via the open staircase winding around the interior courtyard. Crouching low, Hans took the last stack of fly leaves from the suitcase and handed them to Sophie. 'Four minutes before the bell goes,' Hans whispered a warning. 'Be quick.'

'We must get rid of all of them. If someone stops us, we can show him an empty suitcase,' replied Sophie, distributing the final batch along the stairs leading up to the next floor. Hans snapped the suitcase shut. 'Hurry up!' Sophie clutched the last few tracts left in her hand. In a gesture of defiance, she flung a dozen or so over the banister; like paper planes, they spiralled downwards into the interior courtyard. Sophie heard a door open.

'*Komm . . .*' she mouthed to Hans. She hardly glanced at her brother, intent on where she was going; they ran for the staircase and dived down the steps, taking them two at a time. It was at this moment that Herr Schmied, the beer-bellied janitor, stepped into the interior courtyard. He went red in the face when he noticed paper littering the floor. Sacrilege, the university's hallowed ground covered in waste paper! *Hausmeister* Schmied was a stickler for cleanliness and had issued strict orders to his charwomen to keep every floor and even the courtyard of his universe pristinely clean. He bent down, picked one up, glanced at it – and blanched. *Die Weisse Rose!* Treason against the Führer! That's when more sheets came fluttering down. He looked up in time to see someone rushing down the stairs. As quickly as his bulk would allow it he rushed to the stairs to bar the way, when he noticed two students, a boy and a girl, coming down towards him. The boy was carrying a suitcase and Schmied summoned them. None of Sophie's anxiety showed in her calm expression as she coolly manoeuvred her way past him. But Hans wasn't that lucky, the *Hausmeister* grabbed him by his sleeve. '*Was haben Sie da drinnen* – What do you carry in there?'

That was a problem that needed a quick decision. Most likely Hans could have walked out by being polite, but that stupid man irritated him. Instead, he tried to bluff his way out: '*Geht Sie nichts an* – Mind your own business.'

That was the wrong thing to say to a man who believed in his ultimate authority. '*Mitkommen!* – Come with me!' he ordered and pulled Sophie by the arm.

'*Was wollen Sie von uns* – What do you want from us?' asked Sophie in a quiet voice.

Schmied pushed forth his chest. '*Sie sind verhafted* – You are under arrest,' he said, grabbing the girl roughly by her arm. Sophie jerked herself free. They still had more than a minute to make good their getaway. But they froze, or perhaps they thought they could bluff it out with the fat caretaker; whatever, their last chance was gone with the shrill sound of the school bell. The amphitheatre doors swung open, letting out a stream of students. In no time, a ring of the curious surrounded the threesome.

'*Was geht hier vor* – What is happening?' came the sharp voice of a supervisor, probably a Gestapo plant. *Hausmeister* Schmied gave a brief account, waving a tract. Sandwiched between the janitor and the supervisor, Hans and Sophie Scholl were led to the rector.

'*Herr Oberführer*, read this.' Wüst got red in the face as he read the tract. He jumped up and stood himself theatrically against the backdrop of the red flag with its black swastika standing out brightly from the white circle.

'You are a disgrace to this university,' he screamed, 'and you are an even greater disgrace to Germany! Have you no honour?' Hans and Sophie thought it best to remain silent. Within minutes, an *Überfallskommando* (flying squad) raced up to the front gate of the university.

'We're taking over,' announced their chief, looking sternly at the arrested brother-and-sister team. The *Hausmeister*, glowing with pride over his achievement, snapped his heels and the rector nodded approvingly.

A friend of Sophie's, Christa Meyer-Heidkamp, was an eyewitness to the scene:

Every exit from the university had been locked. We were ordered to assemble in the interior courtyard. Anyone who had picked up a tract was told to hand it immediately to one of two Gestapo men, placed especially near a door. They kept us standing in the courtyard for about two hours, when the door opened and Hans and Sophie were led past us, their hands manacled behind their backs. Hans looked straight at me, but his face showed no emotion that would indicate that he recognised me. He knew that even the slightest sign would lead to the arrest of anyone who had been in contact with him.

Cars raced through town, pulling up outside the Scholl flat in the Franz-Joseph Strasse. Searching through it, the Gestapo discovered in a waste-bin under the sink a torn-up draft for the 6th tract. That draft of the *Weisse Rose Flugblatt* was in Christoph Probst's handwriting.

That Germany was not yet ready to listen to the dire warning by a group of students, and was still spellbound by the great magician and his promise of German invincibility over the Bolshevik *Untermensch*, was demonstrated by an event which took place on the same day. Hitler's demoniacal propaganda genius, Dr Joseph Goebbels, addressed a monster rally in Berlin's *Sportpalast*.

'*Wollt ihr den totalen Krieg* – Do you want total war?' he yelled, and a frenetic crowd responded: '*Jawohl!*'

The night was bitterly cold. For the first time in hours or days – Sophie had lost count – they had let her go to sleep. But sleep wouldn't come. In her cell it was dark. She got up, pulled a blanket around her shoulders, and stared into the night sky so full of stars it seemed she could reach out and grab a handful. Only a few days before, she had been so sure of herself, carried along by a euphoric daring; but her life had changed, and now, in the icy white of the cell, she was not so willing to go to her God without a last fight. It had been four days of uninterrupted interrogation, four days of pain and fatigue. She had tried to stay calm, for above all she knew that interrogators depended on the panic of surprise during cross-examination. In the beginning she wasn't sure if she could take the pain. But they didn't use physical torture; her first interrogation started off in a rather agreeable manner. The person who did the questioning acted like a father figure. An elderly man, who kept calling her *mein Mädchen*, and spoke to her in gentle tones. Damn him, it was this gentleness that confused her and she realised that she must make a great effort to stay alert and not be seduced into a false sense of security. Perhaps she could make him believe that she was nothing but a pretty, empty-headed girl and quite harmless. 'Why did you do it?' His voice was soft, mellifluous.

Despite her resolve, she found herself looking up at him like a frightened child. 'Do what? I didn't do anything wrong.'

The Gestapo was playing their subtle game, setting traps by alternatively using persuasion and force. In the end, the brutal investigator replaced the father figure. When she looked up into his hard blue eyes, she knew that she couldn't expect pity.

'Come on, make it easy on yourself, tell us all,' he ordered her in a rasping tone. 'Don't even try to be difficult or you will be hurt. Tell me about the tracts you were carrying in the suitcase.'

'The suitcase was empty. My brother intended to pick up our laundry.'

It came so suddenly, the investigator slapped her hard across the face, and she tasted blood from her cut lips. 'Don't lie to me. You're a member of a network, a criminal working against your *Vaterland* at a time when it is fighting for its survival. Isn't that so?'

'No . . .' He knocked her back and the room turned into a mist of darkness. She heard his voice from a distance. 'Don't you dare fall asleep on me.'

Tears blinded Sophie, she trembled. He waited. He was taking the right line with her. Girls of her class had never been struck before; to them, shock and degradation was as potent a factor in a beating as the pain itself. When the moment of truth arrives, it becomes a matter of a person's inner strength or weakness. But this girl surprised him, her reaction was not what he expected. Her eyes blazed with defiance, not fear.

'Where is your network? Who are its members?' he barked.

'I don't know what you're talking about.'

The next time his voice was a hoarse whisper; he took hold of her hand, and his fingers were ice cold. With his other hand he opened a thin folder lying on the table and pulled out several sheets.

'And how do you explain these? We found them in your room.' She recognised the coloured sheets with one hundred and forty likenesses of Hitler, and so had the Gestapo: one hundred and forty 3-Pfennig postage stamps. Sophie's brain throbbed with the knowledge that she was lost.

Where the Gestapo began, humanity ended and, with

it, logic. A victim bleeding under a torturer's lash is no longer quite human. He enters the silent process of either becoming a hero, or a traitor. And yet, the transformation is unpredictable and sometimes incomprehensible. While to a professional agitator the words 'heroism' and 'disloyalty' are devoid of any meaning and he plays his interrogator like a game of chess, the amateur is the victim of his own noble standards. Honour, decency, loyalty! And these youngsters were pure amateurs, fighting for an ideal. For Hans Scholl, the Gestapo reserved a different kind of treatment from the outset. There would be no sleep for him; he was questioned by relays of interrogators, every one fired with anger over the insult to their Führer.

Müller's appointed investigator was the worst. Tall, broad-shouldered, and as Aryan as they come, he took shifts questioning Hans, but the accused wouldn't talk. The expert of many such in-depth interrogations realised that there were no half-measures in this sister-brother pair. He decided to be relatively gentle with the girl and to torture her brother, counting on the fact that one of them would disclose a single name and then the rest would follow. Having botched it to be the perfect hero, his victim would then turn into a mitigated coward and traitor. Such was the fatal logic of the Gestapo. Under normal circumstances their system worked – but not with these youngsters, taking strength from an inner faith. Their loyalty to friends remained absolute.

For Hans Scholl, time had lost its meaning. 'Who are your accomplices?' a voice screamed into his ear. 'Who is the leader of the *Weisse Rose* network?' Fools, thought Hans, they simply wouldn't believe that there was no network! That there was no organisation! Only a name picked from the title of a novel. They still didn't know that with him they held the key to 'the network', and not a minor cog in a big organisation. Hans shook his head and a fist struck him in the ribs. Still, he continued to deny all knowledge about the tract, or to give away names, until the moment a voice whispered in his ear: 'By the way, we've found the duplicating machine.' It was over.

With the arrest of the Scholls their group had exploded and its members were on the run. Getting caught would be the worst disaster of all – being dragged into the torture cellar. For the Gestapo, no hatred was more intense and no search conducted with greater intensity than for a German who had betrayed his Führer. That's what their Gestapo boss had told them, and they acted on his orders. His agents swamped the university grounds, classrooms were turned into interrogation centres; some students stepped willingly forward, others were coerced into giving information. They took note of all those who, according to statements given by fellow students, had befriended the Scholls. The sum of their interrogation pointed clearly at Alexander Schmorell, Christoph Probst, and Willi Graf.

Schmorell and Probst had vanished, but Graf was still around. During the night of 18 February, Gestapo agents broke into his apartment and arrested him, together with his sister Anneliese. The Gestapo still had no idea how extended the network really was, or the identity of the key to the *Weisse Rose*; they refused to believe that this operation was limited to a handful of university students. They approached Graf with a promise of clemency, counting on him being the weak link. They needed a complete listing of names, the contacts and their habits. Graf didn't break. They tried their harshest methods. Graf limited his statements to facts they already knew; but he didn't disclose names.

Christoph Probst had been avoiding his apartment; he wasn't certain if Hans or Sophie had been made to talk. It just so happened that on this crucial day his wife had entered hospital to give birth to their third child. On 19

February 1943, Christoph's time was up. He walked into the hospital to visit his wife and newborn baby, and to say goodbye to them. At the reception desk he was asked to fill out a form for a visitor's permit, when two men, dressed up as doctors, closed in on him: '*Christoph Probst, Sie sind verhaftet!*' Probst never did get to see his third child.

Following the arrest of Scholl, Probst and Graf, 'Wanted' posters appeared on walls and on public transport, offering a reward of 1000 *Reichsmark* for the capture of Alexander Schmorell: '*Gefährlicher Landesverräter* – Dangerous traitor of the nation'. 'Schurik' was panic-stricken; he knew that Hans and Sophie had been caught, but he had no idea what had happened to the others. He had to talk to Christoph. On the way to the Probst home, he was intercepted in the street by his friend Nikolai Nikolaeff Hamasaspian:

Alex seemed confused and scared. I told him that there had been a wave of arrests. He said that he would make his way across the Swiss border, because he had been there before the war on a skiing vacation. He was wearing a grey overcoat and carried a briefcase. He said to me: 'It would be good if I could change.' I took off my green leather jacket that I had bought in Bulgaria then added some *Speck*, a few cigarettes and 100 *Reichsmark*. I didn't have more.

Alex Schmorell never made it to Switzerland. During a bombing raid on 24 February, while in a Munich air-raid shelter, he was recognised and held for the arrival of the Gestapo. The man who denounced him, justified his act. 'It's not for the money, I did it for the *Vaterland*.'

'Of course you did,' said the Gestapo agent, handing over a cheque for 1000 *Reichsmark*.

The game was up, and it was only a question of time before they would catch the last ones. On 27 February, while Gestapo agents were milling around outside his crowded auditorium, Professor of Philosophy Kurt Huber declared to his student body: '*Die Zeit für hohle Phrasen ist vorüber* – The time for hollow phrases is over.' It was the last lecture he was to give.

'*Recht ist, was dem Volke nützt* – Justice is what is useful for the people.' This was the rule with which Roland Freisler, supreme judge of the *Volksgericht* (people's court), dispensed justice. He had begun his career with a statement, quite unique for a judge in the service of the blindfolded goddess Impartiality. In a letter, he gave a solemn promise to Hitler. 'The people's court will always take great care, to judge in the manner as it thinks, that you, *mein Führer*, would yourself judge each case. *Heil, mein Führer!* Your most obedient political soldier, Roland Freisler.'

Freisler's running of the *Deutscher Volksgerichtshof* was special in that he was not only its final judge, but also acted as its most rabid prosecutor. His favourite method was to shout his accusations at an accused he was supposed to judge fairly and impartially. In doing so, he deliberately avoided all judicial objectivity by calling high treason the smallest offences against National Socialism, a tactic he had acquired from studying the performance of Andrei Vyshinsky during Stalin's terror purges of the 1930s. When Sophie saw the judge, presiding with a swastika pinned to his crimson robe, she knew that this farce of a trial was invested with sudden and wilful death. Freisler read out the accusation to Hans Scholl, Sophie Scholl and Christoph Probst: '. . . *Landesverräterische Feindbegünstigung, Vorbereitung zum Hochverrat und Wehrkraftzersetzung* – Treasonous help to the enemy, incitement to high treason and sabotaging the will of the army', charges, each of which carried the maximum penalty. Freisler's cross-examination degenerated into an emotional tirade of denunciation, a harangue of hatred.

'You are a disgrace to the country and the nation!' he shrieked his accusations; Freisler couldn't contain his paranoid fury. Hans was surprised to hear his own duty defence lawyers murmur in agreement. Freisler pointed at Hans and Sophie: 'There they sit, Judas and the harlot – if God will forgive me for so defaming the name of womanhood . . .'

Hans Scholl interjected: 'Leave God out of this.'

Sophie Scholl defended her right to speak out freely: 'You cannot muzzle us. We think like many others.'

Freisler jumped up from his seat, frothing at the mouth: 'Quiet! Those who attack National Socialism do no longer belong in our midst. Those who attack the person of our beloved Führer . . .'

Sophie interrupted: 'Your Führer better be aware, we're only the beginning.'

Before even coming to a judgment, Freisler spat out with pure venom: 'Such filth as you deserves nothing but death.'

Sophie studied the face of the macabre judge. How could such a man be put in charge of a court proceeding, with the sculpture of a blindfolded goddess of justice holding the scale of Impartiality hovering over his chair? This Freisler was nothing but a party-appointed executioner, blind to any kind of decency and justice.[14] The sentence came as expected: '*Dieses Gericht verurteilt die Angeklagten wegen Hochverrats am deutschen Volk zum Tode* – This court sentences the accused for high treason against the nation to death.'

Freisler didn't waste his time with formalities such as an appeal. The condemned were taken back to their cells. Probst, an agnostic all his life, asked for a Catholic priest; Father Heinrich Sperr, acting for the sick prison padre

---

[14] According to eyewitness Leo Samberger.

Ferdinand Brinkmann, gave him Holy Communion. They didn't have much time. Shortly before five in the afternoon on the day of their trial, Sophie took her final walk down the long corridor in the prison of Munich Stadelheim. In her neat, white blouse, she looked small and fragile, but that was an outward appearance. She turned to her prison guard: '*Il faut avoir un esprit dur et le coëur tendre.*'[15] When the female guard looked at her with a puzzled expression, she translated the French phrase: 'One must have a strong spirit and a soft heart.'

'These young people behaved incredibly bravely,' that female prison guard recorded after the war. 'That's why we took the risk of letting them get together for one final moment, just minutes before their execution. If the people's judge had found out, we would have been severely punished. But we wanted to let them have a last cigarette together – it was only a few minutes, but I believe for them it meant a lot. I remember, young Christoph Probst turned to Sophie and said: "I had no idea that dying can be so easy." To which the girl replied: "In a few minutes we shall meet again in the eternity".'

Sophie left a note behind; in it she told of a dream she'd experienced during her last night:

It was a bright and sunny day. In my arms I carried a child in a white dress on the way to its first baptism. The road to the church led up a steep mountainside. Suddenly I was stumbling towards a chasm. I had just time to put the child down safely before I fell forward into the abyss. This child is our idea, and despite all obstacles it will succeed. We are simply those who show the way and must be willing to die for our ideal.

On 19 April 1943, Willi Graf, Alexander Schmorell and Professor Kurt Huber faced the virulent Roland Freisler

15 Maritain.

and his *Volksgericht*. Huber's defiant address to the court remains a monument to a man's courage:

Any man who feels morally responsible must join his voice to ours and rise against the menacing domination by a brutal force ... for a national community, no sentence is more frightening than to realise that not a single one among us is safe from his neighbour, no father from his own son ... you are trying to take from me the right which is that of a teacher; however the dignity of a university professor, a man who fights openly for the concept of a just state in a just world, no staged process for high treason can take that from me. The march of history will justify what I was trying to achieve, such is my unshakeable conviction.

The accused were tried, convicted, and judged by the dark figure of Freisler in his crimson robe embroidered with the swastika.

Prof. Huber and Schmorell were executed on 13 July 1943.

Willi Graf went to the guillotine on 12 October 1943.

Inside the Third Reich, the trial of the *Weisse Rose* was smothered in silence. Only a short paragraph appeared in the party organ *Völkischer Beobachter* under the headline: '*Gerechtes Urteil für Vaterlandsverräter* – Just sentence for the nation's traitors.' Very few inside Germany ever heard of the resistance movement by a small group of Munich students. Not enough tracts were distributed to make the difference. Of those who did receive them, many called them traitors and dragged their memory through the mud; the majority of Germans were still traipsing after their Pied Piper. Only a few dared silently to call them heroes. But, could they be called heroes? They hadn't performed any superhuman act. They simply defended the right to express an opinion freely. If somewhat confused about their aim at the outset, their line of thought became much more concise in their last three tracts. It pointed out the criminal mind of their nation's leader; their one and only aim was to stop a bleeding to death of the young generation they loved and never betrayed. As partisans to assure their nation's cultural heritage and to conserve Germany's moral integrity, this was a worthwhile task.

To reach the broad masses had been impossible as long as Hitler's armies marched from victory to victory; they had to wait for a reversal of the military situation to bring about a favourable reaction to their cause. They tried after Rommel's setback at El Alamein, and it failed; they thought that they had found it with the Stalingrad disaster, and it failed due to their lack of political realism. Germanic youth movements were by tradition steeped in a kind of Teutonic idealism to which its adherents remained forever faithful. To awaken an opposing political conscience in a youth steeped in the ideology of the Third Reich was an unrealistic hope. That's why they failed.

Their call for Germany's youth to resist Hitler's regime didn't die with them. Several months after their execution, Helmuth, Graf von Moltke,[16] a German resistant, smuggled a copy of their 5th tract to England. What the *Weisse Rose* failed to achieve, relying on the German postal service, British planes tried to accomplish. In the fall of 1943, millions of fly leaves of *A Manifesto by Munich Students*, was dumped over Germany.

The struggle by the *Weisse Rose* showed up the deep problem of a resistance from within Nazi Germany; with the noblest of intentions, they undertook more than their small numbers proved capable of handling. Many claimed that the Scholls and their friends fell short on political

[16] Helmuth James, Graf von Moltke, was executed on 23 January 1945.

pragmatism. That is not so. Deliverance had to come in a just cause; or else it would deny the ideal of charity and faith in the good. The young dissenters' mistake was more due to an ignorance of the endemic support by the nation for a lost cause; Germans in general never believed that they alone had made that war, or that in fact they were losing it.

On 3 February 1945, during an American bombing raid on Berlin, a collapsing cellar beam smashed in the head of *Volksgerichtshof* Judge Roland Freisler.

Gestapo Müller remained in encircled Berlin until 27 April 1945. Then, as if Hitler's *Götterdammerung* wasn't his affair, he disappeared. He was never found.

Three days later, on 1 April 1945, Hitler committed suicide.

The Scholls and their friends rose above the darkness, which took enormous character, and then were caught in a conflict between all those who quite willingly supported evil, and those who recognised it but cowered under the whip of a cruel dictator and his secret police. By their courage they demonstrated that a resistance movement, however small, was ultimately possible; and that there still existed a youth in Germany that was steeped in morality and didn't accept the lies dished out by Hitler and his cohorts. Most importantly, they showed that politics without morality, without the profound basis of that great European humanism, was bound to fail in the end.

Their sacred words that speak of freedom, conscience and humanity, of great courage in adversity, are chiselled into stone at the entrance of the University of Munich. Hundreds pass the inscription on their way to school. The memory of those who risked their lives knowingly, because freedom has no price, is alive. The younger generation may not be aware of the names of those who wrote these sacred words – Scholl, Schmorell, Probst, Graf, and Huber. They only know them as *Die Weisse Rose*.

The *Weisse Rose*'s motivation was an incredible moral fortitude. They knew that their call might expose them to punishment, and death. But nothing could stop them from exposing 'the collective lie'. In this moment of darkness, when nobody dared to speak out, they defied a powerful political machine in a valiant attempt to awake their nation to the fact that a psychopath and his clique were destroying the country and its people. They failed due to the inherent system of any totalitarian regime, which controls the outlets necessary to voice a challenge; but even more so, because a nation didn't care to listen to their prophetic words. Two years later, they were vindicated. The end of Hitler's regime was apocalyptic. Germany's cities were heaps of brick and ashes. People, who had refused to heed their warning, emerged from their mole-like existence in caves to face a nightmare in the stark light of day.

G.F. Duckwitz, The Nazi who saved the Danish Jews

'Ich weiss was ich zu tun habe.'
'I know what I have to do.'

Georg Ferdinand Duckwitz, in his secret diary, 19 September 1943

'We må stå fast ved vores principper, adlyde Herren mere en mennesket.'
'We must stand to our principle, to obey more God than a man.'

Bishop of Copenhagen, Hans Fuglsang-Damgaard, 3 October 1943

Late in the afternoon of 28 September 1943, Georg Ferdinand Duckwitz, a card-carrying member of the Nazi party and special adviser on shipping affairs to the *Deutsche Reichsbevollmächtigte für Dänemark* (the German plenipotentiary for occupied Denmark) picked up the phone. The man he called was a Danish Social Democrat and dire foe of the German occupation of his *fœdreland* (Danish fatherland).

'We must meet – *dringend!*' That was a word that a Dane understood. Something *dringend* was up, in other words: bloody urgent. Late that evening, after the discreet knock on a door in Copenhagen's Rømergade, a man was ushered into the house. At the end of a corridor he entered a comfortable salon with four people present. Three, Duckwitz had heard of but never met before: H.C. Hansen, a prominent Danish politician, Congressman Alsing Andersen from Denmark's *Folketing* (House of Commons), and Vilhelm Buhl; all were members of Denmark's first party, the Social Democrats. It was the fourth, a paunchy man in a grey suit and vest coat, and the man he had called earlier, who strode across the room to greet him. Hans Hedtoft[1] was former leader of the Danish Social Democrats, forced by the Germans to step down. Shortly thereafter, the door opened once more, allowing two latecomers to join them, Frants Hvass, section chief in the Danish Foreign Ministry, and *Kriminelkommissaer* Christian Madsen of the Copenhagen police.

'I don't see the need for introductions,' said Hedtoft, 'I've already told my colleagues about you, so we can get straight down to business. What exactly is it that you wish to tell us?' Six leaders of Denmark, with their eyes fixed on a Nazi, and not a minor one, but the *éminence grise* behind the *Reichsbevollmächtigten*. Not one of the six had the slightest notion what this urgent matter was all about. Was it to be another stern warning to abstain from acts of sabotage? A country as small as Denmark could achieve no spectacular results against an occupying force with the strength of Germany's army. Their best defence was one of passive resistance and, in that, the Danes were true masters. Blowing up a locomotive here, setting a factory ablaze, getting downed British and American aircrews to Sweden, and providing information to the Allies.[2] To

[1] Buhl, Hedtoft and Hansen went on to become Denmark's after-war prime ministers.
[2] It was thanks to Norwegian and Danish coast-watchers that the British Admiralty was first informed about the battleship *Bismarck* breaking out into the North Atlantic.

operate such clandestine channels called for confidence in the individual; whom to trust and whom not to trust depended on bonds of friendship and mutual respect. The six had willingly shown their faces to a German, because Hedtoft had asked them to; and Hedtoft respected Duckwitz.

'There are two kinds of war; one is the confrontation between two enemy forces, leading the conquest of a country. Germany has achieved that goal,' Duckwitz said with an embarrassed smile. 'But there is another aspect that has nothing to do with war; it is one that calls upon the beastly nature of man to show his inhumanity: the elimination of a great number of innocents.'

Hedtoft didn't hide his shock. What was this 'elimination threat' all about? He knew there was something more to come, to which he didn't look forward. 'Are you talking about the elimination of some of my countrymen?'

'Not just some.' Duckwitz took a deep breath. '*Get your Jews out of the country.*'

His statement was met by a stunned silence, before Hedtoft asked: 'You mean . . .'

Inspector Madsen, always a cold police fish, interrupted: 'Confirmed?'

'Unfortunately, yes. A *Führerbefehl*,' replied Duckwitz. 'You've got a few days. The Gestapo has already received its orders. The *razzia* is to take place during the night of 1st to 2nd October. That leaves you three days to get them out.'

H.C. Hansen got up and strolled up and down, deep in thought, before he asked the obvious question on everyone's mind: 'And where do you suggest we should move such large a number?'

'I've already established initial contacts with Stockholm. You will find the Swedes receptive to such a move. I will see if I can be of further help with . . .' he hesitated, '. . . in other ways.'

'You really do care, don't you?' Hedtoft asked Duckwitz.

'It is a sad fact of life that sometimes a man's beliefs must turn, especially when he begins to realise that he is no longer able to change certain things he is ordered to do.' Duckwitz was obviously a man torn by the inner conflict between an honour-bound duty to his *Vaterland* and the even deeper sense of duty towards humanity.

'Is there no hope for them?' asked Hansen.

'There always is. Only *you* must make it happen.'

'We'll do what we can and in every way we can.'

'Better be quick about it; you haven't got much time.'

Hans Hedtoft nodded. The men shook hands, before Duckwitz turned to his friend, Inspector Madsen, and asked him to drive him to C.B. Henriques, the country's advocate of the Supreme Court, who also happened to be the leader of Denmark's Jewish community, in order to appraise him of the looming danger. As he left the room, he looked over his shoulder.

'*Viel Glück* – Good luck,' he said and Hedtoft had the uncanny feeling that they would need a generous portion of it before this thing was over. The men in the room watched Madsen and Duckwitz leaving the house.

'*Kan vi stole paa Tyskeren* – Can we trust the German?' asked Hansen.

Hedtoft glanced at him. 'We don't have a choice, do we?' Such a vast undertaking under the noses of their country's occupier, who had his informers everywhere, would be both difficult and dangerous.

Frants Hvass reacted first. 'So, when do we start?'

'We've already done so, ten minutes ago,' replied Hedtoft.

The same evening, Duckwitz wrote into his secret diary: *Die Vorbereitung für die Judenaktion werden eilfertig getroffen* – The preparations for the Jewish action are rapidly under way. Experts for this unclean undertaking have arrived. I hope they will not find many victims.'

For one week he had worked without let-up, one week of taking risks, and all he ended up with was frustration. He could do no more; now the matter was in the hands of the Danes.

On 9 April 1940, Denmark was overrun by German battalions, despite a non-aggression pact signed between the two countries six months before. The Danes had hardly an army: 3300 soldiers, plus 8000 recruits, defending half a dozen makeshift roadblocks on the main artery leading from northern Germany into Jutland, and one civilian *fort mester* with two soldiers and a few recruits who had never been instructed in the use of the main armament. They manned Masned Oe, a fortress near Vordingborg, to guard the metal span of Europe's longest road and railway bridge across the Storstrømmen between the islands of Falster and Sjaelland (Zealand). The fortress was captured by a German parachute elite, dropping from the sky on half a dozen luckless recruits, in what is best described as using a steam hammer as a fly swat.

The bridge over the Storstrømmen was important for the occupation of Zealand. The Danish government gave in because of the German troops, who landed on Langelinie in the port of Copenhagen, and the Germans' threat of an aerial bombardment of the nation's capital. The main reason for the invasion of Denmark was a strategic one, to get access for the planned invasion of Norway via Jutland and protect the flank of the advancing Germans. Once that was accomplished, the Danes all went back to a normal activity, if one may call the forced occupation of one's homeland as normal. The only noticeable German military activity was on coastal airfields along the North Sea shore;

from concrete strips at Esbjerg and Aalborg, the Luftwaffe launched its bombing raids on Birmingham and Coventry.

Ninety-eight per cent of Danes were (and still are) Lutherans. The rest were Roman Catholics. And eight thousand Jews. In the beginning, the Nazi bosses tried to win over the tall blond Norsemen to their side as prime examples of the Aryan super-race, but also because Hitler couldn't afford to leave frontline troops on occupation duty. Therefore he offered the Danes a conqueror's deal of 'passive cooperation', leaving King Christian X of Denmark and the *Danske Rigsdag* (parliament) in nominal control over the country. The king, the only European royalty to remain behind with his people in a country overrun by Hitler's war machine, was the paragon of defiance; he played a vital role in boosting the country's morale by riding every day through the streets of his capital, never acknowledging the salute by German officers and soldiers.

When a German officer once asked a small boy: 'If that's the king, where is his bodyguard?', the child replied: 'We are all his bodyguard.' The Danes didn't like the Germans, but had no choice in the matter; with wooden-soled shoes and riding on ancient bicycles, they went on with their everyday business, which was principally surviving the occupation. The country possessed tremendous food resources – wheat, milk, butter, and was famous for its Danish bacon. They had little to fear from British bombing raids, as there was no heavy industry the Germans could use to further their war effort. Those Danes who imagined that this status quo would carry on for ever, were rudely awakened on 29 August 1943. That day, German panzers rolled into Copenhagen and the passive honeymoon was shattered when Hitler ordered the dissolution of the *Danske Rigsdag*, and then made it clear that every order by his *Reichsbevollmächtigten* was to be followed as if given by the Führer himself.

This led to a crisis, after the king refused an ultimatum by Hitler's representative, Dr Best, and German army units blockaded the royal palace, making His Danish Majesty their virtual prisoner. Before the German Navy could get hold of the Danish naval ships, their officers had scuttled their patrol boats, anchored in Copenhagen's harbour. The Danish Army was dissolved and its officers given the choice to enter the ranks of the Viking SS Regiment, which none did; so they were interned, and any gathering by more than three persons outlawed. This harsh edict went against the Germans; whatever chance the Germans might have ever had to win the hearts of the Danes, once they touched on the sacrosanct figure of their king, it was gone. A strike brought the country to a standstill, and Dr Best had to ease off. But the mood was no longer the same, it was now one of open hostility, and this was to play a major role in the next storm the country was to weather.

This still left the Nazis with 'the problem of the Danish Jews'. Europe had seen ample proof of what that amounted to. The Nazis didn't even try to hide their ruthless *Ausrottungspolitik* (extermination policy). In carrying out his task as the supreme overseer of the 'Final Solution', SS boss Heinrich Himmler showed himself as the fanatical disciple of a race theory and with an unswerving dedication to its translation into stark reality. This he showed in his address to members of the SS in the Polish town of Poznan (4 October 1943):

Unser Leitmotiv für den SS Mann – Our leading principle for the SS man: we must be honest, decent, loyal, and comradely to members of our own blood and to no one else . . . whether other peoples live in comfort or perish from hunger interests me only in so far as we need them for slaves for our *Kultur* . . . I shall speak to you here, with all frankness, of a very grave matter; I mean the evacuation of the Jews, the extermination of the Jewish people. Many of you know what it means to see a hundred corpses lying together, five hundred, or a thousand. To have stuck it out and at the same time – apart from exceptions caused by human weakness – to have remained decent fellows, that is what has made us hard.[3]

Fortunately, not all Germans were like *Reichsführer* Himmler. There were those who dared to act against the rabid party leaders and their Final Solution programme. One of them was posted in Denmark.

Georg Ferdinand Duckwitz was born on 29 September 1904 in Bremen; his great-grandfather Arnold had founded the family business in 1828, and became lord mayor of the Free Hanseatic Town of Bremen. After studying law, young Georg Ferdinand established himself in Copenhagen to look after the Scandinavian interests of the family's export business. His outgoing nature won him a great number of friends in Danish mercantile and political circles; one was a certain Hans Hedtoft, destined to become Denmark's leader.

In 1933, Duckwitz found himself caught up by the rhetoric of the German dictator and out of conviction joined the NSDAP (National-Socialist German Workers Party). The man who had willingly attached himself to a party's slogans soon discovered the true face of Nazism. And still he remained a member of the Nazi party, since, as a '*Parteigenosse*' (party comrade), he held an entry ticket into the inner circle of power; little did he realise that his decision to stay in the *Partei* would one day be essential to come to the assistance of the Danish Jews. In the opening stages of the Second World War, his position as shipping expert for the Hamburg-America Shipping Line, setting up links between Germany and neutral Sweden, exempted

[3] Wistrich, R., *Who's Who in Nazi Germany*, London, 1995.

him from military service. When German troops invaded Denmark, he was attached to the *Deutsche Auswärtige Amt* (German foreign office) and more specifically to the German *Reichsbevollmächtigten für Dänemark* (the Reich's plenipotentiary in overall charge of Denmark's occupation) in Copenhagen, and Dr Karl Rudolf Werner Best, a super-nationalist and founder-member of the ultra-rightwing *Deutsch-Völkischer Schutz und Trutzbund* (German National Defence Union), which Hitler incorporated into his own party.

Dr Best became a member of the NSDAP in 1930 and joined its enforcing arm, the SS (for *Schutz Staffel*), in 1931. He spent his time in ceaseless political manoeuvres and defeated in turn every rival. He rose rapidly to *SS Obergruppenführer* (Lt-General). On 27 October 1942, Hitler appointed Dr Best as Germany's *Reichsbevollmächtigter für Dänemark*, an ambassadorial title that was a thin veil to hide his dictatorial function. For an overlord of an occupied country, Dr Best had managed relatively well and was counting on continuing thus. As it had for many others, the fall of Stalingrad (January 1943) had severely shaken his confidence; he began worrying that Hitler might lose the war after all and he began making plans which would ensure his survival against such an eventuality. Up until the summer of 1943, he enjoyed a relatively smooth ride, since the Nazi leadership was still exploring means to incorporate the Danes into the *Grossdeutsche Reich*, as they had successfully done with the Austrians and the Sudetens.

In 1943, things went badly awry with Hitler's march to victory. With setbacks in Stalingrad, and British and American troops liberated from action in North Africa, Germany began worrying that the Allies might soon open a second front. The most likely place, the one closest to Germany's heartland, was along the west coast of Jutland. This threat panicked the German leadership into a series of actions; first of all, it ordered that all available occupation forces should be concentrated along the Danish western coastline. A series of sabotage actions by Danish resistance groups, and the execution of a resistance fighter, was followed by massive strikes in factories and on agricultural estates. Afraid that this rebellious outbreak would come to the support of an Allied landing, the Führer ordered Best to clean house in Denmark. At this time Best also received a confidential call from an undersecretary at the German Foreign Office in Berlin, Dr Franz von Sonnleitner, informing him that an order for the deportation of Danish Jews was being drawn up. Whether the Jewish action in Denmark was on Best's direct initiative could never be fully established.

The fact is, that prior to his post in Copenhagen, *SS Obergruppenführer* Best was leading the notorious *SS Einsatzgruppen* in Poland. 'We must clamp down on inferior people,' he said to justify his actions. Best later on claimed that he could foresee major problems on the subject of Danish Jews, and therefore launched himself into an attempt to force the issue by dispatching a telegram to Berlin to settle the Jewish question in 'a reasonable manner'.[4] At his trial after the war, he said that his scheme hinged on the lack of German police effectives in Denmark, and the role the *Deutsche Wehrmacht* was supposed to be playing in the round-up. Best's telegram became the key to the planned pogrom in Denmark:

NR. 1032 VOM 8.9.1943[5]

... *MUSS NACH MEINER AUFFASSUNG NUNMEHR AUCH EINE LÖSUNG DER JUDENFRAGE IN DÄNEMARK INS AUGE GEFASST*

---

[4] The ambiguous role Dr Best played in this affair was never cleared up. Erich Thomson, in his work, *Deutsche Besatzungspolitik in Dänemark* defends Best, while Prof. Leni Yahil in her *The Rescue of Danish Jews* condemns Best's concept and motivation.
[5] German archives AAO Bd R 29567.

WERDEN.[6] – It is my opinion that we must now envisage a solution to the Jewish question as long as the state of emergency exists, for afterwards it will lead to a reaction in the country . . . The Danish government will resign and king and parliament will no longer cooperate . . . To arrest 6000 to 8000 Jews (including women and children) would require a substantial additional complement of German police, as stressed in my telegram of 1.9.1943. Furthermore, the army commander, German Forces Denmark, must put more units of the Wehrmacht at our disposal. For the transport of such a vast amount of Jews it will be necessary to provide a number of ships . . .

Having sent the cable, Best called belatedly for advice from Duckwitz. The two men faced each other across the table in the office on the first floor of a building which Dr Best's predecessor had requisitioned on his arrival in Copenhagen. Both wore civilian clothes instead of the regulation SS uniform. Best's attitude was arrogant, verging on contempt. Duckwitz was outwardly respectful, careful to give his chief no opening for a long lecture on the merits of German occupation. Best studied closely the man across the table. Capable? Of course, extremely so. Loyal to the *Partei*? That was another question. There was no love lost between the two men who were supposed to be working in harmony in a mounting crisis.

'Duckwitz, Berlin will want us to act on the Jews. I've cabled them that before this we will need more effectives for the operation. What do you think their answer will

---

[6] In the orginal text: . . . MUSS NACH MEINER AUFFASSUNG NUNMEHR AUCH EINE LÖSUNG DER JUDENGRAGE IN DÄNEMARK INS AUGE GEFASST WERDEN. DIE HIERFÜR ERFORDERLICHEN MASSNAHMEN MÜSSEN NOCH WÄHREND DES GEGENWÄRTIGTEN AUSNAHMENZUSTAND GETROFFEN WERDEN . . . INSBESONDERS WÜRDE EINE ETWA BESTEHENDE VERFASSUNGSMÄSSIGE REGIE-RUNG ZURÜCKJTRETEN EBENSO WÜRDE DER KÖNIG UND DER FOLK-ETING (PARLIAMENT) IHRE WEITERE MIRTWIRKUNG EINSTELLEN . . .

be?' If Best expected an instant reply, he was disappointed. He was fidgety when he barked: 'I asked you a question, *Parteigenosse*.' The last word put as an afterthought.

'I was considering the implications to arrive at a correct response. The Jews? A sticky matter. You know the Danes . . .'

'You question my decision, and that of Berlin?' Best enquired softly.

'I simply recall the facts. What could possibly be gained by such an act?'

'It's party policy. To serve as a deterrent.' Dr Best briefly outlined the situation, how he was trying to stall a round-up of Jews because of the present explosive situation in the country, by requesting troop reinforcements, which he knew wouldn't be forthcoming,[7] and then showed Duckwitz his telegram to Berlin.

Duckwitz took one look at the text, before he gave his assessment. 'Herr Dr Best, Berlin will never interpret your message in the manner you've intended it. It will not divert their attention, but, on the contrary, it will concentrate them on the issue. That telegram must be stopped before it reaches Ribbentrop,[8] or worse, the Führer himself.'

Best's face turned pale. That man might have a point. Fortunately he had had enough sense not to seek out the help of the Gestapo, who would have jumped on his proposal and reported it to Berlin. 'What's your suggestion?' This time he didn't even try to hide his alarm.

'I've an acquaintance at the Foreign Ministry, I could go and see him.'

---

[7] By the summer of 1943, Germany was afraid of an Allied invasion in Jutland and had massed all its available troops to hold the beaches.
[8] Joachim von Ribbentrop was Hitler's German Foreign Minister.

'Do that, and stop the telegram from going any further.'

Duckwitz flew to Berlin where he met with Foreign Undersecretary Hencke who told him that the telegram had not only passed the foreign minister's desk, but was now on its way to the Führer in his East Prussian HQ. When the telegram reached Hitler, he only glanced at it and decided the future of Denmark's Jews with one brief sentence: '*Die dänischen Juden sind auszurotten* – The Danish Jews are to be destroyed.'

Dr Best received Hitler's order on 18 September 1943:[9]

BÜRO REICHSAUSSENMINISTER. DER FUHRER HAT ANGEORD-NET, DASS DER ABTRANSPORT DER JUDEN AUS DÄNEMARK DURCHGEFÜHRT WERDEN SOLL – The Führer has ordered that the deportation of the Jews from Denmark is to be executed . . .

When someone in Germany received a *Führerorder*, he had no choice but to obey. Once again Best called on his shipping expert for counsel. Best was sitting behind his desk, his head cradled in his hands.

'Just look at this. *Verrückt!*' he pushed the decoded telegram across the desk. 'Don't they know our position in Denmark? Such an act can only hurt our Reich.'

Duckwitz took a look at the *Führerorder* and blanched; he knew that the fate of the Danish Jews was sealed. For him, nothing could match the mindless sickening blood-lust of those who massacred the innocents in the name of creating a superior race, or the beastliness of the man who ordered it.

'Herr Dr Best,' Duckwitz, the civilian, refused to call him by his rank of *SS Obergruppenführer*, 'why don't you give it another try?'

'And go against the *Führerorder*? You must be mad.'

[9] German archives, AAO Bd R 100864.

However, for once Best listened to Duckwitz and he did dispatch another note, expressing his latest concerns.[10]

NR. *1094 VOM 18.9.1943*
...POLITISCH WIRD DER ABTRANSPORT DER JUDEN ZWEI-
FEL LOS DIE LAGE IN DÄNEMARK AUSSERORDENTLICH VER-
SCHÄRFEN – Politically, the deportation of Jews will make without doubt the situation very explosive. We can no longer count on a co-operation from the local government and must expect countrywide unrest and a general strike.

Hitler remained unmoved. Best was told that the *Führerorder* stood.

Best knew that Duckwitz was someone who knew 'everyone in Denmark' from his days before the war:

'*Ich wünschte ich könnte eine Brücke über den Sund schlagen* – I wish I could lay a bridge across the Sund . . .' (the Øresund, the straits between Denmark and Sweden).

Was Best trying to pass on a message? In any case, Duckwitz had already decided to undertake a personal, hugely perilous mission. He was a thorough and conscientious man; everything he undertook was carefully thought out before he acted on it. But for this there was no time. He had to take a gamble to stop a heinous crime, since he knew from experience what the SS squads were capable of in their blind pursuit of anti-Semitic prejudice. In 1938, he had seen from pictures how roughneck brownshirts employed their rowdy anti-Semitic tactics, smashing window panes and burning books, and afterwards he watched in disbelief as the wave of brutalities spread across Germany, until it became a party's terminal philosophy. That day, the madness that he had sensed growing, fanned by a minority of fanatical leaders, had finally surfaced. If their lower-level operatives of terror were coarse and violent brutes, at the

[10] German archives, AAO Bd R 29567.

top they were perverse criminals discrediting his *Vaterland*. The systematic genocide had been in full swing since the middle of 1941; over three million Jews had already been massacred. He simply could no longer remain inactive in the spreading shadow of their villainous deeds, which was putting a permanent stain on Germany. He was a firm believer that 'loyalty to the fatherland must never be confounded with loyalty to a man'. On 19 September Duckwitz wrote the fateful line in his secret diary: '*Ich weiss, was ich zu tun habe* – I know what I must do.' With a single phrase, Duckwitz set off on 'his mission'.

His latest movements had begun to draw the attention of the Gestapo. On 22 September 1943, Duckwitz contacted the Swedish *chargé d'affaires* to Denmark, Nils Erik Ekblad. He briefed the Swede on the urgency of the situation and Ekblad offered to fly with him to Stockholm. Their excuse for the trip: to discuss passage for German merchant ships, since Sweden had stopped all international traffic along its west coast and no foreign vessels were permitted to cross into the three-mile (4.8 km) limit of the Falsterbø channel. Winter storms, snow and frozen harbours made travel other than by small craft virtually impossible, and the Germans had installed a double line of checks along the centreline of the Øresund, after they discovered that downed RAF pilots were using the route to make good their escape. The wealthy Danish Baroness Monica Wichfeldt was hiding a number of British aircrews on her estates, before she had them brought to Sweden on her yacht. A Nazi sympathiser denounced the courageous baroness; she was arrested, sentenced to death, and executed in a German prison.

Before he set off for Stockholm, Duckwitz contacted his Swedish shipping counterpart, Dr Riensberg, to set up an urgent meeting with Sweden's Minister of State, Per Albin Hansson. During this interview, Duckwitz came straight to the point.

'*Statsminister* Hansson, Hitler has ordered the arrest of all Jews in Denmark. You must come to their help.' If Hansson was shocked by the news, he hid it well. In fact, he had always expected something of the sort and had discussed the possibility of providing aid with his ministerial colleagues, but they had failed to come to a consensus.

'I don't really see how we can help,' he stalled with Swedish politeness. 'This is an entirely German affair.' Though Sweden had already accepted a number of refugees from neighbouring occupied Norway, officially it was adhering to its policy of strict neutrality. Duckwitz tried hard, yet Hansson remained non-committal about coming to the help of 'fellow Scandinavians'. It was quite possible, according to a standing international agreement, that Sweden would return the Jews to German-occupied territory.

'Open your doors to Jewish refugees,' Duckwitz begged. 'How they make it across the Sund will be their problem.'

Hansson was well aware of the increasing problems Germany was facing in the conduct of the war. They were not yet losing, but they were certainly no longer winning. He had already decided to exert pressure on his colleagues of the *Landshoevding* (Swedish parliament) to get his country to assist in the Danish exodus; it was a matter of national pride and Sweden was not prepared to take second place when it came to saving human lives.

'I'll see what can be done,' he promised. He knew that it wouldn't be easy. For his initial step, the *Statsminister* ordered to rid his country of doubtful elements; it was widely known that one of the customs officials at Trelleborg harbour opposite Denmark was a Nazi sympathiser. With a phone call, Hansson had the man transferred to northern Sweden where he could do no harm, before he called his ministerial colleagues. While the consultation was in progress, the danger of openly confronting Hitler was discussed, and the wire hummed between Stockholm and the Swedish embassy in Berlin. Duckwitz waited anxiously in his hotel for a reply. He was quickly running out of time. He spent a restless night, unaware that the issue had already been settled; a reply had been received from Berlin, where an official of the German Foreign Ministry had curtly informed the Swedish ambassador 'never to interfere in *innerdeutsche* (internal German) affairs.'

In diplomatic language, this reply was heavy-handed. Calling Denmark *innerdeutsch* was the key to the Swedish decision, because where would Hitler's *innerdeutsch* zone extend to next? Stockholm? Hansson met Duckwitz a final time and promised his government's favourable reception of anyone seeking asylum, who reached Swedish territory. The *Statsminister* was careful never to specify *who* such asylum seekers should be, or that Sweden's offer was principally intended to facilitate a massive exodus of Jews from Denmark.

Duckwitz flew back to Copenhagen and asked for an appointment with the *aide-de-camp* of General von Hanneken, supremo of the *Wehrmacht* in the Danish sector. A civilian aide to the general, Paul Ernst Kanstein, received Duckwitz. As one civil servant facing another, Duckwitz took a calculated risk when he put his cards on the table. 'How will our *Wehrmacht* react to the *Führerorder* regarding the Jews?'

'The troops will obey their commanding general, and Hanneken will not go against Hitler.' Kanstein could have betrayed Duckwitz to the Gestapo, but he was a decent man and did nothing of the kind.[11]

---

[11] It has never been established if Kanstein actually spoke to General von Hanneken and whether his intervention helped to keep German troops in their quarters during the crucial hours.

When they shook hands, Kanstein said: 'I must warn you, do not try to cross Hitler.' Duckwitz grasped the meaning of the warning but still he refused to give in. With matters coming down to the wire, Dr Best ordered him to ready the 14,000-ton *Monte Rosa*, anchored at Aarhus on Jutland, to sail to Copenhagen in preparation for ferrying the Jews to Germany. Luck was on his side; the man in charge of the civilian navigation in Jutland was his old friend, Friedrich Wilhelm Lübke. Duckwitz went to Aarhus to meet with Lübke, who introduced him to the captain of the *Monte Rosa*, Heinrich Bertram, a merchant sailor who didn't hide his feelings for the leaders of the Third Reich. After this meeting, the engine shaft of the *Monte Rosa* was stripped down for urgent repairs and the ship was laid up for several weeks. If Duckwitz had hoped this would buy him more time to plan, he didn't count on Admiral Wurmach's sailing order for two smaller vessels, the *Wartheland* and the *Friedland*, to make from the port of Stettin for Copenhagen.

On 26 September, Bishop Fuglsang-Damgaard of Copenhagen went to see Dr Best, to enquire about the destiny of the Jews. Best answered him with a blatant lie: '*Die Frage ist überhaupt nicht angeschnitten* – That question hasn't even been brought up.'

Each night, Denmark was glued to their radios, tuned in on *Radio Deutschland* (not many) or the BBC (the majority) to listen to the latest news from the war. Neither of the two services told their listeners the truth; both pumped out the kind of propaganda that suited their own war effort. With the BBC at least, there was hope; with *Radio Deutschland* there was none. The fate of the Danish Jews was never mentioned. Not by the Germans because it didn't suit their policy, and not by the British because they didn't know. Only a few in the close circle around Best and the Gestapo did. And those in the German Army and Navy who had been privately informed by Duckwitz, which by now were quite a few. How was it then possible that the efficient Gestapo spy apparatus failed to discover the desperate moves undertaken by Duckwitz?

SS Obersturmbannführer Dr Rudolf Mildner, the head of the German *Sicherheitspolizei*, formerly the Gestapo chieftain in Katowice and political commissar of Auschwitz, stormed into Best's office: '*Herr Reichsbevollmächtigter, ich habe soeben erfahren, dass unser Plan verraten wurde* – I've just learned that our plan has been betrayed.'

Best could only hope that was a Gestapo man's shot in the dark. 'Who is it?'

'We haven't been able as yet to find out who it is. But we must advance the date.'

'We cannot,' replied Dr Best firmly, 'I haven't received the necessary military reserves to assure full success of the operation. The date of 1 October must stand.' Best's reason was more banal; he had engaged in trade negotiations with Danish producers to get food supplies for an increasingly starving Germany. It seemed a logical decision and *Obersturmbannführer* Mildner reluctantly nodded his acceptance to the decision by his superior.

'Just let us make certain, *Herr Reichsbevollmächtigter*, that all prisoners taken are to be delivered into the hands of the Gestapo. We will interrogate them to uncover the conspiracy.' He didn't say what conspiracy he had on his mind, but it was clear that the unfortunate Jews would have to endure brutal treatment and torture by their captors before being shipped off to German concentration camps.

Two days later, Dr Best mentioned the conversation with Mildner to Duckwitz; now the issue had reached panic status. He was sailing on a sea of danger and all on his own; before him lay a sheer unsolvable problem, at the back hovered the dreaded Gestapo, and all the while the clock was ticking away. In the days leading up to the climax, he had become paranoid and with good reason; he had the uncanny feeling that Gestapo agents followed his every step. His nerves began to play tricks on him. But they underestimated his resourcefulness. In these harsh times, Duckwitz wasn't the only one who had lived by his wits, who had got himself out of tight spots by acting nimbly. That night he stood in front of the mirror and stared at a drawn face looking back at him, before he recognised it as his own. Only his exhaustion stopped him from bolting from the room to get away from this image and what this war had done to him. He wanted to go out into the streets and call out his frustration, telling them to leave, and right away.

But, of course, he couldn't do that. He had no idea how much the dreaded Gestapo suspected, or if he was already on their death list. For him that must change nothing; to ensure the survival of many thousands, he had to act and buy as much time as possible. He sent a secret dispatch via the Swede Ekblad to *Statsminister* Hansson in Stockholm, advising him to expect a great influx of Danish Jews within the next few days or weeks. Pushed to the wire, Duckwitz had reached a decision that was to change history. He picked up his telephone and dialled . . .

The fateful meeting between a converted former Nazi and the four Social Democrats, who he suspected were in direct contact with the heads of the resistance movement, the Freedom Council,[12] would take place in the house in Copenhagen's Rømergade on the evening of 28 September 1943. Duckwitz knew that he could trust Hedtoft, but what about the others? Georg Ferdinand Duckwitz had crossed his own Rubicon; he was on the way to the most important rendezvous of his life. He hadn't taken his official car. From

---

[12] And even they were not in complete control of all anti-German activities.

his house '*Friboes Hvile*' (Friboes' Repose) in Lyngby, a quiet residential area of Copenhagen, he took a local bus to the populated downtown section, where it would be easier to lose a trail. At Kongens Nytorv, Copenhagen's busiest intersection, he waited until most of the passengers had debarked, before he jumped off the bus. He turned the corner and submerged in a crowded pavement. Only then did he slow up, trying to catch his breath and gather his wits. He knew that, if caught, he would be made to confess, before they liquidated him with all the others he had confided in. There were many lives at stake, both high-ranking Germans and Danes. Plus 8000 Jews.

Inspector Christian Madsen had provided a safe house, closely watched by his men. It was there that Duckwitz met up with Hans Hedtoft and H.C. Hansen, Denmark's leading politicians. They showed respect for Duckwitz; however, being a 'good Nazi' made him no less of a German.

'This conversation is just between the two of us, I give you my word.' Duckwitz knew that he had to overcome their suspicion. 'Denmark will soon be going through changes,' he began carefully.

'Life is about to change for some of your compatriots.' Hedtoft looked at him quizzically.

'*Get your Jews out of the country*,' Duckwitz said imploringly, knowing that he was actually handing the Dane a grenade with its pin pulled. But he had to be direct and forthright, there was no time for finesse. 'Hitler's orders, his rage will be released against them, and only you can prevent it.' Now that it was out, he felt much better. He could only warn the Danes, but not stop his own Nazi henchmen.

'What about you?' asked Hedtoft.

'Hans, I am still a German, and a responsible one. I will do what I believe in and what must be done.' He had taken the only course of action open to him in order to prevent an injustice to fellow human beings. To do this, he had engaged in a venture with unforeseeable results and hoped that, in a small way, his intervention would help avoid discrimination, or even worse.

Hedtoft had met Duckwitz before the war; he knew that the German was sincere when he told them about the danger; across Denmark, *der Jude* was to be smashed, his economic existence ruined and his family deported, perhaps exterminated. For a carefully reviewed plan of action it was too late. They had to make do with what was available for an immediate action, and hardly a day in which to react.

'We're stretched to the limit,' said Hansen.

'We'll manage something,' replied Hedtoft. Even before he said it, he realised that for it to succeed, they had to count on every hidden source available to them, the resistance movement, the Church, and, most of all, their fellow Danes. They had to move fast before the dreaded Gestapo did their job. The men separated; each was to pick a separate sector of town to take appropriate action.

Hedtoft said in leaving: 'If we're caught . . .' he cut off in mid-sentence. '*Kom så* . . . come on, let's get moving, we haven't got much time . . .'

Their eyes were fixed on the dark streets outside. It promised to be a busy night. The four made a number of stops around town. Their message to leaders of the Freedom Council and the student movement was clear: 'Get to the Jews and tell them to leave immediately for Sweden.' They didn't dare tell them more, or where the information had originated. It is an amazing fact, and perhaps unique in the annals of any resistance movement in the Second World War, that there was no leak, and that their scheme was never betrayed to the dreaded Gestapo. Rapid action was called for. Fortunately, most Jews were concentrated in and around Copenhagen, where 1673 families lived quite openly; only thirty-three families were known to live outside the capital city, dispersed over the many Danish isles. Added to that number were another 1208 Jewish families, who had fled Germany after Hitler came to power, and had settled in Denmark. The Gestapo didn't always know their place of residence since the escapees from Nazi Germany had made every effort to assimilate and melt into the local environment in fear of discovery.

But, who was capable of organising the escape of close to 8000 men, women, and children? Until the days of August 1943, the Danish government had strictly adhered to its 'cooperative policy' in exchange for running its own country, as was promised by Hitler on 9 April 1940. That didn't stop the Danes finding means of opposing the occupier. Resistance movements made their presence felt, organisations such as *Holger Danske*, Bopa,[13] *Dansk-Svensk Flygtningetjenste* (escape help) or the *Studenternes Efterretnigsstjeneste* (students' intelligence network). The clandestine organisations were mainly used for smuggling downed British pilots to Sweden. They had worked out a viable system that cleverly circumvented German maritime patrols. But all their missions had been relatively minor operations, involving two or three British airmen at a time. What they were now asked to do was simply massive: to ferry 8000 people to safety!

Suddenly all of the country was on the move; valuable assistance came from many unexpected sources: Danish civil servants, who had always adhered to their government's passive cooperation policy; railway conductors, customs

[13] *Holger Danske*, named for Denmark's hero, was a nationalist group started by Tom Søndergaard, a veteran of the Finnish-Russian war. *Bopa* was founded by former members of the International Brigade from the Spanish Civil War. *The Student Network* was first begun by Arne Seir, a 17-year-old schoolboy; later it included many intellectuals and writers. All groups were active in sabotage actions, intelligence gathering, and printing illegal pamphlets.

officers and Copenhagen police, which, for once, didn't
spend their time arresting drunks, but instead knocked on
doors to warn the imperilled Jewish population which they
located from their register. Even notorious rum-runners,
making a living running high-speed boats with cigarettes
and booze from Sweden, got in on the act. Much of it was
due to the fact that, in August, Hitler had dared to touch
on the sacred person of their king, Christian X. When
other royalties ran away, the Danish monarch and his
family stayed behind, and the people of Denmark simply
worshipped him for this.

While the Danish resistance raced around on bicycles to
inform the Jewish population, Duckwitz continued to take
great chances with regard to his own safety.[14] He invited
the German harbour commander of the Copenhagen sector, *Korvettenkapitän* (Commander) Cammann, to a private dinner. This was another former colleague of Duckwitz,
working during the inter-war years for the same Hamburg-
America Line as Duckwitz. An officer in the old Imperial
German Navy and, like many, raised in pure Navy tradition
who refused to give the Nazi salute, Cammann was now
the officer in charge of the sleek, grey crafts the Germans
called *Schnellboote*, because of their powerful engines and
high speed, designed to dash up to an enemy convoy or
warship, deliver their torpedoes before making off at great
speed. But they could also be used to prevent small crafts,
such as vessels carrying downed RAF pilots, from reaching
Swedish waters. With their reinforced steel bows they

[14] Not all Danes seem to agree on that today. The assistant director of
Denmark's Freedom Museum, Henrik Lunbak, wrote to the author:
'I think that most people would agree that Best was more or less
aware of what Duckwitz was doing. That does not make the initiative
taken by Duckwitz less praiseworthy from a moral point of view,
but I doubt whether it involved any great risks in regard to his
personal safety.'

could knife through a wooden boat and send it to the bottom. Just the psychological effect of seeing them lying in Copenhagen's harbour was sufficient deterrent to discourage many trawler captains from trying for the impossible. In the opening stage of their conversation, Cammann proved reluctant. '*Mein lieber Georg*, war is a sorry madness, and death is a constant part of it. Of course, there will always be killing in war, with two diametrically opposed causes in which each side believes. If you believe what you do is right, then your action is as guiltless as that of a soldier fighting a war, which he believes he does in a just cause. But you have engaged on a crusade without hope.'

'I do not condemn a soldier because he has killed in battle. But killing Jews isn't war. It is just killing.' Duckwitz eventually managed to win *Korvettenkapitän* Cammann over to his side. On the night of the Great Escape, the *Schnellboot* squadrons were laid up in docks, many with their engines stripped for overhaul.[15] Duckwitz's personal intervention had removed another danger. And if he had considered the outcome of his talks with the *aide-de-camp* of General von Hannecken as being negative, one thing was certain: the troops of the *Wehrmacht* did not search buses and trains that were carrying hundreds of Jewish families, sitting terrified on their suitcases in overcrowded compartments. However, most refugees were taken to departure points by all kinds of motor vehicles, on bikes or they walked. It can hardly be imagined that the *Wehrmacht* coast-watchers should have overlooked this hectic activity going on before their very eyes. Yet, whenever a coast-watcher dutifully called in with 'heavy

---

[15] After the war, a Jewish researcher contacted the Foreign Ministry in Bonn for proof of connivance by German Navy officers in the mysterious *Schnellboote* repair affair, but all orders had come verbally and no documents proving otherwise were left behind. The same goes also for the German Army's inaction on Danish trains.

activity on the Øresund', their officers did not follow up on the report; except for some isolated occasions, the Army did nothing to interfere with the exodus. A good portion of the *Wehrmacht*'s officer caste never hid their abhorrence over the inhuman treatment and mass executions of Jews by *SS Sicherheitskommandos* in Poland and the Ukraine. However, this never stopped other troops of the same *Wehrmacht* from participating in atrocities in Eastern Europe

Until 29 August 1943, the day of the change in venue by the Nazis, the Gestapo in Denmark was only acting in an 'advisory capacity', theoretically without jurisdiction. They could not take possession of evidence, arrest, or take custody of prisoners in the Danish zone of co-operation, which had been agreed on by Hitler in 1940 – unless such prisoners were turned over willingly by the Danes which, of course, they never were. So the Gestapo masqueraded as Danes to perform their dirty work. Their most prominent victim was Kaj Munk, a priest and famous author. He was found lying in a puddle of blood in a growth of pine saplings next to a country road near the village of Paaruphede (3 January 1944). In an effort to pin the murder on the Danish resistance, they left a scribbled note on his jacket: '*Du Svin har alligvell arbejdet for Tyskland* – You pig has always worked for Germany.' The giveaway was in the writing, partly in Gothic letters, which no Dane had ever learned in school! The Danish police arrived on the scene, and discovered almost immediately the identity of the killer gang, but then was ordered to call Munk 'an apparent victim of a shooting by parties unknown'.[16]

---

[16] The four identified as killers were: the leader of the gang, SS-man Otto Schwerdt (going under the covername of Peter Schäffer), Heinrich Söhnlein, Louis Nebel (a Swiss and former member of an American gangster group) and the SS-man Kurt Carstensen. A fifth member of the group was killed in Russia.

In the priest Kaj Munk, Denmark found its martyr figure. But in the case of the 'Jewish solution', the Gestapo and their Quisling informers had slipped up, and remained ignorant that their plan had been crossed – from the inside! By his example, Duckwitz had proved that it was possible to combine inherited cultural and national values and, at the same time, prevent the implementation of barbaric extermination. With his brave conduct he had helped to avert a great tragedy of which there were countless examples all over a Europe suffering under the Nazi boot. Now it was up to the Danes, and they responded as one nation to help those in peril. Human democracy stood its test. For that, the free world would remember them.

The first warning reached a great number of Copenhagen's Jewish community on the morning of 29 September. Copenhagen's Jewish congregation, still ignorant of the thunder about to be released on their heads, had gathered that morning in the synagogue in preparation for the yearly celebration of Rosh Hashana. Just before religious service Chief Rabbi Markus Melchior pulled the leaders of his community to one side: 'Tell everyone you trust to get his families out of the apartment and hide out with his neighbour.' During service, his message was whispered from ear to ear. Within a few hours, Rabbi Melchior's message had reached most of the Jewish community of Copenhagen. The problem was how to get the message to their brothers in the countryside. The Danish Lutheran Church solved the problem: local priests, alerted by phone from their archdiocese, rushed around outlying villages on bicycles, warning Jews of their impending arrests. For a Dane there existed no distinction between Christians and Jews; all were Danes and all were brothers. Hiding them was one thing, but getting them away was yet another.

In the early hours of 2 October, it seemed as if Hitler's

Sicherheitspolizei was present in every corner of Copenhagen: uniformed German police on foot; Gestapo agents in black cars, racing along deserted streets of a blacked-out city. Wherever a German police officer appeared in the entrance of an apartment building housing a Jewish family, the Danes made every effort to divert the Germans' attention in order to give their co-citizen a chance to make good their escape down the back stairs. When agents found vacated apartments, the neighbours gave any excuse that seemed plausible: the child of the family next door had come down with the measles and was taken to hospital. Which hospital? Their neighbours didn't know. Housewives, glowing with feminine boldness, showed their utter contempt of the Germans. As long as there was no Gestapo capo alongside, the attitude of the young police constables was often one of admiration for the women's courage and they halted their search. For a fleeting moment a framed picture on the wall, the photograph of a happy couple on a Sunday outing held their attention, before they departed with a shrug of the shoulder.

All over the country, the tacit complicity to counter anything that smelled of Gestapo, spread. Priests and farmers were hiding Jews, in their homes, in their attics, their grain silos, and hay barns. Hospitals were suddenly filled to capacity. Through Copenhagen's Bispebjerg Hospital alone passed over 2000 Jews; received by Dr Richard Ege and his wife, they were hidden in quarantine wards, in nurses' quarters, even in the mortuary. Medical charts on the beds gave the patients' names as Møller, Hanssen or Jenssen. Bookshops were suddenly high in demand; one of the main dispatching centres was Copenhagen's Nordiske Bookshop, from where the *Holger Danske* resistance group took Jews to various places for embarkation.

However it did happen that some Jews couldn't be reached in time. Christine Thalvard was a Lutheran; but since she had been married to Rafi Seligmann – who had taken off with another woman years before – both she and the son that Rafi had sired, were considered Jewish. She was working as waitress in a café and renting a room from a 69-year-old widower. She was at work when the widower came by and told her to come home immediately. Over the years, he had come to think of Christine and her five-year-old son as his own family.

'You should have left Denmark long ago,' he said with tears in his eyes, embracing the woman and her boy, 'but now you really must go.' He stuffed a handful of banknotes into her pocket. 'Take it, it's all I have to offer.' As soon as they left the house, he buried his face in his hands and wept. Thirty minutes later came a knock on the door. It was the *Sicherheitspolizei*.

'You have a Jew woman living here. We must speak with her.'

'She is not here,' the old widower responded, surprised by his outward calm. The police didn't search too hard, almost as if relieved that they didn't have to take away a woman and her child. Twelve hours later, Christine and her little boy were on their way to Sweden.

Those who helped the Jews to make good their escape came from all walks of life. One was the editor of Denmark's largest daily, *Ekstrabladet*, Leif Hendil. Helped by a local policeman, who kept his eye out for German patrols, Hendil ran an efficient escape route from Snekkersten, north of Copenhagen, to Hven Island; a Swedish boat, the *Julius*, owned by Erik Marx, a Gøteborg Jew, picked up the escapees and brought them to Sweden. One getaway route was handled by another colourful character, Johannes Johannsen, by profession harbourmaster of Denmark's biggest beer brewery, Tuborg, at Hellerup. This jovial, potbellied Dane with the looks of a schoolmaster was one of the main organisers of the exodus. Ever since the

German invasion of 1940, this stout royalist had worked out an escape route, should it ever become necessary to save his king. Now he was given the opportunity to put his plan into operation.

When asked by the director of Tuborg, Henrik Kraft: 'Could you find a ship master who will take some people to Sweden, and no questions asked?' he nodded.

'Send your people over to me.'

From the first days of October 1943, Tuborg beer depots received an unusual influx of visitors; the adults were supplied with workers' coveralls and helped carrying cases of beer past German harbour guards on to ships. The children in kindergarten groups were led aboard 'to take a look at the ship's machinery'. Johannsen's ships transported beer from Hellerup to Jutland, and Jews from Jutland into Swedish waters. His Jewish beer route was involuntarily helped by a quarrel between two German harbour commanders over the question of authority. Johannsen exploited this to tell one German that the other had already inspected his ship. His beer ships, hailing from Grenaa and Saeby on Jutland, made a detour to dump the Jews off on the sand spit at Hven, straddling the Øresund's territorial mid-waterline between Hoersholm (Denmark) and Landskrona (Sweden).

Soon Hven took on the look of a seaside holiday camp. Many Jewish families reached safety courtesy of Harbourmaster Johannsen's Tuborg Route. Another ingenious way was the fireship supply boat, such as the *Gerda* out of Gedser headed for the Gedser *fyrskib*, a floating light tower marking the southern entrance into the Østersøen (Baltic). Not only bread and vegetables was loaded on board, as its skipper waved in passing to the German patrol vessel lying outside the harbour, but a load of Jews, lying flat on their stomachs under oily tarpaulins. The shortest way from Denmark to Sweden was from Elsinør (with Kronborg

Castle of Hamlet fame) to Helsingborg; other embarkation points were from Lund, Dragør, Gilleleje, Bøgeskov or Mosede on Zealand, or from the Isles of Samsø, Møn and Falster with destination Limhamn, Ystad, Malmø or Trelleborg.

Fishermen played a crucial role. Some were paid, many were not. This wasn't a taxi business, this was a highly dangerous humanitarian effort to save lives, and the wealthy Jews paid for the diesel for their poorer brethren. A frequented route was from Copenhagen to Malmø via the offshore sand spit of Saltholm.[17] Waiting on a small pier outside Copenhagen was a group of six, two families with their children. The only thing that could distinguish them from other Danes was their ID cards – not Jensen or Paulsen, but Stern and Posner. All were Danes by birth. Lorenz Stern was a livestock exporter and David Posner owned a fashionable clothing shop in the city. With the Gestapo on their heels, the families fled to the Bispebjerg Hospital where they were hidden in the mortuary. Shortly before darkness, they were told to take the bus to Amager; a teenaged student met them at the bus stop. The student underground movement had done their job well; soon afterwards, a boat came floating towards shore precisely where they had been told it would. They received a shock when it turned out to be a rowboat, so small that they were sure they would never make the voyage across the treacherous current of the Øresund. Two men in all-weather parkas pulled up the boat.

'How many of you are there?'

'Six,' replied father Stern.

'Six? We were told four.' He shrugged his shoulders. 'Well, get in.' He waved them on, but then stopped them

[17] It was there, in 2001, that a giant bridge was opened between Denmark and Sweden.

when he saw the parcels they carried. 'Leave that,' he ordered.

Inevitably, refugees always carried on them what they thought indispensable, such as family photos and other useless mementos. It made sense; at stake were lives, not mementos. They would be eight in a boat that normally held two plus fishing tackle: Knud Rasmussen, Bengt Poulsen plus three Sterns and three Posners.

Bengt installed himself at a set of oars, while Knud pushed the boat from the shallow shore with the length of a pole. With water swilling dangerously close to the gunwale, the refugees perched like frightened sparrows on nets on the bottom of the tiny boat. In silence they left behind Denmark, their homes, their belongings and their memories. The fishermen pulled on the oars; their breathing came in ugly gasps, and quickly their effort had them covered in sweat.

Young Julius Posner, who had just turned nine, crouched between the thwarts on the bottom. He had the impression that they were making straight for the gaping mouth of a monster whale. Within a few hundred yards from shore, they hit rough water. Knud and Bengt nursed the boat right up to the heaving edge of the current, working it slowly forward. A big comber was chasing them; the stern of the boat met the base of the wave while the boat was being pushed onward by sheer muscle power to neutralise the speed of the onrushing sea. The boat was lifted, then momentarily stood still on top of the crest while the wave passed under it.

The two experienced Danes, plying their oars with great strength, had managed to evade being struck side-on by the comber, which would have flipped them over. After the big wave came a series of eddying waves, much smaller and easier to deal with. Both men leaned into the oars and with a mighty heave they headed straight out into the darkness. More waves carried the boat out into the deep water, but also splashed water into the boat, soaking the refugees. Further out at sea they were flung along at great speed by the rush of the underwater current.

For what seemed to the escapees like an eternity, Knud and Bengt moved in unison, their muscles straining in a ritualistic gesture, pulling on the oars, while the perspiration poured down their arms and drenched their eyes. The boy Julius had become seasick and therefore was no longer plagued by thoughts of a monster whale; he strained his eyes ahead into the implacable darkness; he was seeking desperately for a sign that the boat would stop being tossed about by the swell. Suddenly they could see dawn creeping over a long whale; no, not a whale, but a stretch of sand like a whale's hump! With a final pull on the oars, the boat cut across the still water and drifted to a stop on the sandy shore of Saltholm. The two rowers unshipped the oars and then kept clenching and unclenching their tired fists, while the refugees jumped into the knee-deep water to help drag the boat up on the beach. The two fishermen would spend a few hours resting, and then return to Denmark, dragging an eel-line behind them so as not to arouse suspicion. It was different for the refugees. They were overcome by a feeling of great elation. Young Julius, because the sea monster had not swallowed him up, and his parents, because they had made good their escape from Hitler and his black-clad henchmen. The homesickness would come only much later.

A group of twenty Jews reached the railway station at Naskov on Lolland; with nervous hands they passed coins through the ticket windows; the clerk took no notice of them and he didn't ask for the authority's travel permit. They were waiting anxiously for the train to arrive when two German military policemen showed up; however, they were only interested to check the papers of German soldiers departing on home leave. As the train pulled in, the Jews crossed the platform with the commuter crowd and climbed aboard. A *Wehrmacht* patrol aboard the train didn't so much as give them a second glance.

Copenhagen's Skudehavn was a place for departure. Many Jews went there to find a boat. Christine Thalvard-Seligmann had wandered there with her child. She wasn't wealthy like many other refugees; she had only the little money the old man gave her. Shivering with fear for her child, she faced a bearded fisherman

'*Du er e sekerhed* – You are safe,' he said in a calm voice, alleviating her fears. That night, Kastrup fisherman Curt Nielsen in his MÖ 926 took eight Jews to Sweden.

The distance between Copenhagen and Malmø was not so great that it couldn't be done in a night; yet others, departing from islands further down the Baltic, had to face a more harrowing trip. Max Tischmann was warned when he walked into his law office on Falster that the Gestapo was about to arrest him. He managed to call his wife Tuva in Idestrup, located four miles (6.4 km) from his office, to get herself and the children towards Stubbekøbing, a small fishing harbour where they had spent many a summer splashing in the sea. While he was peddling on his bicycle from Nykøbing, he hoped that Tuva and their two children had already managed to reach a friendly harbourmaster. In fact, Tuva and the children had narrowly missed a German roadblock; she took the children through the Corselitze forest, which added miles to the track. The thick forest with its magnificent oaks was like a time warp from the Viking period, with its funeral dolmens, a permanent reminder of the glorious period when Norsemen ruled the seas. But Tuva wasn't interested in Scandinavian lore and her children were at the end of their endurance. This in itself held recompense; the children were too tired to be frightened. They made it to a forester's cottage where his wife gave the children milk and thick slices of buttered bread. More than anything else, she gave them hope that someone cared. She sent her fourteen-year-old son to the harbourmaster's office. Vigo Andersen wasn't surprised; a few hours before the vicar had already forewarned him. Some hours later, stepping off the Bodø ferry, his office was suddenly flooded with two dozen Jews from Copenhagen.

The Danes were a sturdy people with a direct outlook on life. You told a Dane what you wanted, stated the price and he would say 'yes' or 'no'. Don't beat about the bush. Not in Denmark. Vigo Andersen went down to the small harbour. The man he was talking to had the look of a fisherman who knew what he was about. Otto Sylow was standing next to his weather-beaten but seaworthy old craft.

'Otto, all hell's breakin' loose – the *Tyskerne* are going after the *Jøderne*. Can you take care of some? After nightfall?'

'Across?' *Across* for a Dane, in a time of war, always meant Sweden.

'Yah.'

'Long ride. I'll need some diesel.'

'You'll have it,' said Vigo Andersen. The wealthy among the Jews had given him money to pay for black-market fuel. 'Meet me at eight o'clock on Groenesund Faergeplads.'

Otto nodded. This didn't take words, something the Danes were forever careful never to waste. Travelling with human cargo, especially one the Gestapo was chasing . . . the stake was high, and the odds were long. Otto Sylow's fishing boat was a wooden 33-foot (9.9 metre) trawler, with an antiquated, coughing, 35-horsepower glow-plug motor, the NF 24 *Talona*. The war had left him without spare parts, and the engine was running more on hope than on the tightly rationed kerosene.

Late afternoon: Tuva and the forester's wife pushed the

two tired children on bicycles to the edge of the forest. 'Wait here,' said the woman. All was peaceful; the only sound was the gentle splash of waves lapping on the wooden landing stage. Dark clouds began to cover the horizon and a drizzle-like mist drifted in from the sea. It was getting cold. Tuva took off her coat and wrapped it around her children.

Together with his two brothers Hermann, twenty-four, and Gunner, twenty, Otto Sylow set out from the small Stubbekøbing harbour to pick up the refugees on the wooden jetty at Groenesund, off the Corselitze forest. They found Vigo Andersen and Ove Lund from the Haesnes sawmill, where some of the Jews had been hiding out, with twenty people of all ages, perched on suitcases. How could they get them all 'across'? Three Sylow brothers, thirty herring nets, and twenty refugees. But then again, they couldn't leave them behind, that would be condemning them to certain arrest.

'All right, hop aboard! No suitcases.'

'But, please . . .' said a young woman, clutching her small suitcase in her arms.

'But nothing,' growled Hermann, 'we haven't got room for bags. Dump them, or stay behind.' The refugees piled from the pier on to the trawler's deck. An old woman looked so frail that Gunner doubted that she would survive the dangerous crossing. As for the girl, she told Hermann that she was trying to reach an uncle – in Mexico! When the wooden *Talona* pulled away from the jetty, it did so with a loud bang from its tortured two-stroke engine. The refugees worried that the sound could be heard all the way to the German Navy patrol ship at Kriegers Flak.

They emerged from the Groenesund Passage. While Hermann looked after the labouring engine, Otto headed the creaking and groaning trawler past the Møn lighthouse into the open Baltic; they became conscious of a persisting sound building up on the dark sea, the gurgling rush of waves. They were heading into a storm.

The first wave struck. The refugees closest to the railing clutched others to keep themselves from tumbling overboard. Within minutes, everyone aboard was violently sick and Gunner, as the youngest, had to clean up the mess. It was madness to make a run in seas like this. If the waves were high, these were nothing compared to the approaching peril, which they didn't share with their human cargo: between Stevns Klint and Kriegers Flak, cutting across their path to Sweden, the Germans had laid a minefield. That wasn't all; at the ocean-end of the minefield lay a big German ship with an even bigger gun.

Otto and his brothers knew what they could expect if their vessel was spotted and the German alerted one of the 'Schnellboote'. With his coughing 35-hp engine he had no chance against the 600-plus horsepower of the German coastal patrols. The storm, whatever discomforts it brought to his passengers, proved to be a stroke of good luck; the wind's noise covered the sound of their engine and reduced the visibility. This helped them circumnavigate the danger; but it called for a big detour of some 30 miles (48 km), adding five hours to the trip, before Otto dared to head north to make for the Swedish coast at Trelleborg. There was another danger: the English had dropped floating magnetic mines into this part of the Baltic; that wasn't too dangerous for a wooden-hulled trawler, but if one drifted into their path – a fisherman from Haesnes had struck one and nothing was ever found of him. They were eight hours out of Denmark, with the Talona about 15 miles (24 km) from the Swedish shore and steering for the bright lights of Trelleborg, clearly to be seen on the distant shore, when out of the growing dawn rose the silhouette of a warship on the horizon.

They were still out in 'the forbidden zone' and chances were that the German patrol craft would spot them soon. In the face of such unfavourable odds, Otto had no option than to risk all. He had to make a run for the shallows, risking both engine and keel. And if he grounded, they would be a sitting duck for the warship's guns. There were dozens of sandbanks and submerged outcrops, some little more than smooth, rounded rocks, clogging the approach into Swedish waters. Sailing in those channels was dangerous, and they could easily get lost in the darkness unless they followed a Swedish fisherman who knew his way around every rock.

As the *Talona* carried no life jackets, Otto ordered everyone to take off their shoes and strip down to the minimum, in case they were forced to go overboard. After hours fighting a storm, Otto Sylow pushed the throttle to maximum revs, something he had never dared before; the engine vibrated and the NF 24 shook and rattled; but it picked up speed, reaching a full seven miles per hour (11 kph). God was on their side and somehow the old wooden boat stayed in one piece, and his position in the notoriously treacherous shallows removed them from imminent danger. A German warship would hardly risk its keel to chase after a rickety old trawler.

That still left the danger from the flat-bottomed, high-speed patrol crafts. But all went well and they had almost reached Sweden's three-mile (4.8 km) limit when a panicked voice on deck cried out: 'Someone's coming!'

Gunner looked through his glasses and giggled: '*Det er en Svenskaer* . . . That's a Swede.'

Indeed, a Swedish patrol boat was heading for their trawler. The Swedish Coast Guard stayed some hundred metres off and a friendly officer waved to them. 'Do you carry refugees?'

'Yah.'

'Cover your boat's number and name with nets and head for the coaling place.' There was a valid reason for their warning. German collaborators were known to take photos of any boat with a Danish number. As they were approaching the distant shore, a dark, veiled curtain showed that it was raining heavily. That was good, nobody would be standing on shore, watching them. As Gunner wiped the salt from his face, a tense, barely audible sound wafted back from the bow: the sound of relief, joy, and salvation, all wrapped into one. After ten hours the *Talona* slid unnoticed into Trelleborg. A loader at the coaling pier took hold of the boat's painter. People hugged and kissed each other and slapped the Sylow brothers on their backs. With eyes surrounded by dark circles, Tuva Tischmann stared into Otto's face. When she gave him a kiss, a flash of embarrassment crossed the Dane's face. He turned, and walked away without speaking.

Otto and his brothers had their engine overhauled thanks to the generosity of a wealthy Swedish Jew. They made one more trip to Sweden. Several dozen Danes would survive the war because of the Sylows of Stubbekøbing. On his second trip, they were nearly given away by an unguarded remark of someone they had ferried on their first trip to safety.

'That's the boat that brought us over,' cheerfully cried a man, standing among a crowd expecting relatives on the Swedish side, while pointing to the approaching boat. There was a good chance that at least one among the people on the quay was a German informer.

'What are you talking about?' snapped a bystander. 'You have forgotten how you got here or who you contacted, is that clear?'

Carelessly written letters unwittingly betrayed some brave Danes that had risked their lives. Claus Heilesen of the Students' Intelligence Group collected some fugitives to lead them to the fishing port of Taarbaek. Probably inadvertently, someone had given to the Gestapo the registration number of their vessel. The Germans fired on the boat and twenty-year-old Claus Heilesen was killed. The fisherman and fugitives were arrested and the boat blown up.

As an increasing number tried to reach Sweden, risks became greater and passages expensive. One engaged in the rescue operation was Christian Algreen-Petersen, who operated under the covername of 'Christian' for the Students' Intelligence Group. 'My job at first was to deliver messages. After the first days of October, the initial rush was over. Jews were still cramming our apartment, where my mother took their names and asked how much money they had. That was important. Some of the Jews were rich but many had only a few hundred kroner and some had no money at all.'

The first question Christian's mother posed to the newcomers was: 'Har du penge – Do you have money?' Many were shocked by the question – they considered it blood money – but it was a fact that, once the Gestapo became aware, fishermen had to take increasing chances. The search of ocean-going vessels became more rigorous and the Germans began using sniffer dogs. A group of chemistry students went to work on the problem and came up with a mixture of dried rabbits' blood and cocaine. This numbed the dogs' sense of smell. But the danger to the passers was real.

'In exchange for their service, the captains demanded 1000 Kr (US $200 at 1943 value) per passenger.[18] This wasn't blood money and no one got rich passing hapless

[18] Taking into account that – for an overall fee of perhaps US $1,400,000 (1943 value) – 7,200 lives were saved, this sum doesn't seem excessive.

fugitives to safety. It was a kind of boat insurance; anyone caught or suspected of passing Jews had his vessel confiscated, or, worse still, holes punched into its hull.'[19] Mrs Algreen-Petersen managed to collect money from richer Jews to pay for the poorer.

Failing to get the Jews, the Gestapo took reprisals on the land-locked organisers. Christian's group, who had helped forty Allied airmen to reach Sweden, was betrayed and fell into a Gestapo ambush. It came to a shoot-out in the streets of Copenhagen. Christian's two companions were killed; he was badly wounded and spent the rest of the war under interrogation in a Gestapo prison.

One of the escape methods involved Danish fishing vessels meeting their Swedish counterparts on the high seas to swap refugees for the Swedes' fish catch. This provided the Danes with a convenient cover to continue with their 'fishing activity'. A heavily travelled route, involving small embarkations, lay between the Amager Peninsula, directly to the south of Copenhagen, and the small isle of Saltholm with its series of treacherous sand spits, lying halfway across the wide Sund to Sweden. They dumped their fugitives on this bird sanctuary to await their pick-up by Swedish crafts. With the many boats unloading there, the normally off-limits Saltholm took on the appearance of Henley on regatta day.

Without doubt, the most famous of all escapees was the great Danish physicist, Nobel Prize laureate Niels Bohr, a half-Jew[20] and co-founder of the Committee for the Support of Intellectual Refugees. His escape from near-arrest was one of the most remarkable stories of the war. The Germans had allowed Bohr, an absent-minded genius who knew strictly nothing about the problems of the world,

[19] Statement by Christian Algreen-Petersen.
[20] Bohr's mother was a Jewess.

to continue his work at the Institute of Theoretical Physics, studying the theoretical possibilities of the unleashed atom. His German counterpart Heisenberg tried to convince him to work for the Germans during a visit to Copenhagen. When the English found out, they immediately dispatched a secret invitation to him to join a team of nuclear physicists working in England; this message was relayed to Bohr by the *Prinserne* (Princes)[21] resistance network on a piece of microfilm hidden inside a hollowed key. He refused to leave Denmark; however, with Duckwitz's warning, which was conveyed to him by Hedtoft in person, Bohr finally accepted to take his son to Sweden. They hid out in the cabin of Sven Knudsen, who ran an underground escape service in his grey-painted boat with a silenced motor. Bohr and his son arrived in Limhamn near Malmø.

A young Swedish officer was detailed to accompany the famous physicist by car to Stockholm. They stopped en route for lunch, and the officer proudly presented his 'Nobel-Prize guest' to the restaurant owner, who called a newspaper and the secret was out. That's how the Swedish king found out about Bohr's presence and invited him to dinner. That invitation, greatly publicised, solved a tricky problem for the Royal Air Force; while German agents in Stockholm thought their prize escapee was sitting down to a meal in the palace, Niels Bohr was lying in the bomb bay of a British Mosquito bomber, which whisked him across German-occupied Norway to England. From there Professor Niels Bohr went to Los Alamos to help with the birth of 'the bomb'. The rest is nuclear history but not everyone was quite that lucky.

Since, in character with the coolness of Scandinavians, they kept loading their fugitives under the noses of the

[21] The *Prinserne* was founded by a group of Danish ex-army officers under Lt-Col. Nordentoft.

Gestapo, many ruses were employed to mislead the German agents. In spite of every precaution, sometimes information filtered through and a race developed between the blockade-runners and the *Sicherheitspolizei* sent to intercept them. Sometimes the luck failed. It is an unfortunate fact that most of those caught were by denunciations of Danish collaborators. The worst incident took place in the coastal town of Gilleleje north of Elsinør on the Zealand coast. A girl, working as chambermaid, had fallen in love with a German soldier; she was heartbroken when he was transferred to the Russian front. An advertisement published by the Germans in Danish papers, offered a substantial compensation in exchange for information leading to the arrest of Jews. Hoping that her action would bring her beloved back, she went to the Gestapo denouncing eighty Jewish fugitives hiding out in the town church's parish hall and attic.

On the evening of 5 October 1943, German police wagons pulled up in front of the church. They asked the local police to assist them, but the Danes refused. For well over an hour Pastor Kjeldgaard Jensen stalled the German police, which had received no specific orders to desecrate a church. The stand-off was ended when Hans Juhl of the Gestapo showed up and ordered his SS squad to surround the church with flashlights and machine guns. Then they broke into the church. The use of violence generated enough fear for the victims to give themselves up without a struggle. Gilleleje's Pastor Kjeldgaard Jensen described the drama in his church register:

October 5 was a terrible day for the whole town of Gilleleje. On that day, the occupying power carried out a raid here in the town to capture Jews. Further raids were made in the days that followed and many Jews, known and unknown – 1200 at least – were gathered here in town in private homes and the hotel, and unfortunately also in the church loft. It should be noted that the raids only succeeded at all with the aid of informers. May the Good Lord have mercy on His old and stubborn people and keep them from harm.

Only a small number of Jews taken at Gilleleje survived the camps to return after the war.

The role of the Gilleleje chambermaid was the exception; for the rest of the country, Dr Best's warning to the authorities in Berlin was quickly proving correct. The Danes were not taking Hitler's inhuman order lying down. On an official level, the strongest protest came from two sources. King Christian X sent a note of protest delivered to the German authorities by his Permanent Foreign Undersecretary Nils Svenningen. If this was not enough to light the Danish fuse, then it was the pastoral message (3 October) by the Lutheran Bishop of Copenhagen, *Primus Inter Pares* Hans Fuglsang-Damgaard, which was read out during church services throughout the country. The bishop didn't mince his words:

It is the sacred duty of the Christian Church to protest wherever Jews are being persecuted from pure racist or religious reasons, because such is against the justice of the Danish people. Forgetting religious convictions, we must all stand up and fight to preserve an equal freedom of our Jewish brothers and sisters that we ourselves treasure more than life. Our conscience makes it our duty to stand up against any infringement of that right. We must stand to our principle, to obey more God than a man.

When Max Tischmann, who had made his escape by sailboat out of Møn, was re-united with Tuva and their two children in Malmö, the joy of finding them alive overwhelmed him. A similar joy was felt by hundreds of other families, hunted by men in black coats, but who had managed to make good their escape.

Vigo Andersen, the Sylow brothers, or Johannes Johannsen were just some of the many silent heroes. The reaction by the Danish population had been truly overwhelming and heroic. Within days, if not within hours, well over 7000 men, women and children were whisked off. To give an idea of the dimension of the foiled arrests, from a total of 8000 Danes of Jewish faith, the Gestapo located only 481. The people of Denmark stood the test.

'Here was something Eichmann and his men weren't accustomed to: the Jews had slipped from their very grasp and disappeared, so to speak, behind a living wall raised by the Danish people in one night.'[22]

All across the country, Danes had offered refuge to Jews in outlying farms, hospitals, churches, haylofts, city apartments and basements, pastors' and old people's homes; private homes and public buildings were turned into safe houses, and public libraries and brewery depots served as dispatching centres. Danish police, customs officers, and railway controllers 'overlooked' the need to check travel permits and identity papers. Students handled the logistics, while ordinary fishermen became blockade-runners. All of Denmark was on the move, unspectacular and silent.

'It was a nation's fellowship, inspired by a rage against the brutal treatment of an innocent and helpless minority. In all justice, it must be recorded that not a few Germans who disapproved of Gestapo terrorism helped if and when they could, if only by a certain blindness at the right moment', is written in the official account of Danish history.

All of that would have come to nothing, had it not been

[22] Yahil, L., *The Rescue of the Danish Jewry*, Philadelphia, 1969.

for the timely warning by a German, Georg Ferdinand Duckwitz, who betrayed his leader's design, and by helping to 'freeze' the German rapid coastal crafts in their berths, turned the planned round-up of Danish Jews into a Nazi fiasco. In a time of terror and darkness in occupied Europe, he set a monument to humanity. The Gestapo never discovered who was 'the mole' and Duckwitz survived the war.

'*Als ich die Nachricht erhielt* – As I was given the news,' he wrote on 4 May 1945, after he received confirmation that Hitler was dead and the German units in northern Germany had sued for unconditional surrender, 'I felt one of these emotional moments in my life, having the assurance that I have not lived in vain in this world.'

One question still remains unclear: who had actually instigated the arrests? During interrogation after the war, Duckwitz involved the *Polizei* chief of Copenhagen, Mildner, who pushed the blame on the *Reichsbevollmächtigten* Dr Best; Best again stated *Reichsaussenminister* Ribbentrop was acting to please Hitler, and Ribbentrop defended himself (during the Nüremberg War Crimes Trials) that his order came directly from *SS Reichsführer* Heinrich Himmler. And Himmler had swallowed poison. One more of the many dead ends in a dramatic period.

The tragedy that was Nazi Germany cannot be compressed into numbers. But the lives that had been saved by Georg Ferdinand Duckwitz's courage, show what a single man, given the human dimension, can achieve. For this, the Jews awarded him the prestigious Heinrich-Stahl Prize, and Her Majesty, Queen Margarethe II of Denmark honoured him with the Great Cross of the Dannebrog, the highest decoration that is given to non-princely persons. When Duckwitz died, aged sixty-eight, on 16 February 1973, the leading Danish newspaper *Berlinske Tidende* wrote in its lead editorial:

There is no doubt that his courageous act helped prevent a bloodbath among our fellow citizens in Copenhagen. A seemingly insignificant German shipping expert put his hand on the wheel of history. The name of Georg Ferdinand Duckwitz is written in gold letters in our nation's Book of History.

Danish Minister Per Federspiel praised the German's unique achievement before the *Rigsdag*: '*Vi maa I Danmark aldrig glemme Georg Ferdinand Duckwitz' indsats og mod* – Never must we forget in Denmark the part he played and the courage he showed.'

A visitor to the Holocaust Museum in Jerusalem will discover a small, blue rowboat with a bronze plaque that reads:

During World War II, the Danish People succeeded in frustrating Nazi Germany's intention of deporting Denmark's 8000 Jews to death camps in the east. The deportations, which were to be part of the 'final solution' for the destruction of European Jewry, were set for the 1st October 1943. A courageous rescue operation was carried out by the members of the Danish underground which assisted 7200 Jews to escape to Sweden.

Situations exist for which there is no established protocol. Among most of the human race, the conscience about inhuman events is an individual matter. Such people, always in the minority, exert a moral and spiritual influence out of all proportion to their number. Duckwitz was one of that select group. He was a Party man, and the Party's only principle, its sole duty, was to do what its Führer told it to do. This leader believed implicitly that everything the Party did was excellent, because he himself conceived everything. Duckwitz dared to disobey his leader, and that was a dangerous game to play; yet by his scrupulous conscience he helped save thousands. On 5 April 1971, the

State of Israel honoured his humanitarian act with an oak planted in its oasis of memories, *Yad Vashem* – the Forest of the Just.[23] It only gives a name: G.F. Duckwitz.

Duckwitz's motivation was moral courage, which is the provider of strength that makes the strong-minded act. Put into a position where he could help, he knew that what the Nazis were planning was inhuman. Whatever his political belief, his concern was first and foremost to preserve human lives from a brutal fate. When the kind of firmness was demanded of him to disregard the orders of his superiors, he challenged his master. This was something he had to face alone, and he stuck to his decision.

The Danes' motivation was physical courage, in order to save their fellow Danes. And in this, they proved themselves champions.

[23] Altogether 276 Germans are commemorated there.

Aleksandr Marinesko, 'For Stalin'

'Hero-worship is strongest where there is least regard for human freedom.'

Herbert Spencer, *Social Statistics*

Kill them, courageous members of the Red Army. Kill them.
Nothing can make the Germans innocent.
Obey the orders of Comrade Stalin and crush the fascist animals
in their dens.
Destroy the racial pride of the German women. Take them as
legitimate spoils of war.
Kill them.

Ilya Ehrenburg, proclamation on the eve of the attack on East Prussia,
January 1945

Great heroes they all were. Following their moment of grand glory, some of these heroes were most deceitfully robbed of their fame. The Soviet Union had its peculiar way of disglorifying some of its heroes.

His name was Aleksandr Marinesko. He was born in Odessa in 1914, a child of the slums. Aleksandr spent his formative years stealing, and diving in the harbour for coins thrown from passing tourist ships. He became the leader of a street gang, fighting it out with other gangs of Turks, Bulgars or Armenians; they fought over territory and girls. At fifteen, he shipped as a cabin boy on the coastal tramp *Black Sea*. His break came during a stormy night in 1934, when a Soviet torpedo boat capsized off Skadovsk and young Aleksandr jumped overboard to save a number of seamen. This heroic rescue brought him to the notice of the commander of the Black Sea Red Banner Fleet, who ordered the 21-year-old to join a naval school. The training was hard, which he didn't seem to mind, because it gave him a position and a uniform and the feeling that he was finally somebody. He boasted of his prowess in taverns during bouts of heavy drinking, an accepted thing in the Russian Navy. He changed bed partners like he changed socks. In 1936 he was transferred to a submarine training base, and found his true vocation.

Because of his harsh upbringing he displayed a great calm under the most precarious situations. This brought him the favourable attention of his instructors, and he was put as navigation officer aboard the SCH 306 *Pischka*, one of the latest submarines in the Soviet Baltic Fleet. He proved his value and in 1937 was handed command of a smaller sub, the M 96, capable of operating only in coastal waters. Despite the high age of his boat, Marinesko tuned his crew so fine that soon the M 96 became the most efficient submarine in the Baltic Fleet. With the beginning of the war, Marinesko's M 96 patrolled the coastal waters around Leningrad and the Gulf of Bothnia. He had no great success and never sank a ship, but did have a close escape when attacked by a German torpedo boat.

In 1944, Marinesko was made commander of the much larger and faster Stalinetz-class S 13. As irony had it, the boat, which was to do great harm to Germany's Navy, was designed and built . . . by Germans! To circumvent the stringent regulations governing the peace treaty of

England's youngest recipient of the Victory Cross: 16-year-old Jack 'Boy' Cornwell.

A dying 'Boy' Cornwell manning his gun at Jutland, 1916. (Painting by Frank Salisbury for the Boy Cornwell Fund.)

Left: Sergeant Kunze, the man who single-handedly took Fort Douaumont, but was denied any credit.

Below: 25 February 1916, 16.30 hours: the storming of Douaumont. These pictures are all the more remarkable for being taken by a young German officer using only the primitive photographic means available at the time.

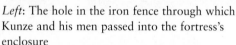

Left: The hole in the iron fence through which Kunze and his men passed into the fortress's enclosure

Below left: Alexander Marinesko, the Soviet sub-marine captain who sank more enemy tonnage than all other Russian warships combined.

Below right: The Soviet sub s-13 that sank the *Wilhelm Gustloff* and the *General von Steuben*, causing over 10,000 casualties.

The hero of Wake Island: Captain Henry T. Elrod, US Navy Flying Corps, who bombed the Japanese fleet with a fighter aircraft held together by spit and wire.

The Wake Island Memorial, showing the smashed propeller of Captain Elrod's Grumman F4F-3 'Wildcat' fighter aircraft of Marine Fighter Squadron 211.

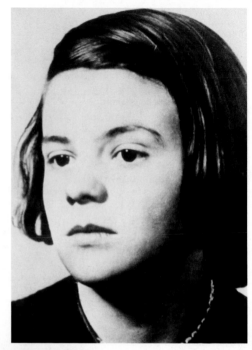

Sophie Scholl, a biology student at Munich's University, a member of the *Die Weisse Rose* resistance movement.

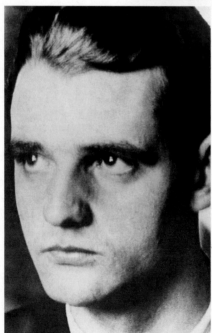

Hans Scholl, Sophie's brother, a medical student at Munich and the avowed leader of *Die Weisse Rose*.

Left: 'I know what I have to do.' This message, sent to the Danish underground, by Georg Ferdinand Duckwitz, a high Nazi official, saved the Jews of Denmark.

Right: Dangerous crossing: a Danish fishing boat ferrying Jews from Copenhagen to Sweden.

Below: Tickling the tiger's tail: Dr Louis Slotin assembling the first atomic bomb.

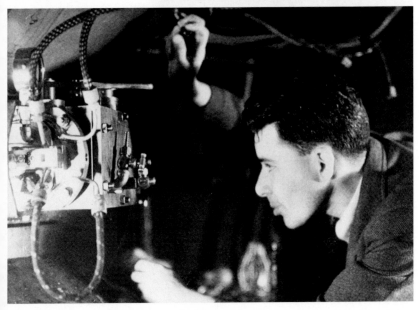

The Long Reveille:
Sergeant Buss on
Gloster Hill, Korea.
(Painting by Ken
Howard.)

Below: The Reverend
Sam Davies, conducting
a religious service one
hour before the final
attack by Communist
Chinese forces on the
Gloster's hill position.

Angel of Dien Bien Phu: Geneviève de Galard, the instant she stepped off the plane that brought her to Hanoi from her Viet Minh captivity.

In the early morning mist, Russian tanks rumble through the streets of Budapest. A few hours later, the Hungarian rebellion will be drowned in blood.

Colonel (later General) Pal Maleter, military commander of the Hungarian uprising, in discussion with officers at his headquarters during the critical days.

Versailles, the Germans had opened a construction bureau in neutral Holland, using the misleading Dutch name of *Ingeniers Kantoor voor Scheepsbnouw* (Engineer Bureau for Shipbuilding). The company belonged jointly to the German Navy and Krupp, and offered some of its output of modern boats to Russia, proving the connivance which existed between Hitler and Stalin before the war.

By the winter of 1944 to 1945, things were going badly for the *Deutsche Wehrmacht*, engaged for the first time in the defence of German territory, East Prussia. General Guderian supported the commander of Germany's 4th Army, General von Hossbach, when he argued with Hitler to order the immediate withdrawal of German troops from the danger of encirclement at Königsberg (today Kaliningrad). Hitler flatly refused: 'East Prussia is an integral part of Germany and will remain part of the German Reich.'

'It is our duty to save our men,' disputed Guderian.

'Save the civilians, if you want, but my soldiers are to hold their position!'

On 12 January 1945, the Russians attacked with nearly one hundred divisions. The first German town they over-ran was called Nemmersdorf. The local German men had marched off with their *Volksturm* units, leaving their women and children behind. The horror done to the town was indescribable. Children were butchered by T-34 tanks rolling over them; their mothers were raped to death or nailed to barn doors. The story of the rape of Nemmersdorf spread throughout East Prussia and within twenty-four hours, a million German refugees, fleeing before the steadily advancing Red Army, jammed the roads leading towards the Baltic harbours. Admiral Dönitz, who had been present during the Führer conference, remembered Hitler's phrase: 'Save the civilians . . .' and ordered whatever transport ships were available to take on refugees in Gotenhaven (Gdingen) and Pillau and deliver them to Kiel.[1]

In what amounted to a superhuman effort, in the period from January to April 1945, German transport ships, without aerial cover and surface protection, managed to ferry over two million refugees and military casualties to safety. The ships mainly used were the 21,000-ton *Hansa*, the 27,572-ton *Cap Arcona*, the 22,000-ton *Hamburg*, the 22,000-ton *Deutschland*, and the 25,484-ton (gross weight) *Wilhelm Gustloff* [2], pride of the German passenger fleet. It had been built on Hitler's order in 1935 for his people's pleasure cruises, an organisation called *Kraft Durch Freude* (Strength through Joy). This time it wasn't on a pleasure cruise, but on a ride from hell.

At the turn of the year 1945, the S 13 lay anchored in the Finnish harbour of Turku, which had been recently stormed by the Red Army. The competition among submarine captains of the Baltic Fleet was fierce, as is so often the case among elite units. Every captain had one aim: to become the 'ace of the nation' – well aware that their task wouldn't be easy, since their theatre of operation was not well suited for submarine warfare; the Baltic was peppered with treacherous sandbanks and, in general, the waters were too shallow for efficient diving.

On 2 January 1945, the commander of the submarine group, Naval Captain Aleksandr Jevstafjevich Orjel, received a direct order from Stalin to engage in activity in

[1] From a captured British document the Germans were made aware of the planned division of Germany into four Allied zones. Kiel was in the British sector.

[2] Launched on 5 May 1937 by Adolf Hitler at the *Blohm & Voss Werft*, Hamburg. Five days before the outbreak of the Second World War, on 25 August 1939, the *Gustloff* was briefly stopped by a British cruiser off the coast of Norway, and told to stop its engines, but then was allowed to pass on direct orders from London.

order to prevent German troop transports from reaching or leaving General von Hossbach's 4th German Army, operating against Marshal Rokossovski's 2nd Byelorussia Front in the Baltic theatre. The subs of the Red Banner Baltic Command were ordered to sail. With Stalin's personal order, competition among the sailing captains was driven on even more. They knew that at the end waited the coveted reward for the one with most tonnage sunk, and everyone wanted to be the submarine squadron's first 'Hero of the Soviet Union'.[3] Until this moment, they hadn't had a chance to prove their valour and raise their boat to the elite rank of the 'Red Guard Class'. Now they were given this chance. All captains were rearing to go – all but one.

The S 13 was loaded, its crew was ready to sail, but its captain couldn't be found. As a matter of fact, Captain 3rd Class Aleksandr Marinesko had been so bored with hanging around idly, waiting for his sailing orders that never seemed to come, that he had told his second, Lev Jefremenkov, to look after the boat, while he indulged in a three-day binge of alcohol and women. While he was lying stone drunk in a bordello, the combat order arrived. Before the day was out, the Russian military police began looking for him, because they had received orders from the NKVD to charge him with desertion and collaboration with the enemy.

When the MPs finally caught up with Marinesko in a Finnish sauna, where he was sweating out his huge intake of *pontikka* – a lethal Finnish concoction that makes vodka taste like baby's milk – he couldn't remember in which whore house he had passed his time, or with how many women he had slept. The suspicious NKVD didn't accept his explanation; they grilled him severely. Where

---

[3] Roughly equivalent to the Victoria Cross, the US Medal of Honour, or the German Knight's Cross.

had he passed the last seventy-two hours? Had he been in contact with foreigners? After all, Turku was a Finnish port, and the Finns much preferred the Germans to the Russians. Commander Orjel wished to calm things down; he needed every submariner to fulfil Chairman Stalin's order. NKVD Commissar Jumkoshian overrode Naval Commander Orjel and kept interrogating Marinesko, who stuck to his story that he had been so drunk that he simply couldn't remember. In their heated exchange of words, Marinesko committed the unpardonable gaffe of challenging the NKVD commissar's courage by referring to him as someone who was quick to accuse others of desertion while he himself made sure never to get too close to the front. This unfortunate incident was to lead to severe consequences for the submarine captain.

Jumkoshian wanted to put Marinesko immediately before a court martial, but his move was prevented by a superior naval officer, Commander Verchovski, acting on behalf of Admiral Nikolai Kuznezov, who feared that shooting an officer, popular with his crew, might lead to an onboard mutiny. His hunch was confirmed when the admiral was presented with a petition signed by the entire crew of S 13, including their first officer, Lev Jefremenkov. This petition saved Marinesko, if only temporarily. As soon as he was let go and returned to his submarine, the S 13 left Turku to join up with a Russian wolf pack off the Bay of Danzig. And there, Marinesko lay in wait for days, without ever spotting an enemy vessel.

He was as undisciplined as he was the type of submariner with that born smell for the hunt. He realised that the Germans were shifting men and material out of Gotenhaven, and not Pillau. He now committed another unpardonable error. Without bothering to inform Soviet Naval HQ in Kronstadt, he abandoned his assigned position and made for the tip of Hela Peninsula, a neuralgic point on the

Baltic's shipping lanes. From that moment on, the Soviet Navy lost all contact with S 13, and the NKVD panicked in the firm belief that their sub-captain had joined the Germans. In fact, what really took place was quite different. He justified his move to his onboard political commissar, Vladimir Krylov, thus: 'The fascists will not come out this way. That's where they are!'

On the marine map he stabbed his finger at a shallows marked Stolpe Bank. 'I'll make for the Hela Peninsula. Of course there is always the danger of mines, but if the Nazi ships can come out, I can also get in. It's worth the risk . . .'

And while the S 13 was sailing south to lie in wait in the obvious position where enemy ships had to pass, the evacuation of thousands of East Prussian refugees had shifted into high gear. Ships were jammed to maximum capacity with valuable *U-boote* crews from the training school,[4] female naval personnel, and thousands upon thousands of women and children, who had congregated along the quays, fearing a similar fate as the women at Nemmersdorf.

One of these evacuation liners was the *Wilhelm Gustloff*,[5] truly a big vessel, with peacetime cabin space for 1465 passengers. But on 30 January 1945, the day it sailed from Gotenhaven, it held nearly eight times as many; 10,582 people had piled aboard and occupied every nook and cranny.[6] Some 370 young women of a naval training school

[4] These crews were trained to take over the new and lethal type XXI and XXIII subs, an absolutely superior type of submarine which caused great anxiety in British marine circles.
[5] Named after the leader of the Swiss Nazi party who had been assassinated.
[6] The total number of passengers was compiled by Heinz Schön, a survivor, who has made it his life's work to collect all data on the *Wilhelm Gustloff* and has created an archive.

had to bunk down in the emptied swimming pool. For the first time, the *Gustloff* was sailing under a dual command; the ship's former civilian captain, Friedrich Petersen, and a naval officer, *Korvettenkapitän* Wilhelm Zahn. This was to create command chaos on board, since Petersen thought himself in merchant naval terms as being 'one captain on board, under God and for the voyage'.

The *Wilhelm Gustloff* left Gotenhaven in a blinding snowstorm. The outside temperature had dropped to minus 20°C and the water temperature was down to a chilling 3°C.[7] As its only protection from marauding Soviet submarines, the *Gustloff* had one torpedo boat, the *Löwe*, as its second protection vessel had sprung a leak that needed repair. To make matters worse, the *Löwe's* submarine detector had frozen solid in the extreme cold and was out of order. In any case, Soviet submarines weren't their overriding concern as they had been mainly inactive. The danger most feared by German captains came from the Royal Air Force, which had dropped altogether 2013 floating mines into the ship channels around Gotenhaven and Swinemünde.[8] And so the *Gustloff* set off at noon on 30 January 1945. With the snow whipping across a wild-gone sea and the light falling rapidly, it was soon dark. The blacked-out vessel slid through the gloom; an argument broke out on the bridge of the *Gustloff* between Captain Petersen and *Korvettenkapitän* Zahn over the use of navigational lights. Zahn, the military man, thought it to be an invitation to give away their position while Petersen feared for a head-on collision in the narrow channel between the minefield and the sandbank. In the end, Petersen won and at 19.30 hrs, near the minefield off Rixhöft, while some ten miles (16 km) off the Pomeranian

[7] In comparison, at the *Titanic* disaster it was 4°C.
[8] German losses to these mines were given with eighteen vessels.

coast, the ship's navigational lights were switched on. Soon they were to pass the dangerous Stolpe Bank, and from there on they would find deep water to the south of Bornholm Island. Petersen wasn't overly worried, he felt sufficiently protected; to the sea side he had the *Löwe*, and towards shore was anchored a wide strip of mines.

The S 13 was riding on the surface, recharging its batteries, and lying in wait twelve miles (19 km) off the Pomeranian coastline on the eastern end of the Stolpe Bank. Suddenly, through the heavy snow flurries, Lt Vinogradov, on watch in the conning tower, noticed lights. He first took them to come from the Rixhöft lighthouse, but when the lights moved, he knew that it was a ship and he informed Marinesko, who sounded the alarm. His plan for attack was clear; in the diffused weather he wouldn't dive, but use his submarine as a surface torpedo attack ship. The Germans had used this technique with astounding success, but the method was contrary to anything laid down in Russian (or British) submarine manuals, as it left a sub wide open to an aerial attack. There was no danger for that in this kind of weather. There was another reason: the Soviet torpedoes were of old design,[9] greatly untested and unreliable when fired at a certain depth, and he wanted to assure a certain kill by firing a shallow trajectory.

A big ship and a smaller vessel were approaching. Marinesko slipped across the bow to get away from the danger of the smaller ship sailing on the sea side, and which he correctly assumed to be an escort. He called for his officers and political commissar to inform them of his decision: 'We have to circle around the convoy and attack

[9] The Germans had sold them the submarines, but not their latest torpedo technique, and the torpedoes of the Soviets were modelled on an antiquated First World War German design, which was highly unstable.

from the coastal side; from there, they will not expect an attack, all their eyes are out to sea.'

The sleek sub sliced through the stormy sea and was soon running on a parallel course some two kilometres from their target, which Marinesko now estimated as an ocean liner of 20,000 BRT. His move put the S 13 between ship and shore, a dangerous position; if anything should go wrong – they were spotted by the escort ship – then they would be caught in a death trap, because he had only 30 metres (about 1000 feet) under the keel, not enough to dive.

The S 13's stern tubes were readied; each held its deadly torpedo, marked with the crew's personal message. Tube one: 'For Mother Russia'; tube two: 'For Stalin'; tube three: 'For the Soviet people', and tube four: 'For Leningrad'. The torpedoes were set for a running depth of three metres. To make certain of a kill, the four torpedoes were to be launched at the minimal distance from target. At 20.55 hrs (German time) Marinesko gave orders to put the boat into attack position. The tanks were flooded and the boat was lowered to the shooting depth, with only its conning tower sticking out above the waves. Within minutes, the big steamer would pass at a distance of only 600 metres (666 yards) in front of S 13's four stern torpedo tubes. The minutes ticked away, when suddenly a huge, black shadow came sliding across the snow flurries. At 21.04 hrs S 13's navigation officer Redkoborodov made a final report of distance and speed of the big enemy vessel. At 21.08 hrs, Marinesko called out: 'Fire one . . . fire two . . . fire three . . . fire four!'

All went, all but one: the number two torpedo, marked 'For Stalin' malfunctioned and was inside the flooded tube, its propeller spinning and thereby arming itself. It could go off at any moment. The next instant, the Soviet submarine was rattled by a series of violent explosions. Through his night glass, Marinesko watched three huge fireballs, and then the target almost immediately began to tilt forward; a big wave washed to the top of the conning tower, soaking the watch. That's when his first torpedo mate, Vladimir Kurotchkin, informed him about the torpedo stuck in number two tube.

Kurotchkin had noticed, when he pushed the high-pressure plunger, that 'For Stalin' didn't make the usual sound of a departing torpedo. He pushed the plunger again, but nothing happened. And then he realised that the torpedo's propeller was running, and that again meant that the torpedo was arming itself – inside the tube! The slightest shock and the bloody thing would explode. He rushed to the conning tower to warn Marinesko of the imminent danger. This turned his captain's attention away from the sinking target and back to his own emergency.

He couldn't make a run without risking an internal explosion. While the thousands of refugees aboard the *Gustloff* struggled in utter despair to make for the life-boats, the crew under Kurotchkin worked feverishly to try and stop the torpedo motor, which, with every turn of the screw, brought them closer to a catastrophe. They were so preoccupied with their own problem that the sub drifted quite close to the first lifeboats lowered into the water. Survivors later told of how they were passed by a submarine with men shouting to each other in Russian. The submariners were luckier than their victims; through another fault, this time in the torpedo's compressed air chamber, its motor stopped. Torpedo Mate Kurotchkin and his helpers, hanging on ropes over the side, somehow managed to shove the greased 'Stalin' back into its tube. The tube was sealed. It was high time to disappear; radio mate Shnapzev called up to the tower that he could hear through his earphones the sound of cracking plates as the target vessel was breaking up, but also the highly distinctive noise of rapidly approaching ship screws.

'Dive! Dive!' yelled Marinesko, sliding down at last from the conning tower. The diving tanks flooded, and the S 13 vanished into the shallows.[10] They left behind a scene of horror, not witnessing a frothing sea covered by thousands of bobbing heads, fighting for their lives in mountainous waves, ice-cold water and darkness. Neither Marinesko nor his crew realised that they had just caused the biggest sea drama ever, one that made the *Titanic* disaster look small.

Sixty-two minutes later, as the *Wilhelm Gustloff* was about to disappear, the dying vessel generators came back on. It was as if the ship refused to die. Her lights shone brilliantly from all her portholes, and her sirens howled. Then the majestic liner, built to give 'strength through joy', suddenly tilted forward and, with lights blazing, slid beneath the waves, taking with her 9582 souls.[11]

Ten days later, Marinesko's S 13 sank another huge evacuation ship. His sonar operator had picked up the sound of screws; a convoy appeared, in its midst a large ship, which Marinesko mistook for an Emden-type heavy cruiser. This time he stayed well submerged. At 00.53 hrs on 10 February 1945, and at a distance of 4000 metres (4444 yards), Marinesko fired two torpedoes. Both scored a hit. One struck below the bridge, the other went into the engine compartment. Only it wasn't a heavy cruiser but the 14,660-ton luxury liner *General von Steuben*, loaded to capacity with refugees. The ship was mortally wounded, and those aboard were already condemned to death in the

[10] This encounter between lifeboats and submarine, as reported by German survivors, remains a mystery, as, according to the log of S 13, she had dived almost immediately after the *Gustloff* explosion.
[11] Although the ship carried no passenger list, the number was arrived at by deducting the rescued from the number of refugees and wounded known to have boarded the ship.

freezing waters. Within minutes, the ship's stern rose high from the water and the big vessel slid down into the deep. A few bubbles marked its grave. Marinesko and his S 13 had struck again, this time causing another 3408 deaths. In ten days, a submarine captain had caused more fatalities than all previous passenger ship disasters of the century combined, including that of the *Titanic*.[12]

When Marinesko returned triumphantly to Turku, with an awareness of having sunk two capital ships, he expected nothing less than a title of 'Hero of the Soviet Union'. His colleagues kissed him and slapped him on the back, and passed around the vodka bottle, while the NKVD waited for him in the shadows to grill him about his disappearance. Marinesko never did get his hero's medal and the fate of the *Wilhelm Gustloff* and the *General von Steuben* was buried in silence; by the Germans quite understandably; the Soviets, never known for suppressing news of their victories, also kept silent. Perhaps they didn't realise the full dimensions of the drama, or, if they did, it was the great loss of civilian life they didn't wish to share with their Allies. It is a curious historic sideline that, for once, the Allies had nothing to complain about Stalin's conduct of the war. Roosevelt and Stalin had pressed him in Yalta to take Danzig, which the British and Americans knew to be the training centre for crews of the revolutionary new type of *U-Boote*, the XXI and XXIII class. Causing great loss among these highly specialised crews could only assist the Allied war effort.[13]

As for Marinesko, he was a submariner who had launched

[12] On the *Titanic*, the total loss amounted to 1517 souls.
[13] The day that the Americans grabbed Werner von Braun and his rocket specialist that helped the USA with its rocket development, the Russians got hold of the German submarine designs, and the Soviet submarine fleet became the strongest in the world, using the original German designs.

his five torpedoes at enemy vessels; he was never told about the true magnitude of the human disaster he had caused. Furthermore, having spent his war years in besieged Leningrad, with its one million deaths by starvation, he couldn't care less about killing a few 'fascist aggressors'. But was the *Gustloff* identifiable as a refugee ship? That question is almost irrelevant. She sailed blacked-out and showed no (clearly discernible) Red Cross markings; she was armed with anti-aircraft guns, which made her into a vessel of war; and, finally, the Soviet propaganda machine could justifiably call her a troop transport, since on board, besides the many wounded, were 1000 active German soldiers from the submarine training school.[14] Given these points, by the international convention, governing the 'law of the sea', the *Wilhelm Gustloff* could be considered fair game.

Marinesko explained his decision for sinking the *Gustloff* before an investigation commission: 'For a few moments it had stopped snowing and I saw the outline of a gigantic ship. I was certain that it was full of men that had once trampled across the soil of Mother Russia and which were now in flight. The steamer had to go down, and I was the man to do it.' He even had the official sanction to kill all Germans; Stalin's court poet, Ilya Ehrenburg, had written a proclamation, distributed throughout the Red Army and Red Banner Fleet, inciting soldiers to violation and death: 'Kill them, courageous members of the Red Army. Kill them! Nothing can make the Germans innocent . . .'

With the war quickly reaching its end, the 32-year-old Marinesko began to badger his naval commanders to present him with the title of hero, which he considered was his

---

[14] After the war, the Soviet propaganda gave out a statement, claiming that aboard the *Gustloff* were 3000 submariners, including 100 sub captains for the new XXI class, plus 7000 Nazi leaders.

due for a supreme deed in the service of the motherland. In fact, as commander of the S 13, Marinesko had sunk more enemy tonnage than any other Soviet submarine or surface ship commander. The suggestion by some members of Baltic Command, including Admiral Nikolai Kuznezov, to honour Marinesko with the citation of 'Hero of the Soviet Union', was quashed by the NKVD, recalling Marinesko's 'lost weekend' in Turku and his undisciplined abandoning of his assigned station off the Bay of Danzig. For Marinesko the situation turned outright dangerous; with the war won, Stalin was no longer in need of heroic defenders, and had given orders to his secret police to hunt out collaborators and dissidents. Because of his insult to an NKVD commissar, a file had been opened on Marinesko.

'Sascha, let it go,' advised his friend Lev Jefremenkov. 'The war is over. Sooner or later they'll make you an admiral.' But the boy from the slums of Odessa wouldn't give in. He so irritated his hierarchy that they kicked him out of the submarines, and finally out of the Navy. He found a job at a building supply depot in Leningrad, drowned his unhappiness in alcohol and women, got into fist fights and was arrested by his nemesis, Commissar Jumkoshian of Stalin's feared NKGB (formerly the NKVD). Jumkoshian framed him, accused him of having stolen building material, a crime which was actually discovered by Marinesko and he was trying to bring to the attention of the local police. However just like in a bad novel where the good guy goes down, assisted by the connivance of the NKGB man, the real culprit, Marinesko's superior, had him charged instead.

Normally, this would have been the end of the story, but in an unusual reversal for a trial conducted in Stalin's Russia, the state prosecutor stood up in favour of the accused and found the charges unfounded. He asked for an acquittal. However the special tribunal, made up of a troika of NKGB commissars, decided differently. They couldn't accuse him of a political crime, their speciality; they could have accused him of drunkenness, and they could have charged him with insulting a state official, their colleague Jumkoshian, but that wouldn't have carried a big condemnation. And the NKGB was after blood. In a secret trial, the three judges cooked up a punishment for stealing government property! And so, the submarine ace, instead of getting his medal, was sent to the worst of all Siberian gulags, Kolyma, or as it was known: the Arctic Death Camp. He was sentenced to three years and served ten. Sixteen hours of work, seven days a week, deep down in the mine, beaten up by brutal overseers, deprived of food for the slightest incident, sleeping on frozen ground in patched-up tents, such was a Soviet hero's fate.

Enquiries by his former comrades-in-arms of their captain's destiny were met with stony silence. Just as it happened to countless others, the whim of some party committee or person of influence had cruelly turned a hero into an 'un-person.' Marinesko was such an un-person, sent out to die in some godforsaken black hole, far away from the sea he loved so well; he missed the ocean's swell and the taste of salt on his lips; most of all, he missed breathing freely. In his moments of despair, he wished that a bomb from that German torpedo boat had struck his submarine. Then it would have been over quickly, without that lingering pain of waiting without hope for relief. But while tens of thousands died of hunger or froze to death in the labour camps, he survived the horrors of the Kolyma Gulag. Two years after Stalin's death, in 1955, a tired and sick Marinesko was finally allowed to return to Leningrad.

It took another six years before he was vindicated by a documentary programme shown on Soviet television about the victory of the Red Army in the Baltic States, which mentioned the 'Wilhelm Gustloff affair'. It named a

Captain 3rd Class A. Marinesko as commander of submarine S 13 involved in the sinking of the ship. In 1961, the Soviet Marine Museum of Leningrad added a painting of Marinesko's sub, with the explanation: '. . . The S 13 which was involved in an attack on the 25,000-ton German fascist vessel *Wilhelm Gustloff*, which the Nazis used to evacuate their military personnel from East Prussia.' The fate of the thousands of civilians on board was never mentioned.

The *Wilhelm Gustloff* affair shows that every war has two facets; while one country mourns its victims, the other glorifies a hero figure. Until the mid-1960s, the name of Aleksandr Marinesko appeared in no official Soviet history book dealing with Russia's war at sea. In October 1963, eighteen years after he had achieved his military feat, he was privately honoured by a number of former senior officers, which included the admirals of the Soviet Fleet Nikolai Kuznezov and Ivan Isakov.

Marinesko was finally lifted from his state of un-person. When asked what he thought of sinking a ship, loaded with refugees, he showed no remorse. He never considered those who drowned in the icy waters anything but enemy soldiers that had done much harm to his country.

'I sank two ships. They were German. For me, and for everyone in Russia, the Germans were our enemy. This line of thought was reconfirmed by a high-ranking official.' The supreme commander of the Soviet Fleet, Admiral S.G. Gorshkov, considers the attack on the *Wilhelm Gustloff* as a heroic deed without compare, which has nothing to equal it in the entire history of naval warfare.[15]

For Marinesko the honours came too late. Three weeks after he was rehabilitated, his rank (retired) and his pension reinstated – and eighteen full years after the event

[15] Baronov, O. and Panov, I., *A Personal Enemy of the Führer*, Moscow, 1967.

finally presented and fed with the traditional 'submariner's suckling roast piglet'[16] – Aleksandr Marinesko was dead, victim of an incurable illness he had contracted during his 'cancer ward years' in Stalin's Siberian gulag. The undisputed 'Soviet king of sunk tonnage' was given a military burial in Leningrad's central cemetery, the victim of a system he had served so well and faithfully, and which finally destroyed him.[17]

It was to take another eighteen years, to the days of *perestroika*, for the seafront in Kaliningrad, formerly Königsberg, to be renamed Marinesko Quay, and for Captain 3rd Class Aleksandr Marinesko to be posthumously awarded the title he so fervently wished for: 'Hero of the Soviet Union'.

Marinesko's motivation lay in the competitive spirit for personal glory. In the ongoing challenge among Soviet submariners to become the king of sunk tonnage, the boy from the slums of Odessa wanted to prove that he was as good, or better than the rest. While others were haunted by a fear of failure, which damned them from taking positive action, his insubordination proved the right approach. He displayed a boldness that was unrestrained by careful forethought, equalling rashness. But then he was betrayed by the system he had served so well. Jealousy and spitefulness turned his exploit into a quick trip down from the top. The medal, and the recognition that went with his heroic feat, came too late to make any difference.

[16] In the Soviet submarine fleet, it is customary to present each crew returning from a successful trip with a suckling piglet.
[17] Marinesko's grave is not far from those of the crew of the ill-fated nuclear-powered submarine *Kursk*, buried in the spring of 2002. Compared to this atomic monster sub, his S 13 would look like a lifeboat.

Dr Louis Slotin, The Chief Armourer of the United States

'He's tickling the tiger's tail.'
Dr J. Robert Oppenheimer, Los Alamos, July 1945

May God receive you, great-souled scientist.
While you were with us, even strangers knew
The breadth of lofty stature of your mind
'Twas only in the crucible of death
We saw at last your noble heart revealed.
The *Los Alamos Times* honouring Dr Slotin, 14 June 1946

Death came at 3.20 pm on a Tuesday afternoon. It did not arrive unexpectedly; in their line of work the danger always existed. The sizzling glow, which suddenly lit up the laboratory, turned their faces to a ghostly blue. Those nearby knew instantly there was no more escape. Death struck invisible and irreversible. And yet, the rapid intervention by one man was to save the lives of thousands.

That hero was Dr Louis Slotin.

There are no neutrals when it comes to 'the bomb'. There are those for it, and those against it. There are no bystanders. For over half a century, the fear of the unleashed atom has enslaved mankind with its terror and, at the same time, has kept the world at an uneasy peace. For good or for ill, the atomic bomb has shaped the destiny of the 20th century. The 'bomb story' is as much a tale of panic, as it is one of invention and discoveries. Only a thin line divides discoveries from inventions. Discoveries lead to inventions, as new inventions lead to more discoveries. This has been a major factor in the mad race for nuclear supremacy. While the splitting of the atom was a discovery, its initial application as a tool of destruction was an invention. Most of all, the 'bomb story' is the legend of men – a collaboration of genius and commitment, of some that dared to challenge the fundamental theories to which science had subscribed for centuries. A tale of trial and triumph, of conscience, persecution and shame.

The story of atomic power began a few weeks before the French Revolution of 1789; a German professor, Martin Klaproth, was handed a pot containing some yellow substance – half clay, half granular sand. It was not sand and it was not clay. Klaproth tried all the known tests, but arrived at no result. Frustrated, he put the pot on a shelf and let it gather dust, when his assistant heated their small laboratory oven for some experiment. Klaproth remembered the pot and exposed some of the yellow substance to great heat. To his surprise he came up with a hitherto unknown greyish metal that oxidised almost immediately. Every base element is known by its symbol, and as the English astronomer William Herschel had just discovered the planet Uranus (1781), Klaproth called his discovery: 'uranium'.[1] He believed that he had isolated the base element itself; in fact, he had only found a compound of uranium oxide.

---

[1] Klaproth also discovered zirconium used in flashbulbs and explosive primers.

In 1841, a French chemist, E.M. Peligot, finally reduced uranium tetrachloride with potassium in a platinum crucible to obtain the base elemental uranium (U-238). Peligot was ill-rewarded by his discovery; little did he realise that uranium was radioactive and highly dangerous. Shortly after his discovery, the chemist 'wasted away' and died soon thereafter of a strange ailment, in what was probably the first recorded case of radiation sickness.[2] Now that the element had been discovered, it was added as U-238 to the table of atomic weights, in operation since 1803, when the English chemist John Dalton proposed an atomic theory of matter. This basis of all modern chemistry was scaled on the lightest of gases, hydrogen, with its specific weight of one. For a century, nothing was done to put it to use.

It can be claimed that the world achieved a great many scientific breakthroughs due to war, but none as significant as one due to the threat of Fascism, which launched complacent Western democracies into the greatest scientific and technical undertaking of all time. In the beginning, Germany had it all – the brains to invent, and the technical means to produce. That was before Adolf Hitler set out to persecute people not for *what* they did but for *who* they were; his racial xenophobia did not spare the most brilliant minds of the century. For the victimised scientists it became not merely a question of conscience, but one of survival in the face of genocide. Had Hitler not hounded physicists from Central Europe, the programme by the Allies to produce the super-weapon might have found itself in dire trouble. In the end, Hitler was confronted with the fact that evil may be a powerful force, but it is not more powerful than genius, creativity and courage.

[2] The first major case of radiation sickness was discovered after the First World War when twenty-four women employed to produce luminous watch dials died of lethal contamination.

'He is no Einstein!' has become a way to describe someone less than brilliant. If ever there was a prime example of a dazzling mind, someone whose ideas reverberated beyond science, it was Albert Einstein.

'I want to know how God created the world,' Einstein declared the day he set out on his long road to discovery. Yes, *create* – not *destruct* – said he whose prediction that mass can be converted into energy led to the most infernal invention in the history of mankind. By 1919, the 'Man of the 20th Century' (Nobel Prize for Physics, 1921) had turned into an overnight celebrity thanks to a solar eclipse that confirmed his theories when light rays from a distant star were deflected by the gravity of the sun in the exact amount he had predicted.[3] Though he was never directly involved in 'the bomb's' creation, the name of this intensely human physicist remains forever linked to the most destructive weapon the world has ever produced.

Alongside Einstein, another important 20th-century physicist was Ernest Rutherford, director of the Cavendish Laboratory in Cambridge, a New Zealander knighted for his achievements as Lord Rutherford of Nelson. He stunned the scientific world when he announced his findings that the entire mass of the atom was concentrated in an incredibly small nucleus, and that a monstrous amount of energy must hold these particles together. What was this nucleus? According to Rutherford's simplified explanation: 'It moves around like our planetary system. Imagine an atom was to be magnified into the size of a large football stadium, its nucleus would still only be the size of a golf ball with a few nervous flies (neutrons) buzzing around.' The

[3] His Theory of Relativity asserts that light moves in a straight line through empty space and at the same speed in a vacuum, and that a light beam will curve where space-time curves. That gravity is a warping of space-time and that this distortion occurs near a massive object, such as a mega-star.

problem was to find a way to release this source of energy. Attempts to split the nucleus by Rutherford's assistants, physicists such as Ernest Marsden and Hans Geiger (who invented the Geiger counter) failed, but these showed that the nucleus remained utterly stable and absorbed more energy than was released. One thing was certain: the energy was there, just waiting for someone to find and release it.

By 1931, Albert Einstein expounded on his theories for the use of a vast source of energy during a state dinner in Berlin as guest of the visiting British Prime Minister, Ramsay MacDonald. The British premier wasn't overly interested in a profound scientific explanation he didn't understand; he had come to Germany to sign a trade agreement. But there was one dinner guest who listened most carefully. Professor Otto Hahn,[4] the prototype of the thorough-minded German professor whose in-born curiosity made him stand out in the scientific community. Hahn used for his initial experiments a hitherto untried heavy element that had been left in the scientific drawer for a hundred years. Relying on the help of two electricians and a lathe operator, he put together a strange contrivance; with steel tubes connected to a central core and dials linked by wires which coiled across the floor in spaghetti-like profusion, it gave his machine more the look of a cement mixer attached to bits collected from a junkyard than a test reactor. Hahn's experiments with his rudimentary reactor and infinitesimal quantities of uranium led to a momentous discovery: the uranium atom split when bombarded with neutrons!

Since the German authorities showed no objection, Hahn proudly announced his finding in a scientific paper, including details of the chemical base element U-238 used for the

[4] He was told about the Hiroshima bomb in a house in Cambridge, where he had been brought as a PoW.

trial. Now that the cat was out of the sack, the scientific community suddenly awoke to the prospect of nuclear terror. It was calculated that one single pound of uranium could release energy equal to 3,000,000lb of coal! If a weapon could be forged from it – God forbid! – especially in the hands of an unscrupulous dictator, like the one who had just marched into Austria and annexed the country, in this spring of 1938 . . . With his sabre-rattling policies Adolf Hitler was provoking a war. He gave the civilised world a fright with a single phrase, by declaring publicly before a huge mass of madly cheering followers in August of 1939: 'The moment might very quickly come for us to use a weapon with which we ourselves could not be attacked!'

In this climate of accumulating wisdom and the spectre of anti-Semitism, a bouncy, 35-year-old Hungarian Jew, Leo Szilard, able to manipulate mentally mathematical challenges faster than most could with a slide rule, worked on an idea so way-out that nobody was ready to believe him. The young physicist was convinced that a super-bomb was ultimately feasible. His thought-provoking source was not Einstein, but a science-fiction novel written by H.G. Wells, *The World Set Free*. In it, Wells expounded on an energy weapon of monstrous dimensions that could wipe out the entire population of the globe. The more Szilard calculated, the more he became convinced that such a bomb *could* be manufactured. Being a Jew, he was not given access to Berlin's university canteen. To discuss his findings, he met with fellow colleagues in a popular coffee shop; he received a shock when some to whom he had revealed his ideas began to show a Führer-worship syndrome. He needn't have worried; as a Jew he was at the bottom of Berlin's scientific pool and his breakthrough thoughts were dismissed as a '*jüdisches Hirngespinnst*' (mad Jewish fantasy).

With anti-Semitic pressure increasing, rumours of 'enemies of the people' being rounded up spread through Berlin's scientific community, and Szilard feared that his time would come soon. Following a dramatic escape, as Gestapo agents knocked on his front door while he belted down the back stairs, he made it with his Hungarian passport across the Danish border, and from there to London in the autumn of 1935. He tried to inform the British about the advanced scientific nuclear experiments going on in Germany, especially those of the Kaiser Wilhelm Institute under Prof. Hahn, and the possible threat this posed. Nobody listened. With a few shillings from a Jewish aid organization, Szilard continued his research in a shabby London hotel room. With pencil, paper and his mental calculator, he concentrated on two theories: 'chain reaction' and 'critical mass'. Simplified, it went like this: one neutron splits one atom – and produces two neutrons which split two atoms – which produce four neutrons which split four atoms . . . once the chain is set in motion it multiplies endlessly. For his paper on theories of 'How to build an atomic device capable of great destructive power', which were finally proven correct in every detail, Szilard was awarded two British patents in February 1936.

The Hungarian Szilard was not the only one trying to work out the secret of nuclear fission. Some were gifted amateurs, such as Franz Simon (later Sir Francis Simon), the scion of a prosperous Jewish family from Berlin, who carried out his first experiment in chemical separation by using soda water and Mother Simon's kitchen strainer. Despite a dearth of results, research not only persisted but also expanded into diversified searches by small bands of dedicated and patient scientists. Every institution worthy of its name rang the atomic bell and opened an atomic research department.

During the inter-war years, physicists began to congregate in the major centres for nuclear research: in Germany at Göttingen, Berlin and Munich with Planck, Heisemann, Pauli, Peierls, Hahn, Meitner and Strassmann; in Denmark at the Atomic Physics Institute under Niels Bohr; in France at the Radium Institute of Joliot-Curie and in the United Kingdom at Cambridge University's Cavendish Laboratory under Ernest Rutherford. And there was also increasing activity under Igor Kurchatov and Yulii Khariton at the Leningrad Physics Institute, as well as at Columbia University, in Chicago and in Berkeley. Princeton could offer as its special attraction Albert Einstein, who had emigrated to the United States.

Every scientist believed that his discovery was for the progress of mankind, not for some crude commercial deal – or worse still, to employ the atom's hidden forces to destroy the world. Such threat was first openly voiced by Igor Tamm (Nobel Prize for Physics, 1958), a top Russian physicist who declared before the Soviet Institute of Science that 'a bomb can be built that will destroy a city out to a radius of ten kilometres'. His worry was well founded. The riddle of the right element for a chain reaction was finally solved in Berlin. In December 1938, Germany's two leading chemists, Otto Hahn (Nobel Prize for Chemistry, 1944), and Fritz Strassmann, finally reached what Hahn called 'a completely new process'. This scientific breakthrough took place while the clouds of war gathered over Europe. With most of atomic research still concentrated in Germany, was it not reasonable to fear that Hitler would speed up his nuclear development programme? The 'German Uranium Project', though way ahead at the beginning of the war, was stifled by an act of intellectual snobbery. In Germany, an engineer was not considered 'a scientific brain', but a bicycle mechanic, and the physicists refused to let them take over and come up with a technical solution.

In 1939, as Germany was marching towards the brink, a meeting was set up in Berlin. The country's leading nuclear scientists, Otto Hahn, Fritz Strassmann and Walther Bothe were ordered to make their presentation to Hitler. Between them they held the key to a force that could theoretically devastate any enemy, regardless of the number of troops or his industrial output. This meeting took place in the vast marble hall of Hitler's Reichs Chancellery. Hitler was surrounded by his closest followers, yes-men such as Goering, Himmler and Goebbels, politicians all, but not one of them with a scientific brain to counsel their leader. But then the Führer thought of himself as the genius-of-the-century and as such he didn't need advice to know what was good for Germany.

When the scientists picked Hahn as their spokesman it proved to be a bad choice. The Fascist megalomaniac and his new world order of *Weltanschauung* had never impressed him and, furthermore, as a scientist, Hahn was incapable of communicating in simple, non-scientific phrases. His complicated scientific definition left Hitler with a feeling that he was wasting his time with another mad scheme. But if the Führer was bored he hid it well; throughout Hahn's narrative he maintained his reserve, that aura of mystery that held an entire nation in its iron grip.

'*Was ist unser Risiko, Herr Professor?* – What is our risk?' asked Hitler with a stern face after Hahn had finished. The question was badly phrased. What he should have asked was 'What can result from it?'

'In something so major, there is no simple relationship between try and risk.' That was hardly a reassuring assessment, but it was the best reply an honest scientist could give. Now only one man stood between an epoch-making discovery and the destruction of the world. The First World War corporal turned nation's leader had suffered through artillery bombardments on the Western Front and knew all about the effect of shellfire. He had seen tanks and planes in action, but this atom thing was not something he could touch or visualise, and therefore even imagine. To Hitler, about to launch his war machine across Europe, this scientific chatter was nothing but distracting fantasy. Whatever power this mysterious atom might conceal, it was hardly the moment to focus part of the weapons programme on a harebrained project without the slightest assurance for success. His engineers were kept busy on inventions of more immediate value: the development of radar, the magnetic torpedo or the proximity fuse.

It is likely, given his aversion to Hitler's personality, that Hahn never intended to present the full details to Germany's dictator. When the physicists presented him with the project – and then failed to mention (or purposely withheld) its weapon potential! – Hitler shrugged it off as 'atomischer Unsinn' (atomic claptrap). The physicist Wilhelm Groth's prediction that 'the country that makes first use of the atom's frightful power will achieve an unsurpassable advantage over all others' was never passed on to the German leader. For Hitler and the Third Reich, the atomic chapter was closed. History threw a dice and the world was spared the horror of a Germanic bomb.

If Hitler was struck by scientific blindness, he was not the only one. Szilard's paranoia had increased immeasurably once he read an article in a three-week-old edition of the *Berliner Tagespost* about a meeting between the Führer und Professor Otto Hahn He was obsessed with the premonition that recent discoveries by the Germans would invariably guide the Nazis to the 'ultimate weapon' – a weapon so monstrous that Nazi hegemony could dictate its will on the rest of the world. Szilard feared, and with justification, that his own theories would end up at the *Kriegsministerium* in Berlin. He delivered his plans in person in a sealed envelope to the British War Office where he didn't get past the reception and was told to slide the secret of 'how to build the A-bomb' through a slot in the window. Szilard insisted on having it marked 'Secret', and he was issued with a stamped receipt. After some considerable delay, he received a reply from an official of the Ordance Bureau: 'There appears to be no reason to keep your specification *secret* as far as the War Office is concerned.'

Such simple-mindedness – not to call it stupidity – was baffling. But then, nobody knew, or feared, a monster called the atomic bomb. The increasingly frustrated Leo Szilard left England for New York where he teamed up with an escapee from Mussolini's Fascist Italy, Professor Enrico Fermi. Together they began work in the field of nuclear fission. Operating an atom-smasher in a laboratory on the Columbia University campus, one considerably less powerful than that of Hahn in Berlin, they principally used mathematical equations to confirm Joliot-Curie's theoretical neutron experiment. The vital information obtained, which made it possible to consider the building of a super-weapon, one that could end the war quickly, was left lying in the 'in-trays' of officialdom – US officialdom was in no way an improvement over the treatment bouncy 'Leo the Bomb' had received in the UK.

Frustrated by a bureaucratic 'we shall let you know', he wrote as final resort to Albert Einstein. Like many refugees from Hitlerism, Einstein was obsessed with the idea that the Germans might find a way to release the atom's energy. The pope of physics studied Szilard's papers and his sharp mind grasped immediately its implications; Einstein wrote a note to President Franklin D. Roosevelt.

Princeton, 2 August 1939.

. . . Some recent work by E. Fermi and L. Szilard, which has been communicated to me in manuscript, leads me to expect that the element, uranium, may be turned into a new and important source of energy in the immediate future. Certain aspects of the situation which have arisen seem to call for watchfulness and, if necessary, quick action on the part of the Administration . . . a single bomb of this type, carried by a boat and exploded in a port, might very well destroy the whole port together with some of the surrounding territory . . .[5]

As it was to turn out, a design by an escapee from Fascism, together with research by other refugees from Hitler's witch-hunt, and furthered by a person in exile and the most prominent spokesman against a dictator's xenophobia, began to turn the tide. War had erupted, the UK government was harried, military production was stressed beyond the limit, and very little moved on the front of nuclear research. In late 1940, two German escapees, Rudolf Peierls and Otto Frisch, outlined in a three-page manuscript the practicality of producing a weapon of enormous destructive force. Winston Churchill recognised its potential and the Peierls Document, together with Szilard's sheaf of declassified material, was dispatched for assessment to America. The Peierls Memorandum went also in another direction. A brilliant young mathematician had joined Prof. Peierls in Birmingham. As this person was theoretically still a German citizen, he was scheduled to be sent to a PoW camp in Canada. Through a last-minute mix-up in his expulsion papers he was not put aboard the *Arandora Star*, which was torpedoed and sank with the loss of all life. Had he embarked on it, Russia would not have obtained possession of the nuclear secret by 1949.

[5] S. Weart and G. Szilard, *Leo Szilard: His Version of the Facts*, Cambridge, 1978

Klaus Fuchs, the most efficient of all Soviet atomic spies, had been passing vital nuclear information to Moscow ever since 1942.[6] Yet at the time, Stalin's thoughts were on the defence of his motherland, and like Hitler, he could only deal with what he could see or touch.

Taking note of Einstein's warning, the pragmatic President Roosevelt acted. He was fully conscious of the political implications should the wrong side get hold of such a super-weapon. With this disturbing thought, and the confirmation from Einstein, he called into being the Uranium Committee. A non-scientific board of military ran the programme and progress was slow to non-existent; in Szilard's words: 'It's like swimming around in syrup.' When he complained, he was told by one of the colonels-in-charge: 'It always takes two wars to find out if a weapon really works.'

This stand-off between scientists and the military took a sudden turn in the spring of 1942, when the US President put the head of the prestigious Carnegie Institute, Vannevar Bush, in charge of the Uranium Committee. In Bush they had found someone who could interface scientific experience with business know-how.[7] Things began to happen; two giant refining facilities grew in the midst of wooded wasteland, one near Hanford in Washington State, and the other at Oak Ridge in Tennessee. The ultra-secret undertaking was provided with a suitable cover name: the Manhattan Project.

It has been said that the First World War was the 'War of the Chemist,[8] and that the Second was the 'War of the Physicist'. Vannevar Bush put a hard-driving military man

[6] Fuchs was arrested in February 1950, seven months after Russia's first nuclear explosion.
[7] Bush was instrumental in creating the post-war military-industrial-university complex.
[8] With the improvements in explosives and lethal mustard gases.

in charge of logistics; Major General Leslie Groves from the US Army Corps of Engineers was called to Washington in September 1942.

'If you do your job right you'll win us the war,' Bush told him. Groves, who knew all about building bridges, but had never heard of nuclear fission, set about gathering 'the bright brains'. At the top of his shopping list was Nobel laureate Harold Urey of Columbia University, the discoverer of heavy water, and Nobel laureate Ernest O. Lawrence, the son of a Dakota preacher, whose life's ambition it had always been to build a 'better mousetrap'. He invented the atom-smasher. Lawrence was put in charge of extracting fissible U-235[9] from the base element U-238 by electromagnetic process; Urey, assisted by Dunning and Keith, suggested another way to produce bomb-grade U-235 by a gaseous diffusion process.

Another Nobel laureate, Arthur Compton of Chicago, brought with him Leo Szilard, Enrico Fermi and Eugene Wigner. Together with Hans Bethe, John von Neumann and Edward Teller, they were told to build a nuclear reactor. The problems confronting these men of science, plunged into the unfamiliar atmosphere of military secrecy, were simply overwhelming. In this uncharted territory nothing was certain; they couldn't share their findings nor discuss these with the rest of the international scientific community. This gigantic undertaking could only be achieved by another 'first' in the history of scientific research: money! Finding the money to win a war was no problem. But it meant that in the laboratory only one certainty counted – to win the nuclear race before the Nazis had the bomb.

[9] U-235 is slightly lighter as it contains three fewer neutrons in its nucleus.

A major breakthrough came at 15.53 hrs on 2 December 1942. In the basement of the squash court, located under the stands of the football stadium on the University of Chicago campus, Prof. Enrico Fermi and his assistants piled 40,000 graphite blocks – around 50 tons of uranium ore. Fermi knew that uranium gave out neutrons, which, captured by other uranium atoms, or 'the critical mass', would split and build up into a 'chain reaction', liberating a tremendous source of energy. That was the principle. Now for the practice. Fermi's first reactor, called CP-1, consisted of a lattice of uranium slugs, dropped into cavities of blocks of greasy graphite to act as moderator; sliding cadmium control rods were used to prevent the (hoped-for) chain reaction from getting out of control. On that historic afternoon, when Fermi climbed down the stairs into the basement room, his heart was beating faster than it had ever done before. Too much was depending on what happened next – perhaps the entire course of the war would be altered, if he read correctly the reactions by all those present. Only a select number had been given access to the control room (the changing room of the varsity's basketball team) to follow the experiment on a large display panel. The pressure created by the constant worry over failure or success showed on everyone's face; some were frightened, but all were anxious. Fermi threw the switch to the relays that slowly hoisted the cadmium control rods . . . suddenly something began to sizzle . . . dials raced . . . critical mass was achieved. *It worked!*

'Insert the rods,' the professor yelled to his assistant. When the control rods dropped and the critical danger was averted, Fermi felt a splurge of happiness. They had achieved it! Everyone rushed up to congratulate him. An excited Arthur Compton rang his contact in Washington: 'The Italian navigator has landed in the New World.'

'Were the natives friendly?'

'Everyone landed safe and happy,' came the cheerful reply.[10]

During the general jubilation, one of his assistants, the Canadian Louis Slotin, remarked: 'The world will change tomorrow.'

'Not for us,' replied Fermi. 'For us nothing changes. We shall always be alone.'

One of the Chicago Group assisting Fermi in his experiment, was a young Canadian from Winnipeg. Louis Slotin was born in 1910 to a couple of Orthodox Jewish immigrants who had escaped from the pogroms of a Tsar. The young Louis grew up in the predominantly immigrant atmosphere of Winnipeg's North End, where temperatures during the winter months favourably rivalled those at the North Pole. He inherited the pioneer spirit of his father, who had taken the new Canadian Pacific to a railway siding in the middle of the Canadian prairies, soon to become the town of Winnipeg in Manitoba. Father Slotin turned his mind to dealing in livestock, but young Louis had other ambitions and showed these at an early age. He was the scholarly little kid on the block, who would rather read books than spend his time running after a ball. One day, teenaged Louis, browsing in a second-hand bookshop, found a volume on basic physics and chemistry. He devoured the book and, through it, discovered his vocation.

'Dad, I want to go to university.'

'To deal in livestock he wants to go to university? The quality of beef you'll learn down in the stockyard.'

'No, Dad, I want to become a physicist.'

'A what?' asked a stunned father Slotin, who had envisaged his son pushing quantities of prime prairie beef to the

[10] A. Compton, *Atomic Conquest*, New York, 1956.

folks in Toronto and Montreal. Yet once convinced that his son wouldn't be a dealer in livestock, he fully supported his ambition by paying his way through school. Louis proved himself as extremely ambitious and studious; this bespectacled youngster was so brilliant that, aged only sixteen, he passed his entry exam into the physics department of the University of Manitoba, where he won the Gold Medal in both physics and chemistry. When Canada's Research Council wouldn't allow him a grant to further his graduate studies, he left for London to join Prof. Allmand at King's College.

While working out in the college gym, he was challenged by the college's varsity coach: 'Forget the push-ups, stick to your books, young man.' He considered this remark as an attack on his skinny frame and it so upset him that he took off his spectacles, folded his books and began serious training; as he did with everything else, he wanted to be better than others and with sheer will he became the university squad's bantam-weight boxing champion. However, this did not gain him the renown of his intellectual output, which won him a medal for his remarkable thesis on the 'Intermediate reaction of unstable molecules during some chemical reaction' – his passport into the nuclear society.

By 1937, Slotin had moved back to America where he joined the University of Chicago as a research associate, spending every moment of his time helping to build the world's first atom-smashing 'cyclotron'. With his dexterity, he became the great expert with paper and screwdriver, an engineer among physicists and a physicist of engineering. There was nothing to stop him from trying his theories in practice, and for this he welded, wired and tested. He built the weirdest contraptions; some worked, many didn't, but never for lack of trying.

'It was hard and often disappointing work,' wrote his

colleague, Henry Newson. 'We did the machine shop work, the wiring, even broke up the concrete ourselves.' The late thirties were hard times for science and research. Untested new projects lacked financing, Louis's income was almost zero, and he had to be supported by a generous allowance from his father, proud to call a member of his family 'my son, the doctor', although old man Slotin had not the slightest inkling of what his son was working on. Louis's enthusiasm and intellectual intake brought him to the attention of Prof. Enrico Fermi, who accepted him into his team at Chicago's Metallurgical Laboratory when the Manhattan Project was launched. And thereby it happened that a young Louis Slotin was in Chicago when Prof. Fermi proved the feasibility of a self-sustaining nuclear chain reaction with his pile of graphite around a uranium core.[11]

For young Dr Louis, scientific challenge was everything in life. From the outset, he was hooked on the nuclear project and eagerly followed the call, first to Oak Ridge, where he worked with Prof. Eugen Wigner on plutonium production, before he was transferred to Los Alamos, and in December 1944 attached to the Bomb Physics Section of Prof. R.F. Bacher. Louis Slotin thus became one of the select whiz kids in their mid-twenties, guided and fathered by some of the greatest brains in science, the Nobel-Prize physicists. His work was covered by the Official Secrects Act. For his family, this meant that their son had 'fallen off the edge of the world'. One postcard from an unspecified place read: '. . . And don't worry, Dad, if you don't hear from me for a while, I'll be fine . . .'. This was followed by more months of silence. They knew that their son was doing research work on some kind of metal, probably designing

[11] According to a Chicago University record, Slotin was present during the Fermi test, although one of his colleagues, Henry Newson, claims that he wasn't.

new wheels for an automobile and the car company wanted to safeguard its secret. The Winnipeg Slotins had no idea that their 26-year-old offspring was about to put together the most destructive weapon ever devised by man.

Following Fermi's experiment, 'the bomb' was no longer the *Hirngespinst* of a mad Hungarian scientist. Now was the moment when engineers took over from the physicists. But the road ahead was hard and arduous. To extract a few kilos of fissible uranium would take three years and two billion dollars. Two elements held potential – the first of which was uranium, which had been around since 1789 and was fairly well known. There was, however, another possible base element, highly unstable, poisonous and deadly radioactive.

In 1940, an American research team under Glenn Seaborg (Nobel Prize for Chemistry, 1951), Edwin McMillan, Joseph Kennedy and Arthur Wahl, made a surprise discovery. Between them they held a dozen lifetimes of experience in chemistry and, yet, they didn't know what to do with their terrifying find. 'It is so bad, so highly unstable, just to mention its name scares the living daylights out of me,' claimed Seaborg. Named after the planet Pluto, plutonium was, without doubt, the most lethal of all known man-made elements. The advantage of plutonium over uranium was that it had a bigger nucleus, thereby promising an even more powerful release of energy.

The next major headache was the separation process. How to isolate fission-grade material (U-235) from its dirty base elements (U-238)?[12] Or how to transmute uranium into the supercritical plutonium (Pu-239)? The electromagnetic process called for giant magnets that sucked up huge amounts of electrical power, enough to run the

[12] Uranium-235 had to be enriched from its normal 0.7 per cent content to more than 90 per cent!

industry of an entire state; that could be resolved with the financial means at their disposal. The second way, gaseous extraction, was a different matter. It required membranes with such minute holes that no drill proved fine enough. This problem had the engineers stymied – until one of them, while sitting down at his daily ablution, leafed through a glossy magazine and, bingo, his magic lantern lit up! Pictures in newspapers were nothing but an amalgam of minute dots. Newsprint and acid led to a dramatic breakthrough in the creation of membranes with millions of holes. Once proven, the gaseous diffusion method beat out the more costly electromagnetic process.

Now that both plutonium and uranium productions were on line, that still left a viable bomb design. At this stage entered a person of pure genius, a 39-year-old physicist from the University of Berkeley, Dr J. Robert Oppenheimer. A Harvard graduate (1925) with an honours degree from Germany's Göttingen University for his thesis on quantum numbers of the nitrogen nucleus, he was told to 'create a device for producing an explosive neutron chain reaction in a fissile material, such as uranium U-235 or plutonium Pu-239'. This confronted him with several challenges: to work out on paper the critical mass necessary to set off a chain reaction of sufficient destructive power and, secondly, to find a way to isolate the two critical masses. After all, the idea was to blow up Berlin, not the State of Tennessee. For security reasons, this operation couldn't be achieved at the site of the separation plants. A new location had to be found.

As a boy scout, Oppenheimer had camped on top of a desolate mesa in the New Mexico desert, named Los Alamos. It was in the midst of nowhere, an ideal spot to guarantee safety and secrecy. It was hard to imagine a more dismal and forbidding place than Los Alamos; everything seemed the wrong way around. In a way, this proved a blessing, since they had to start from scratch. A secret village grew in the desert. Oppenheimer's only run-in with the military chief, Major General Leslie Groves, was over the matter of wearing uniforms. This, his scientists simply refused to do.

The 'bomb squad' received a boost with the arrival of Niels Bohr, who fathered a thesis on the structure and radiation of atoms. For fear that the Germans might find out what went on behind the electrified fence of Los Alamos, the exiled Danish professor was introduced around camp as Dr Nicholas Baker. Everyone felt the pressure – a tension, so Oppenheimer considered, critical to their work. They improvised their way through unknown territory. Nothing worked; special lathes were ordered to handle the new metals, and the machine tools proved too brittle; precision-machined casings didn't pass the stringent tests; the wires on electric circuits were too bulky and the trip switches too slow. It was a nightmare. In the midst stood a calm Oppenheimer, conductor of an orchestra of talented technicians. Every problem was passed his way, and most solutions originated from his suggestion. All was teamwork and each problem a personal challenge. They worked the drawing boards and they worked the lathes, until someone came up with an answer. Dr Louis Slotin, the 26-year-old boy genius from Winnipeg, was put in charge of the delicate operation of monitoring the plutonium chain reaction; the title given to his small but select group was 'combat core team'.

The 'core' of the bomb was made up of two carefully machined, beryllium-coated grapefruit-sized halves of weapon-grade plutonium. The plutonium core was a complex challenge to manufacture, and in its assembly stage infinitely more hazardous than bringing into critical contact two uranium spheres. To install them in the correct position called for the specialist, and Slotin was just the man for this job. Someone had to do it, and he was used to handling volatile plutonium. Counting on both his valuable experience as an engineer and as a physicist on the cyclotron, he was put in charge of designing a viable assembly procedure of the two critical masses. His acceptance of incredible risks was best demonstrated by a bizarre incident. A valve of one of the cooling elements got stuck; to adjust the valve, Slotin stripped down to his shorts and dived into the water container that had been specially installed to absorb radiation. He shrugged it off with 'One of us had to do it'. His colleague Dr Morgan called Slotin 'a cowboy – but a brilliant experimental scientist'.[13]

Slotin thrived on challenge; for him it became a continuous trial-by-error, knowing only too well that an error while handling 'the real thing' would not permitted. He developed a system that was as unique as it could be lethal. Enrico Fermi, watching him performing a trial run, remarked with great apprehension: 'If you keep doing this with the real thing, you'll be dead within a year.' Using his nimble hands, the young Canadian (now a naturalised American citizen) stood up to the task. The fact that this was nothing less than to find out how close a distance from each other the two plutonium halves could be brought together, before the parts went 'prompt critical', became known around Los Alamos as 'tickling the tiger's tail'.

He began by working out in theory how this could be best achieved, before he designed the machine to do the job. In appearance it was similar to a vertical lathe, dubbed with morbid premonition the 'guillotine'. One of the plutonium half-spheres was placed on the bottom of this specially built test-bench, with its flat side facing up. Its twin sister was then attached with a clip-spring to a

[13] The Canadian journalist Martin Zeilig in a 1995 article about Louis Slotin in *The Beaver*.

system of levers which could be lowered – not with the fall-speed of the notorious French instrument of death but very, very gently to measure the gap just before a 'prompt critical reaction' (nuclear explosion) was allowed to set in. If the two halves remained divided by too great a gap, the end result would prove ineffective; like opposite poles they would 'expand' (drift apart).

To explain the effect, Slotin used the preamble of a racing car and its driver. Leaving the halves too far apart was like a racing car starting in reverse gear. To get a good start the driver had to wind the engine to maximum revs until the green light, and then send his car hurtling forward with the sudden depression of the accelerator (the gun effect). The same also applied to the assemblage of the two beryllium-coated hemispheres. Like the car, the grapefruit halves were sitting on the starting grid, waiting for their green light; only here the bomb's accelerator was a tightly packed, standard chemical explosive, slamming the halves against one another. Too far apart and they would 'idle' or fizzle out, too close and they would bring the critical surplus of neutrons to ignite into an uncontrolled reaction. Yet nobody could tell with precision where this gap lay. Scientists had calculated that the 'critical safe point' prior to a 'prompt burst' lay in a theoretical separation of between 3 to 4mm; but that was at best an estimated value.

Dr Slotin and his assistants burned many a night's candles, trying various approaches. During this time, Dr Slotin was a walking laboratory, his pockets on his white smock bulged with pliers, slide rule, screwdriver, electric tape and bits of wire. He was so involved in his work that he missed meal times, and the canteen had to make special sandwiches long after dinnertime; Sunday was an unknown luxury.

Assisted by his team he began by inserting precision-machined spheres made from ordinary metal but of correct size and roughly similar in weight to the 'real thing'. At this preparatory stage it mattered not if things went wrong, other than extra trials were time-consuming. Everything could be repaired, amended or scrapped. They spent endless hours in workshops rebuilding or improving their 'guillotine'; they worked on it until they were confident that they could perform the operation with eyes closed. Those were practice runs with spheres of ordinary steel. Given the inherent danger of radiation exposure, the real operation would be relatively crude and performed without adequate protection. In other words, during his assembly with the real thing, Dr Slotin would be virtually 'flying by the seat of his pants'.

Then came the day when Slotin was given 'the real thing'. Nothing was left to chance; the assembly room with its central guillotine was ready and bathed in near blinding white light. They removed the first half from its container and placed it carefully in its lower cradle on the guillotine. Then came the tricky part, the second half; it clipped into a system of spring fasteners on a movable arm, swinging out from the lathe for added security. Once clicked back in place, and verified for its perfect alignment, a hand-operated sprocket wheel and pinion was used to lower the arm holding the second half into the critical distance. For this first assemblage, Slotin's only reliable measurement tool was an improved Geiger counter and the voice of his 24-year-old assistant, Harry Daghlian, standing three feet behind him and calling out the radiation values as well as the distance shown on a luminous scale, while Slotin's eyes remained fixed on the two halves.

A neutron monitor, which looked like a weatherman's barometer, recorded the radiation increase in red ink on a paper drum. With such simple devices, a great amount of physical courage, and a pair of steady hands, Slotin began lowering the top semi-sphere by the measured turn of the hand-operated wheel on to its waiting sister. Gradually the distinctive crackle of the Geiger counter increased as Daghlian called out the readings of the gauge needle, which still showed an acceptable output of 'rads' (measurement of radiation). Suddenly the crackle of the Geiger counter began to accelerate furiously in volume . . .

'Approaching critical!' announced Daghlian in a steady voice, as if conducting another dummy run.

The counter raced, the needle jumped. Daghlian called out: 'Critical!'

Slotin racked the wheel a fraction back before bringing the operation to a stop. The first 'live test' had been brought to a successfully conclusion. Oppenheimer, Fermi and all the hard-working scientists were the winners. General Groves beamed. So did Slotin; within days, he delivered the first assembled bomb core to the 'Trinity' personnel and for it was jokingly awarded the honorific title of 'Chief Armourer of the United States'.

Oppenheimer's team began to install the core into the bomb mechanism. Actually, there were altogether three bombs. One was made up of 30lb (13 kg) of weapons-grade uranium to provide its critical mass. In their jargon, this became known as the uranium gun-type device, because two hemispherical halves of U-235 were loaded into the opposite ends of a gun-barrel cylinder drilled from tungsten steel. A standard artillery charge was placed behind one half to smash it into the other and thereby create a chain reaction.

The other two bombs were made up of plutonium. Here, the scientist faced a similar problem as with its cousin, the uranium bomb – the firing sequence. To set off the chain reaction of the plutonium centre core was more difficult: the plutonium half-spheres were to be compressed, suddenly and most violently. This process was called an 'implosion'. Its crucial element was timing; the chemical explosive charges had to be fired at precisely one millionth of a second. For a long time, this had them stymied until it was resolved with the invention of a revolutionary electronic micro-switch, called a 'kriton'.

Standard gun explosives were tightly packed around the Pu-239 sphere, and the electronic micro-switch triggers inserted. It was the implosion bomb that was finally picked for the only test run, code-named 'Trinity'. Unauthorised access into the final assembly hall was impossible. Past a guard post, manned by a special unit with orders to shoot-to-kill without challenge, and through a steel door on rollers which could only be opened from the inside, and only after a coded message had been passed from the guard post. After proceeding through a visual check, the way led along a narrow passage into a domed hall, brightly lit by fluorescent tubes. Coming out of the dark tunnel, it took some time for the eyes to adjust to its glaring brightness. It was here that the plutonium bomb had been assembled. The object that caused so much anxiety was lying in its cradle, painted black, with two metal hooks and wires sticking from an external electronic connector box. There was something evil radiating from this instrument of death. Perhaps it was its surroundings, the sinister dark of a prehistoric cavern that had once given shelter to cavemen who used mastodon bones to butcher their foe. Now it housed the ultimate weapon ever devised by man.

The scientists and engineers knew they had 'a big one'; they didn't know how big it was. Nobody ever questioned the truth of applied physics, just as nobody ever questioned that a straight line is the shortest distance between two points. Physics, like mathematics, is neat and logical because it exists only in terms of its own definition. Like most untried things in life, this device depended on definition. In the days leading up to the test, most physicists were overwrought and suffered from lack of sleep; *facts* were their profession – and they didn't have facts, only conjecture and estimates. To claim afterwards that they hadn't understood the full implications of a nuclear blast would be superfluous once it was set off.

When General Groves asked Oppenheimer about the projected force of the blast, he was given a scientist's reply: 'This is hard to explain without mathematics, but if you stand next to an atomic explosion, it makes no difference if it is ten, or a hundred kilotons.' But was 'that thing' really under the control of man, or had they created a monster that would send humanity back to rejoin the apes? Whenever a physicist dared to express his concern, the military hierarchy wrote it off as 'scientist's paranoia'. Added to the many technical problems came the stress factor.

'I've always believed that God is on our side and now we're going to prove it,' Dr Oppenheimer stated flatly on the evening before. One thing all were sure of: from tomorrow at sunrise, the world would never be the same again.

'A big one,' they said. At dawn they would find out how big. 'Wake up the dragon . . .'

'Trinity Day', 16 July 1945, and the first glow of a new day was rising over the Journado del Muerte desert at the Alamogorodo test site in New Mexico. The thoughts of those who were permitted to share this historic day were fixed on the top of a 100-foot (30-metre) steel tower . . . some fidgeted with the zippers on their coveralls, others chewed their fingernails. Slotin was inside a concrete bunker, checking his read-out over and over again to make sure everything was correct. It was.

Oppenheimer's face looked drawn – concentration, fear, or conscience, who could tell?[14] For months he had felt like Robinson on the island, closeted with his calculations and

14 R. Oppenheimer, *The Open Mind*, New York, 1955.

data, developing projections based on what was known – and that was precious little. Now that they were about to enter history, he felt as if some external power was overriding the impulses transmitted from his brain; it left him with a natural fear of woe to come.

The more he had researched the feasibility of an atomic explosion, the more repellent it appeared. 'Stop playing God,' he told himself. Later he would confide to a friend that, at this moment, his mind had turned to a poem from the Hindu epic of *Bhagavad Gita*:

> if the radiance of a thousand suns were to burst at once
>   into the sky
> that would be like the splendor of the mighty One,
> I become death, *the shatterer of worlds* . . .

'Start countdown . . . sixty minutes and counting. Twenty minutes and counting. Power relays all active . . . goggles on. Fifteen seconds, ten . . . five, four, three, two . . . one. 05.29 hours forty-five seconds. *If the radiance of a thousand suns, were to burst at once into the sky*, a pinpoint flash, the explosion of light was so blinding that it ran through all the colours of the rainbow before it became pure white and grew rapidly into a ball of fire. *I become death, the shatterer of worlds*. The earth shook and darkness followed. With a demon's shriek, the pressure wave passed over their dug-outs, a cataract of sound and wind. Those in the open dug-out watched with pounding hearts and eyes protected by smoked goggles; their facial skins were pulled back by the wind's force into ugly masks while they fixed their attention on the terrifying display. The chaos was so gigantic that their minds did not fully react to the enormity of what they had just witnessed.

Enrico Fermi was the only man thinking rationally. He dropped a sheet of paper and allowed it to be blown across the dug-out floor. Quickly he measured the distance from his position to the paper. While those who had observed the flash looked away from the blast to get their sight back to normal, Fermi worked on his slide rule. Triumphantly he held it up before he turned to the others.

'It corresponds to a blast of 10,000 tons of TNT.'

General Groves stared at him. 'What? Oh . . . we must keep this thing quiet.'

'What do you mean, quiet? They've heard that blast in five states . . .'[15]

The United States of America had the 'ultimate weapon.

'The bomb will never go off, and I speak as an expert on explosives,' Admiral William Leahy, his American president, had advised. But it had just done that, and on Trinity Day.[16] Following the test bomb, America still carried two usable bombs in its atomic arsenal: a plutonium implosion device of 13 KT (kiloton)[17] and a uranium fission bomb of 22 KT.[18] Now the question was asked what to do with them?

Nazi Germany lay smashed; it had surrendered two and a half month earlier. That's when something happened to the physicists. The majority of the Los Alamos scientists were European Jews, afraid of the Nazi menace. They had no quarrel with the Japanese. Conscience set in over the horror weapon they had invented.

'The use of any weapon in war may be immoral if it

[15] The explanation given to the local population was that an ammunition dump had blown up.

[16] US president, Harry Truman, was told about Trinity during the Conference of Potsdam, July 1945.

[17] One kiloton equals 1000 tons of TNT.

[18] KT, or kiloton, is the amount of energy released by 1000 tons of TNT. The plutonium bomb was dropped on Hiroshima (6 Aug 1945), the uranium one on Nagasaki (9 Aug 1945).

causes more suffering than absolutely necessary,' became their guiding argument. Spokesman for the dissident scientific community once again became bouncy Leo Szilard.[19] He said openly what was on everyone's mind: they had *feared* that the Germans could produce it; they *knew* that the Japanese could not! When General Groves would not receive him, Szilard went over the general's head to James Byrnes, US Secretary of State.

That sent Groves into a tantrum: 'Since its inception the Manhattan Project has been plagued by the presence of certain scientists of doubtful discretion and uncertain loyalty.'[20] His xenophobic accusation included the man who had been instrumental in its success, but whose moral conscience had forced him to voice his concern, Dr Robert Oppenheimer. This episode was to lead to one of the most shameful events in American history, the witch trials of moral objectors. Oppenheimer and Szilard weren't on their own. Many scientists were now against using their creation. When it was felt that no single nation should hold control over such unbridled power, Niels Bohr had even suggested opening the secret to their Russian war allies. In late June 1945, a meeting was called in Washington. Groves and Oppenheimer were present.

On the way to the meeting, he queried Oppenheimer: 'Are you aware of the plans of that dissident group in Chicago?' by which he referred to the men around Leo Szilard.

'If you talk about their worries, my answer is yes.'

'You want to polish up your conscience while we have the chance to finish this whole thing with one shot?' The

[19] Together with his friend E. Wigner, Szilard received the prestigious 'Atoms for Peace Prize' in 1959.
[20] Groves' anti-Semitic and anti-foreigner xenophobia, in J. Blum, *The Price of Vision*, Boston, 1973.

memory of this particular incident was to carry over into the shameful 'Red scare' period of the early 1950s. Groves ran into more opposition during the high-powered meeting. This time criticism came from within his own camp, the military.

'Whatever will the world think of us? This device is not an honourable way to lead a war,' argued a high-ranking naval officer.

General Groves went red in the face. 'What do you call honourable, admiral? Do you call Pearl Harbor honourable?'

'We must make a public show of the device before using it.'

Oppenheimer sat there and smoked his pipe. So far he hadn't taken a side.

'What about a public test, Dr Oppenheimer?'

'You mean, invite the Japanese, and show them?'

'Something like it, yes.'

'If we conduct a test, invite the Japanese, and we fail, what then? We will have wasted some irreplaceable material.'

'You mean to say, we go ahead and drop it without a test?'

'That is not for a scientist to say, that only a president can decide.'

When Oppenheimer returned to Los Alamos, the first thing everyone wanted to know was: test or no test.

'Yes, we'll do it,' their chief told them.

'Has anybody ever given this a thorough thought? It will affect the lives of thousands, perhaps even millions,' said one of the scientists, Dr Louis Slotin.

Oppenheimer took his pipe from his mouth and pointed with it at the young scientist. 'We've been asked to solve a technical problem, not come to a moral judgment. We assemble it, that's all.'

A barbarous war was still going on in the Pacific. American losses were heavy. To end the war, the United

States was faced with the prospect of an invasion of Japan's home islands, and more casualties. Science was replaced by politics. Now that their job was done, the inventors were told to climb back into their sandbox and play with new toys. All further decisions were reserved for the shapers of a post-war universe of eternal peace. The American president was adamant. In a historic statement Truman declared: 'If a bomb can be built – a bomb can be used.'[21]

Today it is clear that the scientists knew something that the president of the United States either did not know or did not consider: *the moral implications* and, with them, the stigma this would leave on the country that unleashed a monster on humanity. Democracy is based on the principle that if people have enough information, wise decisions will be made. None of the Washington officials had ever been told of the after-effects of a nuclear explosion caused by radiation fall-out. After the test blast, the apparent ill-effects suffered by US troops that had been purposely stationed close to the Trinity blast site, with no more protection than a pair of smoke-coloured goggles, were either ignored, or hushed up. The lesson, that the bomb was the obliteration of all moral issues and could eventually threaten all of humanity, had been understood by scientists but had not been learned by politicians.

An 'interim committee', chaired by the Secretary of War, Harry L. Stimson, met in Washington to decide if the bomb should be dropped on Japan and, if so, where? One side of the table suggested dropping the bomb on to a purely military objective, such as the island of Truk in the Pacific Ocean. Yet to achieve a 'profound psychological impact' on Japan's population, a strike would have to be announced and the military feared that the

[21] H. Truman, *The Year of Decision*, New York, 1955.

enemy would move thousands of American PoWs on to the site so that idea was abandoned. Nothing is known of what really took place in the conference room that day of decision, nor who voted for and who against the drop; the official, declassified archives contain only a brief memorandum:

After much discussion about various types of targets and the effects to be produced, Secretary Stimson expressed the conclusion, on which there was general agreement, that we could not give the Japanese any warning ... but we should seek to make a profound psychological impression on as many of the inhabitants as possible.[22]

Only a small band of nuclear scientists realised that even wars have their limits. On 6 August 1945, at 08.15 am, the world entered the Nuclear Age with a single phrase, yelled by the co-pilot aboard the *Enola Gay*: 'My God! What have we done!?'

'For we cannot control nature except by obeying her,' Francis Bacon (1561–1626) had written in his *Novum Organum*. A small community of scientists had attempted to control nature, and they had nothing to celebrate. Once the world had seen pictures of a nuclear dead zone, it was impossible not to launch into a moral judgment. Of course, there had been other lethal attacks on cities, causing even more casualties, such as the firebombing of Dresden and Tokyo. But that was achieved with 'conventional arms', which seemed acceptable. This, on the other hand, was a test case clearly designed to demonstrate man's scientific ingenuity and industrial might.

Niels Bohr, a visionary, had tried to warn the American president Roosevelt as early as July 1944: 'The fact of

22 M. Sherwin, *A World Destroyed*, New York, 1975.

immediate preponderance is that a weapon of unparalleled power is being created which will completely change all future conditions of warfare . . . any temporary advantage, however great, may be outweighed by a perpetual menace to human security.'

Was this then the greatest invention achieved by mankind? Was the atomic bomb a mere *accident de parcours* brought about by a will to end all slaughter on the battlefield and man's genuine wish to stop the continuation of such barbarous activity? Or was it an unavoidable predicament on the long road in search for 'the ultimate'? One thing was certain: the nuclear threat had modified the realm of warfare in which a gamble was no longer permitted. The trust which the leader of a super-power might place in such a weapon as a deterrent to aggression was merely an illusion. Any contest with atomic weapons would be no duel, but mutual suicide. In pragmatic terms it might be argued that the atomic bombs dropped on Hiroshima and Nagasaki killed many thousands, but in fact saved millions of lives since it did end the war, and prevented the next big one from starting. At least the first bomb on Hiroshima may thus be defended.[23]

'Did you know what you were doing?' Many scientists, directly involved in the monster's creation, claimed afterwards that they had no idea of the awesome power they were unleashing on future generations. Dr Louis Slotin was among them. In a letter to his parents he wrote that

[23] Sir Henry Tizard, wartime chairman of Britain's Air Ministry Aeronautical Research Committee, addressing the Royal United Service Institution a few months after the war, declared: 'It was indeed fortunate that the atomic bomb and the long-range rocket were publicly demonstrated before the end of the war, although they had very little effect on its outcome.' (R. Clark, *The Birth of the Bomb*, London, 1961)

'a tremendous step has been achieved, and I am the proud part of it'. Indeed, for a scientist, 'the birth of the bomb' was a success. Nothing untoward had happened during its creation, and its final result was convincing: two towns had been obliterated, incinerated and blown into smithereens, giving visible proof of the Promethean power of the atom. American political decision-makers were mesmerised and brashly self-confident about the fact that they now held the ultimate weapon. Generals held the unshakeable belief in the inevitability of nuclear weapons according to the military line of thought that 'bigger is better'. Nothing could go wrong. The time of war emergency, where it was all right to 'slap them together as fast as you can', that period was not yet over; the world was still far from being ready for eternal peace.

Physicists and technicians continued their work, still unconcerned about adequate safety procedures. There had been only a few minor incidents, yet no matter how insignificant any one of these mishaps may actually have been, they all were serious, since these were part of an unimaginable force let loose. The nuclear community began having first doubts – were they really immune from mishap? A feeling grew that, whatever the perfection of the system in theory, the practical prospect of ensuring that every component was handled with the same precision was simply too much to ask for in a system reliant on human beings. Distressed over a fight with the wife, an upset stomach, a sweaty hand that trembled; these are just some of the many reasons why things can go wrong.

But habit is the greatest hazard; like any task, performed day in day out, it tends to become routine, and provokes an 'I can do it in my sleep' attitude which can lead to a moment's inattention, and disaster. Even those who advocated guaranteed trouble-free development slowly came to realise the potential danger of a catastrophic accident. As the flow of technical criticism increased, and the radiation after-effects of Nagasaki and Hiroshima were publicised, a general awareness of the danger, and overall hostility to nuclear arms exploded throughout the world with a uniformity and spontaneity that was unprecedented. But it changed nothing; the military made certain that any constructive criticism in the West was written off as the Big Red Conspiracy, designed to weaken America's will to defend universal liberty. The Great War was over; yet another had started the moment the victors began quarrelling among themselves. Churchill gave it a name: 'The Cold War'. America had 'the bomb', which gave it unique super-power status to dictate world destiny. World hegemony was at stake – and its key was 'the bomb'.

The nuclear mill ground on; more tests were made and bigger and better bombs produced. In late 1945 occurred an unexplained mishap. During one of their 'routine operations', something unexplained happened and Slotin's assistant Harry Daghlian absorbed a sizeable dose of 'rads'. Though, by now, the results of exposure to radiation had been observed and studied on the victims of the Hiroshima and Nagasaki blasts, the study of burns by gamma rays and neutrons was still in its infant steps. Many of the survivors died within days after the blast, victims of that new, silent killer: 'radiation'. It was known that a dosage of 1000 rads was life-terminating; at Nagasaki it was found that anyone within a radius of two miles (3.2 km) of detonation point had received 1000 rads and that radiation sickness symptoms became almost immediately evident. As a result of these studies, a scale was established which put nuclear fall-out exposure into four categories:

Level One   (0 to 100 rads), no apparent symptoms, tiredness.
               Chance of recovery: not life-threatening
Level Two   (100 to 200 rads), general malaise effect. Chance
               of recovery: reasonable
Level Three (200 to 600 rads), skin haemorrhage, fever, throat
               swelling. Chance of recovery: 20 per cent
Level Four   (600 to 1000 rads), gastrointestinal symptoms,
               vomiting, nausea, extreme fever, ataxia, bleeding
               in mouth and urine. Chance of recovery: zero;
               death occurs within days

Daghlian's condition, established as 'Level Three', became the first known case directly connected to the bomb production process in the United States. His condition weakened by the day. One of his frequent visitors in the specially designated quarantine section of the camp's hospital was Louis Slotin. The invisible killer defeated every effort to save Daghlian.

With the death of his friend Harry Daghlian, Slotin's heart was no longer in it; he began planning to return to civilian life and work on scientific research projects in Chicago and he applied for a position in Prof. Raymond Zirkle's Chicago Institute of Biophysics. He wanted to explore new fields – perhaps with the dream of eventually being awarded the coveted Nobel Prize for Physics. He agreed to remain in Los Alamos until he had trained a suitable replacement, at least until after 'Operation Cross-roads', the projected 1946 Bikini-test.

'I have become involved in more tests, much to my disgust. But I am one of the few people around here who are experienced *bomb put-togetherers*,' confided Slotin to his friend Philip Morrison in the spring of 1946. Indeed, Slotin's wartime exuberance had evaporated; he and his colleagues had helped his country win the war and then had seen the devastating result caused by their creation.

As for a future peril posed by Stalin's Russians, all he knew about them was what his father had told him about the Czar's pogroms. America continued assembling more and bigger bombs, and Louis Slotin, America's 'Chief Armourer', continued 'to screw these things together'.

'How can you do it, day after day?' asked a colleague every day.

'There's little difference between a car assembly line, and what I am doing. It's routine.' Indeed, routine, but of a most lethal sort, because routine makes for carelessness. And his routine was not putting cars together, but tickling a tiger's tail.

On the Omega Site, the super-secret assembly location in the Pajarito Canyon off Los Alamos, was located a concrete laboratory with a small steel door and an even smaller lead-glass window. That day, eight persons were in the room: Slotin, standing at the assembly lathe; slightly behind to observe the operation was his 'trainee', the man designated to take over from him, Alvin Graves; behind Graves stood another scientist, Allan Kline. Also in the room, but slightly further apart, were other nuclear scientists: Cieslicki, Young, Schreiber and Perlman. There was also a security guard, Patrick Cleary. Over the months it had become a pattern before every assembly – a great tension was built up and could only be discharged by a successful finish. Again, like the times before, all felt this tension.

Dr Slotin had never played poker with the laws of physics. He had performed the operation a hundred times and the actions were almost, if never quite, mechanical. Slotin was too good a 'mechanic', too experienced, too aware of pitfalls and hazards, to do what only idiots do and neglect the checks. He knew the checklist by heart: 'You make sure everything's done by the book before you even think of putting this thing together.' He'd always preached it and always done it. But that day he didn't. Nobody knows what made him forget to insert the two safety clips, that 21 May 1946. Perhaps for him this was just a repeat of a familiar event, and he considered himself so experienced by now that he didn't need the added safety device, which only slowed him up.

On that fateful day, Dr Louis Slotin, America's avowed 'bomb put-togetherer', became a tightrope artiste without his safety net. According to Allan Kline, who was present in the room: 'This assembly had been run so many times before that all its characteristics were well known. But this time Slotin did something different. *He improvised.*' Indeed, Slotin inserted his left thumb into a notch on the top of the sphere and then jammed a heavy screwdriver between the halves to restrain the hemispheres from coming into direct contact. His hands moved easily, confident and steady. He stopped for a moment to take a deep breath, and then concentrated even harder as the half inched slowly downwards. Another turn and the critical distance would be reached. Slotin, wearing protective goggles over his spectacles, bent forward, getting ready for the final turn of the wheel.

That's when it happened. It is not known what distracted him while he was worming the conical screwdriver further out in order to decrease the distance between both halves. He might have been distracted by something and his hand became momentarily unsteady, or a drop of sweat seeped from his forehead and fogged up his glasses. His right hand slipped from the grip of the screwdriver. It clattered to the floor while the top half hung suspended, its descent slowed up only by a flywheel without a safety stop. All those in the room heard the frightening telltale crackle. It came from the centre of the work table as the two halves had almost made contact. A painfully bright blue halo burst from the centre, and a sudden flux of heat swept across them as the needle of the Geiger counter jumped off the scale. Everything happened so fast that most were incapable of seeing what really took place.

'*Critical!*' yelled Slotin at the top of his voice, struck out with his left hand and knocked one of the beryllium halves to the floor. In the split second he moved forward, his body shielded the others, at least partially, from the radiation burst. His lightning reaction had stopped the unthinkable from happening – he had prevented the charge from turning critical and disintegrating in a 'prompt burst', which might well have doomed the entire compound of Los Alamos and crippled America's nuclear capacity. From the moment he threw himself against the lethal halves and thereby prevented a premature chain reaction, Slotin had saved the lives of all those on the base, but his own chance of survival was zero.

'It's safe,' he said, trying to catch his breath. 'And I'm done for.'

What happened next became blanked out in the panic and the confusion that reigned. There was only one thing they were all sure of: something terrible had taken place. Forgetting about the danger of radiation, Slotin picked up a Geiger counter to take a measurement. Then he felt something he had always dreaded, something he never thought could happen to him – the first tiny pinprick of pain in his stomach. A few moments passed before he felt nausea climbing up from deep inside, like an iron hoop gagging him, nearly preventing him from breathing. He could feel himself being dragged down, while the pressure became stronger and more unbearable. Was he already entrapped in the inexorable, icy grip of the invisible killer?

He stumbled for the door and out into the open . . . blood came streaming from his nose. But he was alive . . . alive . . .

A voice came from somewhere: 'Louis, talk to me, please talk to me. Tell me if you're all right. That's all I want to know . . .' and Louis Slotin weakly gestured with a hand that burned like blazes.

An immediate black-out was clamped over the affair. There is, however, an official report (declassified in 1985) and some statements, given from memory years later by the men present, of the events inside the room:

'Kline, Cleary and Young ran out of the east door of the laboratory as soon as they could react after the accident . . . Perlman had run up the northeast corridor . . . Slotin, Graves and Schreiber had followed him to the main laboratory from where Slotin called for an ambulance. He then called the others back (Cieslicki, Cleary and Kline) and prepared a sketch of the approximate positions of everyone present at the moment of the accident.

The security guard Cleary confirmed this version:

I ran out the east door and down the ramp. This probably took me five seconds. I was followed by Cieslicki and Kline. Kline told the MP to open the gate, who had trouble getting his whistle out of his pocket before he opened the gate. He then blew the whistle. I ran 1000 feet [300 metres] up the road, when Dr Slotin and Mr Young came out and called us back into the laboratory. But before they had a chance to go back in, Slotin vomited violently and complained of a strong burn in his left hand. When we drew the diagram of our position, the only conversation was who had absorbed how much of the radiation.[24]

Schreiber went back in to take a reading with his Geiger counter and left immediately when the needle hovered near

[24] From newspaper articles by Barbara Moon in *Maclean's* Magazine (October 1961) and M. Zeilig in *The Beaver* (Aug. 1995).

a critical point. In the meantime, Slotin made another phone call to his friend, the physicist Philip Morrison: 'There's been an accident. It's gone "prompt critical". You'd better come down here.'

'Did it really go critical?' enquired Morrison with a worried voice.

Slotin's answer said it all: 'There was a blue glow . . .'

Morrison then knew that it was serious. Within the hour, all those who had been inside the laboratory were locked away in quarantine inside the green barracks of the Los Alamos Medical Center, not only for check-ups but also to stop the mishap from becoming public knowledge. Slotin and Graves were put into the same room.

'Al, I'm sorry I got you into this,' said Slotin, once they were alone. 'I'm afraid I have less than a fifty-fifty chance of pulling through this one.'

It wasn't long before Slotin showed a high fever and a red rash broke out on his abdomen, together with continuous vomiting and severe diarrhoea. Everyone still hung on to the slim hope that his absorbed dose wasn't too great, but Slotin already suspected that it had been over the limit. When the station's radiobiologist, Dr Wright Langham, walked into the room, Slotin looked up and said: 'I know why you're here.' Like all those handling 'it', he knew that there was no antidote for radiation burn. Three hours after the accident his left hand was fat and red; by night-fall his abdomen was hard and swollen. Dr Langham applied ice packs and injected morphine to lessen the pain. Slotin took it reasonably well; he certainly didn't look depressed.

The entire hospital staff, as well as every physicist on the base, worked feverishly to find a solution, until Dr Langham, using Slotin's ring and some loose change that the physicist had carried in his pocket at the moment of the accident, concluded that the physicist had absorbed a dosage four times as strong as the one that had killed Daghlian.

Schreiber, Cieslicki and Kline had sketched their own approximate position in the room. Upon comparison of the drawings, it showed clearly that Slotin had protected them with his body, thereby acting much like a shield, while absorbing the maximum rads. Those standing nearest to Slotin had been his two principal assistants, Kline and Graves. Working with a slide rule based on the individual sketches, with equations and comparisons by taking in everyone's distance from the centre and the probable length of critical contact, radiation counts were established.

Kline was about five feet (1.5 metres) from the critical point, circa 90 rads, or upper Level One. All others were Level One on a low scale, since they were far enough from the critical point.

Graves, at three feet (90 cm), but partially shielded by Slotin's body, 166 rads, Level Two.

The radiation flash struck directly only the man who knocked over one of the two grapefruit halves. Dr Louis Slotin was Level Four.

Inexorably the terrible sickness grew in Dr Slotin, a devouring, agonising pain that tormented his insides, and a fever that shook him and soon left him so weak that he could no longer move his hands. The news of a serious accident spread throughout the compound. Slotin's colleagues, gathered in front of the hospital to get the latest medical report, refused to accept Dr Langham's diagnosis.

'Hell, that can't be,' said his friend Morrison; those who had been with Slotin inside the assembly hall stated that it had only been a millisecond of blue light; that couldn't have been enough to cook a human. It had been found that only those Nagasaki victims who had been exposed to several seconds of radiation incurred a lethal dosage.

A news black-out was installed. After Philip Morrison threatened to go to the press in order to set a monument to the bravery of his friend, the US Army issued a statement, which was as lame as only a public-relations department can concoct. Four days passed, before an official release was handed to ANS (All News Services) in mid-afternoon of 25 May 1946: '... An accident occurred during a laboratory experiment with fissionable material. At the moment of the mishap, Dr Slotin, in charge of the test, dispersed the material to avert serious consequences by radiation to other members of the group ...'

The press release further mentioned that four of the eight men exposed to the radiation in the accident had already been released from the US Engineer Hospital in Los Alamos. They concluded: '... All technical personnel involved are in satisfactory condition.' By this time it had become clear that Louis Slotin was slowly dying and medical experts were called up nationwide to examine the stricken scientist. That the government was fully aware of the doctor's terminal condition became clear when Dr Hermann Lisco, a renowned pathologist from Chicago, was flown to Los Alamos to perform the autopsy, if and when ...

Following the press release, Slotin was finally allowed to contact his parents. He dictated an ambiguous telegram: 'MY TRIP TO PACIFIC INDEFINITELY POSTPONED. WILL WRITE DETAILS. LOVE. LOUIS.' More pressure from colleagues made General Groves agree to permit Slotin a phone call. Thursday night, forty-eight hours after his accident, a nurse held a receiver to his ear while he spoke to his father. He told him about a minor accident, and since he couldn't come home, perhaps his parents should come down to see him; he would look to it that they got permission to enter the base. His parents, Israel and Sonia Slotin, arrived on the day of Sabbath. They were shocked by the condition of their son. They had last seen him many months before, bouncy and full of energy; now his drained body lay pale and helpless, racked by frequent convulsions, his grossly swollen left arm packed in ice. When his father spoke to him in his heavily accented English, Louis smiled, a father trying not to embarrass his son by their East European background; he recalled his childhood and the language they had spoken at home: 'Pappa, red Yiddish!'

There were long stretches when Louis was coherent, even trying to comfort his father and mother. Contrary to his parents, devout Orthodox Jews,[25] their son had never been spiritually strong. But the prospect of death brought Dr Slotin back to reach out for the Jewish rite. Since the accident, his faith had become so essential to him that he could hardly imagine being without it. He was certain that he was dying, and that the medical staff tried to keep him artificially alive with constant blood transfusion. Morrison had told him about the long queue outside the blood donor centre – everyone on the base lining up offering their blood to save their colleague who, by his courageous act, had saved their lives.

In a desert like Los Alamos where no flowers grow, except those planted and nursed by the wives of scientists in their front yards, the flowers were cut and brought in large bouquets to the hospital, together with get-well notes. The local plant photographer took hourly pictures; alas, not

[25] When it was explained to Israel Slotin that an autopsy should be performed to establish the precise circumstances and level of radiation damage, the father said that such was against his religious belief; yet, for the sake of science and to honour his son's life work, he agreed to it (statement by Prof. Morrison).

to remember him by, but to allow a study of the victim's galloping disintegration. On the fifth day, his permanent nurse, Anna Mae Dickie, when checking on his count of white blood corpuscles – man's lifesavers – noticed that it was plummeting out of control. The platelets were being destroyed faster than they could be replaced. On day six, the pulse rate rose, his breathing was irregular and his frame shaken by violent convulsions. His body turned into a sheet of deep purple and his lips turned blue. His body was passing into the final, toxic stage. A haemorrhage was momentarily stopped with the use of a new drug, which had been tested on radiated animals: 'Toluidine Blue'. The relief was short; when the next haemorrhage began, it was because all of his blood-clotting platelets had been used up. On the seventh day his digestive system broke down completely; the last thing to go was his mind. Eight days after the mishap, his main bodily functions failed and he descended into a coma. He was placed in an oxygen tent. Nine days after the accident, at 11.00 hrs on 30 May 1946, Dr Louis Slotin was dead.

Bob Stewart was one of the young scientist trailblazers at Los Alamos, working as Slotin's assistant. 'Louis was a source of inspiration to all of us, he would always insist upon taking the greatest risk himself. With him, the world has lost one of its foremost scientists,' he said. After the initial shock of a great personal loss followed years of silence. Why was it that none of his colleagues ever talked at any length about the 'Slotin incident'? It wasn't that they were unwilling or ashamed. It was because they simply didn't wish to go on thinking about it.

Philip Morrison, who ended up as professor emeritus at Cornell, spoke of it many years later: 'It was the most painful time of my life and I don't like to go back to it.'

In September 1946, Prof. Robert Brode of the Physics

Department at Berkeley, attacked the government's secrecy, pointing out the likelihood of similar accidents:

I believe that more good would be done in establishing an award to be given each year to the outstanding contribution towards safety in handling hazardous radioactive materials or in recognition of successful accident-free programmes. Some publicity of the outstanding ideas or of the successful research programmes with hazardous materials will certainly help to reduce the type of accident in which Slotin died.

In fact, Dr Slotin's death did result in one safety measure: his unique thumb-and-screwdriver method was replaced by a remote-controlled robot arm.

For years an official veil of invisibility and oppressive silence was clamped on the Slotin affair. Similar secrecy, like the one that plagued the American nuclear establishment, also managed to put the lid on a disaster that happened in Stalin's Soviet Union. The worst nuclear accident in history was not that of Chernobyl, but one that took place in December 1957, near the main industrial centres of Chelyabinsk and Sverdlovsk (today's Ekaterinburg).

In 1948, at the height of Stalin's uncontrollable panic to catch up with the West, a plutonium-producing reactor, Chelyabinsk-40 (CIA codename: Post Box 40) was put up near Kyshtym in the Ural Mountains. In an operation that came straight from the pages of a Solzhenitsyn-type gulag saga, and in which lives simply didn't count, over-tired, hard-pressed workers dumped truckloads of atomic waste wherever a convenient place could be found. Water seeped into the storage space and eventually activated the radioactive material. In late 1957, a chain reaction was accidentally set off in a waste dump. It released a great amount of Strontium-90 into the atmosphere and a large area was contaminated, causing many thousand cases of radiation sickness. An entire area of Russia was sealed off and no one was allowed to leave the stricken region. Overall casualty figures are not known but it is now certain that these must have been huge. In an ill-tempered outburst, the chairman of the United Kingdom Atomic Energy Authority, Sir John Hill, called the initial reports of the Kyshtym disaster 'pure rubbish'. In November 1976, a Soviet defector, the biochemist Zhores Medvedev, inadvertently told the story of the Kyshtym accident to the *New Scientist*, and the tragic truth was revealed.

In the post-war world, the United States was uniquely powerful, with a near-monopoly on the ability to project force globally. With the preponderance of power the US now enjoyed, the American administration made its case with the subtlety of a sledgehammer, according to the dictum: 'Might is right'. By 1946, the fundamental nuclear issue was no longer of a scientific order, but the political decision of how the United States would employ the amazing power it now exercised. America had shown that its industrial might and its vast resources could enable it to win wars. The question was whether the new world order would rest on a threat of nuclear deterrent, or if the super-powers possessed the intellectual and political dynamism to evoke a real conversion of values. Because Hiroshima had proved once and for ever that there was no hole deep enough to protect blast survivors from the follow-up wave of radiation and that it might well be better to be fried or smashed by the blast, than to die a slow death from radiation sickness.

The story of Dr Slotin is not only one of death and destruction, but also the tale of a spectacular technical and organisational triumph; critics may say that the atom was harnessed for the forces of destruction, yet their ideas, research, development and revolutionary technology provided a new impetus for generations to come. It offered a new source of much-needed peaceful energy to drive machines and light up cities. It also turned future global war into an impossible gamble that could not be won, or only at the price of self-immolation. It kept major powers at peace with each other, and the Cold War remained what it was called: cold.

The great minds of the Atomic Revolution transformed the 20th century the way that their forebears of the Industrial Revolution had transformed the 19th century. Many individuals contributed to the process. Behind every monumental invention, for better or for worse, stands the extraordinary human mind that overthrows inherited ideas about logic, space and energy. Dr Louis Slotin was an emblematic figure in that select group of men. He was someone who lived life to the full, gave his all to any task, and could get the best out of others. Everything he did was planned down to the final detail. Afterwards they said he took one risk too many. It is his epitaph that, half a century after his death, whenever the scientific community talks about heroes, his name rates high among them.

For many years, the American government put a lid on the affair.[26] Only his colleagues and his family knew Slotin's name. And they weren't prepared to talk about it; they avoided all reference to him. For the specific purpose of putting an end to a horror, physicists and technicians had taken the right decisions and come up with the correct answers, only to find that they had created chaos. For many years it seemed that the nuclear scientific community had finally lost its innocence.

In August of 1986, the US Office of Special Investigations declassified (partial) files of the 'Slotin Incident', including a personal diary with excerpts of Hitler's maniacal threats:

---

[26] There were some enterprising journalistic enquiries, such as Barbara Moon in Canada's *Maclean's* (1961).

'The moment might very quickly come for us to use a weapon with which we ourselves could not be attacked!' Next to it Slotin had scribbled: 'Not likely!' That was his credo. To save the world from a menace. As he lay in intensive care, his father said:

'You've worked too hard.'

With tears in his eyes, Slotin Jr replied: 'We had to get *it* before the Germans.'

In the end, that 'it' was his life. In a quest for greater knowledge, and to defeat evil, he staked his own life.

In the end, Dr Slotin's motivation came down to a question of personal reliability. A pioneer, setting out with naïve faith, working through disappointments, achieving breakthroughs, he entered into the secretive world of the scientific merry-go-round, always in fear of what a technical breakthrough out of control can do in the time of nuclear Armageddon. He realised that all could end with a sudden blast from the siren. Once he engaged in work where mortal dangers were known to exist at all levels, but were untested and unconfirmed, he had to be prepared for such eventuality. When it did come in a sizzling blue flash, he acted on the spur of the moment, because he was prepared, and it was all he could do to save others from suffering a similar fate. A clever scientist paid with his life so that wise men might live.

On 14 June 1946, three weeks after Dr Slotin's death, the head of the US President's Atomic Advisory Panel, Bernard Baruch, addressed the delegations of the United Nations Atomic Energy Commission: 'We are here to make a choice between the quick and the dead. We must elect world peace – or world destruction.'

The Glorious Glosters, Heroes all

'The 1st Battalion, Gloucestershire Regiment, British Army and Troop 'C' 170th Independent Mortar Battery, Royal Artillery, attached, are cited for exceptionally outstanding performance of duty and extraordinary heroism in action against the armed enemy near Solma-Ri, Korea, on the 23rd, 24th and 25th of April 1951 ... Without thought of defeat or surrender, this heroic force demonstrated superb battlefield courage and discipline ...'

Citation by Harry S. Truman, 1951

They had been steeped in the principles of duty, honour and country. Sheer willpower became their mainstay for tenacity. And tenacious they were, persuaded that there was no substitute for victory. This is not the story of a single soldier, but of an entire battalion of heroes, because, in the beginning, they were just that: a battalion.

At the end of the Second World War, the victorious powers had separated their spoils into an 'East' and a 'West'. The most noticeable partition was 'The Iron Curtain', which divided Europe from the Baltic to the Adriatic. There was another wall, perhaps less visible, but potentially just as explosive. It divided the peninsula of Korea into a 'North' and a 'South' along the 38th Parallel. In August

1945, the Japanese in the south of Chosen[1] had surrendered to American troops; those above the parallel capitulated to the forces of the Soviet Union. While the United States, tired of war, kept only a small number of support troops stationed in the South, a Korean Communist leader, Kim Il Sung, riding into the capital city of Pyongyang on the back of Russian tanks, had usurped power in the North and created the Korean People's Army, armed and trained by the Soviet Union. Encouraged by his increasing military power he began to cast his eyes on the rest of the country. This, and the promise of support from his Socialist brothers, launched him into an ill-advised adventure. The peace in the 'Land of the Morning Calm' (Chosen) was shattered.

The war in Korea began before dawn, on 25 June 1950, when shells from North Korean guns came hurtling across the demarcation line and regiments of Kim Il Sung's Korean People's Army (KPA), supported by T-34 tanks, surprised the world by crossing the 38th Parallel. By nightfall Kaesong had fallen; three days later the North Koreans captured Seoul and the United Nations reacted. But that took time. In the meantime, the few badly organised South Korean and American units were quickly pushed into the perimeter of Pusan on the southernmost tip of the Korean peninsula. And that's where they stayed until 15 September. That day, in a brilliantly executed operation, United Nations troops under General Douglas MacArthur landed at Inchon. This sliced the country in half, pinning down much of the North Korean forces in a hopeless position, cut off from their supply bases.

With Kim Il Sung's defeat imminent, the Communist rulers of Beijing decided to come to his assistance, not to shore up the tottering North Korean dictator, but to

---

[1] Ancient name for Korea.

avoid having an American-controlled regime as their direct neighbour. The buffer of a Communist North Korea served China well. In his country, Mao Zedong's decision to enter the Korean War was praised as *vingming juece* (a brilliant decision), an accolade reserved for truly great feats of the past. Having just emerged victoriously from a devastating civilian war against the nationalists, it took something spectacular to consolidate Mao's personal cult. Perhaps most vital of all, it would give him a chance to test his country's own security strategy, and find out exactly how much he could count on the support by brotherly Russia.

Though Mao Zedong had received a personal assurance from Stalin that he would supply the 'Chinese volunteers' with as much military equipment and ammunition as they needed, should they enter into the conflict, Russia would not consider sending its pilots to fight in Korea. For Mao it was a clear signal that he could not count on Russia in case of a much wider conflict; this created the initial break in the Socialist brotherhood, which was to be confirmed in later years. However, Stalin added an addendum: 'The Soviet Air Force will assure an aerial umbrella over China's national territory, especially over important industrial centres in the coastal areas.'[2] Stalin's single phrase had the potential to lead to an all-out global conflict.

The Sino-American confrontation began with a telegram by Chinese Communist Party (CCP) Chairman Mao Zedong to his army commanders, Chinese People's Volunteers (CPV) generals Peng Dehuai and Deng Hua, dispatched at 21.00 hrs on 18 October 1950:

---

[2] By 1949, the Soviet Union had the atomic bomb. This specific clause was eventually 'leaked' to an American source, resulting in Truman's decision to fire MacArthur.

IT HAS BEEN DECIDED THAT THE FOUR ARMIES AND THREE ARTILLERY DIVISIONS WILL FOLLOW OUR ORIGINAL PLAN TO ENTER NORTHERN KOREA FOR WAR OPERATIONS. THE TROOPS WILL START ACROSS THE (YALU) RIVER FROM THE ANGDONG-JI'AN SECTION TOMORROW (19 OCTOBER) EVENING. IN ORDER TO MAINTAIN STRICT SECRECY, THE TROOPS SHOULD START TO CROSS THE RIVER AFTER DUSK . . .[3]

Mao dictated that the national media was to adopt a policy of 'only act but not talk'. Boxcar loads of fake Korean People's Army uniforms were delivered to the Chinese staging areas for the CPV soldiers, in order to take the Americans by surprise. The deception worked – the Americans were caught asleep.

Shortly after midnight on 19 October 1950, the Chinese People's Volunteers (CPV) – a title created to hide the fact that this was the regular Chinese Army – launched a massive assault across the frontier separating North Korea from the People's Republic of China, and CPV General Nie Rongzhen was able to report to Chairman Mao that all was proceeding according to plan. Some 180,000 Chinese caught the over-extended US Eighth Army of Lt Gen. Walton H. Walker unawares and pushed it back from their position on the Yalu River. A few days later, Gen. Walker died in a car accident and a tough paratrooper, US Lt Gen. Matthew B. Ridgway, took over command of the US Eighth Army (27 December 1950). He could do little to stop the 'Chinese flood' and, for a second time, South Korea's capital Seoul had to be abandoned. Fighting delaying actions, Ridgway tried to slow up the human wave of Chinese pouring down from the north. The next stage of the war turned into a contest of American firepower versus Chinese manpower. Ridgway called this strategy his 'meat-

[3] Chen Jian, *China's Road to the Korean War*, New York, 1994.

grinder'. If artillery and planes weren't enough, there was always 'the big one'.

It was the spectre of a confrontation with this ultimate deterrent, which brought General MacArthur to fall. When the Chinese began employing 'privileged sanctuary' tactics, using Russian-made MIG fighters, but with Chinese aircrews flying from Chinese airstrips along the border, bombing the United Nation forces in Korea before retreating back into their 'neutral' Chinese sanctuary, the Supreme Commander, Korea, Gen. Douglas MacArthur, launched the call for a 'Let's bomb the Chinese back into the Stone Age!' Such a demand was politically unacceptable.[4]

US President Truman stated: 'We are trying to prevent a world war – not to start one!' and then fired his famous general (11 April 1951). MacArthur had never learned the lesson of higher politics: politicians will interfere in military matters, while soldiers must stay clear of political affairs.

Once MacArthur was gone, Matthew Ridgway took over Korea Command. A strong believer in offensive tactics – 'static warfare is bad for morale' was the way he put it – he ordered a general advance north. In December, the Chinese had poured across the Yalu River with enough weapons and men to conquer the earth and yet they were unable to draw visible benefit from their numerical advantage in the face of stubborn resistance and superior firepower. Buried by an avalanche of American 155mm shells, napalm and bombs from Sabre jets, their brotherly Korean haven was quickly turning into perfect hell.

On 14 March 1951, UN troops liberated Seoul and, on 3 April, they crossed once again the disputed 38th Parallel into North Korea. Ridgway's objective was to

[4] Truman was aware of the secret clause in the Stalin–Mao agreement. Flying into China would have brought the US Air Force into direct confrontation with the Soviet Air Force.

prevent the Chinese from massing up for another major offensive and to grind their armies into dust with the help of his superior firepower. Indeed, 'Ridgway's meatgrinder' rolled forward and all along the frontline the Chinese took a severe beating. But they weren't finished. Rumours grew of a massive Chinese counter-offensive; the date most frequently mentioned was 15 April 1951. In fact, under cover of night the Chinese had managed to bring forward 700,000 troops under CPV General Peng Dehuai, who had received his baptism of fire as a divisional commander under Chiang Kai-Shek fighting the same Chinese Communists he was now leading into battle. His offensive plan was in two stages: the breakthrough, and the consolidation, each portion employing 350,000 men. General Peng was a good strategist; however, he was one who cared little for the lives of his men, and who stuck to the ancient belief that winning battles calls for massive human sacrifice. To emblazon his tarnished image, following his loss of Seoul in March, his principal target became once again Seoul.

The task for the initial breakthrough was allotted by Gen. Peng to his 63rd CPV Shock Army, the cream of Chinese troops made up of the battle-hardened 187th, 188th and 189th Divisions. Maj. Gen. Frank Milburn's 1st US Corps held the sector around Seoul, with several British units, belonging to Brigadier Tom Brodie's 29th British Brigade Group, attached to Milburn's Corps. The British Group was made up of three battalions of infantry and one of cavalry: the 1st Battalion Royal Northumberland Fusiliers, the 1st Battalion Royal Ulster Rifles, the 1st Battalion Gloucestershire Regiment and the tanks of the 8th King's Royal Irish Hussars (of 'Charge of the Light Brigade' fame). In support was the 45th Field Regiment, Royal Artillery, the 170th Independent Mortar Battery and the 55th Field Squadron, Royal Engineers. Furthermore it had an 'A-Piss', as the soldiers called the Aerial Photographic Interpretation

Section, and, most importantly for the soldiers' wives, it had a detachment from the Royal Army Pay Corps.

The British brigade sounded impressive – on paper. What Tom Brodie lacked most of all were men, men and more men. He was handed an amalgam of post-Second World War peacetime units, which had been demobilised and cut to the bone in order to save the British taxpayer money, and then, as a hastily constituted 29th Brigade Group, was rushed off to take part in a new war. The positive aspect about its soldiers was that they all brought with them the experience of battling it out with the Germans in the Second World War. In their opinion – and before they met them for the first time – 'them Gooks ain't no Krauts'. They were soon taught a different view, when all the support units, from signalman to paymaster, mechanical repairman, cook, photographer, even chaplain, priest or rabbi, were called upon to pick up a rifle and fight for their lives.

The Americans' overwhelming firepower covering the main approaches to Seoul decided CPV General Peng to opt for two secondary dirt roads through the mountainous region to the west. He had received intelligence about the presence of the British Brigade Group in the Imjin sector, but he knew that they were not thick enough on the ground to put up the challenge that could be expected from Maj. Gen. Milburn's American battle force, backed by their heavy artillery and jet planes. Peng's offensive plan was based on the assumption that the British, faced by a huge numerical superiority in men, would turn tail and run.

Allowing for a rolling start to reach the necessary striking momentum, Chinese units were to move out late in the afternoon and hit the British line across the Imjin shortly after dusk on 22 April 1951. They would crash through the British line, overrun the rear echelon, and from there flood forward to strike into the soft flank of the Americans around Seoul. They were scheduled to reach South Korea's capital within thirty-six hours, or by noon on 24 April. Peng's plan would not allow the Americans to shift their defences; by his rapid advance he would crush the entire 1st US Corps between two pincers. Speed was the key, and the Chinese general had no reason to believe that his plan wouldn't succeed, faced by nothing more than a thin screen of under-strength Commonwealth battalions. Peng savoured the thought of victory. Having failed in a similar move on the Yalu River in December 1950, the People's Army of China would this time achieve victory. With the 1st US Corps eliminated, the entire US Eighth Army front would crumble. On Sunday, 22 April 1951, with preparations completed and three divisions within striking distance of the Imjin River, General Peng Dehuai issued the order for the massive assault. The War in Korea was about to enter into a new phase.

'Here is where we shall launch the initial assault,' Peng pointed on a wall map to the hamlet of Choksong and its narrow mountain road leading south. And that was precisely where Tom Brodie's 29th British Brigade Group had dug in and thrown up a blocking position, anchored on the hills on the southern bank of the 300-yard-wide (270 metres) Imjin River. Reconnaissance patrols by the Glosters had found that the river was only knee-deep in a number of places and could be forded on foot. This news was passed on to Ridgway's HQ and became the integral part in designing a start-off point for the planned American spring offensive. But what if the Chinese got there first . . .

A series of tree-covered rock piles fell steeply away towards the valley of the Imjin.[5] On its southern embankment, parallel to the river, ran a dirt road to the hamlet of Choksong. In April 1951, much of this west–east traverse

[5] The author visited Gloster Hill in 1961.

road and the hills behind it was held by the 1st Battalion Royal Northumberland Fusiliers, supported by 'A' Troop of 170 Independent Mortar Battery. Further to the east was another road. It led from north to south, through a knee-deep river ford, grandly baptised 'Gloucester Crossing' when a platoon of the Glosters waded across 'looking for Chinks'. From the hamlet of Choksong, the road snaked through a defile between hills, towered over by the 650-metre Kamak-San peak (675 metres), to Solma-ri and from there to Munsan-ni. It wasn't much of a road, more a cart track, muddy and with deep ruts, and couldn't take heavy equipment. Basically unsuitable as a major assault axis, it was never considered to be the enemy's principal target. But since it was a road that could become a potential danger for a diversionary flank attack on the 1st US Corps by lightly armed Chinese units, the four companies of the 1st Battalion, Gloucestershire Regiment (better known by their abbreviated name: the Glosters) were ordered to set up a blocking position, straddling the road between Choksong and Solma-ri.

On their approach march to their assigned position on the Imjin, the 1st Battalion Glosters had pressed on through the countryside; their battalion ate up the kilometres in a punishing sun and driving rain, across hill and flatland, mostly in a single file, hoping that nothing unforeseen would happen. If they had the feeling that a thousand hostile eyes were closely watching them, they found only hamlets touched by a war without people, but many dead pigs that stank, their legs stiff with rigor mortis. One of the men, walking on point through a rice paddy, stepped on a land mine. His leg was blown off and his face destroyed.

They found the Imjin valley ravaged by war, with bomb craters and black scars from napalm, bearing witness to the furious battles fought here during the previous autumn. Its hillsides were covered with some vegetation and gnarly trees. They established a hill position two kilometres (1.25 miles) back from the river, and 270 metres (300 yards) straight down to the bottom of the valley; on the downslopes, the Glosters took their entrenching tools and went to work. They dug their hole deeper, anticipating that they might stay on for a while. This was not a time to become complacent. The dominant elevations along the river line were now fortified, solid enough to stop minor incursions, but never meant to withstand a major assault. In an extended forward position near the river crossing, located on Hill 148,[6] known as 'Castle Hill' due to a concrete observation bunker built months before by Americans, was Maj. P.A. Angier's 'A' Company, Glosters. A few hundred yards to their east, on Hill 182, was Capt. M. Harvey's 'D' Company. Posted on Hill 144 was 'B' Company of Maj. E.D. Harding, covering the gap between their hill and that held by a company from the Royal Northumberland with a Vickers machine gun. Maj. P. Mitchell's 'C' Company was held back in a covering position further south of the narrow defile. Spaced out over the hills were Capt. Graham Lutyen-Humphrey's heavy mortars and Capt. Theo Littlewood's machine-gunners.

Slightly ahead of the hamlet of Solma-Ri was Hill 235, the rock pile that was to go down in glory as 'Gloster Hill'; a few dozen men of the battalion's assault pioneer platoon under Capt. 'Spike' Pike had dug in on its northern slope; most of them had been recalled into active service and, being used to shovel-work, their foxholes were the most elaborate, and their trenches strung like a lace curtain across the hillside. 'Spike' Pike was a popular character; his relationship with his men was one of father and sons. The CO had just informed this veteran of Lord Lovat's

---

[6] On military maps, hills are always numbered by their height in metres. In other words, Hill 148 equals 148m.

Second World War commandos that his transfer had come through.

Touring the trench with his replacement, Lt Alan Blundell, he said jokingly: 'God help you with that lot', without realising how much he and his men would need the help of God. Battalion HQ, communication centre, as well as the support mortar units of 'C' Troop 170th Independent Mortar Battery under orders by Capt. F. Wisbey, were put in position at the base of Hill 235. For artillery support the battalion counted on 29th Brigade's three batteries of 25-lb howitzers, a handy gun which had proven its worth in mountainous terrain during the Second World War. Including supporting personnel, cooks, corpsmen and signallers, 1st Battalion, Gloucestershire Regiment, came to a total of 773 men under the command of Lt Col. James Power Carne, known to his staff as 'Fred', and much respected by his men. During the Second World War, 'Fred' Carne had served as battalion commander in Burma, gathering experience slugging it out in wooded terrain. This 45-year-old softly spoken man, with a blond-grey mustache and a bony, if gentle face that belied his toughness, proved himself an inspired leader, genuinely caring about the well-being of his men. In this he stood in stark contrast to his foe, General Peng Dehuai, for whom lives were but a statistic, and who didn't rely on courage, but on the quantity of human flesh.

On Saturday 21 April, Lt Col. Carne had sent out a reconnaissance party. Skirting the fields they moved into the abandoned village of Choksong. To their utter relief they found no sign of an enemy and the Gloster Crossing on the Imjin was deserted. Sergeant Jack Eames, the patrol leader, could report 'no enemy activity'. The sergeant, decorated with a Military Medal in the Second World War, was ordered to set up an observation post in an isolated hut north of the hamlet, near the Gloster

Crossing, and to stay there for the night. One of his men was new to the unit; Roger was practically a baby among the grizzled veterans. But Roger wanted to be where there was action and the way he figured it, the Glosters were the ticket. He volunteered for Korea and had joined the unit only two days before. The older soldiers took him under their wing and shared the watch with him. It happened just before dawn; Roger had just been relieved of guard duty and was taking some shut-eye inside the hut, when a number of artillery shells slammed into and around the hut. The boy was killed before he could get his boots on. In a brief skirmish, when a Chinese patrol tried to sneak across the river, the Glosters killed four and the current washed away their bodies. For the rest of the night, all remained quiet.

Sunday, 22 April turned out to be a bright, sunny day. Brigadier Tom Brodie had to face a few early-rising journalists, eager for snippets to feed to their readers back 'in the real world'. They had heard some bangs during the night: 'Brigadier, there has been sporadic artillery fire.' They were referring to the incident involving Eames' reconnaissance patrol. 'Is that a sign for a forthcoming Chinese offensive?'

'Well, gentlemen, it seems to have been random fire. We have no further indication . . . yes, it was in the Gloster sector. Now if you will excuse me . . .' Brodie wasn't convinced it was 'random fire' and neither were the journalists. The instructions from Combined HQ on how to handle the front-line press was to let them have it 'straight and simple', not endangering the situation, and without creating panic. Brodie wasn't panicked, but he was concerned.

He called his superior at Corps HQ for reinforcements, and a sympathetic American voice replied: 'Brigadier, it isn't that we don't want to let you have more of our guys, we just ain't got any to give to you. We know that you're gonna hold with what you've got. But we'll get some 155ers over to you.' Brodie could use a heavier hammer, and the new American 155mm howitzers would do just great.

'Random fire' was also the explanation given that Sunday morning by company commanders to their units along the line. Colonel Fred, never seen without his briar-pipe, which he used for smoking as well as a map pointer, discussed the shelling with his staff, ADC Capt. Antony Farrar-Hockley and Intelligence officer, Lt Henry Cabral. The soldiers sat around, cleaning weapons or writing home to tell their loved ones that nothing much of great news was going on and that 'quiet flows the Imjin'. After all, there wasn't anyone who had so much as seen a Chink. Dead ones, yes, but no live ones. They did know that somewhere to their north hung a Great Chinese Dragon, but until this St George's Day, all was perfectly quiet.

A jeep with the Reverend Sam Davies drove up. The Glosters' chaplain was young, tall and handsome – just 'one of the boys'. More than that, this man of God was also a provider of cigarettes and something to whet the whistle. Holy water, they called it, and never tried to enquire where his treasure hailed from; to them it mattered not if it was obtained by Christian means. For the companies sitting on a hill, picking fleas, the appearance of the pastor was always welcomed. It couldn't be stated that the men were overly religious; in private life they went to church whenever it suited them or whenever a cousin was getting married. Their language was soldier's language, not something to be practised in church. But this was different, the Chinese were somewhere out there, and there was always the off chance that it might well be the last time the men from Gloucestershire, Berkshire or Wiltshire would be able to speak to their God through the good shepherd with his holy water. So it was, this clear, sunny

St George's Day, 1951, in the hills of Korea. Surrounded by a group of bareheaded soldiers, the padre donned his white habit, put up his fold-up table altar in front of a bombed-out temple, and began to read from the Bible. It was a simple sermon: *all people that on earth do dwell, fighting the good fight.* It was a language the men of 'A' Company understood, and they replied with the rousing hymn 'Oh, Valiant Hearts'. The padre raised the chalice and shared Christ's bread with the kneeling. One of them was a 24-year-old reservist, Lt Philip Curtis.

For the rest of the day they were sitting around, joking, smoking and brewing up tea, except those on guard duty – and even they got their tea. The main activity came from two quarters; on 'Pike's Peak', marked as Hill 235 on military maps, Capt. Pike was trundling around a youngish 2nd Lt Alan Blundell. From the next day onwards Lt Blundell was to take over his 'broom and shovel squad', because 'Spike' Pike was going home. Private Jack Biddle, 'Uncle Jack', took one look at the young second lieutenant, and remarked drily: 'We'll have him trained in two days.' The other party was going on in the 'Grand Hotel' of RSM Jack Hobbs, a tent with a four-poster bed and a bar dispensing ale twenty-four hours a day, at least such was the scuttlebutt. The Regimental Sergeant Major was giving a bash for his departing buddy, Orderly Room Quartermaster Sergeant (ORQMS) Taffy Evans, who had done his thing 'for King and Country' and was scheduled for home transfer. Was that not reason enough for a hefty celebration and a get-together of all the ruling sergeants? – old-timers such as Signal Sergeant Jim Smyth, Provost Sergeant Bill Peglar, who looked after 'law and order', CSMI 'Muscles' Strong, the commander's personal body-guard, and Drum-Major Philip Buss, who blew a mean bugle. One who did not feel like celebrating was the pipe-smoking battalion commander. For almost a week he had received disturbing information of enemy troop concentrations to the north of his own holding position. There was no indication yet how big or how far away. Just a dry: 'enemy activity reported'. The longer he kept studying his map the more he worried about the gaping holes in his lines. He called Brigade HQ and was passed through to Brigadier Tom Brodie. 'Sir,' said Carne, 'I've got gaps wide enough to allow an entire Chinese division to slip through.'

'I've taken it up with Corps HQ, they haven't got manpower to spare. We must make do with what we've got.' Brodie knew that Carne was right, 13,000 metres (about 14,400 yards) along an easily fordable stream was a lot of frontage for two battalions to hold. As soon as he got off the phone, Brodie turned to his ADC. 'Still no news of those Yank guns?' he enquired. The ADC, with a tired and dispirited face, who had spent the whole day on the phone, had something forlorn about him.

He shook his head. 'None, sir.' For twenty-four hours, ever since the danger first became apparent, the brigadier had been impatiently expecting the arrival of the heavy artillery pieces. The route across the passes, made soggy by spring rains, was delaying their arrival.

'Captain, get me aerial recon on the line.'

Just before darkness on 22 April, the field telephone rang in Col. Carne's HQ; Brigade HQ was on the line. The American aerial reconnaissance squadron had just informed them that one of their planes reported 'signs of enemy concentrations ten miles (16 km) north of the river'. How big, it didn't say. Ten miles could mean two days, but Col. Carne was not prepared to take a chance. The Chinese had done it before and surprised the Allies on the Yalu. He ordered Number 7 Platoon under Lt Guy ('Guido') Temple to establish an ambush at the Gloster Crossing. The lieutenant moved into a forward position. It was a moonlit night and the visibility was good. They dug in along the south bank of the river and had been lying in wait for almost three hours when, all of a sudden, the opposite shore seemed to move; Lt Temple couldn't believe what he saw through his field glasses. Masses of the enemy popped up like mushrooms after rain – human forms that were unreal, more like an army of ghosts. A horde of Chinese was moving towards his side of the Imjin – Temple's two dozen Glosters against all of China, or so it seemed. There was still time to pull back, but they wouldn't. Their advantage lay in surprise; the other side didn't know that the Glosters were lying in wait across a river's breadth.

'Hold your fire until the lieutenant gives the order,' went a whisper along the line. The soldiers hunkered down, safety-catch off, fingers wrapped around the trigger. The first Chinese wave came wading across the knee-deep ford, four dozen in line. They were halfway across when Lt Temple yelled: 'Free fire!' The initial effect was terrible; the automatic-like precision fire of the Glosters was awesome; they didn't need to pick targets because there were so many. Their single Bren-gun raked the mass of flesh. Scythed by the merciless hail of slugs from chattering guns, the Chinese toppled like grain.

The follow-up wave got to within fifty yards (45 metres) of the Glosters and then their strength seemed to fail. Bracing their rifles against the earthen parapet, the Glosters were picking them off. The river was awash with corpses. The moon vanished behind a passing cloud, and under the cover of darkness more Chinese surged forward. The leading enemy was only a dozen yards from the Glosters, howling madly as they charged, when the moon came back out and bathed the landscape with its blue light.

A Chinese had almost reached Len Allen's hole when the private shot him in the chest. 'Keep shooting those bastards,' yelled a commanding voice. Chinese lurched, spun and collapsed. Still more came across; their determination was truly incredible. The men of Number 7 Platoon did not hear the explosions nor feel the wind of passing bullets; their breath came in gasps and they went on bravely with their work, which was killing the enemy. The initial assault was followed by three more human wave attacks and three more times the men of 'Guido' Temple dispatched them to their death. They worked their bolts and sent bullet after bullet slamming into bodies. Pfc Len Allen, who had once claimed that he had nothing against 'blinkin' Chinks' and whose gun barrel was too hot to touch, yelled: 'Them fuckers must be breedin' over there.' In front of his foxhole lay ten mangled corpses. All of China had come at them and the thin line of Glosters had stood. Down to five bullets per man and one charger for Allen's Bren-gun, it was time to 'bug out'.

Lt Temple's order was passed along the line: 'We're pulling back.' Number 7 Platoon, 1st Battalion Gloucestershire Regiment had faced an entire enemy battalion, and survived. Unknowingly, they had just endured the curtain raiser to one of one of the largest offensives of the Korean War.

The night had just begun. The worst hit was Major Pat Angier's 'A' Company. Their hill lay closest to the river crossing and Angier's boys held the key to block the enemy's advance. Although the previous action by Lt Temple had slowed up the initial rush, two more CVP battalions had managed to cross the river further downstream. They were rapidly advancing towards Hill 148, 'Castle Hill'. The landscape in the valley lay bathed in moonlight like an enormous panorama. The only thing that spoiled nature's beauty were the many figures coming across the valley floor.

Maj. Angier blew into his mike to test the radio. Lt Philip Curtis got ready to fire the Very pistol, signalling 'free fire'.

With a loud click, the bolt of a machine gun snapped into readiness. The sweat of nervous tension was pouring into the men's eyes; their anxiety showed. Hanging halfway out of his hole, Private Charlie Edkins was watching. He saw what looked like marionettes sliding across the valley floor, silent as the night. Then the first wave reached the incline. A star shell burst, a bugle blew, then the Chinese started uphill. Sporadic bursts zipped uphill, through the shrubs and over the trench. From the valley in front of the hill emerged massive groups of Chinese, probably the better part of two battalions, at least a thousand soldiers, going up against sixty men.

Charlie Edkins cursed under his breath; he had a pack of 'Old Golds' in his pocket, saved up for a nice day when he could lay back and enjoy it, and now perhaps he would never again get the chance to smoke them. Shooting in every direction, the Chinese came scrambling up the steep slope. Explosions echoed back and forth.

'I'm hit!' groaned the man next to him. Blood soaked through his tunic; he had been hit in the chest and in the shoulder. Edkins crawled to the man, ripped open the shirt, and slapped a bandage over the wounds. They had only been inches apart when the bullets struck, and Edkins wasn't even scratched, such are the fortunes of war. He kept his head under the lip of the trench. If he'd get hit in the body, perhaps he would survive; his body was big and strong and could take a few bullets, but not in the head. Bullets whined. A shadowy figure passed in front of his rifle and disappeared up a traverse. When the enemy was fifty yards (45 metres) below the trench line, Gloster machine guns opened up, hammering out belt after belt until the barrels were glowing hot and jammed.

Troop 'C' of the 170th Mortars lobbed clusters of bombs into the advancing hordes on the hill and in the valley. Yet nothing seemed to be able to halt the enemy's advance;

their bugles drove them into the mouths of the guns. A lot died while ever more came up the hill. Soon they had reached the first British positions and their human wave virtually blasted the British off 'Castle Hill'. With it, the Chinese took the single prominent feature of 'A' Company's position, the concrete pillbox. Within minutes they set up a machine gun and were using this bunker to pour a deadly stream of bullets at the men of 'A' Company; the trench leading to the bunker became the focal point of an intermittent line of tracers.

'A' Company began to take heavy casualties. John Maycock's platoon was down to six men before he was cut in half by a burst from that machine gun. The platoon nearest this gun was that of Lt Philip Curtis. With his platoon decimated to twenty, Curtis made contact with his company commander. Maj. Angier's orders were curt: 'Shift them off the top!' Curtis replied with a single word: 'Right!' then collected whatever was left of his platoon and said: 'Let's go!' They stuffed their pockets with all the grenades they could find and crept forward. They had made thirty yards (27 metres) when they were slashed by a burst from that cursed machine gun. Three men died instantly, four more were wounded, including Phil Curtis, who was struck in his side and his left arm was shattered.

A vital organ must have been touched, as blood was pouring from his side in little squirts. Most of his men were dead, his pistol was empty, and with his shattered arm he could no longer hold a rifle. But he had said that he would silence the machine gun, and silence it he would! Slowly he scrambled back on his feet, his shattered arm dangling uselessly by his side . . . he stumbled forward, with a grenade clutched in his good fist, making in a straight line for the concrete box on the hill. The gun kept firing squirt after squirt, but miraculously not at him. Nothing could stop him. He left a trail of his life's blood trickling to the ground. What gave him the strength to move was a mystery, a dying man on his most glorious mission. He raised his good arm, brought the grenade to his mouth pulling the pin with his teeth and suddenly stood within five yards (4.5 metres) of the machine gun. That's when the Chinese saw him. Their gun swivelled and fired a burst point-blank into the heroic lieutenant – at the moment he let go of his grenade. While Phil Curtis collapsed, mortally wounded, the grenade rolled into the pillbox, exploded, and wiped out the gun crew. Lt Philip Curtis's funeral pyre was a stack of exploding grenades and ammunition that ripped the concrete bunker apart in a display of fireworks.[7]

On nearby Hill 182, where Capt. Mike Harvey's 'D' Company was dug in, silence prevailed. The most effective military stratagem would have been to send an ambush patrol downslope to alert his company of an attack. Two, three men with a couple of hundred rounds of ammunition could take out a dozen enemies before they even fired back. But he refused to risk any more people or split up his forces, when suddenly clusters of mortar bombs came shrieking down, blasting the hill and its defenders. The Chinese scrambled up the slope in pairs, spread far apart. Only their muzzle-flashes could be seen clearly in the darkness. They fired long horizontal burst over the slope and used ammunition as though it was sand. With their overwhelming superiority of manpower and bullets, they could afford to fight a battle of attrition. In minutes, 'D' Company took severe casualties. When the first waves of attackers moved out from the cover of the trees, the men of 'D' fired point-blank into the masses.

But the attack against 'D' wasn't conducted with the same vigour as the main drive to force the passage, which

[7] For his action, Lt Phil Curtis was awarded posthumously the Victoria Cross.

was still directed against 'A' Company. There, the British heavy mortars had become embroiled in the fight; the bombs of the 170th Battery exploded a mere thirty yards (27 metres) in front of the men of Maj. Angier. The acrid fumes of cordite hung heavily over their slit trench; bullets kicked up dirt next to them, above them, around them. They stood, they killed, and they were killed. For them it was over, and that made them fight so much harder. From all over the hillside came yells and curses, but also cries of agony and frustration. Men shot to shreds were tumbling down on top of those who had fallen before.

With the company down to thirty able to stand and shoot, Maj. Angier got one last message through to Col. Carne. 'Colonel, I have to report that our position is in danger. If I am to remain, then I must have reinforcements. I'm down to two dozen men and ammunition is critical.' In what was perhaps Col. Carne's toughest decision in his entire military career, he had to condemn the remainder of a company to save the rest of his units from annihilation. His face underwent a change; his mouth hardened and his eyes became narrow slits. In a clipped voice he spoke into the microphone: 'You will make a stand until further notice.'

'Yes, sir,' acknowledged Angier. 'Don't worry about us; we'll be fine.'

Ten minutes later, Major Pat Angier was dead.

It was at the moment when 'A' Company was virtually wiped out and without defence, that Chinese bugles blew and the attackers turned around, tearing down a torn-up, bloodied slope. The Glosters were stunned. A minute before the enemy had almost broken through their line, and in the next moment they were gone. The 105mm howitzers, which had stood by idle due to a gun's shallow trajectory, began firing shells into the patch of land between the retreating Chinese and the river. Some of them ran into the explosions and were torn to pieces, others veered off, recoiled, and stopped just in time to receive the full impact of the next salvo, sent a hundred yards short in anticipation of just such a panic stop. Only half of the Chinese were lucky enough to get clear. The other half were killed or maimed. In the ensuing silence the once scenic panorama of nature's beauty presented the picture of a medieval battlefield strewn with corpses.

The last dozen of 'A' Company couldn't believe their good fortune. They were barely alive, staggering around dazed. A dead Chinese, hanging halfway into the trench, was pushed out; a worn cloth purse fell from his pocket. A few coins, a staged photo, badly faded, of a girl holding a child, a wedding ring fashioned from copper wire; those were the dead man's only worldly possessions. Like the many hundreds, lying all over the slope, this Chinese would never again sit with his wife and baby. Near him, a Gloster was lying face down, shaking uncontrollably. His head was turned to one side and his mouth was open, sucking in the earth, his lungs pierced by a bayonet. They bandaged him and draped him over two rifles used as a makeshift stretcher. They found their major; for him help was too late. One of their party bent over his dead body, putting his mouth to that of the major, trying to blow life back into it.

'Benny,' cried another, 'he's dead, dead. Let's get out, they're crawling all over the place.'

The respite gained by the sacrifice of 'A' Company allowed Carne to pull back his other companies. The fury of the assault, and the mass of attackers, had made it plain that this was no diversion; this was the real thing. His battalion was lying in the direct line of advance of a major Chicom[8] Battle Group. Carne couldn't afford to have his companies isolated from each other and then let the Chinese destroy them piecemeal.

[8] Chicom for Chinese Communist.

Pulling them back proved a sage decision. Only much later in the day did confirmation reach him that three Chinese divisions, 60,000 fighters and support troops, were moving in on his Imjin sector. He received the order to 'consolidate the line'. The only way to do this was to pull back his three mangled units and put them into a single blocking position further down the road. For all practical purposes, 'A' Company had been annihilated; 'D', though badly mauled, was still functioning as a unit; only 'B' and 'C', which had been lying slightly back from the road entrance into the defile, had been spared major casualties. For his 'blocking stand', Carne picked Hill 235. It would shorten his frontline from over six kilometres (4 miles) to a mere 600 metres (666 yards). For this he could muster at the very best 350 men. That still left wide gaps . . .

Throughout daylight on 23 April, there was a certain amount of skirmishing but no major assault. The survivors of the three point companies had pulled back and took up their new position. Now that all were together, their mood became unbeatable, an imperceptible lessening of tension, together with the most primitive of beliefs that if you anticipate something bad, it will never happen. They knew they were much better than any 'gooks'; they were Glostermen and would hold out against whatever the Chinks had to throw at them. When one called the hill 'The Rock of Gibraltar', the voice of Sgt Major Mike Gallagher cut through the babble of voices: 'Soldier, this ain't no Geebroltaar. This is Gloster Hill.' The men cheered. It was by this name that a Korean rockpile went down in the annals of military history.

While most were detailed to dig their new holes even deeper, others looked after the many casualties, from scars and scratches to shredded limbs. The light casualties were given an aspirin and a plaster, and told to get back on line. Those who had trouble standing were propped up on ammo boxes with a clear view over the trench and handed a rifle. There were also the serious casualties. Many had received deep wounds that put them beyond recovery. The medical officer, Capt. Bob Hickey, ably assisted by Medical Sgt Baxter and a team of volunteers, cut and patched, while Chaplain Davies comforted the dying. Someone began humming a song and soon the haunting melody of 'Amazing Grace' floated over the trenches.

On the night of 23 April, Chinese General Peng got ready for another assault, and once again, his men would march nowhere except into oblivion. Down in their holes sat the Glosters and waited. Most were too tired to eat and too tired to feel bad. Some thought about what had happened and how they had been graced to live a few more hours. Because come again the enemy would, that much was certain. As the night shadows fell, a tension hung in the air, so palpable that it could be heard in beating chests and felt on sweaty brows. Eyes stared into the growing darkness. Men were blowing into their cold hands, with rifles in the crooks of their arms. Somewhere, 10,000 miles (16,000 km) back, there was light and heat. But here it was dark and cold. The minutes ticked away slowly. Sgt Jack Eames looked around at flickering shadows. He sat down next to a young recruit.

'How will this end, serge?' asked the boy, more for assurance. 'I'm frightened.'

'So am I, son,' said the sergeant, 'but we'll never give them an inch, will we?'

The Chinese had managed to install a mountain gun battery on a ridge overlooking the British position. Throughout the day, artillery explosions harried the men on Gloster Hill. The Chinese artillery had sighted them in their guns, but they waited for darkness before they opened up in serious. In the trenches all hell erupted. The dark night was lit up with crazily zigzagging fireworks. More flares bathed the scene in ghastly blue light. By the fire of exploding mortar bombs and artillery shells, the hilltop shone like the rim of a volcano. Some shells of the first salvo landed short, but thereafter every projectile was on target, blasting the men; a flash of light, an explosion, shrapnel slashing through the dark. Followed by another, and another, a chain of deafening explosions.

For the Glosters in their holes, time stopped, seconds became minutes and minutes turned into hours. That was shortly before 'that sound' came out of the night – unreal and eerie, a sound they would carry with them all their lives. The sound of Chinese bugles, followed by whistles, ten, twenty, a hundred. Charging uphill, in a wild rush of screaming death and energy, came the horde. The enemy was silhouetted in the glaring white light of parachute flares and the Glosters fired and fired and fired, magazines dropped and new ones snapped into place. The desperation and frustration poured from their barrels and the only thing they felt was their guns' recoil. Tracers shot out in streaks, marking the targets. Mortar rounds popped, arched, and exploded with incredible rapidity, blasting great gaps into friend and foe.

An entire enemy squad was buried in a hail of fire from a short round of their own mortars as they came scrambling uphill. Bullets flew like sheets of steel designed for slaughter. Screams of pain and yells of death were heard coming from the Chinese lying on the slope. From behind every rock, every tree, spilled forth Chinese, dodging bullets, running for cover. Groups were caught in the murderous crossfire of machine guns. Where they went into hiding, British bullets shredded the shrubbery. Some tried to fight it out in the open; these were instantly killed. But the Glosters were running out of ammunition. Their decreasing rate of fire encouraged new Chinese endeavours.

One of their company managed to steal silently to within

yards of the trench. When those irritating Chinese bugles blew, the Chinese rose and, like a human avalanche, rushed up to the Glosters' trench, shooting, throwing grenades, bayoneting. A grenade landed at the foot of a soldier and he jumped back just as a mortar bomb went off. The blast caught him in the waist and bowled him over. He lay still and suddenly he screamed. Not because it hurt, but because it didn't. He screamed when he realised that he was paralysed.

The stream of fire 'walked' up and down the trenchline. The noise was ear-shattering. The bullets kicked up the dirt and made thunking sounds as they slammed into trees. The firing shifted back to Sgt Eames' position and a round grazed his shoulder. It threw him back, his helmet popped off and the back of his head was smeared with blood where he had crashed into a stone. A throbbing pain ran from the back of his skull to his eyes and he feared losing consciousness. A shot passed inches over his head. That woke him up. He rose, steadied himself on the edge of the trench, and emptied his automatic rifle into the onrushing shadows. He cut a handful of Chinese in half only yards from him.

On the eastern approach of the hill, Chinese with planted bayonets advanced steadily uphill. They moved cautiously, bent over, faces drawn taut. After two days of frightful losses, they had become reticent and reluctant. They leap-frogged from crater to crater until they were close. That's when they were spotted. Only thirty yards (27 metres) of churned-up earth separated the Glosters from the Chinese. But the British were in their holes and the Chinese were not. Lt Cabral pulled the pin on a grenade and let it roll down the slope. It made *pop!*, and a group of five Chinese moved no more. With bullets smacking all around him, a Gloster medic bellied to one of his wounded. He couldn't pull him out, so he patched him up and gave him a morphine shot, before he crawled back to provide first aid for others. To drag a wounded under his armpits to a safer place the medic had to raise his own body. That's when he got hit. He uttered a bubbling moan, his mouth opened, and his face contorted in pain; with a low grunt he sank to his knees and died.

The force of this indescribably courageous defence was too much for the Chinese; despite the furious screams by their officers, entire units began to run. It turned into a deluge of flight. The rest sought shelter wherever they could, in shrubs and behind rocks along the slope. God had sent a miracle. Private Jim Walker noticed a few Chinese, cowering in a depression, watching the fire-lit skies, chattering excitedly. He bellied into position, raised his Bren-gun and mowed them down with a single burst.

Dawn came much too slowly, setting the scene for a repulsive view of mangled, sprawled bodies in front of the trenches or hanging out of foxholes, mostly foes, but also many friends. The lull in the fighting gave Chaplain Davies time to conduct a service for the dead.

'I will lift up mine eyes unto the hills from whence cometh my strength,' prayed Padre Sam Davies. The men looked at the hill, their hill, thinking of the men who had died there, and how close to death they had been themselves in these past forty-eight hours. The chaplain's prayer was heard, because, at daybreak, a flight of US Air Force F-80 Shooting Star jets roared overhead, lining up on smoke markers sent up by Carne's men. The planes came down in tandem, swooping out of the sky like birds of prey. They screamed over the hill at low level. Instinctively, the men in the trenches threw themselves flat to the ground as silvery cylinders dropped from the jets' wings. The slope erupted in a searing white flame. In seconds the wood in front of the trenches changed into a roaring gale of yellow tongues of fire. Chinese smeared with incendiary liquid dropped screaming and were transformed into black mummies. A curtain of acrid black smoke hung over Gloster Hill from the lethal napalm wing-tanks, having cut a fiery swath through the re-forming CPV battalions. A thin snake of black smoke crawled over the Glosters' trench, bringing an oily smear, a reddening of eye and a taste of burnt flesh that reached into the back of their throats. Where the jellied liquid clung to trees, it flickered like private hells. By its light they could see shrivelled up bits of carbon that had been human. On the northeastern slope, Chinese were running down the hill in the hope of finding a way out of the holocaust.

Up until now, the attackers had suffered atrocious casualties; forty per cent of their attack force was either dead or put out of action. In fact, of the two divisions that had been engaged in this sector, one was almost completely wiped out, trying to pave its attack with casualties, feeding in battalion after battalion to achieve the breakthrough. The CPV front commander had called his severely mauled attack battalions back to regroup, and then decided to use a fresh division, and concentrate everything in one more attack on the British line.

For the soldiers on the hill, everything was quiet: 'They've buggered off!' The few hundred survivors of the battalion couldn't believe it. Seven times they had tried and seven times they were repulsed. The British survivors hung over their rifles, dazed, shocked and exhausted. A soldier sat down next to a severely wounded; he lit a cigarette for the wounded, holding the man's head and watching him die. Sgt Jack Eames was on guard duty. Their wounded had been moved behind the shelter of some rocks where it was felt they might have a better chance to survive the next onslaught. The others, tired and worn-out, lay in the trench, half-asleep on top of their weapons, waiting for a sunrise that might bring relief. As he looked down the slope, it occurred to Eames that the Chinks could be ten metres away and no one would see or hear them. It was just too quiet to be real.

This calm didn't last long before all hell again broke loose and a firestorm came down on them. The shells from the Chinese battery on the nearby mountain exploded like volcanoes. The soldiers kept their heads down while shrapnel, bits of wood and rock splinters flew everywhere. A soldier came running up to Eames' lot, breathing hard, his face black from cordite. He didn't say a word; he just grabbed half a dozen grenades from a wooden crate and ran back. They never saw him again. Suddenly there was a tremendous roar of a plane skimming overhead and Private Jim Walker went flying into the opposite wall. The earth convulsed, before clumps of it came thudding down around his body. For a while he lay the way he had fallen, gurgling sounds forcing their way out of him; blood poured down his face, he jerked himself up and forward, without noticing the pain.

'I'm hit,' he heard himself cry out. Bloody hell – he had been hit like a prize fighter gets hit and, just like a boxer, all he had to show for it was a nosebleed! Not much of a heroic wound. When the explosion died away and the earth stopped raining down, the soldiers in the trench lifted themselves up, shaken and stunned. Some of them were wounded. The Chinese however were less fortunate. The American bomb had struck smack among them. Their corpses were smeared all over the bushes.

More US planes came howling through the air, their blazing wing-guns mowed the enemy like grass. That didn't stop the Chinese artillery from pouring more shells into both defenders and attackers. They were now too close together to be separated with accuracy and the Chinese gun commanders didn't seem to care who they hit. Bodies were tossed into the air as dozens of impacts tore the hill apart.

Some swore afterwards that they could see the souls of the dead ascending to heaven, a weird trick played out on their imagination with their nerves at full stretch.

Sergeant Jack Eames, the military medallist from the Second World War with a voice that could pierce barrack walls, and known as 'the indestructible man', had a look at these shredded bodies lying in front of his men. Eames was turning away, when suddenly more gooks appeared in front of him. He backhanded two grenades at them. They went off with a double *pop!* The Sergeant was already searching out new targets. More Chinamen came rushing at him; he jumped up, shooting from the hip, and killing most. One Chinese got through, one with a planted bayonet. Pain came over Eames in scalding waves, blood pumped freely in little spurts from the gaping wound in his side. He had no morphine; he took a piece of hard wood and bit into it to stifle his scream of pain.

For the moment there was no firing, a sudden stillness had settled over the trench line. The only sounds were those of men breathing and the gentle sobs of the wounded. A medic came rushing up, tearing open the plastic wrapping from a battle dressing and slapped it over the gaping hole. A breeze came up, and the men were thankful for the gentle wind, blowing away the acrid fumes.

'Left flank!' someone yelled and they fired at whatever was piling over the edge of the trench. Sgt Eames, propped up against the trench wall, felt an unparalleled surge of adrenaline. Nothing could hurt him any longer, nothing could stop him; he felt that any bullet would simply bounce off him. Weakened by a severe loss of blood, his arms strained from holding the heavy gun; he forgot all about his terrible wound while he pumped bullets into the breach and released round after round. Everyone else was blasting away in a deafening surge of firepower. He could see bodies scrambling uphill, getting hit, and rolling down the steep incline. More Chinese were running in his direction. He got caught up in the madness, in the howling and dying. Figures were running everywhere, only to be reduced to piles of human debris. Then his strength failed and he collapsed. Two men grabbed him under the arms and pulled his limp body into a shelter behind a rock. He lay there, with his eyes closed and his chest rising and falling very slowly. A young soldier, the same sergeant he had told that they wouldn't give an inch, sat next to him, tears flowing down his cheeks.

'God, please . . . Do something. His heart is going . . .' No one heard his call – no one but the battalion's padre. Chaplain Sam Davies knelt down beside Sgt Eames and took a look at the wound. He tried to stop the blood, but the wound squirted like a spring tide. The sergeant opened his eyes; with great difficulty he put on a brave face.

'I'm all right, padre,' he whispered. 'You can leave me now.' And then he died. Indestructible Jack Eames wasn't the only one. Chaplain Davies found a young soldier, clutching his rosary beads in death.[9]

All along Gloster Hill, machine guns brushed away every living thing coming at them. Nothing helped. The guns overheated or ran out of bullets . . . and the Chinese jumped into the front trench!

'Evacuate!' came the call. Everyone who could move scrambled uphill, shooting and running. One, Private Jim Walker, always the individual, grabbed his Bren-gun and raced downhill, straight at the mass of Chinese, firing madly from the hip. Suddenly it was over.

Lt Col. Carne pulled the men from the forward trench

[9] The beads accompanied Chaplain Davies throughout his captivity and, afterwards, were returned to the dead soldier's parents.

line, shortening his perimeter even more around the crest of the hill. The last survivors used their bayonets to dig holes in the hard ground and build breastworks from rocks; Carne divided whatever was left of his battalion between Capt Wilson, defending the southeast spur, and Maj. Harding covering the northwestern approach. They had to hold out until relief came. Tom Brodie had promised a push by a battalion of Philippine reserves supported by the tanks of 8th Hussars.

In early afternoon, a troop of M-24 Chaffee tanks advanced bravely; explosions ploughed up the ground close by. The lead tank had just entered the narrow defile, its tank commander scanning the area through his periscope, when his tank received a direct hit and burst into flames. For a while the rest of the tanks performed a kind of mechanical dance, jerking backwards and forwards, in an effort to avoid the missiles and mortar bombs. The enemy was somewhere near but not to be seen, not firing directly, but from the flank – or the rear! Seeing red flames licking the armour of the M-24 not thirty metres (33 yards) distant, and blocking the advance, the rescue attempt was called off. With it, the final hope for relief was gone. From now on, the Glosters were on their own.

Major Harding's 'B' Company had fulfilled their order and held out as long as their ammunition lasted and his men could stand. Explosions crashed all around them, cloaking them in choking smoke and fine dust; it was a miracle that anyone survived in the open trench. Maj. Harding ordered his radioman to establish contact with battalion HQ. He received no answer; either he was on the wrong frequency, or they were dead.

'Conserve ammunition, pick targets carefully,' Harding ordered. Seven consecutive battalion-sized waves dashed up against 'B' Company's position. The world around them seemed to disintegrate as the Chinese mortar gunners launched a near inescapable spread simultaneously. The blast threw Company Sergeant Major John Morton off his feet. A shell had exploded behind him. Morton found himself dazed, his rifle thrown a few metres away. A wet spot spread on his battle tunic. When he low-crawled to his rifle he could feel the blood flow from a wound in his side. He picked up his gun and pushed himself to his knees. The man next to him was wounded. Then another, and another . . . One of his original platoon, who'd been missed by the shrapnel, clawed his way towards them. Everyone else was beyond help. The Bren-gunner slumped over his rifle, with a large hole in his back. Another flailed around with his arms, fighting for life, while blood gushed from his throat. The man spat blood and lost consciousness.

'Come on, talk to me,' pleaded his buddy, holding him in his arms, like a father comforting a child. 'Don't you dare die on me. You're going home, lucky bastard.'

'There's nothing more we can do here,' said the sergeant major. When 'B' Company of Maj Harding finally joined the rest on Hill 235, it consisted of fifteen men and four bullets. 'No one but the Glosters could have done it', wrote Brig. Tom Brodie in his report, after he had given them permission to break out. For that it was too late. The road out of the defile was blocked; the best Brodie could do to help them get through the ring of steel was to order up more aerial bombing runs. At the same time, the Chinese commanders had ordered several more battalions into the fray. It was intended to give the last defenders the *coup de grâce*.

For the Chinese, Gloster Hill acted like a magnet; they could have bypassed it to the left and to the right, but they wanted to take it! They began by mortaring the summit. Drum Major Buss was lying in a shallow trench. The first bomb landed a hundred yards away, the second fifty. 'The next will be bang on,' he thought. He heard the explosion but couldn't see it. He looked in front of his parapet to see a black hole and wondered how on earth the burst had missed him. Then there were more explosions and shrapnel flew over the piled-up rocks in front of him. Suddenly the mortaring stopped. The silence worried Sgt Buss as much as the shelling. Because it signalled that 'they were coming'. He looked towards the others who were nearby.

'Go on, kill them,' he snarled. 'Kill the bastards.'

Once Col. Carne knew that no help would come, he had to come to a decision. Wait for the end? Counter-attack before they were down to the last grenade, the final bullet? He knew that the situation was going downhill fast. It was only a question of time; their defences were weakened and the ammunition was running out. During the next attack, or the one after that, they would be swamped. A break-out under these circumstances was impossible. However dramatic the outcome, it was he who had given the order to make a stand; it was he who risked the lives of his men, and he would suffer the consequences. That, and that alone, was the lot of a commander. The situation around the summit was no longer desperate, it was hopeless. By 10.30 hrs the Chinese had broken through the northwestern spur and were about a hundred yards from the top. Lt Col. 'Fred' Carne picked up the rifle of a fallen, stuck several grenades into his belt and then gathered some soldiers that could still walk, as well as sundry cooks and mortar men from the 170th Battery, who had buried their tubes once they had run out of bombs to throw at the enemy.

'How are your men?' he asked the only surviving sergeant, arming the hastily assembled group with anything he could lay his hands on.

'Frustrated and enraged, sir.'

'Enraged is never a bad thing.' He turned to his small group. 'Ready?'

'Sir!' came their reply.

'All right. Let's go!' That moment a jet roared overhead. A napalm canister went off a hundred yards away, but to Carne and his hastily assembled group it felt as if they were in the middle of an erupting volcano. Carne rose to his knees.

'Glosters forward!' A yell, and they raced over the parapet, across the trench, over earth mounds and corpses. They ran downslope, bellowing and roaring, their primeval sounds mixed with most expressive invectives. They fell, rose, fell again, slipped and rolled downhill. They emptied their magazines.

The Chinese were paralysed by the sudden attack of an enemy they thought was already dead. Their mortars barked hollowly; bomb splinters hissed past them like angry wasps. When the telltale whistling came, the Glosters dived into the nearest shell hole and lay flat on the bottom, pressing their faces into the earth. Two were killed trying to get out of the hole, a third was wounded. Carne's men continued running down the rock-strewn slope. They no longer gave it a thought that they could be blown to bits at any moment. They gained on the enemy and were halfway down when an enemy machine gun opened up from another hill, its tracer bullets whistling past. As if in a dream, they kept on running, screaming, shooting and throwing grenades. Their mad charge managed to push the Chinese from the upper portion of the spur. Twice more the Chinese tried and twice more Carne led his 'mad squad' in a suicidal chase, throwing them off 'their hill' . . . until they ran out of bullets and grenades. With a wry smile Carne looked at Capt. Harvey of 'D' Company, who had followed his colonel.

'I think we should clear out now, Mike.'

Capt. Tony Farrar-Hockley, the colonel's ADC, had taken leave from his post; with the batteries of his radio finished, and his superior leading 'the Charge of the Light Brigade', there was no further reason for him to hang around HQ and stare at a dead radio. He had taken over the pitiful remains of 'A' Company. The Chinese came up against him, blowing their damned bugles. He hated that racket; it was a thing to focus his fury on; their noise annoyed him no end.

'Drum Major!' he yelled. A clipped sergeant's voice came from higher up on the crest.

'Sir!' Drum Major Philip Buss grabbed his rifle, jumped to his feet and raced down the slope.

'Got a bugle, Sergeant?'

'Sir!'

'Then blow it, Drum Major, blow it!' It was an order Drum Major Buss readily obeyed. As the battalion's Mozart he also couldn't stand that noise; those were no bugle calls, just offending, screechy sounds. He couldn't fill his lungs to the fullest, crouching down in a trench, so Sgt Buss jumped to the top of the parapet, took a deep breath, and the first notes of 'Reveille' rang out over the hill. The reaction was incredible; all along the trenchline, the harried soldiers cheered Sgt Buss, with his legs straddling the ground and his bugle raised to his lips. The following minutes opened the door to a Drum Major's military fame.[10] Philip Buss played 'Cookhouse' and 'Officers Dress for Dinner'. Fittingly, he ended his bugle concert with 'The Last Post'.

The morning was cold. The chill crept through their uniforms. The hill looked dreadful. The slope leading up

[10] An oil painting in the Gloucestershire regimental museum recalls this unique event.

to the Glosters' position was carpeted with dead Chinese; their rifles bristled erratically skyward, clutched in frozen hands. Torn apart by grenades, the corpses weren't human any more, but then, what was? The trench was no different. Littered with empty ammunition boxes and spent cartridge casings; bodies, and bits of bodies draped over the sandbags; in machine-gun emplacements were stiffening corpses. The survivors' movements had become exaggerated and heavy, as if time had slowed up; everyone got the feeling that his whole life had led up to this moment in time. And now it was over; in this sudden silence, there were so many to be patched up or buried, no one took any longer count.

'I hurt!' moaned one, lying on his back, his chest heaving spasmodically. Another sat in silence, grasping his side with a distorted face before falling back to lie unmoving. And yet another, moaning, rocked from side to side, his fists pressed to his temples. Still further on, a young soldier, half hanging out of his foxhole, screaming to God or anyone who would hear him, his left side all mangled and covered with thick slabs of congealed red. Every heartbeat brought forth more blood. One man was sitting quietly, trying to write a note to his wife: 'My sweet, I'm too tired to write . . .'

'Go and find your own escape route,' Col. Carne ordered his company commanders, 'and may God guide you through.' The casualties were to remain behind, counting on Chinese military courtesy to keep them alive.[11] Capt. Hickey, the medical officer, and Padre Sam Davies offered to stay with them. The last one to set off with eighty-one men was Capt. Harvey. He was the only one to get through. When he finally reached the American lines,

[11] Chinese were considered more human in the treatment of prisoners than their Korean comrades.

his roll call came to five officers and forty-one rank and file.[12]

Then the Chinese guns boomed for a last time; their rounds came crashing down on the last two hundred. And when the firing stopped, Gloster Hill was crawling with Chinese . . .

At mid-morning on 25 April 1951, the hill was wrapped in frozen silence. What was left from the 1st Battalion of His Majesty's 28th Regiment of Foot, the Glosters, was trudging down the hill that had become their sacred funeral pyre. For three days they had held the hill. Was that yesterday or last month? They couldn't remember; too much had happened. They were desperately tired. The silence of death blanketed the valley and the hills beyond. Now they were headed into captivity. Ahead walked Lt Col. 'Fred' Carne, whose citation for the Victoria Cross was to read: 'He showed powers of leadership which can seldom have been surpassed in the history of our Army.'

The 'Glorious Glosters' exemplified the spirit of resistance. Any task they were asked to perform, they did well and with pride. They had lived with each other, they had cried with each other, and they had learned to depend on each other. They stood and they fought and they died. During three memorable days on the Imjin River in April 1951, they bought time for the rest of the United Nations to rally their forces. Of the Glosters, only a mere handful came back. Of the 622 fighting men that held up a Chinese Army, forty-six made it to safety; the others remained were they fell, or suffered long months in captivity.

A battalion demonstrated spiritual courage, physical endurance and unmatched battle skill. Their individual

---

[12] The losses inflicted by 29th Brigade on the 63rd CPV Shock Army were 11,000 killed.

acts of heroism do not require embellishment; their deeds speak for themselves. The Glorious Glosters, heroes all.

The Glosters' motivation was tenacity, fortified by a 'last stand syndrome'. The officers knew that they could rely on their men's quiet steadiness and excellent fire routine. Yet firepower alone was not self-sustaining. It took leadership of a high order to ensure that the defence held out. Tenacity or not, Lt Col. Carne could not have conducted a last-stand defence without the inbred sense of duty of these rightful heirs of the tradition and steadfastness of the British infantry. Once the Glosters were told to make their stand, thereby saving the entire Allied frontline from collapse, they held out, selling their lives dearly. Of the many feats of individual heroism, it would be hard to single out one.

Geneviève de Galard, The Angel of Dien Bien Phu

'Dien Bien Phu is a symbol – the symbol of the fight by the free world against a totalitarian world. Today's youth must admire the courage of these brave men that fought and died for an idea.'

Geneviève de Galard, January 2002

It was hell. The shells came down in clusters. The phone rang in the first-aid ward: eight wounded, twelve more, then it was suddenly forty; they stopped counting at a hundred. A long line of walking casualties waited in the open trench leading down into the tunnel. There was no more space inside the underground shelter. They were lying everywhere, twenty in the storage room, four in the tiny radio room; one of them was a soldier with his face blackened by powder and his leg torn off, blood gushing from the stump. Next to him lay one with a gaping stomach wound. He didn't move because he was already dead. From another stretcher reached out an arm, making signs in the air. And always more fire from the sky and more calls for stretcher-bearers and more demands for blood plasma and morphine and sulphur drugs. The sharp crump of exploding shells drowned out the screams, the calls for help, the agonising pain, the shock and the fear.

'*Mademoiselle, moi beaucoup peur* – Me much afraid . . .' It was Phuc, an '*octoctone*' (native) ambulance driver who had lost part of his right arm. The nurse was sure that any moment now one of these monster 122mm shells would come through the roof and down into the ward. Then all would be over, the pain and the suffering. She had no time to worry; her task was to reassure her wounded, not herself. She stepped over the stretcher of a man who had lost both legs, then climbed over more wounded, placed pell-mell in the ward and along the long slit-trench leading down into it. There were just too many casualties and more were brought in by the minute. The medical staff was exhausted, even the tough Médecin-Caporal Sioni; an hour earlier he had told her: 'I can no longer stand on my feet.'

She too felt so numb that she could no longer smell that stinging odour of urine and excrement mixed in with the sweat of fear. She stopped near Sgt Moret, a brave man; with a bullet through his stomach, he had stood his guard and fired belt after belt until the enemy was pushed back. He would probably survive. The Algerian Legionnaire Mokhtar was less fortunate; shrapnel had torn apart his intestines and he was drowning in his own blood.

'*Mademoiselle, de l'eau* – Water . . .' She couldn't allow him water; it would kill him. Anyway, what difference would it make, now, or in an hour. And all the while, the bombs exploded overhead. Suddenly, silence. The enemy had vanished into the darkness. There was also silence down in the underground hospital; they either slept, or they were dead.

When the world woke up, that 8 May 1954, they saw

the picture of a middle-distance runner splashed across the front pages of their newspapers:

THE CONQUEST OF THE EVEREST OF ATHLETICS
ROGER BANNISTER RUNS MIRACLE MILE:
3 MINS 59.4 SECS!

Further down the front page they discovered a column that announced a Viet Minh offensive on a beleaguered fortress in the jungles of French Indochina with the unpronounceable name of Dien Bien Phu. Little did the world realise that the imminent fall of this French colonial bastion was to lead to the longest war of the 20th century, one that was to last 8000 days, causing millions of dead – including 55,000 American GIs – and would redraw the political map of South-East Asia.

The Korean War had left in its wake shattered illusions and an escalation in the East-West crisis, but it also brought about a heightening of tensions between China and the Soviet Union; their struggle for Communist hegemony created new political challenges for supremacy in the Asiatic region. The analysis of the military lessons and political implications of the Korean War led to evaluating the failings of strategy, the role of sophisticated armament and the fighting ability of armed forces. In delving into the part played by Communist China, when it quite willingly unleashed a round of fighting in this sensitive part of the globe, it raised many questions about future warfare in South-East Asia. Following the end of the Korean War, the leader of Indochina's liberation movement, Ho Chi Minh and his military commander, General N'guyen Giap, received tons of Chinese war materiel that was no longer needed on the front in Korea. Even more crucial, the 'human factor' came into play.

Very much like the British, who had never learned their

lesson during the Boer War, the French greatly underestimated their 'barefoot foe'. General Navarre, France's commander in Indochina, was a man who held the peasant army of Chairman Ho and General Giap in total contempt. It is true; two years before, the Viet Minh had suffered a severe setback fighting the French. But this time it was to be different. A status quo between North and South had been established in Korea; for the planners of an Asian Communism, Indochina was the ideal trouble spot to rattle the Western powers. With this in mind, Ho had received tacit backing from both the Kremlin and Beijing. Their previous military setback had taught the Viet Minh commanders a valuable lesson; they withdrew from the cities, held by strong French garrisons, and faded into the jungles along the border region. The area along the Laotian border was such a place.

Experts on military incompetence may be forgiven for thinking that after two disastrous world wars there was nothing more to learn. There was. The French did it, at Dien Bien Phu, an obscure outpost in what was then called French Indochina. The fortress had been established at the border junction between Laos and Vietnam. Politically it made sense; France wanted to hang on to its colonial empire, and that included Laos. Militarily it was madness; the place was located in the worst possible position, a bowl of rice paddies surrounded by heavily wooded hills. When it rained the bowl became waterlogged, and when it didn't rain a tropical sun fried the indigenous' brains. That's why they always wore conical straw hats. The plan of French strategists was to cut the road to the Laotian capital of Luang Prabang and deny the Communist Viet Minh their supply of rice. Unfortunately, their planners ignored a local wisdom: 'Trying to block a road in a country where peasants walk barefoot around a roadblock, is a European idea.'

On 20 November 1953, the French High Command launched 'Operation Castor' by parachuting two battalions of French Colonial Paratroopers (paras) into the paddies around an obscure little border hamlet, Dien Bien Phu, in order to establish a fortified base along the Laotian border, and to deprive Ho Chi Minh and Giap of the vital supply line from China via Laos. Choosing the site, the French never imagined that anybody could penetrate the jungle wilderness, least of all occupy the base's surrounding hills; a certain General N'guyen Giap was to prove them wrong. He achieved what the French considered impossible. He moved four entire divisions plus all their heavy equipment through the roadless jungle. On the evening of 12 March 1954, he had completed his build-up.

A total of 48,000 Viet faced 12,000 French. It wasn't only a numerical superiority in men; the main difference was in artillery. Giap's support army of human ants, those 'barefoot peasants' the French officers held in such utter disregard, dismantled the cannons and then pushed them piece by heavy piece through the jungle – on bicycles! Operating by night to protect the secrecy of their approach, General Giap planted his eighty 105mm howitzers and twenty 122mm heavy mortars on the heights looking straight down on Dien Bien Phu!

On the night before Giap struck, a hill tribe *montaignard*, barefoot and armed with a spear, arrived at French headquarters, babbling in an excited voice. The French officers didn't have the faintest idea what the man was trying to tell them, but the colonel didn't like it. By the time he found an interpreter it was too late. The attack caught the French completely by surprise. So much so that, on 13 March, the day the Viet began their devastating rain of fire, the French artillery chief, who had always claimed that he would 'wipe the Viet from the face of the earth with his heavy guns', pulled the pin on a grenade and held it against his chest.

The way he died was kept hushed up and he received a hero's funeral.

Following a series of suicidal attacks, which culminated in overrunning the outlying French strong points, the Viet moved their guns even closer and thereby could bring the garrison and its two metal-grated airstrips under direct fire. In a replay of Verdun 1916, Giap's cannons turned the fortified fortress into a meatgrinder. Every day, the noose tightened a bit more around the defenders. Within days, the French could get neither in nor out of the valley, and the French Air Force didn't have what it took for the support of the beleaguered fortress; their infrastructure in both planes and landing strips was simply not sufficient to handle an operation of such scope. That fact came as a severe shock to their High Command. They finally asked the Americans to bail them out.

'This isn't our war, let's not get involved in an Asian conflict,' advised General Ridgway, who had learned his lessons in Korea. President Dwight D. Eisenhower took the general's advice and refused America's military assistance.

The causes of the French failure were many, but the most obvious was their persistent underestimation of the enemy's potential. The major factor in favour of the Viet Minh was their ability to move around the jungle with the greatest of ease. And while the diplomats slid notes across baize tables, thousands of defenders waited for relief; however, they did everything they could to prolong their survival and to wait 'for *the* day' by performing incredible feats of heroism. One of them was a woman.

She was born in the lush, green fields of southwest France, the land of d'Artagnan and Cyrano de Bergerac. Like the two great heroes, she too was the daughter of old nobility, dating back to the era of Jeanne d'Arc. Her studies in a private Catholic school in Paris were suddenly interrupted by the Second World War and her family moved from Paris to Toulouse. Having witnessed the ravages of war, the girl developed an urge to come to help people in need and, rather than marry into nobility and become the titled mistress of a château, she passed the state exam as *infirmière* (nurse). Her destiny was decided the day she met a school friend who told her about the 'flight nurses in the French Air Force'[1] or, as they were called: *convoyeuse*. The official title gave her the rank of a sub-lieutenant, and combined a thorough medical knowledge with exhaustive flight training, including how to handle seriously wounded in non-pressurised aircraft. Geneviève de Galard passed the test and asked for a posting to Indochina. Why Indochina? 'Because it was there that a war was being fought and I could be of most use to help suffering soldiers.'

Arriving in Indochina on 7 May 1953, she was stationed in Hanoi and flew as *convoyeuse* between Pleiku and Hanoi, evacuating the casualties of 'Operation Atlantide' from the Central Highlands. The first time she flew to Dien Bien Phu was on 20 January 1954. From then on, the Dien Bien Phu run became routine for her. In the beginning it was mainly for the evacuation of dysentery or cholera cases. But then everything took a turn for the worse. Following three days of murderous combat for the outlying strongpoints around Dien Bien Phu (between 13 and 15 March), nothing was ever the same again. Giap's hordes neutralised the positions and brought the main base camp under the direct bombardment by his massed cannons. French casualties kept mounting by the hour.

On 17 March, a white-painted DC-3, bearing a huge Red Cross on its fuselage, managed to land on the airstrip in

---

[1] Flight nurses were started by the US during the Second World War, and a school for flight nurses existed in the USA.

Dien Bien Phu, where it unloaded cases of medicine and bandages, and collected thirty-two wounded. Compared to the number of overall casualties, thirty-two wasn't many, but at least it marked the start of a medical evacuation process. While the wounded were still piled up in the back of the DC-3 aircraft, the Viet artillery opened fire and shells began to fall near the airstrip. The pilot raced the engines and had a trying time to lift the tail-heavy plane over the perimeter wire; he was so low that the barbed wire shredded his tail wheel. Two more planes managed to land on 18 March, both subjected to heavy artillery fire, where shrapnel injured a male nurse aboard the plane.

On 19 March, Geneviève de Galard volunteered to accompany the in-bound flight to help evacuate more of the seriously injured. She took over from her colleagues who had done the round-trip the day before. For the first time, this operation was to be flown by night. Its pilot was the commander of the Gia Lam airbase, Col. Descaves, with Galard as the plane's *convoyeuse*. They knew that there were at least 400 casualties awaiting evacuation. They were hoping to bring out forty. Their approach was to be made in complete darkness, guided into the metal-grated airstrip by three flashlights – two at point of landing to indicate the width of the strip, and one at the very end to make certain that the plane stopped in time. To cover the noise of the aircraft's approach, a second aircraft was to circle overhead. The delicate part of the operation was the touchdown; the pilot had to cut the twin engines on approach, and virtually fly as glider over the last hundred metres to bang the heavy craft down on to the runway. Considering that such an operation was attempted at all pays a high tribute to the skill of French aircrews.

Geneviève received her call late in the evening; she picked up her oxygen bottle and medical kit, and a military car sped her to Gia Lam airport where the plane, a C-47, the military version of a DC-3 'Dakota', was ready for take-off. She climbed aboard and the plane took off.

'We have three minutes on the ground, not a second more,' Col. Descaves told her, 'then we're off again. So make certain that everything is ready.' The landing was a nightmare; for the pilot, but even more so for those 'sitting in the back of the bus'. At least the pilot could see out of his window, but those in the enclosed back[2] had no idea where they were, or what was going on around them. It was like riding in a subway through a tunnel. When the engines cut, all Geneviève could hear was a howling of wings slicing through air. If ever she needed to pray, this was the moment. It was the bounce and rattle on the landing grid that finally assured her of their safe landing.

But that was not her only shock of the night.

'When I saw the medics who had accompanied the wounded, and discovered what state they were in, un-shaven, with fatigue drawing deep lines, I felt as if I had not landed on earth but instead descended into hell. Of course, this was only my initial impression – I was to see much worse.'

With feverish activity the medics pushed nineteen wounded through the hatch; thirteen were walking casualties and six were brought aboard on stretchers.[3] It took only two minutes, but even that was too long. While they were about to take on the last casualties, Viet artillery spotters discov-ered their presence and guns began shelling the airstrip. Their plane took off and Col. Descaves ordered two more evacuation planes, which had been hovering overhead, to head back to Hanoi without attempting a further landing. The 340-mile (544 km) turnaround from Hanoi to Dien

[2] The cargo section of the Dakota's military version, the C-47, carried no windows.
[3] Geneviève de Galard kept a detailed diary.

Bien Phu and back took them two and a half hours. For the following week, one or two planes ventured into the besieged camp every night. On the night of 26 March, three planes made the trip; one circled and two landed. The two took off with a minimum charge as the pilots had to abort their stay on the ground given the concentration of incoming fire. The following night brought more of the same. Two Dakotas had already landed and taken off with their load of wounded; therefore, the ground staff didn't expect a third aircraft. So when Geneviève's evacuation aircraft landed, there were no waiting ambulances near the strip.

What had happened? Where had it gone wrong? For hours, those to be evacuated had been waiting in the base shelter, when a message came through: 'Aircraft on approach.' Normally, such warning came thirty minutes prior to the loading operation, this time it came three minutes before. Four ambulances raced to the airstrip, bouncing from pothole to crater. 'I wonder when those air jockeys take more of a risk, to land without lights at night or to make for a perfect target in a day approach?' mused one of the drivers.

'Ask the pilots,' replied the accompanying lieutenant. That night, they didn't get any more out. Flashes in the mountains were a sure signal of imminent trouble. The plane couldn't wait. The pilot swung the aircraft around and took off with shells exploding around them. The men in the bouncing ambulance saw only the exhaust flames of the rapidly disappearing plane.

Geneviève looked out of the still open door. 'It was at this moment that I saw ambulances speeding towards us, but then it was too late, the plane was in the air. I felt absolutely terrible, having left behind all those hoping for their exit from hell. Many of them, especially those who couldn't be operated on in the camp, were thereby condemned. It was because of that incident that I asked my *chef d'équipe* to put me on the next flight, a flight that proved to be my destiny.'

A solution had to be found, because the Viet gunners ignored the large Red Cross signs painted on the planes' fuselage and were firing at the white painted DC-3s. Dr Paul Grauwin, the chief of the surgical theatre in the field hospital, together with Padre Heinrich, went to see Colonel de Castries.

'*Mon colonel*, we cannot get enough wounded out.'

'How many can we evacuate by night?' asked the colonel.

'Not enough. In the end, all depends on so many factors, the *sang-froid* of the pilot, the speed of the stretcher-bearers, the reaction time of the Viet gunners. Last night it wasn't a pretty sight; the plane was already rolling when a few walking wounded ran after it, hanging on to the open door to be pulled in. *Eh bien . . .*' said the doctor with a deep sigh. 'We should open a first-aid station halfway between strong point Isabelle on the plain outside the perimeter. A kind of neutral territory where both our men, and wounded Viet can come for treatment.'

Col. de Castries gave it a thought. 'Not bad, it might solve a major problem. I'll pass it on to Hanoi. But I doubt that the Viet will go for it. Giap doesn't seem to give a damn about his losses.'

'They're shooting at our Red Cross planes.'

'Uncle Ho claims our Dakotas are bringing in ammunition. For them any excuse is good enough to ignore the Geneva Convention.'

It was the morning of 29 March. A C-47 under the command of Commandant Blanchet, with the board-mechanic Chauvin and the *convoyeuse* Geneviève de Galard, took off just before 05.00 hrs. It was very late to complete the round-trip in darkness, but technical problems had delayed the take-off. Their landing at Dien Bien Phu was projected for precisely 06.15 hrs. It was this late landing, just before daybreak, which was to prove fatal. For weeks now, just before sunrise, a dense fog had blanketed the bowl, and hid the runway. On the initial approach, the pilot made two futile attempts to bring the aircraft down, but because of the dense fog bank in combination with the two feeble landing lights he couldn't make a visual approach and feared that he wasn't lined up correctly for a landing. He tried for a third and final time. They had to get down, many wounded depended on them! That's when the accident happened. The plane touched down, bumping along the metal strips, but the blind landing had brought it too near the barbed wire entanglement protecting the edge of the runway.

Geneviève heard a sharp crack, as one of the stakes holding the wire entanglement sliced through the left engine cowling. They bounced to a stop and soldiers were already pushing the plane around into its take-off position. They had no idea about the seriousness of the damage, until the board mechanic took a look, while they were already loading up the wounded. 'The oil pan is damaged, oil pressure's down to zero,' was the verdict of mechanic Chauvin. 'It'll take at least two hours to patch it up.' And two hours they didn't have; daylight would come in twenty minutes.

Cdt Blanchet called Geneviève. 'Move the wounded off the plane and get them back into the ambulances.'

'But we cannot . . .' she tried to protest.

The pilot shook his head. 'I cannot get this thing to lift off on a single engine.' He shook his shoulder. 'Sorry, but we're stuck.'

What might have been repaired during the night, had they not been delayed by a late take-off, was now out of the question. The sun was about to come up, its heat would quickly dissipate the fog, and they couldn't endanger the lives of a mechanic to repair the aircraft in plain view of the Viet artillery. The damaged plane was pushed to the edge of the strip. At 10.30 hrs, the white plane with the big Red Cross painted on its side, sitting like a dead duck alongside the field, was targeted by the Viet artillery; the third round struck the wing, the aviation fuel exploded in an orange flash and a great black plume rose over Dien Bien Phu. This time the Viet made certain to knock out the runway: 122mm mortar bombs landed on the strip, slicing up the metal grid and making it unusable for future landings. This marked the end of any further attempt to fly out more casualties.

With the destruction of the airstrip the base was now hermetically sealed off from the outside world. Nobody could any longer get in, nobody out. Everything depended on an efficient and sustained aerial supply mission. All the needs of a base, counting ten thousand men, every shell, loaf of bread and medicine, every gallon of drinking water, had to be flown in and then delivered by air drops. A scarcity of fighter aircraft and atrocious meteorological conditions reduced greatly the efficiency of targeting air drops on the landing zones, especially in the face of a lethal anti-aircraft barrage. Because of the anti-aircraft barrages put up by the Viet, the C-47s had to dump their supplies from an altitude of between 6000 to 9000 feet (1800 to 2700 metres), using a pyrotechnical delay fuse to open the parachutes and thus assure that munitions and food dropped into an increasingly smaller base perimeter. Due to prevailing winds, more than half of the parachuted supplies drifted off and were lost to the enemy. A further handicap lay in the aerial congestion over a rapidly diminishing drop zone, with planes circling and flying in all directions. Some C-119s managed to fly at lower altitudes and assured a relatively 'safe drop', but their cargo capacity was considerably less great than that carried by the Dakotas. Another problem that faced the defenders was the recovery of munitions in the rainy season. Deep mud had made truck traffic impossible and everything had to be carried on the backs of men, exhausted from their daily firefights. And then even the last general drop zones were overrun by the enemy, or lying under his direct artillery fire. The only drop zones in use were the strong points still in French hands. Finally, even these air drops became impossible and the aerial supply bridge ceased to operate altogether. That day the fate of the men fighting on the ground was sealed.

Since 29 March, the night the last flight into Dien Bien Phu had landed on the strip, Dien Bien Phu counted two more residents: one was the Dakota's pilot, Cdt Blanchet. The other was a female medial flight escort, Geneviève de Galard. The *convoyeuse* turned into an *infirmière*, a nurse. From the airfield she had hitched a ride to the hospital of the *Médecin-Commandant* Dr Paul Grauwin, in order to offer her services; it was the only place where a stranded flight nurse could be of assistance.

'Dr Grauwin, since it seems that I shall be staying on for a while, I put myself at your entire disposal.'

Grauwin could certainly use a trained nurse, but he wasn't sure if she could take it; it wasn't a hospital with broken legs, these were casualties with ripped-open bellies and torn-off arms. The place looked more like a slaughter-house than a field hospital, where the suffering was great; men were brought in hourly with the most horrid wounds and then died like flies. The chief surgeon decided on a shock test: he put Geneviève into a ward with a dozen of the worst casualties, men with gaping belly wounds and not expected to survive,[4] and the earth had soaked up the blood of the last casualties.

The base hospital was a confusing labyrinth of tunnels, storage space for medical supplies, a preparation room,

[4] Dr Paul Grauwin, *J'etais Médecin à Dien Bien Phu*, Paris, 1992.

a surgical theatre, and wards for the wounded. When Geneviève first entered the long tunnel, lit by naked bulbs, a repugnant odour of human sweat, excrement and ether stifled her. She sat down on the blood-soaked ground beside a badly wounded and held his hand. Next to him, a shroud had been placed over a dead comrade; only his arm stuck out from under the sheet. On the arm was a wristwatch – still ticking away. The whole was a scene from Dante's *Inferno*, but she stood the test.

Dr Grauwin observed her from the entrance:

I confided to her the worst possible cases; in a small shelter were ten casualties with open stomach wounds, jammed together on stretchers. There was hardly enough space to move in between them. Bandages covered their intestines, and these bandages needed changing twice every day. They required constant observation and injections; they couldn't move without help. But most of all, they needed kind words. While shells rained down on us I kept watching her, and I was astonished by her calm. She moved from wounded to wounded as if nothing special was going on. She had *la geste* that it took, the kindness, understanding and precision, but she had something else: the pureness and the freshness of a young girl.'[5]

Indeed, Geneviève had *la geste*, the soothing touch, the ability to heal by providing words of encouragement in her fresh, youthful voice.

'Let me give you an injection . . . where do you want it, in the leg, in the arm, oh . . .' she blushed. 'I see . . . here, it didn't hurt, did it?' And the soldier, who had been cringing with pain, smiled bravely back at her. She knew that she couldn't help everyone to survive, but at least she could help them to die in peace.

Once Dr Grauwin had seen her at work he gladly

[5] *Médecin-Commandant* Dr Paul Grauwin.

accepted her offer. It was settled: Geneviève de Galard
would become his assistant. But even this caused a problem:
Geneviève de Galard was the only woman in a camp of
12,000 men, and macho paras at that. Certain arrangements had to be made to ensure that she was treated as
a nurse, and not a female intruding into the all-male society. Grauwin briefly introduced her to his staff: Sergeant
Deudon, twenty-four, was assisting during operations. Sergeant N'Diaye, twenty-three, from Senegal was in charge
of post-operative care, and also looked after the hygiene
of the patients as well as the primitive means allowed
it. He was helped by *Caporal* Abbou. *Caporal* Lachamp
kept books on the number of casualties and their operational needs. Private Perez was the anaesthetist; Sergeant
Kabbour was steriliser, *Caporal-chef* (Master Sgt) Arriba
was in charge of thirty local coolies working the stretcher
parties. The nineteen-year-old Algerian Lahcen, strong as
an ox, received the arriving casualties. Julot was the radio
operator. And there were four Vietnamese general aides:
Hoang, Minh, Muon and Binh, the oldest being fifty-three
and the youngest seventeen. The team was rounded out
with an Italian, Sioni, and a Spaniard, Cortes. Though they
were legionaries without medical training, they soon turned
into a valuable addition to Dr Grauwin's *équipe*.

The first night in the shelter, the medical helpers stared
at Geneviève with open hostility. In her flight uniform, a
prim white blouse and blue skirt with ordinary city shoes,
she looked a rather useless addition.

'*Une vierge* . . . a virgin,' referring actually to her lack of
combat experience, was *Caporal* Sioni's initial judgment.
'She doesn't even have the strength to lift a stretcher. Now
we're stuck with her. Where are we going to put her up?
You can be sure that I'll not give her my stretcher to sleep
on . . .'

A week passed, when the same Sioni who had thought

of her as a useless thing hanging around their necks, asked to be attached to her service; he was to become her most faithful assistant. Julot found her suitable trousers and N'Diaye a T-shirt. Levasseur 'liberated' a pair of basketball shoes. A sergeant of the 2nd Para presented her with a camouflage coverall.[6] Bacus offered her his stretcher bed; Sioni produced a clean sheet and a soft pillow. One thing was sure: she had been fully accepted into *l'équipe*.

She didn't have to wait long before her presence became invaluable. The 30th of March marked a harrowing day. VM General Giap had decided that it would be the day he'd bring Dien Bien Phu to fall. At 16.00 hrs a deluge of fire began raining down on the camp and the surrounding strong points. Within no time, the underground hospital was receiving hundreds of wounded, especially those who had managed to survive the attack on strong point *Dominique* which, following a heroic defence, had been overrun by masses of Viet. In an indescribable carnage, the African gunners of Lt Brunebrouke had fired their 105mm cannons point-blank at the advancing enemy. They loaded and fired, loaded and fired, until the tubes were glowing.

'Fire, damn you!' screamed Brunebrouke, when one of his guns fell silent.

'The piece is overheating,' protested a chief gunner.

'Then piss on it,' yelled the lieutenant. 'But keep firing!'

The enemy was upon them and turned the battle into hand-to-hand butchery. Those who survived dragged themselves into the hospital and ended up in Geneviève's ward. Lt Brunebrouke died on 13 April, having received the last rites from Father Trinquand. '*Ego te absolvo . . .*'

The day folloing the attack of 30 March was a horrid experience for Geneviève. Casualties arrived with bleeding

6 See her photo (inset section).

heads and open bellies. Most of the time the wounded were hovering on the edge of consciousness. It was horrid. Stacks of limbs were lying in a bin. To whom belonged that smashed leg, or whose was the arm cut under the elbow? The team of surgeons worked day and night, patching and cutting, and she cleaned, bandaged, and applied sulphur drugs. In all of her twenty-eight years, she had never imagined anything like this could happen. There were wounded, waiting to be patched or cut up, lying throughout the underground passages, suffering, moaning, dying. No comfort, no hygiene, and the wounds infected themselves. There should have been many more deaths. How they survived was the miracle of nature – certainly the only miracle in this *trou d'enfer*, this hell-hole.

One who knew her well described her as '*Elle n'était pas autant forte en geule* – She didn't have coarse features, or the build of a rugbyman and she wasn't convinced of her own importance. On the contrary, everything was only *douceur* on a Madonna face.' Even in her baggy coveralls, Geneviève was a pretty girl with cropped auburn hair, and a slightly upturned nose. It was in her eyes that the pain showed, forced to watch the suffering of the many overflowing wards and trenches. Fatigue was written all over her face; her body felt as though it wanted to fall. Still she knelt down beside her wounded, wetting their lips from a water bottle and feeling their pulse. One young *légionnaire* was in shock, but he was young and healthy-looking enough to come out of this. She ministered to him as best she could, cleaned the wounds, and applied a bandage to stop the flow of blood. Later, when no one watched, her body shook and tears came streaming down her face. She had spent so much time caring for the wounded and watching them suffer. She had nursed them and had seen them die.

How this had changed the protected life she had been offered at home to one of sacred duty towards fellow humans.

After a few days in the underground hospital, she asked Grauwin: '*Commandant*, where are the other casualties?'

'They are all over the place, some at HQ, some at 2nd Para.'

'Can I go and pay them a visit?'

'Don't you realise that the Viet are firing at us? What if you get a shell on your head?'

'*Oh, mais non*, I do have my helmet . . .' Nothing, but nothing could stop her.

'*Mademoiselle, qui êtes-vous*? – Who are you? A nurse? Incredible. You must come and visit us often . . .' With it, her visits became a daily happening; casualties spread throughout the base waited anxiously for her visit, to confide in her and listen to her words of comfort. Dr Grauwin suppressed a joyous grin; after his *équipe*, his patients had adopted Geneviève. Colonel Langlais gave her packs of cigarettes to distribute. The story of the 'miracle nurse' spread throughout the base, and she was solicited to visit units in the trenches who weren't even wounded. Many claimed afterwards that it was the words from this tough slip of a girl that instilled them with hope and made them pull through. In no time she was known under a new name: *l'ange d'espoir* – the angel of hope.

During the days of heavy bombardment, one of the main problems she had to put up with was personal hygiene, and since there was no way to go to an outdoor latrine during the day, that caused a problem. For the men this wasn't an overwhelming problem; there were enough empty medicine bottles to be filled up, but for her, it was different. Her needs had to be performed outside, and then only during the cover of darkness.

'Of course, there was always the risk of getting hurt. But to fulfil certain needs that we all have, I had to go outside. For that I had to wait for nightfall which wasn't always simple.' For the first few days she slept on her stretcher among the casualties, being kept up most of the night by their agony. And then, one day, she discovered a small cubicle in the cave wall, covered with a parachute. The men had dug it especially for 'her personal comfort'. From then on, it became her home away from home, decorated with a simple wooden cross. Yet, many nights, sleep evaded her as the thoughts of her wounded kept flooding her mind; she had confused dreams and half-awake periods. Then she turned to the cross to pray to the Lord. Please, let the slaughter end. *Requiescat in pace.*

Lt Chevalier had covered the evacuation of his men from the strong point trench through a tunnel, acting like a Horatio at the bridge. He kept the escape tunnel open until he could tell by the sounds that the Viet had entered it. Then he blasted it. Part of the blast went his way and he had received a wound in his neck. Shrapnel had pierced part of his backbone and left him paralysed. Two of his men dragged him back. He arrived in great pain. Nurse Geneviève tried everything: phenergan, dolosal, morphine, sedol and gardenal. Nothing helped. Chevalier's life was slowly fading away. Twice every day, Geneviève sat by his side, feeding him a teaspoon of soup at a time.

'I'm finished, I know it,' he said to her in one of his lucid moments. 'May the Good Lord bless you.' He lived for another six days. He died in the last hour of the night, before morning came. He died hard and no one could help him. He held Geneviève's hand fast, but he did not know any longer that she was with him.

Then someone said to her: 'He is dead.'

'No,' the French nurse replied, 'he is not dead yet. He's still holding my hand fast.'

Ecoutez tous, vous qui êtes à l'abri.
La sombre histoire des Mystères de Paris . . .
Listen, all you out there in the trench
The sad story about the Mystery of Paris . . .

That jingle was the last message the men on strongpoint
Dominique received from a programme, aired over Radio
Hirondelle from Hanoi, with the intention of cheering up
the troops. That was moments before the 306th Viet Minh
Division struck.

'*Couchez-vous . . . les grenades, bon Dieu!* Get down . . .
the grenades. Fire to the flank . . .' It was night. First came
the ear-splitting howl of projectiles, and then short flames,
white and yellow, followed by the blast of hot air, and some
parachute flares to bathe the horror in their ghostly blue
light. Then followed the screams from the wounded.

'Medic! *A moi . . .* help me, I'm bleeding . . .'

'*J'ai un balle dans le ventre . . .* I'm shot through the gut.
Medic!'

'*Bon Dieu*, don't let me die, *mes copains . . .*'

'Withdraw to the summit trench . . . take the wounded
with you . . .' They pulled their downed buddies by an arm
or a leg or slid on the belly up to them.

'*Couche-toi sur moi* – Lie on top of me,' and then
crawled with their load and with their nose in the dirt
to safety.

'*Commandant Médecin*,' the call came from one of
Dominique's forward position under attack by mortar
shells and machine guns, 'I have a case of open fracture.
What am I to do?'

'I'll send out a stretcher party.'

'No, he cannot be transported.'

'Describe his wound.'

'The muscles of the thigh are destroyed, his tibia is bust
and the arteries are severed.'

'You must amputate.'

'What?' came a panicky voice. Lieutenant Corbineau was trained to shoot at enemies, not cut off the legs of his own soldiers.

'*Bien*, I'll send someone out to you.' Dr Grauwin did just that. *Médecin-Sergeant* Fleury went.

'We've put on a tourniquet,' shouted Lt Corbineau over the noise of exploding shells. The young soldier was in great pain.

'Put him in that trench,' Fleury said, turning to the stretcher-bearers. 'Let's have a look.' He took off the tourniquet. The blood spurted. '*Mon pauvre vieux* – my poor friend, nothing doing, you're already practically amputated. I am simply going to regularise the question.'

'The hell with it, go ahead, doc.' The man was operated on in the open trench, as more shells whistled overhead. Miraculously, the man survived. Sgt Fleury, who braved the bullets to perform the operation, died.

Geneviève was a woman made of truly stern stuff, resourceful and decisive, the kind of person who refused to stand by and look helpless. When Dr Grauwin ran out of blood conserves for transfusions, she found donors. When a stretcher case needed to relieve himself, she found him an empty bottle. She was mother, sister and angel all wrapped up in one.

'For me,' she said, 'the hardest thing to take was the suffering of the others.'

Her main task was to 'disconnect the wounded',[7] including the artificial slow-up of the rate of pulse of a wounded that helped him overcome his initial trauma, which followed all shot wounds. This was achieved by injecting them with a cocktail of phenergan and dolosal,

[7] The 'disconnection method' was invented by Prof. Laborie.

potent drugs that helped to reduce their heart rhythm and put the patient into a state of 'slow-motion life'. The patient fell asleep; he no longer suffered, and it prevented the dangerous shock effect that sudden injury brings. To administer the dose, she had to kneel next to the stretcher, often in the mud, injecting by the light of a torch buttoned to her blood-splattered, muddied coverall.

Lt Col. Bigeard, commander of the paras, paid her a great compliment: 'I want you to know that you are held in high esteem by my men, including the many who have never met you and whom, hopefully, you are unlikely ever to meet.' Such words warmed her so much that she didn't mind being so exhausted that she felt like falling asleep standing on her feet.

After every treatment, she had to rinse her hands in alcohol before taking care of the open stump of another amputee. She scraped the infection from the festering sores and administered sulphur drugs. One of her patients was Heinz Haas, a lean and lanky boy, who had always been good for a joke before a shell exploded near him. When they found him he was lying in a pool of blood, a pitiful sight. The explosion had torn off one arm and shrapnel punctured his legs. A comrade applied a tourniquet to his bleeding stump and carried him piggyback to an evacuation point. The medic N'Diaye put him on the operating table. Dr Grauwin checked the leg; the femoral artery had been damaged and the man was losing much blood, but no other vital organ had been touched. His other arm had also absorbed much of the explosion and was so badly mangled that the only way to save his life was to amputate both his arms and one leg, or risk gangrene. The man was tossing around in delirium.

'*Bitte, mein Kommandant, nicht abschneiden* – Please don't cut it off.'

Grauwin didn't have a choice – not with the means at

his disposal. Cpl Sioni attached the wounded with straps. Geneviève got ready with sterilised scalpels and bandages. It was the first time that she had had to stand by watching a man lose his limbs. The operation went well, but then came the great danger of infection, because Grauwin no longer had sufficient antibiotics to seal the stumps; so it was entirely in her hands to keep the young man alive by changing his bandages twice a day, a terribly painful process, both for the patient and the nurse, watching him suffer. Haas did his best to demonstrate the courage shown by all.

One day, when the shelling was not too bad, he begged Geneviève. 'Please help me get some fresh air.' She lifted him upright, he then put the stump of an arm around her shoulder, and on his single good leg, Haas hobbled along the trench to the exit of the shelter to gulp in a lungful of cordite and dust. For him, this was the closest to clean air he had come across since they had brought him into the shelter.

'Thank you,' he said to his nurse, 'this is the nicest thing that ever happened to me. And when this is all over, I shall take you dancing.'[8]

Another legionary was paralysed by shrapnel in his spine. One day he called out excitedly to Geneviève: '*Venez voir!* – Come and see!' and with it he wiggled his toe. He had to share his happiness with someone, and Geneviève was just the person for it. A shell explosion had blinded a young sergeant; Geneviève found him something to do for which he didn't need his eyes – a mouth organ. He became quite good at it and his music helped to brighten the sinister atmosphere of the underground shelter and aided in recovering the man's spirit.

Dr Grauwin had two major worries. One was that the

[8] Haas survived, and Genèvieve de Galard saw him regularly afterwards.

incessant shelling from the 105s would make his hospital collapse, the other was that Geneviève, who had turned into an irreplaceable asset, would get herself killed on one of her daily visits to off-lying aid stations. Geneviève was never overly worried about her personal safety; she felt that God was on her side. Even a simple chore such as walking in the protection of the central trench was not simple. The trench leading to the operating theatre was jammed with stretchers and Geneviève had to step over the many wounded to get to the assistance of Dr Grauwin. The wards were jammed to the limit with many of the seriously wounded; some sobbed openly, others tried to laugh and joke, others just crouched on the ground, overwhelmed by pain and grief. Only her native patients, *les montaignards*, were silent; those tough wiry men from the Central Highlands that volunteered day in and day out to go out into enemy territory to bring back information and sometimes came stumbling back from a *sortie* with the most atrocious wounds. Pain, which would have sent a European raving mad, they withstood without a moan.

A young African had been brought in with a deep chest wound. Geneviève gave him various pills, but the young soldier went wild and threw them in her face. She ordered a medical orderly to give the man a force injection to reduce his fever; this calmed him down, but then he cried out in his delirium and tried to get up. Dr Grauwin diagnosed that soon he would die. Geneviève refused to give in. She and the orderly N'Diaye took turns to look after him. The African survived.

She helped N'Diaye and his coolie squad to clean up the ward, to make the casualties as comfortable as possible. At first, the appearance of a female startled the men and occasioned some whistling. But then her soothing remarks helped to make their sores and aches less painful. She gave them sleepy-time shots, cleaned wounds, spoke a gentle word here and added a female touch there. Many were from the Foreign Legion and didn't speak any French; still, they all understood what her calm voice tried to tell them. She was always by their side and, when the time came, she closed their eyes for the eternal rest. No wonder that she sometimes felt every ounce of strength draining from her; then she just stood in their midst, immobile, with great sadness, thinking why all these brave young men had to die, and for what? For the honour of a uniform and a flag, which more often than not wasn't their own flag. No, it was this unexplainable phenomenon of camaraderie under fire which, for them, made all the difference.

One of the many problems was available space; the furious hand-to-hand slaughter in the trenches produced an unusual number of casualties; they needed more wards. That was solved with the fall of strong point *Dominique* on 30 March, which left its radio-relay post inside the base unused. Normally, Dr Grauwin would rely on Fleury to help him clear out the underground post, but the brave Sgt Fleury was dead. He had gone to the assistance of the man with the serious leg injury and then had stayed on until waves of Viet overran the trenchline. He had just time to empty two magazines from a submachine gun he had grabbed off a fallen, before he himself was struck by a burst from a machine gun.

In addition to all her other duties, Geneviève volunteered to take on Fleury's job. With some of the walking casualties, she took on the backbreaking chore of throwing out the gear and map tables from the radio post that was no longer needed. The new ward provided space for fifty stretchers. Then came a day when their own 155mm howitzers were knocked out; that freed the munitions preparation shelter for more stretcher cases. However, it was so far removed from the hospital that Dr Grauwin never got to see that

ward, and Geneviève became his only liaison with the
casualties there.

The worst cases were always those with stomach wounds.
The immediate shock invariably produced a trauma that
not many survived. Those who did, were operated upon
and put into a special ward. Three times a day Geneviève
had to remove the soiled nappies and change their bandages. She performed her task always with a gentle word.
Peritonitis was the worst killer, but the second was the
shortage of serum.

One tough para, Lt Rondeau, walked into the hospital
as if nothing had happened: 'Doctor, I've got this small
shrapnel in my belly. I don't think it is much, but you
better have a look.' Dr Grauwin examined the wound;
granted the entry hole was quite small but that was still
no indication of the possible damage inside. Suddenly the
lieutenant collapsed on the ground with terrible cramps.

'Geneviève, *deconnectez* the lieutenant. Be quick.' She
injected the lieutenant with the customary dose of phenergan-
dolosal. As soon as his pulse rate was down, Dr Grauwin
made the incision. What he discovered was serious, an
intestinal tear of almost twelve inches (30 cm). It took him
one hour to remove the piece of jagged metal. 'Geneviève,
put him on a drip.'

Of all her many patients, why did she remember him?
Because on the 1st of May, it is customary in France to give
a girl a bouquet of *muguets* (lily of the valley) and the young
lieutenant had fashioned a small bouquet from paper and
wire for her. She wasn't there when Lt Rondeau died.

At the height of the shelling, Col. Langlais came to the
hospital for a brief visit.

'*Mes respects, mon colonel*,' saluted an exhausted Dr
Grauwin.

'You annoy me with your respects. For that will be time
when we have nothing better to do. I want you to write

me a text for her citation . . .' He nodded his head in the direction of Geneviève. He then strolled around the casualties. '*Alors, comment va notre convoyeuse* – How is our flight nurse?' Langlais asked some of them.

'*Mon colonel*, she is our good-luck charm. You can't find any better.'

Langlais invited her for lunch in the HQ mess. The boys at headquarters had given up their precious chocolate rations so that the cook could make a cake for her.

'You don't know what you've done for our men; your mere presence has made this hell seem more humane,' said the colonel. Humane? There was precious little of it around. When she returned to the hospital shelter, she was met by sour faces.

'What have I done?'

'From now on you're going to have lunch with the officers; you've just dropped us,' complained *Caporal* Sioni.

Later, Dr Grauwin took her aside: 'Don't worry about their petty jealousies; they consider you one of them. *Ils vous aiment, prêts a se fair tuer pour vous* – They're willing to let themselves get killed for you.'

'*Mon commandant*,' Sgt Kabour presented himself before Dr Grauwin. 'My men can no longer stand the stench. Can't you order N'Diaye to fill in the hole?'

'*Le trou* . . . the hole!' he said, and what a horror it was. *Le trou* in question was two metres (six feet) wide and two metres deep. There were so many amputations that Dr Grauwin had ordered a hole dug for the cut bits and pieces of mangled limbs. That's why the hole became known as '*Le trou des amputés* – The hole of the amputees' – where Sioni and Bacus, N'Diaye and the other medics disposed of the members cut off from living bodies. A diabolical mixture of legs, arms, hands and feet, that gave off an unbearable stench. Dr Grauwin had told N'Diaye not to fill each layer with earth, because he needed the space for more of the same kind. Once the first limb pit was filled, they had to dig another, and then a third one . . .

Towards Geneviève the wounded behaved utterly bravely; they bore their pain and suffering in silence. '*Quand il y'a la vie il y'a l'espoir* – Where there is life there is hope, and there was always hope.'[9] Though many of the wounded must have known that there was no hope of them making it through the trial, they never showed it openly or complained about their fate. As in similar situations, more and more rumours were rife that the US Air Force was coming to their aid, that the rainy season would halt the combats, that the Geneva Conference on Indochina would bring about an honourable settlement,[10] that Americans would parachute in their elite regiments for a combined break-out operation, and that Col. Crèvecoeur was already on his way from Laos with four battalions to punch a breach through the Viet ring.

The tighter the ring became, the more such rumours were believed, since it was their only *espoir*. In fact, Col. Crèvecoeur had launched 'Operation Condor' and Lt Col. Goddart was indeed on his way to relieve Dien Bien Phu with four battalions, marching in from Laos. For three weeks, Goddart's men slashed their way through the dense mountainous jungle region, and had reached a point only two days' march from Dien Bien Phu, when they ran into a series of ambushes. Faced by the prospect of encirclement by an entire Viet division, coming down on them from the last series before the besieged fortress, Goddart had to abandon his attempt and turn back; he did

[9] Geneviève de Galard's interview with the author.
[10] In fact, Giap was kept abreast of the negotiations, and Ho Chi Minh pushed him to bring Dien Bien Phu to fall before the conference could decide on it, presenting a *fait accompli*.

however manage to collect several hundred escapees from strong point *Isabelle*, who had managed to slip through Giap's ring.

Meanwhile, the fight for Dien Bien Phu continued without let-up. The hospital, the trenches, and rapidly emptying ammunition storage spaces were overflowing with casualties. After Giap's attack on strong point *Huguette*, of the 300 paras that had held it, 106 were dead, 79 missing, and 49 wounded. The survivors, calling themselves '*les évadés d'enfer*', the escapees from hell, stumbled into the hospital, the walking wounded carrying their badly hurt comrades humpback. Commandant Vadot, who had received shrapnel in his thorax, asked Grauwin if those of the wounded who still walked could be used for frontline duty.

The doctor shook his head. 'They are not wounded. They are dead on their feet.' In fact, after having spent their last reserves, they dropped where they stood, snuffed out like candles.

Geneviève took her helmet from a peg on the wall. 'Mademoiselle, please stay with us,' pleaded one of the wounded.

'I have to go, there are others who also need my help.' There were always others, and then more again. They never stopped bringing them in. Bacus, Gindrey and Levasseur were lifting those who had died from the hospital shelter, twelve in one ward alone. They had to make room for others. How many wounded did they have to look after? 2000 ... 3000 ... ? When would this carnage stop? Padre Heinrich was kneeling next to a dying soldier who whispered: '*Seigneur, donnez-moi le danger* ... Lord, give me danger, but grant me a final hour without pain ...'

Geneviève went with a stretcher party to a particularly vulnerable position. When she got there, she found a Moroccan sapper who couldn't move. A mortar bomb had impacted in the trench behind him, smashing part of his vertebrae. 'I don't want to die . . . please, help me . . .'

How could she? His back was gone, for him it would have been better had the shell landed directly on him. She administered a hypodermic shot; his pain went away and he looked at her with grateful eyes. He lasted for almost an hour. His clouding eyes reached out for Geneviève before he died. For a long time she was haunted by the look of those eyes, searching for a glimmer of hope. That night, Geneviève heard a voice: '*Je voudrais tant m'endormir* – How I would love to fall asleep, never to wake up again . . .' Then she realised it was her own voice she heard.

On 29 April, Col. Langlais came to the hospital to ask Geneviève to go and see the commanding general – de Castries had just received his general's stars – who had something important to tell her. When she arrived at the *Poste de Commandement* (HQ) she couldn't understand why everyone had a smile on his face. She was welcomed – if this was the word to use given the circumstances – by the commander of Dien Bien Phu, General Christian de Castries. He handed her an envelope.

'I opened the envelope and I saw the *Croix de Guerre* and the *Légion d'Honneur*.'

'*Au nom du President de la Republique . . . pour services de guerre exceptionnels*,' the general said. And with it, the general pinned the crimson ribbon with the medal on her dirty, muddy coverall and gave her the obligatory kiss on both cheeks. She couldn't get over her surprise, especially as there had been only one recent air-drop, and the parachute with the medals, intended for the brave soldiers, had ended up in enemy territory. She finally found out that her *Croix de Guerre* was that of Col. Langlais and that Capt. Bailly had willingly given up his own *Légion d'Honneur* medal to decorate a heroine. When she returned to the hospital, she showed a certain embarrassment. She shouldn't have worried; *l'équipe* had been informed. In fact, the whole camp had known about her honour before she found out. The '*garçon d'équipe*' had made a cake, salt biscuits stuck together with melted chocolate, decorated with a candle wrapped with a red ribbon. And provided a *breuvage* of unknown source, medicinal champagne liberated from God-knows-where. For Geneviève it was the most memorable celebration of her life.

'No one has ever deserved the *palme dorée* more than you.'[11] The next evening, 30 April, was the *Day of Camerone*.[12] Lt Col. Bigeard and the parachutists of the Legion, always in a macho class of their own, honoured Geneviève de Galard by making her '*Première Classe de la Légion*', the first woman ever to achieve such distinction.

It was 5 May, after darkness. The military intelligence had informed HQ that something special was up; their *montaignard* scouts had reported major enemy troop movements in the past twenty-four hours. Down in the shelter, a dozen of the ambulatory wounded got up and crowded around the surgeon: '*Si nos copains doivent y rester, nous voulons être avec eux* – If our buddies will fight it out to the very end, then our place must be with them,' they said, rising from their cots and somehow finding the strength to hobble from the wards and rejoin their units for the final stand. The one-eyed, one-armed, one-legged joined their *copains* on strong point *Eliane 2*. They picked up weapons and stripped the dead of their helmets. This was not a gesture of defiance, but the emotion of a last-stand camaraderie, that said: 'If we go, then let's all go together'. *Eliane* was the final barrier between the Viet and the main camp. From the original three-company unit there were

[11] *Palme dorée*, or gilded palm, is the French *Croix de Guerre*.
[12] Camerone is the 'holy day' of the French Foreign Legion.

only sixty left; of those, most were so seriously wounded that they hunkered down with their bodies supported by sandbags, just high enough to shoot over the top of the trench. Not one of them returned, true to the principle of the uniting brotherhood of combat.

The end of Dien Bien Phu began at 16.00 hrs on 6 May. The signal for the all-out attack came with a terrifying howl of rockets launched from batteries of Stalin-organs. The initial salvo struck the perimeter and the world of Dien Bien Phu blew apart in a white-hot flame. An exploding volcano engulfed the trenches; the base was hidden behind a curtain of fire. Within minutes, the camp was turned into a sea of flames. Fuel drums burst and burning diesel oil penetrated into underground shelters like lava. The explosion of ammunition dumps shook the ground in a continuous earthquake. For the men of Lt Marcel Edme's *2me Companie des Parachutistes Coloniaux* the strike came so suddenly they didn't even have time to seek protection. The Viet Minh had dug a tunnel beneath their hill and filled it with two tons of TNT.

At 16.03 hrs, the summit of strong point *Eliane 2* came apart in flame and death. Clumps of earth and human debris flew through the air. It lasted only seconds but, when it was over, what was left of Lt Edme's company was a large, black crater. The men on nearby *Eliane 4* had looked on in horror at the deflagration. *Capitaine* Pouget called his section commander, *Commandant* Vadot.

'It's most urgent. I cannot hold my position without reinforcements.'

'We don't have any to send to you.'

'Then let me withdraw to *Eliane 3*.'

'Negative. You hold. After all, you are a para and you hold out. That's an order.'

'Understood. If you have nothing more to add, then for us it's over.'

And a clipped voice replied over the radio: 'For us too . . .'

The combat increased in violence. Giap's mountain artillery, firing now point-blank, shattered the last trenches. Shrapnel and showers of stones whizzed around the men. This time they were done for!

For those inside the perimeter, the stifling smoke of bursting rockets and burning fuel oil blacked out the sky. The smoke penetrated into the hospital wards, adding choking and dry coughing to the suffering.

Around 23.00 hrs, on 6 May, Geneviève, put on her helmet, pulled her head down between her shoulders, and ran along the covered trench to HQ to find out from Col. Langlais what was going on, so that she could inform her wounded. The officer looked at her with a sad smile.

'*Geneviève, vous êtes notre porte-bonheur* – You are our good-luck charm. As long as you here, the chance will smile on us.' But he knew that even her presence couldn't alter the outcome. For thirty-six hours, as combat raged on a rapidly shrinking perimeter, she sat up with her wounded, suffering with them the final agony, these moments of great sadness, the moving *adieus* by unit commanders, coming into the ward to bid farewell to their wounded soldiers.

'*Les Viets sont a quelque metres* – The Viet are only a few metres off.'

'Geneviève, if I don't make it, embrace my family . . .' Many left letters with her, because they didn't plan to be taken captive. One had a roll of film. Geneviève slid the film into a plaster cast around his broken arm.[13] With Lt Col. Bigeard in the lead, a '*perce de sangue*' (a 'bloody break-out') was planned and anyone who could still walk and fire a gun was to accompany him. They would blast their way through into Laos. The entire medical staff

---

[13] These were the only pictures of the final combat that survived.

volunteered to remain behind with their casualties. General Christian de Castries made it clear that he wouldn't leave; he hoped that his presence would vouch for the safeguard of the wounded. In a last-minute change of mind, de Castries called off the planned Bigeard break-out, knowing it would lead the men only to their death.

It was 7 May 1954, 09.45 hrs. The Viet were now masters over every strong point on the opposite shore of the Nam Youm River. Only *Eliane 4* held out, hoping for relief or a sudden change in weather. Neither happened. For a moment, time seemed to falter . . . everything, their futures and perhaps the future of their nation's hold on Indochina, depended on what took place in the next half hour. The grim-faced paras on strong point *Eliane 4* stared into the dense curtain of dust whirled into the air by the preparatory artillery barrage on the slope fronting them, when, out of the dust, appeared the first waves of howling *bo-dois*

'*Tiên lên! Tiên lên!* – Attack! Attack!' Many of the attackers were green recruits, without an idea what hand-to-hand combat really meant; they had been brought forward the night before and were sent into the slaughter without preparation. From a network of trenches, spreading like an immense spider web around the French positions emerged a cloud of human ants with conical hats.

Giap had chosen strong point *Eliane 4* as target for a concentrated charge. Its defenders had never seen that many Viet from so close. A rolling barrage of 105mm artillery shells and 122mm mortar bombs flattened Eliane's outer defences. Some fell short, right into the ranks of the tightly bunched-up *bo-dois*, adding greatly to the confusion. Behind the curtain of fire, the defenders felt rather than saw the waves of Viet; the mangled barbed wire entanglements presented no obstacle; the enemy came on like a steamroller, lines of tracers tore into them. Regardless of the staggering losses, they 'flowed' across the defences like a spring tide, shooting, stabbing, maiming, killing and being killed. It was the negation of any type of war Occidentals knew how to fight; against this human ant assault, a soldier's instruction manual became obsolete.

A hundred, a thousand *bo-dois* ran forward, into explosions and death all around them, hell-bent for the trenches to kill the French. The defenders got caught up in the madness of the instant. Giving off infernal yells, many jumped over the trench, shooting from the hip while storming forward. Only those who have lived through an Asiatic war can have an idea of its brutal horror. While the first Viet wave attacked with bayonet, a second wave, only twenty metres (22 yards) behind, poured bullets into strong posts and often into the backs of the men in front of them. For a few more moments, isolated nests of resistance managed to hold off the first, then the second wave. But there were simply too many of them for the worn-out defenders.

Cries for help vied with the stuttering of machine guns. The last defence of strong point *Eliane 4* had to give way; the men retreated, and retreated, until there was nowhere else to retreat to. In the confined space of the final trench, a group of paras fought with the strength of desperation. A desperate call for God to stand by their side went out. God wouldn't listen. One by one they fell. Despite a sucking chest wound, Lt Corbineau stood tall and tossed his last grenade into the on-rushing horde. Then the Apocalypse was upon the last of the French paras.

On 7 May, shortly before 17.00 hrs, General Christian de Castries radioed his superior, General Cogny in Hanoi: '*Mon géneral, situation grave, combats confus partout. Je sens que la fin approche. Nous nous batterons jusqu'au bout* – General, situation serious, combats everywhere confused. I feel the end is upon us. We shall fight to the very end . . .'

Cogny: '*Bien compris, bien compris. Vous lutterez jusqu'au bout. Pas de question de hisser le drapeau blanc* – Understood. You fight to the end. Out of the question to raise a white flag.'

'*Non, nous détruisons les canons, le matériel et les postes de radio-telephone a 17.30* – No, we will destroy the cannons, all material and radio telephones at 17.30 hrs.'

After a momentary silence, General Cogny said: '*Merci!*'

The commandant of Dien Bien Phu had the final word: '*Au revoir, mon géneral. Vive la France!*'

At 16.45 hrs, Lt Col. Bigeard, 'Bruno', received a call from an outlying post that somehow had been by-passed by the massive assault on the other side of the river. Sub-Lt Allaire of 6 Paras wanted to know if he should try a breakout to rejoin the battalion at base. He couched his message in words only a legionnaire such as Bigeard could decipher: 'Shall we perform a Camerone[14] and get our feet wet?'

'Bruno to Allaire. No attempt authorised. A ceasefire about to come into effect.'

'Received, *mon colonel*,' came the reply from a shocked Allaire, who simply refused to believe that French paras would surrender. '*Mon colonel*, I request a written order.' It was this order that became the only official document of surrender.

'*Pour Allaire. Cessez-feu a 17 h 30. Ne tirez plus. Pas de drapeau blanc. A toute à l'heure. Bruno* – For Allaire. Ceasefire at 17.30 pm. No further shooting. No white flag. See you. Bruno.'

Beneath this note, an honour-bound but thoroughly distraught lieutenant-colonel of *la Légion* expressed his feelings in four simple words: '*Pauvre 6. Pauvre paras!* – Poor 6th. Poor parachutists!'

---

[14] Camerone in Mexico where, in April 1863, the Legion made a famous last stand.

War had been their universe, the Legion their fatherland and the regiment their family. For Sub-Lieutenant Allaire, and all the others who had survived fifty-seven days of hell, their world stood still. France had sacrificed 12,000 of its best soldiers to a hopeless cause, and then abandoned them to their fate. At 17.30 hrs, the survivors destroyed their weapons. It was a moment of vanishing *gloire* for the Foreign Legion and those who had held it dear. The medical staff shared their feeling. They were surprised when, at 17.00 hrs, a relative calm fell over the base, interrupted by occasional bangs that didn't sound at all like incoming artillery shells. The thuds were somehow heavier, thumpier. Down in their shelter they didn't know that the order had gone out to destroy all weapons and ammunition depots, and that around the camp demolition work was well under way.

The *Médecin-Commandant* Grauwin called his staff into the operating theatre. '*C'est fini* – It's over.' His announcement was met by stares of incredulity.

A young parachutist, fresh from an operation, raised a bandaged arm from his stretcher: 'But, *mon commandant*, there are still many *gars* (men) among us who can put up a fight.'

Grauwin shrugged his shoulders. 'We have been told to prepare for the arrival of the Viet. I want one *infirmier* (medic) in each of the wards. Geneviève, you stay with me.' He added under his breath, 'And don't you move an inch from my side.'

They used bandages to fashion white armbands and then added red crosses with Mercurochrome. They had no idea if the Viet soldiers would recognise the Geneva Convention, or even know about it, but it was worth the try. By 17.25 hrs, an ominous silence descended over the base, when they suddenly made out a jumble of voices, Vietnamese voices, coming down through the aeration shaft. Footsteps trampled across the shelter's roof, like ghosts walking over their grave.

'They're outside. I'll have a look,' Grauwin said. From the shelter's entrance he saw how General de Castries was led at gunpoint past the hospital compound. His captors wore green uniforms and bamboo helmets stuck with leaves.

Geneviève heard a voice behind her: '*Di ve!* – Get out!'

She turned and saw a figure in a green uniform, trousers rolled up to his knees, and feet covered in mud. In his hand was a submachine gun pointed at her midriff. He motioned with his gun towards the exit. '*Di di! Maulen* – Get going!' At gunpoint Dr Grauwin and Geneviève were pushed from the dug-out. In the slanting rays of an evening sun she discovered the new Dien Bien Phu. As far as the eye could see, men in green uniform rushed about, an army of ants, with ever more streaming down from the hills and stepping out of the conquered French trenches. The hillside of nearby strong point *Eliane 4* was strewn with hundreds of corpses, defenders and attackers, united in death. A Viet officer stopped them.

'*Vous êtes le commandant Grauwin* – Are you Cdt Grauwin?' he barked.

'I am.'

'By order of the High Command of the Army of Liberation of Viet Nam, you must return to your hospital to look after your wounded.' That was the only positive news of the day. They would be allowed to take care of the men who had been under their care. From the hole into the underground shelter spilled a nauseous smell of drugs and death, a smell they had never noticed before, or had chosen to ignore, during their fifty-seven days down in the hole.

Now the war was over. That night, exhausted as she was, sleep would not come for Geneviève. Her body shook with emotion, her thoughts centred on her wounded, and what the next day might bring. In the middle of the night, a Viet came to escort her to de Castries' former *Poste de Commandement*, the same place where she had been honoured – how long ago? She couldn't even recall it, all seemed so vague. The place had been turned into the command centre of the Viet. She met two senior people in the map room; one was the head of the military, the other a political Viet Minh commissar.

'*Nous avons faire vous venir* – We have asked you to come because we've heard that you have well taken care of the wounded, and we are utmost concerned with their continued well-being.' And then they asked her to collaborate with them, a request which she refused. The ploy was all too obvious; they would use her for propaganda.

'If you wish to demonstrate your humanity, then let the wounded go, they can no longer do you harm.'

From a flight nurse she had become a field nurse and now a prison nurse. Back down in the shelter, the soldier who had been blinded by a grenade and didn't know what was going on around him, complained bitterly: 'Why doesn't anybody look after us?' Geneviève explained to him the situation. The worst cases were allowed to remain in the shelter and, despite her refusal to cooperate with the demands of the victors, Geneviève was given a certain leeway to look after her casualties. But she had no further medication to administer; the Viet had stripped the shelves of all their medical supplies and drugs, as they had to look after thousands of their own wounded and the fighting Viet Minh were notoriously short of drugs. Once again Geneviève proved her mettle; when she noticed how the Viet began to raffle antibiotics, bandages and other vital supplies, she hid some of the big bandages and sulphur drugs, used on the freshly amputated and those with stomach wounds, under her stretcher bed. After three days, the Viet commander ordered a tarpaulin strung up on poles and, for the first time in sixty days, the serious casualties were carried from the underground shelter to breathe fresh air.

Figures with haggard, stubble-covered faces emerged from the opening of the tunnel, blinking in the sudden brightness; with their skeleton arms they were trying to shield hollow eyes. The reason for this astounding, humane gesture all too soon became apparent with the arrival of a Viet film crew to take pictures. Everything had been perfectly set up by the political commissar, including the visit of French casualties by a benignly smiling Viet Minh military commander who had given permission for Dr Grauwin and his medical helpers, dressed in clean white smocks, to rejoin their wounded.

On 14 May, after a number of PoWs was put to work to patch up the 1000-metre (1111-yard) airstrip, a single-engine Beaver aircraft landed at Dien Bien Phu, carrying aboard a medical officer who informed Dr Grauwin that the evacuation of the worst cases had been negotiated, and that from now on daily flights of small aircraft would rotate for pick-up. Professor Huard, the dean of Hanoi's Medical University, had arranged the humanitarian act. Among his former pupils he counted many Viet commanders that had remained admirers of this outstanding man. This gave him the confidence of the Viet Minh hierarchy. All in all, the airlifts managed to liberate 858 French casualties, which – considering that only 3000 out of a total of 12,000 survived – was one-third of all those who came through the battle. For all others began their long march into captivity.

On 24 May, a Beaver with Professor Huard aboard landed in Dien Bien Phu to conduct a personal inspection of the camp – and to collect Nurse Geneviève! When he presented her with the good news, she refused to leave; she insisted on remaining behind, looking after her wounded, and furthermore, it was out of the question that she would take the place of a wounded on the plane. It was her superior, the *Médecin-Commandant* Grauwin, who decided the issue. 'Get on that flight, and that's an order! You've done more than your duty.' He grabbed her by her shoulders, pulled her close and kissed her on both cheeks. When he let go of her he had tears in his eyes.

'Geneviève, none of us will ever forget you.' For the first time since she had arrived at Dien Bien Phu, forty days before, Geneviève de Galard cried freely. Throughout the ordeal she had clung to her faith, and nothing could shake it. No shells and no horror. The moment she stepped off the aircraft in Hanoi, this slip of a girl in a baggy uniform much too large for her, an American reporter cried out:

'Here comes the Angel of Dien Bien Phu!'

That name stuck.

Geneviève de Galard's motivation was a quiet resolution and calm determination to help those in dire need, the kind of courage seldom observed by fighting men. It exists in the mind and the heart. As a devout Christian and trained nurse, the suffering that she had to observe, day after day, was trying, but with her strong character, she overcame all hardship placed upon her. She was indeed invaluable, healing and soothing, not asking for recompense, and not expecting any. Hers was a quiet heroism.

Colonel Pal Maleter, A whiff of freedom

'This we swear, this we swear—
Slaves we no more be!'
Sandor Petöfi, during the revolution of 1848

'We will bury you.'
Nikita Khrushchev, 26 November 1956

The full horror of their situation finally dawned on them. A crowd poured into the square, carrying a bloodied corpse above their heads. The Hungarian crisis of 1956 was one of the main events in the East-West conflict following the Second World War. It turned into a test case of the West's willingness to come to the assistance of a nation trying to free itself from a Communist yoke. The students had started it and the workers had joined in. Soon near on half a million Hungarians were taking to the streets of the nation's capital, Budapest. They were of all ages, and came from every social strata. They chanted the Hungarian anthem and danced around a giant bonfire, its flames fed by party membership booklets. The workers from the 'Red Czepel' steel mills came marching to Stalin Square equipped with their acetylene torches. They hurled themselves in fury on the monument.

Blue flames bit into the bronze ankles of the 10-metre high (11-foot) statue of the defunct Soviet dictator with his arm pointing towards a bright socialist future that had never been theirs. A young man shimmied up the statue, the end of a rope clutched between his teeth. He looped it around the red dictator's neck, while others wound the other end around the bumper of a truck. A cheer, a pull, and Stalin tumbled.[1] The first act of the Hungarian Revolution was utterly symbolic: by knocking down the overpowering figure of Stalin, they said that they would no longer be slaves of the Soviets and their local stooges.

It was 20.30 hrs. A portion of the huge crowd had surged into the square in front of Radio Budapest, located in a red-brick building. Leading the demonstrators was a group of youngsters, no more than fifteen or sixteen years of age. One of the secret police guards in front of the building fired a salvo into the air to halt their progression. Shaken by the noise of the gun, a young agent of the feared secret police, himself not much older than the boys below him in the square, and who had been strategically placed on the roof overlooking the square, pulled the pin on a stun grenade and let it drop on to the crowd. A sharp explosion, a second of stunned silence, followed by the piercing scream of a girl. In front of her, held upright by the push from behind, stood a corpse without a head. The grenade had exploded in his face. This teenager was the first casualty of many thousands in the bloody battles that were to last thirteen days. The Hungarian Revolution had begun. Its shock waves reverberated around the world.

* * *

[1] Like the pieces of concrete chipped from the Berlin Wall, the most treasured possession of a Hungarian is a sliver of bronze cut from Stalin's statue. Many carry it on a neck chain.

In Hungarian, revolution is known as *forradolom*, which stands for 'the boiling over of the masses'. Like volcanoes, all victorious revolutions of the past have had an active period during which the destruction of the old order went on. The initial phase was always the spontaneous eruption of a large part of the population, putting power into the hands of a revolutionary multitude. It may not have a leader in its initial outbreak, but soon people up in arms, unless guided, lose their will and their initiative without one. That's when a man must step to the fore, to give direction to the popular stream. In these moments, a revolution turns speedily into a boiling over of the masses. And in Hungary, boil over they did, in late October 1956.

Just as years before the Nazis had pushed aside philosophers and humanitarians to have a single-minded dictator ruin Europe, the liberation from the Nazi yoke was exchanged for a Communist despot, transforming Hungary with a similar single-minded ruthlessness. For years, the 'Stalin of Hungary', Matyas Rakosi, had taken a lesson from his Soviet namesake and eliminated anyone within his own party apparatus who posed a danger to his brutal rule. His power base was the secret state police, certainly the most hated force in the country. This organ of terror, the *Allamvedelmi Hivatal* (AVN, or Authority for the Defence of the State)[2] (popularly still called by its former name, AVO), had been instituted, and modelled on Russia's KGB, by the Hungarian Communists in 1946. AVN candidates trained for months in the manipulation of the political, economic and social forces that could bear on the security of the party structure. The AVN force was made up of heavily armed squads, recognisable by their blue shoulder

---

[2] People still referred to it by its former name AVO (for *Allamvedelmi Oztaly*), ironically named the Section for the Defence of the State.

tabs; its agents planned their operations shrewdly and then cold-bloodedly executed them without regard to ethical considerations. No one was safe from arbitrary arrest, neither the intellectual community, always a favourite target in a totalitarian society, nor the working class that the party had promised to defend. It was quite obvious that these terror squads would turn into the mob's instant target to exact frightful revenge in case of a popular uprising.

At the time of the outbreak of trouble, Sandor Kopaci was prefect of police of Budapest:

Our political regime functioned on fear. Everyone was afraid, and at every level. The minister was afraid of the Central Committee, the Central Committee was afraid of the Politburo in Moscow. Intrigue was everywhere, and throats were cut in the grab for power. We lived a permanent conflict of interests. In other words, everyone was afraid of everyone else. Many times we were closeted in meetings, trying to come up with a solution because, if not, we knew that the street would find it for us, and that would be a terrible shock to us all.

The Hungarian terror purges began in 1949 with the trial of Lazlo Rajk, then in line for the leadership of the Communist Party; in the power struggle, Stalin's puppet Rakosi accused him of leading a (non-existent) anti-Socialist conspiracy. Together with 3000 party members, loyal only to him, Rajk was executed. The Rajk purge turned Rakosi into Hungary's dictator. Rakosi's taste for power, and the trappings of power, had eroded all commitment to earlier Socialist ideals. Using his feared secret police with utter brutality and ruthlessness, for years Rakosi kept a tight lid on the hidden unrest. In the spring of 1956, Rakosi unwisely took on the writers and poets of the Petöfi

Club,[3] who used their *Irodalmi Ujsag* (Literary Gazette) subtly to suggest a change in government policy. They dared to propose replacing dictator Rakosi with Imre Nagy, a Communist, but also an anti-Stalinist and truly patriotic Hungarian. The day before the Poznan riots, in an earthquake which not only made Poland tremble, but spread its waves into every one of the Eastern Bloc countries, the Petöfi Club held a demonstration in favour of Nagy. It was only the direct interference of the Soviet ambassador Andropov (later Russia's premier), seeing the downside of starting an open fight with Hungary's intelligentsia, that stopped Rakosi's henchmen from arresting Nagy and four hundred of his followers. But the signal was set.

Moscow recognised the problem that might arise in Hungary, should they follow the Polish example. Hungary's nationalistic trends were not transitory and there was a strong, if latent, nationalist sentiment in the country, exacerbated by the presence of Soviet troops on its territory. Should the Hungarians, as members of the Warsaw Pact, become 'bloody minded', an awkward situation would be created for the Soviet Union. With their minds focused on checkmating the upheaval in Poland, Moscow had had its fill of Rakosi, their faithful lieutenant. For years, the all-powerful Communist king of Hungary had been propped up by a conniving Moscow Politburo until his stock began to fall; at this point, as sudden as it was suspect to Hungarians, the Communist Party of Hungary (and Moscow) reversed itself. But then the Russian party bosses committed a serious error; rather than replace Rakosi with the immensely popular Imre Nagy, in July 1956 they picked as new head of the Hungarian party Rakosi's second-in-command, the sinister

[3] Named for the 19th-century Hungarian poet and freedom fighter Sandor Petöfi.

Ernö Gerö, who had learned all the dirty tricks from his master.

For the Hungarian leadership, the situation was growing increasingly worrisome. Witness to it was Enver Hoxha, the Communist dictator of Albania, a life-long Stalinist who hated Khrushchev for having betrayed his idol Stalin, who visited Budapest in June 1956. Dined by party boss Gerö under the painting of Attila the Hun in the Parliament Building, the Hungarian told his Albanian comrade: 'Our army is weak, we have no cadres. The officers are the old ones from the Horthy army.'

'Without a strong army, Socialism cannot be defended,' Hoxha replied. 'You should get rid of the Horthy men. You must recognise that the internal reaction, supported by the clergy [Cardinal Mindszenty], the powerful kulak stratum and the disguised Horthy Fascists, set about undermining your leadership. Your country has become a field for intrigues by Khrushchev, who wants to put your country under his control, and Tito, who wants to destroy the Socialist camp.'

Gerö shrugged it off. 'There are groups in the party, writers, etc., who are not on the rails and want to avail themselves the XX Party Congress.'[4]

Hoxha's annoyance showed clearly on his face. 'How can you sit idle in the face of this counter-revolution which is rising? Why are you not taking measures?' To the hardliner, steeped in political intrigue and willing to commit murder, it was as if his Hungarian comrades had lost all of their sense of direction. 'You must close the Petöfi Club immediately, arrest the main troublemakers, and bring the armed working class out in the boulevards. If you can't jail [Cardinal] Mindszenty, what about Imre

---

[4] Khrushchev's famous de-Stalinisation process of the XX Party Congress.

Nagy, can't you arrest him? Have some of the leaders of these counter-revolutionaries shot to teach them what the dictatorship of the proletariat is?'[5]

'We cannot act as you suggest, Comrade Enver, because we do not consider the situation so alarming. We have the situation in hand . . .'

They didn't, and it soon came to the test. Two events played together. The first happened on 6 October, during the annual commemoration of the 1848 to 1849 Hungarian Uprising against their Hapsburg overlords. It provided the occasion for a big demonstration, which quickly turned against the Gerö government. Thousands of flag-waving workers and students assembled on Kossuth Square in front of the Hungarian Parliament, shouting: 'Nagy! Nagy! Nagy!'

Who was this man the great crowd clamoured for? Imre Nagy was by far the most popular personality of his time in Hungary. He envinced an unusual, modest charm and the self-confidence of men who naturally attract a following and as naturally command respect; a rotund little man, fifty-seven years old, sporting a bushy moustache and a pair of steel-rimmed pince-nez, whose peasant's accent belied the intellectual, he was someone who liked the arts, the theatre, and taking tea at the Gerbaud, the *café chic* with its Hapsburgian *gemütliche* past and its delicious *strudel*. Nagy could never be called a reactionary – he was a dedicated Communist of the old school, yet openly hostile to the idea of Hungary being subjected to a permanent Russian occupation. His reasoning was simple. Hungary was truly Socialist and, as such, dedicated to remain within the Socialist bloc. Their direct neighbour Austria was not. Yet, only the year before (1955), the

[5] From a personal account by Enver Hoxha in his *The Khrushchevites*, Tirana, 1984.

Austrians had managed to rid themselves of the Russians. So why not have the same thing take place a few kilometres down the blue Danube? Nagy planted this idea during his days in the government, because Imre Nagy had been in and out of politics all his life. In October 1956, he was definitely out.

The second event that shook the Communist empire came on 20 October, with the announcement that Wladyslaw Gomulka – the Polish mirror image of Imre Nagy – was voted in by the Polish Central Committee as its new chairman. His first act was to declare 'Poland's independent road to Socialism', a courageous statement, which set the Hungarians on their road to freedom, a freedom they coveted, and were increasingly unlikely to enjoy any time soon. The Rakosi years had been too despotic for this freedom to come quickly. Over the years, it had begun to dawn on the masses that 'individual freedom' depended not on the skill of a few politicians but on the willingness of millions who saw their future in a different way from their past. Therefore, if Hungarians wanted their freedom, they had to come by it in their own way.

Janos Kavoc was a 22-year-old student leader in Budapest's Technical University. Endowed with sturdy independence of character, and an awareness of honour and dignity, he possessed the twin attributes that were fundamental to the Magyar (Hungarian) nation. The universe of the average Hungarian was down the long path of despair, disillusion, and the legacy of fear. Young Kovac dreamed of an alternative reality, a world where no terror existed, a world without official lies. All it took was the courage to speak out, and make the rest realise that they mustn't continue to tolerate oppression; a challenge that faced every Hungarian and brought forth a new vision.

'Aren't you a bit of an idealist?' asked Sandor Bekesi, his physics professor.

'Of course. I'm also a Socialist. But that doesn't mean that I like our present situation. They will not give it to us, so if we look for a brighter future, we must fight for it.'

The professor proved a wise prophet: 'Russian rule in Hungary will never be ended merely by the struggle of the Hungarian people alone. However, world conditions are bound to change so fundamentally that nothing will be able to prevent Communism's total disappearance.' For that to happen, it would take another thirty-three years.

Some violent events are morally and intellectually justifiable. For instance, if a university devotes its teaching to propagate the idea of oppressing its own population, this is far more obscene than the students of that university demonstrating against their teachers, however violent. In the lands of Eastern Socialism, universities had become mere offshoots of the Communist Party, fountainhead of doctrines and decisions. Not like in democratic countries, where students were always vigilant and active at every level of the protest chain, from ideologists to planners, and cadres to foot soldiers to cheerleaders. In Hungarian universities, the era of quiet acceptance was about to change. With the beginning of the new university term, Budapest's student movement became more dynamic and outspoken, demanding openly a truly independent, democratic-Socialist Hungary, based on the solid foundation of a newly negotiated Hungarian–Soviet pact – but on an egalitarian basis. The youngsters approached their goal with emotionally inspired faith that the righteousness of their cause must eventually lead on to victory. They spurned violence, and the unethical use of terror was considered from the outset as being unworthy of their crusade.

With this uppermost in their minds, they called for an assembly of the student body in the Building Industry Technical University for 22 October. It turned into a heated debate, which lasted all day and ended by drawing up a resolution of sixteen points. One of their demands was uniquely symbolic: the removal of the oversized bronze Stalin statue in the centre of Budapest. While this meeting was in progress, other students were mimeographing the 'sixteen points', before pasting them on tree-lined boulevards throughout the city. They called for a demonstration that very afternoon, in order to add popular pressure to their arranged presentation to party boss Ernö Gerö.

October 23 1956 dawned with clouds hanging heavily over the Danube city. Radio Budapest forecast rain for the afternoon. That suited the Communist officials, gathered for an emergency meeting of the party's central committee, as it accorded with Talleyrand's immortal dictum that 'rain is counter-revolutionary'. The Communist leadership hoped that the weather would put the damper on a massive response to this afternoon's marching call. Because, just like everyone else that morning, they realised that a student revolt was brewing. To be prepared 'in case of wider disturbances', Gerö ordered armed AVN units to guard public buildings and to occupy rooftops around the parliament and radio station. Since the student body numbered in the thousands and a majority could be expected to participate in the protest march, this posed a severe problem to the security forces; the Budapest AVN lacked readily available manpower. Therefore, its commissars pulled in young trainees, as yet unused to crowd control. They then committed the unpardonable error of supplying these raw recruits with real bullets. Scared, trigger-happy recruits and live ammunition make for a lethal combination. It was to become the spark that set off the explosion.

The weather did nothing to inhibit the fervour of the students. Shortly after lunch, first groups began moving from the Technical University towards the centre of town. The crowd swelled by the minute and, like the wide Danube, which they crossed by the ancient Chain Bridge, it swept everyone with them, pensioners, civil servants, housewives, high-school kids cutting their classes, and even two football teams. No one was left untouched by the event. For once, the street belonged truly to the masses. They sang, they waved flags, and shouted slogans. Those who didn't march, because they were too old or had to look after their babies, were hanging out of windows, waving handkerchiefs. From the Grand Boulevard spilled another river of flag-waving humanity; this was support from a most unlikely quarter, and came as a complete shock to the authorities: the steel workers from the red suburbs, yelling: 'Russkies go home!'

At Rakosi Street, the crowd split. The main body headed for Parliament Square, while others turned off to make for the radio building, where they found their access sealed off by heavily armed AVN units, carrying batons and automatic rifles. The demonstrators started a shouting match with the secret police, trying to win them over to their cause: 'It is true that Stalin has moved mountains, but he had millions of enslaved Hungarians do it for him' and 'Here in Hungary we do not have capitalists and landlords, we call them party secretaries and commissars'.

The authorities were getting flustered; never before in the history of the People's Republic of Hungary had there been anything approaching this spontaneous manifestation. By the time the majority of that immense throng, by now well over 300,000, assembled before the Parliament, it was getting dark. In front of this neo-gothic Hapsburgian building on the Danube embankment, the mass jostled on the beautifully gardened Place Kossuth. They ignored the signs: 'Don't walk on the lawn'. They lit torches from rolled-up pages of the latest edition of the party's *Free People* newspaper, with its editorial about the latest achievement by the government, citing the progress in the living conditions of the same workers that were now standing down in the square, lighting the torch of rebellion. A voice called out the name of a man, and was answered by a dozen, a thousand, a hundred thousand: 'Nagy! Nagy! Nagy!'

Josef Fedor, a student representative from the medical faculty, was standing in front of the Parliament building under the arcades: 'It was a fantastic feeling just to be there, among that immense crowd, a feeling shared by everyone present that day, with everyone shouting: "Nagy!" His name was pure magic, it was as if it cleared the horizon and a new sun was beginning to rise over our future.'

It wasn't the sun that rose, but the opening to a Greek drama. The man for whom the crowd clamoured, Imre Nagy, arrived around 20.00 hrs; because of the masses blocking the front gate, he had to make his entry through a back door. Once it became known that he was inside the building, three hundred thousand voices clamoured for him to step on to the ceremonial balcony.

'Why me?' he asked those assembled around him in the room. 'I have no power, and I am no longer a member of the party.' In fact, he had been publicly chastised and expelled from the Communist Party of Hungary. 'Who gives me the right to address the people?' Imre Nagy could easily claim this right for himself, since he and no one else was the people's choice.

When the yelling of 'Nagy! Nagy! Nagy!' continued and pressure began building up, inside and outside, Nagy finally stepped out on the balcony. For minutes, a tremendous roar, accompanied by the hysterical waving of thousands of flags greeted his presence.

When the crowd calmed down, he said haltingly: 'Comrades!' Catcalls and whistles answered him. Nagy recognised his mistake, held up his hands and pronounced with his gravelly voice the magic words: 'Citizens! Hungarians!' That's when the crowd went wild. Many had tears of joy in their eyes – redemption had finally come!

At the same moment, while Nagy was addressing the crowd, a deputation of students, which included 22-year-old Janos Kovac, was standing in Party Secretary Gerö's office, pressing him for immediate reforms. He promised that he would consider their demands, but that this would take some time. And time was what he didn't have. Ever more students were gathering on the Technical University compound; rumours and rousing speeches inflamed them. It was like letting the Genie out of the bottle; shouting slogans, they spilled from the university grounds and headed for the blocked-off radio building to join their fellow protesters and get their message read on the air. When they reached the initial crowd, who had been there since mid-afternoon and were still restrained by an AVN barricade, the new arrivals had no idea what was going on in front and kept shoving forward. By 22.30 hrs the push became so great that the metal barrier gave way and the crowd spilled over it and raced towards the radio building.

For the hard-pressed AVN police, this flouting of their authority was as infuriating as it was unexpected. Nobody could afterwards tell how it happened. Shots rang out, a grenade exploded. Then another shot and a student leader, waving a flag, fell over dead. With a cry of pain and fury the crowd surged forward, pushing aside the cordon of AVN and making for the entrance door of the radio building. One of the recruited AVN gunners, placed on a rooftop opposite the building, panicked, and without awaiting an order from his officer, opened fire with his machine gun. Other agents heard the shooting. In the belief that the order to open fire had been given, they began hosing down the crowd with their automatic rifles and a thousand students found themselves at the wrong end of gun barrels.

Bullets whipped into the dense crowd, shredding bodies and tearing youngsters apart. A dozen staggered and fell, then a dozen more spun about and dropped out of sight. The crowd made for doorways; some were struck only steps away from sanctuary. From the roofs all around came the vicious clatter of machine guns. At this moment, several tarpaulin-covered trucks loaded with automatic rifles and bullets appeared down the street: it has remained the single greatest mystery of the Hungarian Uprising where these trucks hailed from, or who had dispatched the weapons into the eager hands of an over-excited crowd. All hell broke loose. Gunfire rattled. Tracers scored the air. The crowd fired by instinct. The AVN replied by instinct. The whole thing turned into a ghastly nightmare. Bullets dealt death. The sharp staccato of machine guns could be heard clearly in front of the Parliament; it could be heard all over Budapest and, from there, the sound was carried by telephone wire across Hungary, into Austria, and from there, to the world. In a hail of bullets any chance for a peaceful settlement died. Radio and television networks interrupted their programmes, bells on teletype machines rang in newsrooms around the globe: 'RUSH RUSH RUSH 23.10/2200GMT REVOLT HAS BROKEN OUT IN HUNGARY. ASSOCIATE PRESS REPORTS GUNFIRE HEARD IN BUDAPEST . . .'

'Where are you going?' worried Hungarian mothers asked that night. Their young sons and daughters invariably replied: 'To the barricades!' Teenagers had broken into police stations, overpowered the duty constables, and armed themselves with their guns. Others picked up the weapons from the dead AVN men in front of the radio building. They tore up cobblestones and piled them into street barriers. They overturned streetcars and trucks and set them on fire. Young army call-ups left their cantonments and joined the students, bringing with them their weapons. They waved flags and sang a patriotic song, written a century earlier by their great freedom fighter, Sandor Petőfi, with its words more relevant than ever before: 'This we swear, this we swear/Slaves we no more be!'

The situation in Budapest was slipping from the grip of Party Secretary Gerö. In the next hours, he made calls around town to gather his faithful for an emergency meeting. He acted like a man drowning, fidgeting with his pencil, and he didn't look up when he said: 'I have asked our Russian comrades for their brotherly help.'

'My God, Ernö. Stop the tanks!' shouted one of his old guard.

'Too late, they're on their way.'

'There's going to be a massacre. It's our people . . .'

Gerö shrugged his shoulders. 'Nothing will stop them now.' He hesitated for a moment. 'Furthermore, I shall make Imre [Nagy] president of the state council.'

That announcement struck the hardliners like a bomb.

It was 05.00 hrs, 24 October 1956. To the east of Budapest, a pale grey ribbon announced the dawn. The din of street fighting continued ever since the first barricades had gone up around midnight. The police and AVN were outmatched by a steadily growing number of armed insurgents. Units sprang up on every street corner. At the Museum Crossing, a priest had joined a barricade put up by students from the Technical University. He held up his hands and recited the canticle of Zachariah: 'For the love in the heart of Our God, who cometh with the rising sun, help enlighten those who hover in darkness, in the shadow of death, and guide our path on the road to peace.' The young insurgents listened and a voice intoned: 'Amen.' Janos Kovac thought of a more appropriate phrase his farmer father had told him: 'At dawn the wolf comes to feed.'

That wolf was awake. Before dawn, the Soviet commander in the Budapest sector, General Tikhonov, ordered the Soviet MVD, the Russian army's security police force, to move a great number of tanks and armoured personnel carriers from their station in Szekesfehervar to the centre of Budapest and disperse the rioters 'by the use of force'. The first units reached the outskirts of town and started shooting up the barricades. By 09.00 hrs, three full Soviet divisions were fighting street battles in the centre of town. The Russian tankers had been trained to fight in open territory; now their task was to engage in urban guerrilla fighting in a densely populated sector of an ancient city, where streets were narrow, snipers lurked on rooftops and teenagers threw bottles filled with petrol from open windows.

Maria Wittner, a nineteen-year-old student, was one of the 'flame-throwers'. She had received her training, as did every school pupil in Hungary, from Fadeyev's 'Young Guard', a how-to-make-petrol-bombs manual, which the party leadership had made compulsory reading in class. They siphoned petrol from vehicles into a beer bottle, with one or two ribbons protruding from the top and its neck blocked airtight with rolled-up newspaper. The gasoline soaked the ribbon, which was then lit and thrown. A formidable weapon if handled right. And the kids who used it, many of them only ten, twelve years old, soon became experts. All over the city, Russian tanks were turned into flaming death traps, set alight by children and teenagers, rushing with Molotov cocktails at tanks from their blind side.

Students of the chemistry faculty came up with a variant

to stop tanks by pouring liquid soap on cobblestones in streets with an incline; it made the heavy tanks slide helplessly backwards to end up stuck in house fronts. Then, the students mounted the helpless tanks, poured petrol through turret slits and dropped a match – *Boom*! Construction workers arrived with hardhats, boxes of dynamite and blasting caps. They bundled sticks of explosive, tied them to the end of a thin, invisible string, such as a fishing line and, when a tank passed, pulled on the line from a basement window to explode the charge under the tank tracks. In lanes too narrow for tracked vehicles, snipers manned rooftops and picked off Russian MVD foot patrols. Nests of resistance sprang up all over town; however, they lacked coordination and overall guidance, and each group fought their individual stand. Explosions shook house fronts, echoing and re-echoing down the long brick-and-concrete gorges of the wide boulevards; smoke and fire was rising beyond the Danube.

To advance on the Parliament and the radio station, the Russians had to take the Avenue Soroksari where a number of tall buildings, the Corvin Mansions, blocked their way. The insurgents had a saying: 'There are three great powers, the USSR, the USA, and the Corvin Passage.' This strategic bottleneck was anchored on massive blocks of flats, with streets too narrow for a tank to manoeuvre, even to turn its gun turret. A petrol station was conveniently located on the nearby corner, where insurgents went to fill up. Not cars, but Molotov cocktails.

The Budapest revolution was like a forest fire out of control; radio reports helped to spread it quickly into the major cities. Gyor and Magyarovar were in uproar; gunfire was reported from Debrecen. A countrywide curfew was declared until 14.00 hrs. All the while, a nation was sitting anxiously by their radios. Radio Budapest continued its running commentary of the various battles.

One hundred and twenty teenagers had stormed across the old Chain Bridge and strung a white banner across its centre span. The national football squad, participating at the Melbourne Olympics, called on the population to show their patriotism. A furious battle erupted between Stalin Bridge and Elisabeth Bridge along the banks of the Danube, where fifteen tanks, captured earlier by insurgents, faced a vast superiority of Russian tanks. The Russians took on the untrained Hungarian tankers, recaptured the tanks, and then shot the makeshift crews. The fight wasn't as unbalanced as it seemed. The Russians never really knew where their enemy was and with the element of surprise preserved, the irregulars were strong enough to hold out against a regiment of regulars. The sporadic firing lasted for hours, and then suddenly everything fell silent. An eerie mood settled over a beleaguered city.

In dire need of popular support, having called on the Russians for added muscle, and failed, Gerö stated in a message over Radio Budapest that he had 'suggested to the party and the workers' councils the installation of Imre Nagy as president of the ruling council'. With this political move he hoped to bring Nagy under his control. The effect of this announcement was magic and stopped the fighting.

'To Parliament Square!' was the call, and then: 'Let's hear Imre speak.' Nagy wasn't only a patriot; he was also his country's most charismatic politician. When he stepped out on the balcony of the Parliament and addressed the crowd, it was as if spring had come. He promised that he would permit no obstacle to hinder his programme of 'one people, one nation, one Hungary'. The crowd cheered, and sang the *Marseillaise*.

Nagy had found out about his political appointment by radio; after his speech, and in the company of his son-in-law, Ferenc Janosi, he went to see Party Secretary Gerö in his offices. Gerö was furious at Nagy's addressing the crowd without his permission. 'You are the instigator of these riots,' he yelled at the man he had just appointed his new prime minister.

'I've started nothing, and you bloody well know it,' replied Nagy, equally furious with the accusation.

'How dare you excite the masses? You hold neither function nor office!'

'I thought you'd just appointed me premier,' smiled Nagy. He knew he was getting the upper hand. Their meeting was not only cold; it was bound to fail, since Nagy had already decided never to become part of an already discredited government. Neither he, nor Gerö, was aware that Moscow's special envoys, Mikoyan and Suslov, had arrived by jet at a Soviet airbase near the Hungarian capital. A tank convoy brought them into Budapest. Arriving at military headquarters, they took one look at the rapidly deteriorating situation and decided to replace Gerö with Janos Kadar, who they knew was pro-Russian and, so they believed, acceptable to both party and country. For that it was now too late; the street had made its choice. Imre Nagy was the man of the hour, and the only one acceptable to Hungarians.

A knot of foreign reporters idled around the entrance to Imre Nagy's house. Only one television had been allowed inside. Something was up. Their tension grew, and they weren't a part of it. Listening to their radio, Hungarians, as the foreign press corps, tuned in to the Munich transmitter of the 'Voice of America' for a reaction from the outside world; they had to endure endless swing music, interspersed with half-hourly news flashes that continued to treat Hungary as a by-line. It quoted a CBS report from 'a well-informed source in Budapest' about an imminent change of government. A photographer from *Paris Match*, Jean-Pierre Pedrazzini, complained to an equally disgruntled colleague from Vienna's *Kronenzeitung*: 'Always the same, everything for the Americans. They're the big boys now. Nothing for us.'

They sipped hot coffee from a thermos, then started on beer, and did what every reporter has been forced to do throughout the ages: they waited. Around midnight, full of strong Hungarian brew, the journalists returned to their lodgings to file their copy of the day's events. Despite their articles, forecasting an upheaval that had to end in a great spilling of blood, there was a failure in the West to comprehend the young Hungarians' aspirations. Few outside the country realised the looming danger. Albert Camus, who followed the development by radio, wrote: 'The moment of despair is alone, pure, sure of itself, pitiless in its consequences, it has merciless power. Liberty is dangerous, as hard to live with as it is exciting.' It was meant as a warning to all sides.

October 25 was to become the decisive day of the revolution. It began early in the morning. A throng of workers from the Czepel Island Steel Works, accompanied by their wives, marched on Parliament Square, past Soviet tank units guarding it. Twenty-four hours before, they had been good, card-carrying comrades; now they had exchanged their red workers' banner for the red-white-and-green Hungarian flag, with its central sickle and hammer cut-out that was to become the banner of the revolution. They had adorned the flag with black ribbons to honour the dead of the previous two days' fighting.

The Russians proved exceptionally friendly. Their commander even promised that he would not be using force as long as nobody took a shot at his men. But that's precisely what happened; only it wasn't the workers, nor their wives, but AVN men, placed behind several machine guns on the roofs surrounding the square, who suddenly opened fire on Hungarians and Russians alike. They got what they were after, the start of a massacre. The Russians slammed down their tank covers and fired into the crowd. Eighty-two died immediately. Then an AVN man leaned over the parapet and dropped a few grenades. He was spotted and a man pointed him out. The fury of the workers was impossible to describe.

A thousand workers armed with hammers, metal bars and automatic rifles they had picked up off the dead, rushed towards the building. A machine gun fell into their hands and was turned on the door of the guards' barracks. Some AVN came yelling out of the door, hands held high, and ran straight into the stream of machine-gun fire. Another attack was under way on a nearby block of flats where a machine gun had been spotted. They used an army vehicle to slam through the wooden door of the building, then dashed up the wide stairs, killing everyone in their way. The last of the AVN had barricaded themselves behind the chimneys on the roof, firing their machine guns until they ran out of bullets. All but two were hurled on to the pavement below.

It was certainly not a foregone conclusion that the entire country would be aroused to a revolt, or could stand up to the might of the Red Army. The Communist Party had practised ruthless liquidation of any source of opposition for so long that an alternative leadership would be hard to establish – unless a dramatic event provided a powerful stimulus. Such an event was not far off. While the Parliament Square massacre took place, an event of far-reaching consequences occurred inside the largest Hungarian military complex in the centre of the city, the Kilian Barracks: its regiment joined the revolutionaries.

The troops' morale was dented by years of having had to align with the Soviets' training routine – for instance, the Hungarians were used to eating hot meals in the evening; instead they were given their hot meal in the morning. However, the event which was to follow, could not only be attributed to an army's low morale. The truth was much more complex. When the recruits had received their order to march out and support the hard-pressed Soviet tank troops, they said no. They were first and foremost Hungarians, and not prepared to defend some nebulous image of the Warsaw Pact. This defiance to Socialist unity dealt a crushing blow to Gerö's Communists, and was a complete reversal of Communist strategic thinking. From the beginning, the Soviet leaders had made sure that any potential opposition to their satellite satraps would never get the chance to develop a successful counter-revolution by denying them heavy weapons. They were unsuccessful at preventing it in Hungary, where workers gathered in factory militias received weekly training in methods of urban defence, and schoolchildren had to read DIY bomb-making manuals. The Russians and their local stooges were stuck, having no alternative but to gird themselves for a protracted struggle, which now seemed inevitable. From basements and doorways, the insurgents were in a position to strike where and when they wanted. Though they were still unable to meet the enemy in open combat, or even to defend a barricade against a major tank assault, they harassed the Soviets like 'innumerable gnats, which by biting a giant in front and in the rear, ultimately exhaust him'.[6]

Top floors and roofs became prime locations to control the streets. Sewers provided underground passages and communications for the local guerrillas, allowing them to move from block to block, transport ammunition and evacuate if necessary. For a Russian, it was not a good idea to go down there and hunt them. This they dealt with either by simply blocking some of the sewers or flooding them. Then there were the snipers. Most of the Russian casualties were killed with shots in the head or neck. The

[6] Mao Tse Tung.

Hungarians were not all just shooting their guns in the air; many of them actually knew how to use them; during the day most of the sniper shots were concentrated in two places – head and groin. Groin injuries were incapacitating; it took two people to take care of a wounded soldier, and it was humiliating. At night, most shots were in the lower jaw. Which went to show the real dangers of smoking.

When the Russians rushed into the building in pursuit of a sniper, the chances were that the stairway was booby-trapped, and the sniper had escaped by a route the Russians didn't know about. This is where the tanks came in handy. The Hungarians used obstacles to stop their advance. In city streets, concrete blocks and debris, sandbag barricades, trenchers, or a combination of all these, effectively stopped the movement of armour and troops. They didn't block all the access routes at once; using a system of blocked streets they managed to lead Russian tanks into a pre-defined killing zone. As more people joined the uprising, they began to force the Russians on to the defensive, while themselves consolidating their forces and increasing the size of their units from tiny bands into regular workers and student battalions. Every successive strike raised their morale and restored the confidence of the civilian population. And now a regiment of the Hungarian army had shown open defiance of an order!

Soon a kind of conventional warfare would replace irregular combat and the outcome would depend not only on the comparative strength, but the ability and will to win. But it took a military brain for that to happen. Until that moment, the insurgents had acted in dispersed groups, unconnected with each other. The intervention by Soviet tank troops (at dawn on 24 October) united them in a loosely connected revolutionary front. But more than anything, they lacked a coherent plan that only a military leader could provide, one who was versed in strategy, coordination and logistics. Such a man was about to come to the fore, and from the most unlikely place, the army's high command.

As more reports were coming in of sporadic attacks – for instance, a 'freedom brigade' had stormed Gyustafoghaz prison and liberated four hundred and fifty political internees; another group of insurgents had broken into the party's newspaper, *Szabad Nep* (*Free People*) and lit a bonfire with its furniture and files – the report of a soldiers' revolt in the Kilian Barracks located in the heart of the city put the loyalty of the entire Hungarian Army into question. A thoroughly shocked Janos Kadar ordered his Defence Ministry (for political reasons the Russians couldn't be asked to do the job) 'to move an available Hungarian tank unit to the caserne and put down the rebellion'. The call was put through to the commanding general, but was finally taken by Pal Maleter, a young colonel in the Hungarian Army, who was standing in for his boss while he was temporarily out of the office.

At thirty-nine, Pal Maleter was exceptionally tall; his handsome face had the look of a tough, determined individual – the toughness of a soldier who, during his spell in the various forces, had seen the rougher side of life. He spoke little; his eyes darted around with a sharp, shrewd look and he listened to anything that was said. He had the inherent qualities of a natural leader who tends to attract followers and inspire loyalty. Russian military academies rarely produced a leader with such natural talent as this young colonel. For the monolithic structure of the party, with its strict internal prerogatives, assured that a subordinate's authority derived not from his personal qualities, but from his appointed party position. Therefore, Colonel Maleter, lacking the right ingredients to be a good party cadre, had been shuttled on to a siding. His expectancy in the army was to be a desk-bound colonel, never a commanding general.

Maleter was born in the Austro-Slovakian town of Eperjes, and studied medicine in Prague. Shortly before the Nazi takeover of Czechoslovakia, he moved to Budapest, where he continued his medical studies. When he ran out of money, he volunteered for military service in the Army of the Hungarian regent Admiral Horthy, a dictator who had always aligned himself with whoever was in the wind. At the time the wind blew for Hitler. Joining the army was Maleter's way of continuing his studies and obtaining Hungarian citizenship. By 1944 he was a lieutenant with the Second Hungarian Army on the Eastern Front fighting alongside Germans against the Red Army. One night they were roused from their sleep by a blaring voice from a loudspeaker: 'Hungarians! We know where you are. Don't obey your German commanders, or you will regret your excursion into our motherland.'

Next morning Russian battalions crushed the Hungarian positions with their tanks. Lt Maleter was one of the few survivors. He had never denied his leftist leanings and readily accepted the Soviets' proposal to trade his prisoner-of-war existence for one fighting Nazis in his homeland. After extensive partisan training, he was airdropped over Transylvania and fought an outstanding guerrilla campaign. His heroism was honoured with the Soviet Union's highest order for valour, presented to him in person by Marshal Malinovski. Maleter moved with the Red Army on Budapest and, in January 1945, having gained the Russians' confidence, was put in charge of a brigade protecting the Provisional Hungarian Government. It didn't take him long to become aware of the oppressive regime that Stalin was installing throughout his satrap lands, the ruthless politicians maintained in power by the iron fist of the Red Army. Captain, then Major Maleter, a man of honesty and high intelligence, combined a strong personality with a deep, if concealed, detestation of Marxist humbug. However he wasn't someone who would ever betray his allegiance to the flag he had sworn to defend. In the Army, no one trusted anybody. To obtain proof of his continued loyalty, the Rakosi regime tested Maleter with traps.

One morning, as he was having breakfast, someone knocked on his door. It was a friend from his student days at the Ludovika Military Academy. 'Maleter, we know your political feelings. We all want to live in a free world. You must help us to get rid of the Russkies.' Maleter pulled out his gun and escorted the man to the police station. Next morning, a high party man came to congratulate him on his proven loyalty. His 'friend' had been an AVN plant sent to test him.

By the early 1950s, Maleter had reached the rank of colonel. He was quiet, preferring to work alone, even though it was a genuine pleasure being around him and he seemed to enjoy working with others. He also had the ability to turn off any secondary distractions and focus his entire attention and brainpower on the important matter at hand, be it a hypothetical plan to attack across an enemy border or to squash a real riot at home.

In the months leading up to the crisis, mainly brought on by the events in neighbouring Poland, higher circles within the Army were developing a totally new awareness. There was even critical discussion on matters that had long been kept out of sight, an increasingly vocal expression of discontent with the system under which they lived, compared with the life in democracies in the outside world – which, of course, they were prevented from seeing, or only under the strictest surveillance. This discontent also grew in the lower echelons, the vast majority being young, unmarried conscripts. With Poland uppermost in their minds, soldiers were convinced that a similar revolutionary situation was unavoidable and that out of it a new Hungary would arise. Therefore, it was no wonder, once the October riots broke out, that many young recruits threw in their lot with the insurgents. And when this happened, the call went out to crush the Hungarian mutineers under the cleats of Hungarian tanks. And so, because of the absence of the commanding general, the man who received the order from a panicked party leadership to take Hungarian tanks and put down a mutiny at the Kilian Barracks was Colonel Pal Maleter.

Col. Maleter had five tanks under his command. He went into action wearing his cap. Steel helmets made thinking difficult, and if anything explosive was to hit his vehicle, a steel helmet wouldn't be of any help. His column was rolling past the destruction in the centre of town. Hundreds of shop windows were broken but, amazingly, nothing had been stolen, proof that this was a revolution of the pure, and not given to looting. The interior boulevard was strewn with overturned trams and burnt cars; fallen trees had been pushed across the pavement to obstruct tanks. The National Museum was in flames. A fierce battle had taken place just outside the Technical Institute and the bodies of the fallen revolutionaries had been covered with Hungarian flags. In front of the Hotel Astoria, dozens of youngsters were sitting on Russian tanks, waving red-white-and-green flags with the by now customary cut-out in the centre. As a military man of acumen, but also as a Hungarian, Maleter looked on this devastation with alarm. In Lajos Kossuth Street, his column passed a group of armed students, cheering at the sight of tanks with Hungarian crews. A boy jumped on the lead tank and handed the gunner the national flag with a 'Hungary forever!' There was something touching about the naïvety and pureness of thought of this young boy. And in the circumstances surrounding this minor event may be found much that probably altered the course of the Hungarian Revolution.

The column continued along Üllöi Boulevard towards the Kilian Barracks. Located across from the caserne were the heavily fortified Corvin Mansions. This building complex had been turned into a fortress by steelworkers, under the leadership of the Pongrazc brothers, and two union foremen, Marton and Solymosi, calling their militia unit the 'Corvin Regiment'. Earlier that morning, when they had tried to take over the strategic complex and found the main door barred by an AVN unit, the Pongracz placed a satchel charge against it. The explosion blew down the door and the two AVN guards standing behind it. Two more agents stood in the courtyard, their faces mirroring fear. They were cut down by a burst from the automatic that an insurgent had recovered from the dead AVN man inside the doorway. They heard before they saw Maleter's column of five tanks rumbling up the boulevard. The Pongracz hadn't heard of the trouble in the nearby Kilian Barracks, and were sure that the tanks had come to oust them from their fortress. Fighting AVN armed with automatic rifles was one thing; facing tank guns was another matter.

Maleter knew a problem when he saw one. With the Kilian Barracks on one side, held by rebellious soldiers, and the Corvin Mansions on the other, held by insurgent workers, the Corvin intersection had been turned into 'Budapest's wall of Thermopylae'. He had two options: either to talk his way through or shoot his way through, and was still undecided when the wide door of the Kilian Barracks swung open and out stepped a young man waving a Hungarian flag with a hole in its centre. A moment later, another man appeared from the Corvin Mansions. Both headed for Maleter's lead tank.

Revolutions do happen with lightning speed; days become hours and hours shrink into minutes. A single moment of decision – or indecision – can win a combat or condemn it to failure. This was such critical moment. Faced by a soldier and a worker, something snapped inside the colonel. Perhaps he was tired of the accumulation of acts of hardship on his own troops – or it was simply because his mind was sharper and could foresee what was coming at them, and the country in general. Whatever it was, he knew that he could never give the order to fire on fellow Hungarians!

The moment that Pal Maleter joined the revolution, the tide swung in favour of the insurgents. In him, the movement had found its military leader. Maleter was a successful commander and his methods worked, even if they were occasionally unconventional. His military brain was no longer doing battle for meaningless territories in a Soviet satrapy, but for his family, his people, for Hungary! He knew well enough that to defeat Soviet armour in the middle of his hometown would need a miracle. A miracle was what Maleter demanded of his fates. Before he had always laughed at the notion of some kind of spiritual guidance; he was an intensely practical man. Now he had a deep inner feeling of doing the right thing. Weird certainties came upon him: the conviction that chance had chosen him to emulate the great Kossuth; but also that he would die in this struggle for freedom. Perhaps it was because of this certainty that he could accept his fate calmly. His men cheered when he told them that they were given the glorious task of liberating Hungary. From this moment on, they would fight, if need be, Russians, but never again Hungarians.

Maleter assembled the rest of his officers. 'There is no reason for all of us to stay here. What we need most is to gather up arms and ammunition from the depots. Those still guarded by government loyalists, talk to them, tell them how things have changed. I'll make a few calls. Don't forget the AVN warehouses. As for anti-tank weapons, we must make do with what we have, the Russians have sealed our artillery in their cantonments.'

Maleter, with characteristic clarity of vision, went directly to the root of the matter and struck his initial blow. The Army, as it was constitutionally obliged to do, had to protect the government. By seizing control of the weapon depots of the city, and the ammunition stores, he seized command of the Army, a critical factor in every upheaval.

It took only ten minutes for the news of the Maleter affair to reach Janos Kadar. With Maleter gone over to the revolution, the Communist boss felt helpless. A meeting was arranged and Maleter went to see Kadar. In the course of their discussion the colonel refined his proposal. He argued that the government should call up all available reservists and constitute a 'People's Militia', should Moscow respond by an invasion of the nation's sovereign territory. Whatever the political risks, he argued, the Hungarian Army must be used, and all restrictions on them lifted. Its Army was the only organised power grouping inside Hungary, capable of bringing down the entire Socialist system. Kadar was faced with a dilemma. An Army which is allowed to think is a danger for a politician. Yet Kadar understood that if he didn't give in, Maleter would proceed independently to form his militia.

The colonel pointed at some Russian tanks parked outside the window. 'What good are Russian troops? We need to make a call over the radio and we will soon have all of Budapest, if not all of Hungary with us.' With this threat, Maleter put his finger on the strength of the insurgency, and from that moment on managed matters with the skill and energy of the born revolutionary. He took full advantage of his opponents' weaknesses, using their precepts as ammunition for his own guns.

His initial task was to clear the centre of Budapest of

Russians. Key were the Danube bridges. A major tank action took place on the Danube embankment; Hungarian T-34 tanks were shooting it out with the much superior Russian T-56s across the river. Tanks were destroyed and burning oil sent black clouds into the skies over Budapest. Then the Russian tanks backed off, heading away from the fighting, with dozens of wounded stacked behind their gun turrets.

'The Russkies retreat!' screamed a student, jumping on to the earthen embankment, madly waving a Hungarian flag; seconds later he was cut down by a burst from across the water.

The pattern of events changed rapidly once Maleter took control of military actions. There was noise everywhere, of shells exploding and tracks clanking and squealing as Hungarian tanks took up strategic positions. They were not firing directly from the front, but from the flank or far back, in well-chosen positions along boulevards they knew so well. There was no longer the weariness of struggling with uncertainty and responsibility. Whereas before, usually decisive men had been left in a state of uncertainty, now everyone was told what to do. They drew on their reserves of self-control and stamina, and quickly exploited their advantages.

As the pattern became clearer, Col. Maleter could view the outcome of his operation with some satisfaction, even if his hopes were far from being fulfilled. There was no sign yet of any opening which could be exploited against the Russian tanks, but gains had been made, particularly in the centre of Budapest, where Russian units had been isolated and left uncertain of their fate. The Hungarian snipers were well sited and inflicted many casualties, while the Russians' morale showed signs of cracking. It was a demonstration that the Red Army was neither omnipotent, nor invulnerable, and that was an encouraging sign.

Newspapers around the world carried headlines. Their

conclusion was that the will of Russian forces to resist a popular rising was so low and the inner strength of the Communist regime so decayed, that they would be unable to put down the student and workers' rebellion, especially with the support by the Hungarian army. When the political aim of the enemy involves a comparatively smaller sacrifice than the probable outlay required to defeat him, the will to resist him will be correspondingly smaller. That was the manner in which Hungarians, but also politicians around the globe, saw the beginning of an astounding withdrawal of Russian forces from the centre of Budapest. One day they were there and the next day, the powerful Red Machine was gone. Hungarians didn't care about the reason for the Russians' withdrawal; they only had time for celebrations. By the last days of October, Budapest was awash with a wave of euphoria. With Maleter in military control, the mood took an upswing. Jokes floated around. The favourite story was that of teenagers ringing the doorbell of a spinster known for her fussiness.

'Miss Kodaly,' said one, 'if we wipe our feet clean, may we come in and shoot out of your window?'

The reporters of Radio Budapest had entered into the jubilation, keeping up the nation's morale with a stream of positive announcements. They broadcast feats of individual heroism, such as when youngsters jumped on to Soviet tanks, brandishing flags and practising their school Russian on the soldiers: '*Zdrastvuite, tovarich* – Have your masters told you who we are? Fanatics? Fascists? Or mercenaries in foreign pay trying to destroy Socialism? Our leaders are Imre Nagy, who fought on the side of the Socialists in Spain, and Pal Maleter, who combated the Nazis with the Red Army!'

Since the days of the nation's greatest hero, Lajos Kossuth, who, in 1849, took on the might of the Austrian double-eagle, nobody had enjoyed greater popularity than

Imre Nagy and Pal Maleter. That fact was reinforced in Moscow by a report from Russia's intelligence service: 'Nagy and Maleter's status as a symbol of defiance has been strengthened with the Hungarian people; these men are also turning into symbols in the neighbouring Socialist People's Republics.' Romania and Czechoslovakia? That was downright seditious. Suslov and Mikoyan conferred with Khrushchev behind the Kremlin walls. Their problem was not only Hungary, but also the threat of a potential contagion: the Hungarian crisis could push the Socialist hemisphere into a conflict beyond their control. But dare they move, they asked themselves? They still lacked a clear picture of the West's reaction. What if America was to send its armoured divisions to the Czech and Austrian border? This could be done without any intention of actually fighting but it could provoke a war. In a sense, the Muscovites had become prisoners of their own hard-line propaganda. Moscow couldn't give in – and they couldn't let it go. The consensus was: Strike now!

'Patience,' counselled Nikita Khrushchev, aware that Eisenhower's America was preoccupied with his campaign for re-election, and that France and England were grumbling about Nasser's nationalisation of the Suez Canal. His spy service had informed him of an imminent invasion of the Sinai by Israelis, coinciding with English and French forces bouncing on Suez. The estimated timing for such an operation was between 28 and 30 October. In the confusion of a war in the Middle East, and with attention diverted by special news bulletins from Cairo and Tel Aviv, with political commentaries from London, Paris and Washington, nobody in the world would give a damn about Budapest.

Late on the afternoon of 29 October, Maleter stormed into Nagy's office: 'A combined English and French force has landed at Suez.' It was at this moment that Maleter must have realised that their dream was over. With fighting going on in the Sinai and along the Suez Canal, Hungary lay wide open and helpless. The Soviets had ostensibly 'pulled out' – because they had known all along about Suez! They were just waiting for the right moment. With universal attention diverted to Egypt, the Russians would never allow such an opportunity to slip past them.

On 29 October, under the guidance of General Bela Kiraly and Major-General Pal Maleter – he had been promoted overnight – a Central Revolutionary Armed Forces Committee was constituted, which from then on became the unique command body of the Hungarian Army. Later that evening, Kadar handed the task of re-establishing order in Budapest to Maleter and his Hungarian units. On a diplomatic front, Hungary found itself completely isolated. Under such circumstances, it was difficult to envisage how a peaceful solution could be achieved. Perhaps time would work in their favour and it was in their ultimate interest to minimise the concessions that would have to be granted to the Russians, to let Hungary rule over its own destiny.

And then something unexpected happened; to their utter surprise, Suslov and Mikoyan arrived unannounced on 30 October, to announce that Moscow was willing to accept the Hungarians' proposal in most points: 'All Soviet troops will be withdrawn from Hungary – all but those that are vital to assure the Socialist world's protection as stipulated by the agreement of all Warsaw Pact nations.' That was more than Nagy could ever hope for. In the company of Zoltan Tildy (the only non-Communist in the government) and Pal Maleter, they met the two Soviet emissaries to study the proposal. This took several hours.

Finally, Tildy addressed himself to the Russian parliamentarians: 'You must have faith in our desire to remain good friends with the people of the Soviet Union and its leaders. Hungary has no intention of pursuing any anti-Soviet policies.' Spoken by a non-Communist, the statement carried weight. Suslov showed his usual sour face, and Mikoyan smiled. Maleter felt a knot in his stomach: the Russian's smile was too sincere to be real – because this agreement amounted to nothing less than a Soviet admission of defeat, and a Russian would never surrender! And yet, everyone was taken in, including the CIA's super-spy Allen Dulles, who assured President Eisenhower that this was the most significant treaty ever agreed upon by the Soviets and that it constituted a serious step forward. In fact, Russian tanks were seen moving out of Budapest, and his agents reported that one of their divisions was loading its tanks on to special trains at the border town of Zahony, band, flags and all. At a Budapest street intersection, a metal Red Star from a government building lay on the pavement. Three Soviet tanks approached, some of the last to leave the city. The first drove over the star, as did the second. The third swerved to avoid it and instead drove over a parked motorcycle. Its owner picked up a paving stone and threw it after the tank.

That evening, Radio *Miksolc*, located in an industrial city, transmitted: 'Stop the massacre of our Hungarian brothers in Budapest. Let the Soviet contingent leave Hungary. Force them into a ceasefire. We've had enough autocracy by our chiefs. Yes, we want Socialism, but let this be a specifically Hungarian Socialism, reflecting the interests of the working classes and our most holy patriotic feelings.'

Rumours were rife in Budapest that the country was returning to a pre-war capitalist society. Maleter squashed these rumours; during a press conference he declared: 'We are out to create a Socialist Hungary. Nothing about this can be left open to discussion. We will neither return lands, nor banks, nor factories to their previous owners.' As the days went on and an eventual victory became more than just a dim hope, they began to plan for the future. The new leaders of Hungary didn't lose sight of their ultimate goal: truly to liberate the country from its Russian occupation and afterwards restore Hungary into the Socialist fold.

Then an incident occurred which the Russians would later use to justify the reversal of their position. Despite its outward calm, Budapest was still in ferment; in the outskirts of the city, vigilante groups were chasing down AVN agents. This took on the aspect of a bloody stag hunt, where the outcome was invariably a bullet in the head. In a bloodstained settlement of accounts, swift and cruel vengeance was everywhere. Two hundred and thirty-four AVN agents were killed in Budapest and the provinces. A particularly vicious incident happened on the Place of the Republic, where the office of the Communist Party for Greater Budapest was located. The building itself was solidly built and still guarded by the hated agents of the AVN, armed with machine guns.

Early in the morning, a large crowd had gathered outside on the square, also bent on squaring up accounts. Inside the building was the local party secretary, Imre Mezö, who telephoned to the party's Central Committee for immediate help. The Central Committee called on the Defence Ministry and got through to Pal Maleter, who hurriedly dispatched three tanks to the site to preserve what could be saved and avert a blood bath. However, the tank crews joined the insurgents and turned their cannons on the building. Faced by a mob of thousands and tank artillery, it left Secretary Mezö and his old guard with no alternative but to surrender. Many party cadres were bludgeoned to death or thrown down from windows and rooftops. Others were lined up around the square, and executed. Men who only the day before wielded unrestricted power, kept creeping out, white and shaken, Mezö and his top party cadres among them. They were greeted with much laughter from the gloating crowd, then pushed against the front door and gunned down. A French photographer covered the massacre. His pictures made headlines around the world. The cold-blooded execution of Mezö resulted in grave repercussions.

While the inner city of Budapest was pervaded with the smell of burnt houses, of fire and corpses, the shock wave of Hungary's ideological explosion flowed back to Moscow, exposing serious doubts and enhancing the potential of Soviet military leadership. The decision for the pull-out had been strictly based on political expedience, and the CPSU (Communist Party of the Soviet Union) leadership was seen to have made a faulty assessment. Their generals were furious over the public outcry that the Red Army had shown feet of clay, a view shared widely by the Western press. The military forced their Central Committee into a direct, brutal intervention. It was now a question of timing.

One person who felt ill at ease about the Suslov-Mikoyan Agreement was the US ambassador to Moscow, Charles Bohlen. That night, at a Kremlin reception, he met Marshal Zhukov, who took a strident 'anti-terrorist' line and didn't mince his words about showing 'a firm hand'. The Soviet hero, who had forced the military might of Nazi Germany to its knees, couldn't stand the shame inflicted on the powerful Red War Machine by a fly like Hungary. 'Enough is enough,' he said. His thoughts, backed by strategic considerations, were strongly supported by others inside the Kremlin. Ambassador Bohlen advised Washington of this, but his warning wasn't taken seriously by Secretary of State, John Foster Dulles.

By midday on 31 October, the last remaining Soviet tank had been withdrawn from Parliament Square. Budapest was free of Russians! But was it? At the time that the last Russian tank moved from Budapest, Maleter received a call from one of his unit commanders in the border town of Zahony. He learned that fresh Soviet tank units had crossed *into* Hungary. The principle of conceding immediate and total independence to Hungary would never find acceptance in the Kremlin. A perilous strategic vacuum would be created in an important part of the Soviet empire. Yet, there was a faint hope that some sort of understanding might still be possible between the Russians and the new Hungarians. And perhaps it would have happened, but for the conflict that had exploded in the Middle East: the Suez crisis.

The archbishop of Esztergom and Primate of Hungary, Cardinal Mindszenty, who had been held under house arrest for over a year, met with Maleter. His imprisonment had not broken the intransigence of the churchman, representing a 1000-year-old Hungarian Catholic tradition. 'In two days I shall speak to the people and offer a solution,' he promised, thereby solving the tricky problem of combining state and religion in a highly religious environment, especially in farm communities.

On 2 November, Imre Nagy delivered a memorandum to Soviet ambassador Andropov, protesting at the continued Russian troop movements, including the occupation of rail lines and stations, which was contrary to the earlier Suslov–Mikoyan agreement, and setting out a proposal to resolve the crisis. Finally, on 3 November, Imre Nagy constituted a new government. General Maleter became his Minister of Defence. Nagy sent off a message to the Secretary-General of the United Nations, declaring Hungary's neutrality. It was a daring move, because it put Hungary, in effect, outside the Warsaw Pact Alliance. In case of an East–West conflict, Hungary, together with neutral Austria and Switzerland, would become a combat-free buffer zone. Strategically, that had to be unacceptable to Moscow.

*   *   *

In these first days of November 1956, Budapest enjoyed its 'whiff of freedom'. The cafés reopened, the newspaper boys called out their headlines and rushed between tables. Throughout the country, people were elated and came out into the streets with banners and songs. Nagy and Maleter were the heroes of the day. Intoxicated with the joy of simply talking to one another, perfect strangers dared to discuss the situation openly, another 'first' inside the Soviet Bloc. The city had become a giant village of two million people who all wanted to meet each other. Every passer-by had another story to tell, be it about a battle or a punitive action. In the streets the people enjoyed the sunshine; in parks and squares were crowds, discussing and arguing. Standing on the platform of a truck, farmers from a cooperative were giving away apples and chickens.[7]

For nearly a week, the country's workers had been on strike. Maleter launched an appeal by radio, urging them to go back to their factories 'for the good of Hungary'.

Trains ran again. New political parties mushroomed and started on their favourite game – bickering. There was now a national peasant party, called the Petöfi Party, and a Social Democratic Party and a Small Proprietors Party. There was also a New Communist Party. Imre Nagy slipped up only once in his distinguished political career, when he overlooked the fact that the leader of this so-called new Communism was none other than Janos Kadar, who had been ousted by Nagy from his top position. It proved a fatal oversight; Kadar was not someone who took things lying down; with his party, which still held the majority in parliament, Kadar held a potent political instrument in the ongoing struggle for power. It also gave him an opening with the Soviets. On the evening of 1 November he mysteriously disappeared from Budapest.

[7] György Konrad, *Le Complice*, Paris, 1980.

The news reaching Budapest from border railway stations was increasingly alarming. The Russians had requisitioned Czech railway lines and were deploying a tank army from the north throughout Slovakia. They crossed the Danube and moved into Esztergom and Rajka. Tanks crossed the Danube at Komarom. More tanks were reported on the Romanian border near Nyirbator and Debrecen. Smaller armoured units were already moving towards Szolnok, only one hundred kilometres (62 miles) from Budapest. Increased air traffic was reported from the Soviet airbase at Szekesfehervar, forty kilometres (25 miles) from the city. *Hungary was again being invaded!* Only this time, the Soviets were serious about it. They came with 2500 tanks, 1000 armoured vehicles, and their overall troops effectives were 75,000 men, plus back-up reserves.

By the evening of 3 November, the day that Nagy had proclaimed Hungary's neutrality and formed his government, the only link between Budapest and the provinces was by a single telephone line. Maleter was in conference with Imre Nagy. For the last few days he had tried to warn Nagy of the downside of the Hungaro-Soviet 'friendship pact'. According to him, the Soviets had no intention of letting go of part of their empire. He argued that it would create a precedent and a severe loss of prestige in the game for global strategy of a super-power. Maleter spoke in a quiet tone, without creating panic, explaining to Nagy how best to cope with the situation.

'The tanks are the Soviets' muscle to exact retaliation for their shameful setback. Their hard-liners don't care about public opinion in the rest of the world; they intend to use us as a lesson for other satrap states. I assure you, the danger has not diminished, quite to the contrary, it is getting worse.' He was sure that it was Khrushchev's intention, on advice by Suslov and Mikoyan, to stage a counter-coup and put some handpicked stooges in place.

'But we have an understanding with Moscow,' said Nagy, still trusting in the validity of a piece of paper as only a politician would and, not like Maleter, the military strategist.

'They are Russians and we are Hungarians. We don't speak the same language,' said Maleter. Nagy wouldn't listen; the old Communist couldn't imagine that the Soviets would break their word, because he wanted so much to see his dream come true. For this, it was now too late. Once they had crossed the Czech-Hungarian and Romanian-Hungarian border, the Soviet leaders had shown their perfidious face. When Maleter finally presented him with undeniable proof of an invasion, Nagy's face turned pale.

'We must move immediately into action.'

Maleter looked at him: 'What action do you have in mind? At this very moment, hundreds of tanks are moving in on us.' Even Maleter had no idea of the real dimension of the invasion: more tanks were moving on Budapest than the tank forces of Rommel and Montgomery combined at El Alamein! Khrushchev was determined to stop the contagion and this he could only achieve with brutal force. He was out to demonstrate that the Soviet Union mustn't be trifled with and, for this, he had accepted the option of the big hammer.

He had waited for the appropriate moment and then moved with exceptional speed. And yet, the Russians still resorted to diplomatic delaying techniques. While the Soviet tank force moved into Hungary, the Soviet ambassador informed Imre Nagy that the Soviet government had accepted the Hungarian's proposition and was willing to negotiate on its basis. For this it was necessary for the Hungarian premier to form a delegation, made up of political and military experts. Ambassador Andropov suggested Maleter as leader of the team; it would be easier for a military man to negotiate with another military man.

His move should have been only too obvious for an old fox like Nagy: decapitate the military, and then take care of the political authority left without back-up. Yet Nagy fell for the trick and picked his team. Interior minister Ferenc Erdei was to handle the political aspect, and Defence Minister General Pal Maleter was picked for the military details. The meeting between the two delegations was arranged to take place at the Tököl military compound, beyond the southern suburbs of Budapest. Geza Losonczy, one of Nagy's inner circle, showed his misgivings: 'Tököl is a Soviet base. What if they arrest you?'

'I cannot imagine such low betrayal on their part,' replied Maleter. But he added, 'Unless . . . of course . . . Who knows?' He did know, of course, since there had been many such precedents in the Soviet Union during the Stalin era. Maleter realised that his was not only a mission of despair; it was also a mission of last resort. After two weeks of fighting, the boys and girls manning the barricades deserved more than to die for nothing. To Maleter, the military man, the Soviets' intention was clear. They were coming back and nothing would stop them before they had achieved their goal, which was nothing short of the suppression of the revolution. For this, they were coming with tanks and shells and bullets. The Hungarians had three options: fight to the last man, without hope of outside help; give in and rely on the Russians' clemency; or make for the Yugoslav or Austrian border – a general exodus – but that couldn't be achieved in the time available.

Tököl, 22.00 pm, 3 November 1956. Maleter had been worried about this meeting from the start; unreasonably, maybe, because there wasn't a thing he could do. No way he could guess, either. Maleter was a gentleman. Sometimes he would ignore small transgressions of his men so long as they didn't get in the way of important things. But there were the rules of honour a general would never bend. He could only hope that the other side would behave similarly. Things seemed reassuringly quiet at the Tököl base. A Soviet honour guard met the Hungarian delegation. There was nothing, not the least sign of danger, no reason for Maleter's nagging disquiet; but still, it was there. Such thoughts were distracting; there must be no weakening now, he told himself as he entered into the arena of his adversary. It was his mark of courage that he controlled his fear, which again enabled him to go ahead and do what duty dictated must be done.

The Hungarians were led into a large room and, following the usual shaking of hands across the table, installed themselves opposite their Soviet counterparts, along a large baize-covered table with its standard display of soft drinks, flowers and little flags. The Soviet delegation, led by General Malinin, opened the negotiations with the customary declaration reserved for such an austere occasion, a statement of eternal Socialist brotherhood between their great nations. The difficult part, the haggling, was to follow. Before they got started, the door opened to an uninvited arrival: Soviet General Ivan Serov, head of Russia's secret police. He walked to General Malinin and whispered into his ear. The Russian chief delegate gathered up his papers and got up; without a further word, he and his delegation left the room.

General Maleter was thunderstruck. He burst out angrily: 'What is this all about?'

'The meeting is closed. You are all under arrest,' announced Serov.

Maleter laughed curtly, but there was no fun in his laughter, only the bitterness of disillusion. Intrigue was part of his existence; it had been for much of his life. But always the game had been played by certain rules. He had stumbled into a human jungle in which even the most basic rules of decency had no meaning. A savage wilderness of promise and betrayal. Before he was able to contact Budapest, General Maleter and his colleagues were led *manu militari* from the room, put into a sealed bus, and driven off. Two hours later, the first Russian tank column rumbled into Budapest. They came with motorised infantry on troop carriers, tractor-drawn artillery, and tanks. This time, the Soviets intended to apply brute force without regard for constitutional or other legal restraints, justifying their brutalities under the slogan of 'fighting fire with fire'. This would appeal to all those for whom civil rights had little meaning. Their force was not only directed against military combatants, but also against all those suspected of supporting or sympathising with the insurgents, by the expedient use of reprisal and terror – indiscriminately and without judicial constraint.

Things moved with lightning speed. At 03.30 hrs, a military aide rushed into Nagy's apartment, where he was working on a speech he was to give next morning, and announced the deal with the Soviets.

'The Russkies have returned!'

Twenty minutes later a further message arrived.

'Janos Kadar has formed a counter-government at Szolnok.'

If Hungarians still hoped for a miracle, a loud explosion shattered their dreams. At 04.25 hrs the uncertainty ended with a hail of tank shells, aiming to spread confusion and insecurity. A Soviet tank unit had reached a southern suburb of Budapest, cluttered with workers' flats, and opened fire on the city blocks without prior warning. The first shots were quickly followed by a series of heavy explosions from many directions. Soviet tanks were advancing on the city from all directions.

Jean-Pierre Pedrazzini, a photographer for *Paris Match*, was shaken awake by the first explosion; he knew what this meant – exclusive pictures. He was one of the few who had stayed behind in Budapest; Hungary had seemed settled and the eyes of foreign news editors were fixed on another emergency. Nearly all his colleagues had decamped for the Suez Canal. This was what the planners in Moscow had counted on. Jean-Pierre Pedrazzini walked in the direction of the Kilian Barracks. Karolyi Street was deserted; its barricades had been taken down during the days of 'phoney peace' to allow the flow of normal traffic. The rumble of gunfire was coming from the direction south of Buda, where Hungarian troops were holding out in the Budaörs Barracks. The increasing howl of heavy engines told him that the tanks were coming closer. He reached the Calvin Square. It was clear of traffic and he kept going, trusting his instinct to find action; he was paid to get pictures. And then, two bright circles lit up before him, and behind the circles was the shadowy shape of a monster T-56 with its gun pointed at him. He heard the increased roar of its engine as it came towards him, gathering speed. With a sickening feeling, he realised the driver's intention. The heavy, bulky vehicle ploughed through two burned-out cars, crushing them beneath its steel cleats. It was making straight for the French photographer, hiding out behind a tree, with his camera pressed to the eye and his lens sticking out menacingly like the tuba of a bazooka . . .[8]

A hundred miles (160 km) from his beleaguered ministerial colleagues, General Pal Maleter was on his way into captivity. His bus sped past convoys of tanks rumbling towards Hungary's capital. He stared from the car's window. What a terrible price to pay for liberty. His thoughts were filled with sadness. Fools they had been, trusting a piece of paper; instead of liberty, they had brought madness, destruction, and executions upon their country. The

[8] Pedrazzini died in hospital, after having been shown the special issue containing his last photographs.

price they had asked had been too high. Russian hegemony was to be preserved and now his beloved country would die. Hungary's thirteen days of freedom were only one heartbeat in as many years of despondency.

Geza Losonczy jumped in his little Fiat and raced ahead of the tightening circle of tanks. When he reached Parliament, he found Nagy, with Tildy, Bibo and Szabo. All the others had been caught in various parts of the city by the Russians' rapid advance.

'How bad is it?' was the first question they all asked.

'Worse than you can imagine. They're all over the place. Nothing but tanks, and they're shooting at anything that moves,' replied a badly shaken Losonczy. 'Where is Janos [Kadar]?'

'He's disappeared.'

'Where's Maleter?'

'We don't know; we haven't heard from Tököl and must assume the worst.'

'We must get hold of [General] Kiraly . . .'

Nagy shook his head in resignation. 'No, no more blood. I shall address the people by radio.'

'Imre, you must leave the city,' advised Losonczy, but Nagy had already decided to stay in Budapest and direct negotiations from there. There was nothing to negotiate and time was running out. Nagy was on the telephone to his ambassadors in the various foreign capitals, hoping that their appeal would prompt the international community to intervene and stop what he feared was about to take place. The Russians had timed it well; it was 03.45 hrs in London and 22.45 hrs in Washington, not the best time to get through to world leaders. When they finally replied – Eisenhower through the voice of his foreign secretary, John Foster Dulles – other than offering empty phrases of protest, they did nothing. For Nagy, and for all of Hungary, a vision died. Maleter had been right all along; the Kremlin wouldn't permit a portion of the Soviet Bloc to slip from its hegemony.

At 05.20 hrs, the people of Budapest, who were woken over an hour ago by the rolling boom of gun fire, heard the voice of their prime minister. 'This is Imre Nagy, speaking to you. At dawn today, Soviet units launched an attack against our capital with the obvious intention of over-throwing the legal government of a democratic Hungary. Our troops are counter-attacking. The government mans its stations. I must warn the Hungarian people and inform the entire world of this unprovoked aggression.' Fact was, the government of Imre Nagy had no means to combat this new invasion. A message was delivered to Imre Nagy from the Soviet High Command: unless he surrendered by midday, the Soviet Air Force would bomb Budapest. It showed his integrity that he made a final attempt to prevent bloodshed; at 07.12 hrs in one last message to his people, mainly intended for the invading Soviet troops, Radio Free Kossuth went on the air. Nagy spoke in both Hungarian and Russian: 'Don't fire. Avoid a blood bath. Russians are our friends and will remain our friends.'

Another message went out over the same radio trans-mitter at 07.56 hrs, a pathetic final appeal by the Union of Hungarian Writers: 'We're calling on every writer and intellectual wherever he may find himself at this tragic moment. We beg of you, rush to our assistance. There isn't a moment to lose. By now you must know what is happening in our country. *Help Hungary*. Protect its writers, its scientists, its workers, and its peasants. Save us. Please help, please help, please help . . .' After this message, Radio Free Kossuth went silent.

But another radio station came on the air; it was located in the east of the country and carried the voice of Ferenc Münnich. He announced that Janos Kadar had formed the Revolutionary Government of Workers and Peasants:

'Events have forced us to accept our responsibility; we find it impossible to support any longer the reactionary pressure put on the Nagy government. We are standing up against all counter-revolutionary activities which threaten our People's Republic, in order to protect the power of the working and peasant classes and to safeguard their socialist conquests.' Kadar went on to accept all points laid out by the Nagy cabinet, but with one noted exception: he didn't mention free elections. This first broadcast was followed almost immediately by a second, which made Kadar's position crystal clear: 'In the name of all the workers and peasants of our nation, we address ourselves to the high command of the Soviet army to come to our aid and smash the sinister reactionary forces in order to re-establish calm throughout our land.' This was a blatant lie, since it was precisely the workers who had been the first to man the barricades against the Russians! However, the puppet's appeal justified Moscow's brutal suppression of the individual freedoms in a brotherly nation.

It was still dark. The harsh white light from a tank projector scanned over the shelled flats and on the jumbled pile of corpses in the park. The group's last hope was to scatter, to trickle through the Soviet cordon as individuals. In those early hours of the return of Soviet tanks, Janos Kovac, the student leader from the Technical University, didn't know where he put his own two feet, that's how exhausted he was. Janos sat motionless behind the corner of the Corvin Passage. With him was his friend Josef Fedor. In his mind Janos kept recalling the last few days, the sweet moments of freedom. Gone was the dream; now it would be back to the old repressive system, the rule of unjust law; the law of oppression and moral corruption, a law that enslaved man because more than anything he wanted to be free. They couldn't achieve it on their own and they couldn't expect help from outside. The time had come to give his final order, the disbandment of such units as still existed.

'Go, Josef, go and try to stay alive.'

'I won't leave you.'

'I'll knock your teeth in if you don't move out. Now!'

'And you, what will you do?'

'I will submit to my fate.'

Josef embraced his friend and ran crouched along the house fronts. It was not sweat running down Janos' cheek and dripping on his shirt; he wondered unashamedly when last he had wept. It did not seem important now, not with most of his friends dead. A few tank shells burst not far away, but he was too exhausted to take cover. Soviet tanks had surrounded his last dozen, all that was left of his original group of two hundred; between them they had one RPG (rocket-propelled grenade) and a dozen Molotov cocktails. The rocket launcher could account for at least one tank, but as for the rest? He didn't know why the tanks were not advancing.[9] Janos knew that whoever won, or whoever lost, the fight would not be over when a ceasefire was finally proclaimed. There would always be another shot that had to be fired – perhaps by the execution squad.

Janos grabbed the RPG and moved out with his men to prepare for the tank attack. Dead tired, he leaned against the wall of a building. All he saw was a lot of bloodstained, battle-weary kids facing up to the monsters of a mechanised age. Suddenly the tank engines sprang into life and as the first tank turned the corner, its eye-searing lights beamed upon him. Janos aimed and pulled the trigger; there was a searing flash, a deafening explosion, followed by a thunderous whoosh of fiery flame. The lead

---

[9] The Politburo, still uncertain of world reaction to their rape of Budapest, was holding back on the order for the final assault.

tank disintegrated. The second tank fired. Beneath Janos's feet, the earth rocked. His back hurt, his skin was singed from his scalp, he couldn't hear a sound; the explosion blocked his eardrums. But he could taste the trickle of blood that ran from his nose into his mouth.

Slowly the feeling was flooding back into his numbed back. He felt a strong vibration; the concrete of the road seemed to be cracking beneath him. Although he could not hear them, he saw the rest of the tanks swinging around the burning T-56. Heavy black smoke rose from what was now the broken shell of a tank. Four tanks fired simultaneously. A wall sheltered Janos from the worst of the blast. He was luckier than most of his young fighters. Two were instantly burnt to death by the scorching blast. Three were swept across the street, their bodies shattered by fragments of flying steel and masonry; the rest were crushed by the falling concrete slabs as the front of the building caved in. The first of the tanks was coming up to where Janos was hiding. All he had left was a bottle filled with petrol. He moved slowly along the wall of the house. When he looked around the corner, he saw helmeted soldiers scattering through the street. He lit the wick and began to run for the tank. The moment he threw his bottle he heard the *whoosh!* The shell exploded just opposite him in the street; Janos felt a stab in his chest . . . he staggered back to the house and sank down, his head against the wall. A trickle of blood came from a corner of his mouth, an indication that shrapnel had torn into his lungs. A face lay a foot away from his own and it was turned towards him, with unseeing eyes. He closed his own aching eyes.

Janos Kovac was one of thousands of young revolutionaries buried in Budapest's *Kerepesi* Cemetery.

Maria Wittner, the nineteen-year-old, had been asleep in her home, her first night in a bed in over a week. When she heard renewed firing, she quickly dressed to rejoin her unit in the Bem Barracks.[10] Approaching the Corvin Passage, she passed by a body that lay sprawled across the sidewalk. There was another corpse around the corner, and then another. Maria broke into a run, her breath coming in short gasps. Suddenly she stopped, rigid with shock. She had expected to meet tanks, but not one with its gun pointed directly at her – a Russian T-56 tank, but it wasn't moving. Behind it was another, with its turret blown off. The fried bodies of its crew lay nearby; something else moved around the corner. The suddenness of another tank gun's appearance had a paralysing effect on her limbs. Then she saw the Hungarian flag flying from its turret, and a man waving to her, a maniacal grin on his face.

This makeshift tank crew, manning the last of the Hungarian T-34 tanks of WW2 vintage, had lain in ambush and, with a few salvoes, had blown away three Russian tanks. The buildings around showed the extent of the shelling; upper floors teetered on smashed foundations. Maria heard a scream, and then the crash of broken glass as a body fell from an upper storey on to the street. This was followed by more shooting. The roof of the house next to her collapsed in a storm of flame and sparks, and the glass of the windows exploded outwards, tinkling on to the street. She was seeking refuge inside a doorway. To her persistent hammering, a man opened a side door. He had the looks of a madman, with his scraggly hair and a fixed stare from a haggard face. He and his family had nothing to eat, no water and no electricity. 'It's not the first time,' he lamented, as he calmed down a bit. 'I remember the Russians in 1945 when they came into Budapest. I know their methods. To them, my life isn't worth more than a two-*kopek* bullet.'

---

[10] Named after the Polish General Josef Bem, who joined the freedom fighters of 1848

The tanks kept on smashing their way into the centre; houses were gutted by shells, entire sections of town reduced to rubble, leaving but derisory traces of its inhabitants: children's clothes, a pot, some broken glass; torn photographs of smiling couples, taken on a day of happiness. In houses which had been spared, overturned crockery cupboards and broken furniture bore witness to the fury of the invading Russians. There were signs that a family had fled in haste; an unfinished meal on a plate next to an opened tin. The whitewashed walls of staircases reddened with smears from bloodied hands, where someone had tried to make it downstairs.

A nest of last resistance was in the Kilian Barracks, where Pal Maleter had joined a doomed revolution. Russian tanks and half-tracks surrounded the building from all sides, firing at will. Then it was over, a white flag appeared from a window. Through the gutted walls filed out the defenders, hands held high. Most were hardly old enough to shave and everyone wore a bloodied bandage. The Russian tank commander motioned them to continue along Üllöi Avenue, away from the buildings. Two armoured personnel carriers were placed further down that road. With the vicious rattle of heavy machine guns, the unarmed soldiers were mown down to the last men. Only one survived: George Molnar had offered to stay behind in order to destroy compromising documents. Through a shell hole he looked on in horror at what happened down in the street. He bowed his head, tears flowing from his eyes, dripping on his leg bandage. He hid for two days beneath the rubble and thereby became the only witness to the massacre of the Kilian defenders.

The panic of the past days was nothing compared to the tragic pandemonium that was to follow. Thousands were fleeing the city, fortunate to have been warned in time. Family groups dragged themselves painfully from the ruins of the city, fathers pushed carts, mothers hauled on ropes, children and old people rode in carts, some wailing, other just staring with vacant eyes. Perhaps some teenagers thought of faces that were no longer there. Many of them were used to death, though. After their days on the barricades, they knew how easy it was to die. Very few had not lost someone – a family member, a school friend. Many disappeared in the panicky exodus or were lost in the migration to other countries: Canada, Australia . . . But Budapest was a big city and the thousands that had time to escape were but a small proportion of the millions who had been caught without warning. Then there were always those who, no matter how sorrowful a situation, were quick to make a profit from misery. The people-smugglers; curs with a promise: 'I'll get you across the Austrian border, but it'll cost you . . .'

With Budapest completely cut off and escape no longer possible, Imre Nagy and his closest collaborators were left with no other option than to seek political asylum inside a friendly Socialist embassy. There was only one representation open to them, the embassy of Yugoslavia, whose President Tito was no friend of the Soviet government. For the time being, they were safe. There was another prominent 'escapee'. A young army lieutenant, Palinkas-Palaviccini, received the order to arrest Cardinal Mindszenty. He picked him up and led the nation's highest Catholic priest through backstreets to the US embassy. The cardinal was to spend many years locked inside the American compound, while the young lieutenant was executed by the direct order of a livid Kadar.

Erzebeth Pongracz could no longer cry. Her husband was gone and nobody could tell her where he was at this moment. Was he still alive? She hadn't seen him in two days. She stood inside the room, watching tanks roll by, her plates in the cupboard rattling from the heavy vibration. Her cousin Eva, staying with her, wanted to close the window. 'No,' said Erzebeth, 'please leave it open. At least we can see when they come to get us.' In that way she could check the movement of Russian tanks, passing in front of her house on the way towards the city centre where she knew her husband was fighting.

'Will they ever stop?' she sighed. 'They're after us,' she said, more to herself than to Eva. 'Let's not be under any illusions, we're all targets now.' Eva had given in. She cowered in a corner and seemed no longer to care; she pressed her hands over her ears, she couldn't take the screeching noise of steel cleats sliding on paving stones. In fact, Pongracz and the 'Corvin Regiment' were fighting to the last bullet and the last man. When the Russians finally stormed into the building, they found three hundred dead. And those who weren't already dead, they shot.

Judith Maleter, the young wife of a heroic colonel, remembered the last time she had been with her husband. It had been a few days before the last trouble. He had told her what was happening, doing his best to keep his voice calm and assured; she realised that circumstances were directing his actions and that they no longer had the power to control their destinies. They wasted little time saying goodbye, for the temptation to shut their door on the outside world was too great. Then he was gone and her nightmare took on a new dimension. Now she couldn't take the stifling enclosure of their apartment any more. It was the feeling of emptiness that was most frightening. Alone, without the man she loved by her side to protect her, a woman was walking into a world of infinite darkness.

It was mid-morning on that 'bloody Sunday', 4 November 1956 and, one of the last nests of resistance in the city was in the Bem Barracks. Maria Wittner, the nineteen-year-old student, had managed to get past the tanks

and was filling bottles with petrol when a tank shell
blew a big hole through the wall. Those nearer the wall
thrashed about until a machine gun silenced them for ever.
Covered with dust, she rose from the subsiding blast. For
her, the revolution was over. Maria, dazed and shocked,
staggered outside the building, hands held high. That's
where a Russian trooper shot her. She played dead and
became one of the lucky ones who survived. Eventually
she ended up in a hospital, where Kadar's secret police
picked her up. For her part in the revolution, she was
sentenced to death. Her sentence was commuted to life
imprisonment because she was the mother of a two-year-old
baby. Fifteen years later, she was pardoned and released.

Of the last few hours of the heroic stand in Budapest,
Laszlo Nemeth [11] wrote: 'I am thinking of a young girl,
fighting on the Calvin Square roof. Her comrades had been
killed by her side but she went on firing until her young
body crumpled, too. In my heart, it is this little girl who
speaks; it is she who has sent the message from the rooftop:
"Go on, old candidate of death. If I give my fine young life,
what does it matter if you, poor human relic, do your own
duty?"'

It was 9 November, noon. Over Budapest hung the ominous
silence of death; nothing was left as a reminder of the glorious revolution, only shattered trees, dusty ruins and unbur-
ied corpses. In a whirlwind of bullets and exploding bombs,
thousands had fallen in the last, desperate hours: students
and pensioners, girls and boys, workers and their wives.

The radio broadcast a speech by Münnich, accusing
the striking steel workers of the giant Czepel industrial
complex of being inspired by Fascists. They put up a giant

[11] Laszlo Nemeth, an outstanding Hungarian novelist, in *Irodalmi
Ujsag*.

banner: 'The 40,000 aristocrats and fascists of the Czepel Works strike on.'

Sandor Szilagy and his friend Emre, both armed with sniper rifles, were hiding out in the place of last resistance, the huge steel-mill compound on Czepel Island, where a few thousand workers had barricaded themselves inside the vast montage halls. 'We must hold out until Wednesday!' Sandor had said trustingly, a few days before.

'Why Wednesday?' asked Emre.

'Because that day Eisenhower will have been re-elected president of America.'

'So what?'

'So what? Then it's going to be war. The Americans will not let us die. Eisenhower will take on the Russkies.' Sandor was still looking to America as the Lord Deliverer and Protector. America was big and it was wealthy; but size and wealth are not always the precondition for power and will. Rome was big and rich – and the barbarians destroyed it. Sandor was only expressing the hopes of millions of Hungarians who longed for a brighter tomorrow. Indeed, Eisenhower was re-elected, and then did nothing.

'You'll see, everything will look better tomorrow.'

Tomorrow – what was this tomorrow that would be different from today? For thousands of Hungarians there existed no tomorrow. Only more combat, more dead, more frustration.

A Russian emissary showed up at the Czepel Iron Works under a flag of truce.

'Give in, our intervention is in your own interest.'

'Whose interest?' shouted a worker.

'We are your friends, only protecting your achievements and victories. We've come by direct request of your government.'

The Russian was cut off by Sandor: '*We* didn't ask you. And *we are the people*.'

That afternoon, Russian tanks were ferried on to the island and then blasted their way into the factory grounds. The worker brigades emptied their last charges at the light-skinned personnel carriers with a red star. Many died on both sides. The battle lasted two hours. The last few hundred defenders came out with hands raised. The Russians didn't take prisoners. Night descended. For endless thousands, that night was eternal.

'The counter-revolution has been crushed,' announced Moscow radio. In Paris, *Le Figaro* wrote: '*L'armée rouge occupe maintenant Budapest. Elle est rouge du sang des travailleurs* – The Red Army now occupies Budapest. It is red with the blood of its workers.'

A dream had died. The workers suspended their last line of defence: the general strike that had paralysed the country. It was that, or committing national suicide.

If the fate of the dead was sealed, that of the living was left in suspense. For a week, the Yugoslav undersecretary of state, Viditch, and the Yugoslav ambassador, Soldatitch, had been in daily conference with Janos Kadar, searching for an 'acceptable way' to deliver Imre Nagy from his self-imposed exile inside the Yugoslav embassy. In the end, Viditch obtained the signed assurance from Janos Kadar for a free passage for Nagy and colleagues, in exchange for a mildly written *mea culpa*, which would suffice to make him an ordinary Hungarian citizen again. He was even offered a seat in the new Kadar government, something that the old Hungarian Communists would not accept. The Kadar writ was delivered in Belgrade and stipulated that the political refugees inside the Yugoslav embassy in Budapest were free to regain their homes and, furthermore, would not have to face prosecution.

On 22 November 1956, 18.30 hrs, two buses provided by the Hungarian Health Ministry, pulled up outside the

Yugoslav embassy gate. To make certain that nothing untoward would happen to Nagy and his colleagues, two embassy cars with high Yugoslav officials were seconded to accompany the convoy. Ten men, fifteen women, and seventeen children walked out of the gate and piled into the buses, when, suddenly, two Soviet armoured personnel carriers surged forth and blocked their way. A Yugoslav diplomat jumped from his car and walked over to the commanding Russian officer. 'This is a diplomatic convoy protected under the Yugoslav flag. Its safe conduct has been assured by a written accord between the Hungarian and the Yugoslav government.'

'You have not to intervene in this affair,' growled the Russian lieutenant, pushing his way past the official into the first of the two buses. He ordered the driver: 'Follow the armoured cars.' The convoy drove off and headed straight for the Soviet military HQ, where a colonel told the two Yugoslav officials at the gate 'to get lost'. From there, Nagy and his companions were bundled into cars and delivered by heavily guarded convoy to Romania. The Nagy affair led to a worsening in Yugoslav–Russian relations. In an address to marine personnel, given at the naval base of Pula, Yugoslav President Tito accused the Kremlin of being directly responsible for the Hungarian drama. Moscow replied by charging Tito with upholding 'revisionist ideas'. With this exchange of insults, the break between Moscow and Belgrade was made final.

Around the world, the Hungarian Revolution was an event of lost illusions and lost convictions, and gave rise to a new bitterness. In the West, it led directly to the creation of a form of open Socialism called 'The New Left'. The effects of film and television coverage of the Hungarian Revolution decimated the membership of Western Communist Parties. Old comrades couldn't take what they had to watch on the air – the pitched battles between Socialist workers and Socialist oppressors, the Soviets. In the years leading up to the drama they had held them up as paragons of anti-capitalist virtue, and now they saw them grinding the desire for liberty under steel cleats.

Thousands returned their membership cards; leading members of West European Communist Central Committees resigned. The famous French philosopher Jean Paul Sartre, until that moment an avowed Russian supporter, wrote a scathing condemnation of the massacres committed in the name of Socialism. The fall-out showed also in the polling booth: Communist Parties lost out in national elections in France and Italy. The Communist trade unions of western Europe, the great after-war workers' force, lost over half of their adherents.

There has never been an official count of battle casualties, just as there has never been an account of the number of out-of-hand executions of surrendering insurgents; such deeds were mainly committed by the Red Army. According to an escaped insurgent,[12] a figure of 50,000 to 60,000 dead, plus another 150,000 wounded, was generally accepted as being on the low side. Added to this figure came at least another 10,000, rounded up and executed in batches during the months following the uprising (the winter of 1956 to 1957). Many of the fallen and/or condemned were youngsters between the ages of fifteen to twenty-three. All those who hadn't as yet reached the age of sixteen – Hungary's legal age for administering the death penalty – had to await their sixteenth birthday in prison to face the hangman. Tens of thousands were sent to forced labour camps in Siberia; 230,000 managed to escape to Austria and Yugoslavia.

Seven days after Soviet tanks crushed Budapest, a beaming Chairman Khrushchev received the new Hungarian

---

[12] George Paloczi-Horvath, in his book, *Youth in Arms*, London, 1971.

strongman, Janos Kadar, in Moscow. But at home, his perfidy was to cost him the confidence of the people he was supposed to guide. Peasants and workers would never allow him to forget his sell-out to the Russians. For all his backing by Russian bayonets, Kadar's puppet government was powerless in the face of stubborn resistance which centred around the Workers' Councils, and was deeply rooted in the Hungarian working class. Threats, promises and appeals were alike unavailing. He could never efface the memory or rub out the consequences of those fateful weeks of October. In the end, Kadar went back on every one of his promises and plunged the nation into a dark age under the Soviet gun.

The Hungarian Uprising was a shocking event to both the Soviets and the West alike, because it came about so unexpectedly. It is a great pity that the Western powers did not fully and immediately realise the enormity of this breach of ideology and doctrinal orders. For once, the Communist Party apparatus in a Russian satellite state had shown itself powerless, divided and incapable of decision. It had made the country ripe for a takeover by pure nationalists such as Nagy and Maleter.

While Hungary's freedom hung in the balance, the grim scenes of an all-out war in the streets of Budapest had a depressing impact on Western governments from Vienna to Washington. Moscow had been quick to instruct its ambassadors to call on Western leaders, stressing that they must 'consider the consequences' of involvement in an internal Communist Bloc affair. France and the United Kingdom were up to their necks in a crisis that had been provoked by Nasser's nationalisation of the Suez Canal on 26 July 1956. That left the USA. Moscow wanted to test Washington's steadfastness over its declaration to back up any movement set on 'the liberation of countries under the Soviet yoke'. When it was put to the test, America showed that it was only willing to follow a policy of containment; it recognised the separate spheres of influence, as had been laid down between Roosevelt and Stalin in Yalta. From the moment that President Eisenhower declared before the United Nations (25 October) that 'America is full-heartedly behind the people of Hungary' – without coming out with a strong condemnation of Soviet interference or a remark about providing aid – it was obvious that the Hungarians couldn't count on the United States.

Bordering Austria declared its 'benevolent neutrality', opening its borders to refugees and helping them to reach sanctuary. Many thousands, taking with them only what they could carry, crossed swamps, lakes and rivers to reach *Niederösterreich* and *Burgenland* (the provinces of Lower Austria). Austrian border patrols helped them across – as, frequently, did Hungarian customs officials, by-passing known Russian guard posts. This was considerably more courageous than the stand taken by the United States.

The White House under President Dwight Eisenhower tiptoed around the issue, calling the Hungarian Revolution 'a family affair', and assured the Soviet ambassador to Washington that America had no intention of getting involved in an internal Eastern Bloc struggle. It was a feeble attempt to assuage Moscow for letting the United States handle affairs in their own sphere of interest without outside interference. It left the United States losing all along the line; it smacked of duplicity, even a lack of courage, and it alienated many nations in the West. In a frenzy of banner headlines, Eisenhower's America stood accused that it could not be counted on to defend a people's freedom.

In all the Cold War years, American foreign policy reached its lowest point in the week of Suez and Hungary.

The country's ethic of aggressive vigilance was discredited; its image as the defender of individual liberties lay in shambles. To any outsider it seemed as if General Eisenhower had willingly stood aside to await the outcome of the fighting on the assumption that the two sides would bloody each other into a kind of mutual submission. The Second World War general didn't count on Moscow being prepared to send thousands of its tanks to put down a rebellion by Communist comrades. Hungary was a bitter lesson for America, and a monstrous setback to its credibility. If America wanted to conserve its role as a world leader, it had to look for some answers.

For over a year, nothing was heard of Pal Maleter. He vanished as if he had never existed. After two years came a brief statement by the Hungarian News Agency MTI; on 17 June 1958, Hungary announced the execution 'for high treason and sedition' of Imre Nagy, Pal Maleter and the journalists Miklos Gimes and Jozsef Szilagi.[13]

Moscow had decided on their death. Two days before, the four had faced the Hungarian People's Court chief judge, Ferenc Vida, to answer to charges of initiating and leading a conspiracy, rebellion and treason. The government of Janos Kadar was guilty of suppressing and distorting defensive evidence. Pal Maleter, and all those accused with him, became the victims of a gross miscarriage of justice, and were sent to their deaths.

At his moment of glory, Pal Maleter, the popular hero of Hungary, disdained the praise he so deserved. He travelled the long road from Communism, not because of doctrinal doubts and disagreements, but because its doctrines

---

[13] The fifth principal accused, Geza Loconszy, was already dead; he had gone on a hunger strike, and when they tried to force-feed him, a tube punctured his lung and he died of internal bleeding.

were an obstacle in the path to the practical achievement that mattered most to him – the liberation of his
country. In the beginning of the uprising, Maleter found
himself cast into the role of a misfit, leading his troops
against the rebellion. Driven by his own weariness with
a brutal ruler for whom he had little but contempt, and
who was hanging on to power with the assistance of
Soviet tanks, he reached for the opportunity to join the
good, if final struggle. It was a bitter irony that he was
killed by the very people he had spent a brief but vital
period of his life trying to help ousting the occupier.
That he succeeded, even only for a 'whiff of time', was
a measure of the magnitude and resolution of a people's
determination, against every argument and obstacle however powerful, to achieve their just political and cultural
independence. With his death, and that of the patriots,
the cleats of Soviet tanks flattened Hungary's hopes. For
the Magyar nation the sun had set and there was no
moon.

They struggled in their own fashion – some outspoken,
others silent, against dictatorship and injustice. A fading
photo on the mantelpiece. Judith Maleter, her life before
1956 is like that in the photo: a family life of happiness,
love, marriage, and passion. Then came the fault that
opened that tragic day in November 1956, when Soviet
tanks raced for Budapest. Afterwards, the dictatorship,
the arrests, tortures, disappearances, and deaths by the
thousands. 'Memory should not become a black-and-white
photograph that yellows with age. A nation could not
demand everyone to be a soldier. I am no longer a *militante*.
It is as if all the problems of our defeat have finally found
their solution.'

One of the children of the barricades, Maria Wittner,
remembers today the heroic days of October:

Only the young can make a revolution, full of enthusiasm. We weren't heroic, wishing to die on the field of battle. We didn't even think about that. I'm asking myself today if we actually feared death. We weren't courageous; we hid behind doors every time a tank took us for his target. We ran, but we also fought. It is for this I say, that it is not by accident that it is always the youth that makes a revolution. Yes, for me, our revolution was glorious.

Fatherland is nothing. It is a piece of land. But it is full of memories. Tradition, history and heroes. And a crowd turned into a nation. Those who stayed, those who left, who fought, who trembled with horror, became heroes, all of them, with the exception of those who turned their weapons against them and called foreigners to help. There is no explanation, no absolution. Neither for you, world, nor for you, God. Bless the Magyars.[14]

The fact remained that after ten years of Soviet domination, the common people of Hungary had risen to a man, and fighting with rifles and Molotov cocktails against tanks and artillery, against the whole overpowering apparatus of the Soviet state, had defied their oppressor. Nothing could wipe out that inescapable and triumphant fact. Brave men like Pal Maleter had broken the spell, destroyed the vacuum, and let in a whiff of fresh air. For the first time since the October Revolution, it was the turn of the Communists inside the Kremlin to be haunted by the spectre of freedom.

Until the fall of the Berlin Wall in November 1989, and the collapse of Communism in the satellite countries, Colonel Pal Maleter remained a non-person. The Communists were careful not to create a martyr. They had him buried in an unmarked grave. After the demise of

14 Zsolt Bayer, *1965 – To leave a sign*, Office of History, Budapest, 2000.

their Communist government, the people of Hungary were either too young to remember, or much too busy celebrating their newly gained freedom to recall the names of Imre Nagy, Pal Maleter or Janos Kovac.

They have a saying in the Balkans: 'Behind every hero stands a traitor.'

Pal Maleter, traitor or patriot? From the Communists' point of view, the man could be justifiably represented as a traitor, since he had sworn on the old flag to uphold the constitution. But to the people of Hungary, Colonel Pal Maleter was a national hero twice over.

Pal Maleter's stamp of the hero was boldness, directed by intelligence and a profound sense of patriotism. 'That which is most desirable, and which instantly sets a man apart, is that his intelligence or talent, are balanced by his character or courage,' stated Napoleon. Maleter's courage was enough to match his tactical skill in the face of impossible odds. He used his personal example to force a change and bring order out of potential chaos, when the situation called for a strong man to take the lead and give impetus to a nation's drive to rid itself of foreign occupation and party oppression. In that, he almost succeeded. He transcended the consistencies of men less farsighted than himself; for that, he was lured into a trap, and silently removed. For years, his name wasn't to be pronounced, not even in whispers.

A few still remember. As for the rest, it is too late . . .

Epilogue

'It is fortune (or chance) chiefly that makes a hero.'
Thomas Fuller, 1608–1661

The screen goes to black. An announcer comes on: 'We interrupt this programme to bring you this special report . . .' The camera cuts to: a child, its arms flailing, drifting helplessly in a river covered by ice floes. Zoom back: a man dives into the water, swims towards the youngster. Quick zoom in on the swimmer: he reaches the child, pulls it to shore, where helping hands reach out for it. Close-up of shaking child. Close-up of saviour, in a dripping suit and shivering with cold. 'Now there's a true hero,' says my wife. So he is, since 'an event only happens when shown on the Evening News . . .'[1]

What had made that man dive into the icy waters? Did he know that the observing lens of a camera was present to record his valiant feat? No. This wasn't one of those stage-managed events where a hero's image was more tightly controlled than man's first trip to the moon, down to its (impromptu) outburst: 'That's one small step

---

[1] Television publicity slogan, USA, 1982.

for man . . .'[2] In no way will this diminish their achievements; the first moonwalkers were true heroes, as was
Columbus, who didn't know if somewhere beyond the sea,
he'd sail over the edge. That took courage and forethought.
Prior reflection is what activated the Scholls, Duckwitz or
Maleter. The man, diving into an icy river to save a child,
acted spontaneously, as did Kunze, Elrod and Slotin.

Individual heroism remains an unexplained phenomenon. It is in human nature to perform feats of courage in
the face of impossible odds. As in every human endeavour,
chance and opportunity play an important factor. Some
might call it destiny. 'It is fortune (or chance) chiefly that
makes a hero,' wrote Thomas Fuller in 1650.[3] The fortune,
of course, to be in the right place at the right time, doing the
right thing. The making of a hero not only takes courage
of conviction, energy, will and intellect, it also needs the
chance factor – because the vital ingredient to bring a hero
to our attention is another man's presence who will bear
witness to it afterwards. Such was true for Leonidas and his
three hundred heroic Spartans, and such holds true today.
Only now it is called the lens of a camera.

Time and circumstances can play a critical role in spreading (or withholding) the news. On Wake atoll the entire garrison was taken prisoner, and their account of individual
heroism had to await the return of the survivors after the
war – by which time the story was cold. Nurse Geneviève
de Galard comforted dying men; her quiet heroism was
drowned out by cheers over a record-breaking 4-minute
mile. The stand by the Glosters was glorious indeed, but
there were too many acts of personal heroism to single
out one. Time and again, exploits were simply concealed

---

[2] 'That's one small step for man, one giant step for mankind,' Neil
Armstrong, on the Moon, 20 June 1969.
[3] Thomas Fuller, *Gnomoloeia*, 1650.

from the public because the truth was politically inconvenient. The Scholls' act to raise their nation's conscience was understandably suppressed by Hitler's propaganda machine. 'The bomb' was supposed to be failsafe, and Dr Slotin's feat was not revealed to the public. A KGB commissar gagged Captain Marinesco, because he didn't like him, and neither did the system. Party bosses silently removed Colonel Maleter as a hindrance to their political ambition. The Gestapo never discovered who betrayed their plan to arrest the Danish Jews, and *Parteigenosse* Duckwitz wasn't about to expose his involvement. Inexcusable oversight happened in the case of Boy Cornwell's mother. That leaves a sergeant who blundered into an 'impregnable fortress' and then single-handedly took it . . . did somebody say Kunze?

Throughout history, men and women have shown an impressive gallantry – fighting, suffering and giving their last full measure of devotion. These brave men and women were not part of the specific hero-cult of the 'warrior saint'. Nor were they inspired by a desire for glory. Their unique motivation was a strong sense of morale, stubbornness, and devotion in which duty became the better part of valour. They dared to stand up to injustice, fight hypocrisy and had to pay the bitter price for remaining loyal to their principles.

The characters in these chapters represent but a few of the names entered into some Great Book of Honour. We don't even know the names of many others, but their list is long. They are the unsung millions who must fight, day after day, for their survival, and they are those who work hard to better the life of others. More than anything shown on the Evening News, these are the true heroes. Unknown, unsung, and often forgotten.

Heroes also there are who perished unknown.
Their sacrifice is not forgotten.
And their names, though lost, to us are written in the books
   of God.[4]

[4] Inscription in 'The Shrine', Scottish War Memorial, Edinburgh.

Bibliography

Kunze

The main source is an account, written in 1938, by an eyewitness, Major Kurt von Klüfer, *Seelenkräfte im Kampf um Douaumont – II/IR 24 seine Nachbarn und Gegner am 25 Februar 1916*. The precise timing of events was established on hand of photographs taken by Lt Voigt, a pioneer platoon commander of the 4/PI 22.

Archives Nationales, *Les armies françaises dans la grande guerre*, Paris 1927–33.

Deutsches Reichsarchiv, *Douaumont*, Berlin-Oldenburg 1928–29.

Brandis, C., *Die Stürmer vom Douaumont*, Berlin, 1934.

Beumelberg, W., *Douaumont*, Oldenburg, 1933.

Crown Prince Wilhem, *The Memoirs of the Crown Prince of Germany*, London, 1922.

Klüfer, Kurt v., *Seelenkräfte im Kampf um Douaumont*, Berlin, 1938.

Lefebvre, J.H., *L'Enfer de Verdun*, Paris, 1960.

Péricard, J., *Verdun 1914–1918*, Paris, 1933.

Radtke, E., *Douaumont wie es wirklich war*, Berlin, 1934.

Rougerol, J., *Le drame de Douaumont*, Paris, 1931.

Ziegler, Dr. W., *Verdun*, Hamburg, 1936.

Boy Cornwell

The Imperial War Museum, London.
Alboldt, E., *Die Tragödie der alten Deutschen Marine*, Berlin, 1928.
Carroll, F.G. et al., *The Register of the Victoria Cross*, London, 1988.
Dimmock, F.H., *The Scouts' Book of Heroes*, London, 1947.
Macintyre, D., *Jutland*, London, 1957.
Service, R., *Collected Verse of Robert Service*, London, 1930.
Winton, J., *The Victoria Cross at Sea*, London, 1978.
Article in *Navy News: Boy Cornwell, the Making of a Hero*, Portsmouth, May 2002.

Wake Atoll

A series of articles written by Robert J. Cressman, historian at the Marine Corps Historical Center's Reference Section, as well as several training booklets published by the History and Museums Division, HQ, US Marine Corps, Washington, DC.
Costello, J., *The Pacific War*, London, 1985.
Cunningham, W.S., *Wake Island Command*, Boston, 1961.
Devereux, J., *The Story of Wake Island*, Philadelphia, 1947.
Kessler, W., *To Wake and Beyond: Reminiscences*, Washington, 1988.
Lundstrom, J., *The First Team: Pacific Naval Air Combat from Pearl Harbor to Midway*, Annapolis, 1984.
Schultz, D., *Wake Island – The Heroic Gallant Fight*, New York, 1978.

Scholl

Interviews with contemporaries, conducted by the
    author. Notes by their sister Inge Scholl and their
    brother Werner Scholl.
Bussmann, W., *Der deutsche Widerstand und die Weisse
    Rose*, Munich, 1968.
Scholl, H. & S., *Briefe und Aufzeichnungen* (ed., I. Jens),
    Frankfurt, 1984.
Scholl, I., *Die Weisse Rose*, Hamburg, 1953.

Duckwitz

Most of the material for the crossings comes from
    interviews conducted by the author in Denmark.
Deutsche Biographische Enzyklopädia, Darmstadt,
    1995.
Deutsches Bundesarchiv, Berlin.
Archiv des Deutschen Auswärtigen Amts, Nachlass
    Duckwitz.
Scandinavian archival material (the restrictive period is
    fifty years).
Royal Danish Ministry of Foreign Affairs, *Rescue of
    Danish Jews*, Copenhagen, 1993.
Besser, J., *G.F. Duckwitz – Diplomat ohne Konformismus
    (Die Welt)*, Hamburg, 1958.
Dose, J., *Georg Ferdinand Duckwitz in Dänemark*,
    Bonn, 1992.
Federspiel, P., *Widerstand in Dänemark im 2 Weltkrieg*,
    Copenhagen, 1983.
Henriksen, H. B., *Duckwitz rolle for danskerne
    (Berlinske Tidende)*, Copenhagen, 1973.
Pundik, H., *Gilleleje 43 (Politiken)*, Copenhagen,
    1991.

Svenningsen, K., *Duckwitz in Dänemark*, Copenhagen, 1984.

Thomas, J.O., *The Giant Killers – the Danish Resistance Movement*, London, 1975.

Thomsen, E., *Deutsche Besatzungspolitik in Dänemark 1940–45*, Düsseldorf, 1971.

Wistrich, R., *Who's Who in Nazi Germany*, London, 1995.

Yahil, L., *The Rescue of the Danish Jewry*, Philadelphia, 1969.

Marinesko

Baronov, O. and Panov, I., *Geroi I podwigi – A Personal Enemy of the Führer*, Moscow, 1967.

Brustat-Naval, F., *Unternehmung Rettung*, Hertford, 1970.

Dmitrijev, V., *U-Boote im Angriff*, Moscow, 1964.

Dobson, Miller, Payne, *Die Versenkung der Wilhelm Gustloff*, Wien, 1979.

Germanov, V., *Die Heldentat von S 13*, Kaliningrad, 1970.

Golovko, A., *With the Red Fleet*, London, 1965.

Kron, A., *Alongside the Heroes*, Moscow, 1966.

Lass, E., *Die Flucht: Ostpreußen 1944–45*, Bad Nauheim, 1964.

Lehndorff, H., *Ostpreußisches Tagebuch*, Munich, 1961.

Schön, H., *Der Untergang der Wilhelm Gustloff*, Göttingen, 1951.

   SOS Wilhelm Gustloff: grösste Schiffskatastrophe der Geschichte, Stuttgart, 1998.

Smirnov, N., *Sailors Defend the Motherland*, Moscow, 1973.

Article in *Stern* (Sandmeyer), January, 1993.

Dr Slotin

Much is based on the recollections of Beth Slotin, Dr
    Slotin's niece, his nephew Israel Ludwig, and the
    Canadian freelance writer Martin Zeilig.
Articles from *Winnipeg Free Press* (1946), *Los Alamos
    Times* (1946), *Maclean's* (1961), *New Scientist* (1976),
    Toronto Star (1986) and *The Beaver* (1995).
US Government archives (declassified 1985).
Blum, J., *The Price of Vision*, Boston, 1973.
Clark, R., *The Birth of the Bomb*, London, 1961.
Compton, A., *Atomic Conquest*, New York, 1956.
Jungk, R., *Brighter Than a Thousand Suns*, New York, 1958.
Masters, D., *The Accident*, New York, 1955.
Moon, B., article in the October 1961 issue of *Maclean's*
    (Toronto, Canada).
Oppenheimer, R., *The Open Mind*, New York, 1955.
Sherwin, M., *A World Destroyed*, New York, 1975.
Truman, H., *The Year of Decision*, New York, 1955.
Weart, S., and Szilard, G., *Leo Szilard: His Version of the
    Facts*, Cambridge, 1978.
Zeilig, M., article in August 1995 issue of *The Beaver*
    (Canada).

The Glosters

Contemporary articles from *The Back Badge*, and the
    Sphinx and Dragon, journals of the Gloucestershire
    Regiment.
Carew, T., *Korea – The Commonwealth at War*,
    London, 1967.
Chen Jian, *China's Road to the Korean War*, New
    York, 1994.
Cutforth, R., *Korean Reporter*, London, 1957.

Davies, Padre S., *In Spite of Dungeons*, London, 1955.

Dille, J., *Substitute for Victory*, New York, 1954.

Farrar-Hockley, A., *The Edge of the Sword*, London, 1954.

Goulden, J., *Korea: The Untold Story of the War*, New York, 1982.

Kahn, E., 'The Gloucesters', article in *The New Yorker*.

Hastings, M., *The Korean War*, London, 1987.

Hollands, D., *The Dead, the Dying and the Damned*, London, 1956.

Stueck, W., *The Korean War*, Princeton, 1997.

Voorhees, M., *Korean Tales*, London, 1957.

Galard

The principal portions derive from a personal account given by Geneviève de Galard to the author in Paris in January 2002. The author draws also on his visits to Dien Bien Phu and his conversations in Hanoi with Vietnamese Prime Minister Pham Van Dong (1977) and General Giap (1978).

Service Historique de l'Armée de Terre, Vincennes.

Bergot, E., *Les 170 Jours de Dien Bien Phu*, Paris, 1964.

Bodard, L., *La Guerre d'Indochine – L'Humiliation*, Paris, 1965.

Grauwin, Dr P., *J'etais Médecin à Dien Bien Phu*, Paris, 1992.

Maleter

The author's particular thanks go to Mme Judith Maleter, wife of General Maleter, for adding her personal notes during an interview in 2002. Much is based on the author's visits to Budapest, and

his interviews with contemporary participants in
the rising.

Aczel, T. and Meray, T., *Révolte de l'Esprit*, Paris, 1962.

Bayer, Z., *1965 – To leave a sign*, Office of History,
Budapest, 2000.

Bernadac, C., *L'exécution de Budapest*, Paris, 1961.

Fejtö, F., *La Revolution Hongroise*, Paris, 1966.
Budapest, L'insurrection, Paris, 1990.

Hoxha, E., *The Khrushchevites*, Tirana, 1984.

Konrad, G., *Le Complice*, Paris, 1980.

Meray, T., *Budapest* (23 October 1956), Paris, 1966.

Molnar M. & Nagy, L., *Imre Nagy, Réformateur ou
Revolutionnaire?* Paris, 1959.

Paloczi-Horrath, George, *Youth in Arms*, London, 1971.

Turbet-Delof, G., *La Révolution Hongroise de 1956*,
Paris, 1996.

Tyrenczi, L., *Vérité sur l'Affaire Nagy*, Paris, 1957.

Contemporary articles in *Irodalmi Ujsag* (Literary
Gazette) and French papers.

PHOTOGRAPHIC ACKNOWLEDGEMENTS

Page 1 above, 6 below: Imperial War Museum, London. Page 1 below: Courtesy Royal Navy Trophy Centre, HMS Nelson, Portsmouth. Page 2, 8: Private Collections. Page 3: US National Archives & Records Administration NARA, Washington. Page 4: AKG, London. Page 5 above and centre: The Museum of Danish Resistance 1940–1945. Page 5 below: Courtesy Beth Slotin. Page 6 above: Courtesy Soldiers of Gloucestershire Museum. Page 7: ©Bettmann/CORBIS.

Every reasonable effort has been made to contact the copyright holders, but if there are any error or omissions, Hodder & Stoughton will be pleased to insert the appropriate acknowledgement in any subsequent printing of this publication.

INDEX

Index